INTRODUCTION

Welcome to the opening chapter of my  you'll embark on a thrilling journey thro woven with personal reflections, vivid ir adventures.

This memoir is an intimate exploration of my experience, shapeu by my unique perspective and interpretations. As you delve deeper, you'll encounter vivid descriptions of political landscapes, historical events, and the human drama of wars. These elements serve as the backdrop to my life story, providing context and depth to my narrative.

While I strive for accuracy, I must confess that there may be unforeseen errors scattered throughout these pages. Rest assured; these are unintentional, mere blips in the vast canvas of my memories. I have written without prejudices, non-biased, racial, political or gender mindset. Some names are fictitious, others might be incorrectly drawn from my memory, but I mean no ill will or aggression to anyone or party.

Prepare to traverse continents and cultures as you journey alongside me from my humble beginnings to the far reaches of the globe. My adventurous spirit has led me to every corner or the earth, each expedition teetering on the edge of peril. Brace yourself for the unbelievable as I recount not once, not twice, but four near-death encounters that have shaped the very fabric of my being.

Through my travels and trials, I come to embrace a profound truth; that travel is the ultimate educator, the university of the world. I fervently hope that you, dear reader, will find inspiration in my odyssey-a call to seize the day; embrace the unknown, and live life to its fullest.

So, I extend an invitation to join me in unravelling the tapestry of my life. Together, let us explore the depths of human experience, guided by the timeless mantra: Carpe Diem.

CREDITS

For the book browser, I challenge you to read this story and travel the road of a Nomadic adventurer who has lived 10 men's lives. Crisscrossing every continent of the world.

Publisher = Amazon.com

To complete the book, I owe credit to an ex-aviator and old friend for assisting and editing its contents.

Keith Chiazzari.

For the cover assembly computer work and help with a name, Twins

Kerith & Aden Alcorn

To my wife for the support and help in information over the last ten years of writing.

Clare Evans

For my deceased wife "Josie" who stood by me for 33 years, with 7 country moves.

Josie

To my two sons for the ups and downs, changing social life, schools and countries.

Scott & Grant

BY THE SEAT OF MY PANTS

South Africa to the United Kingdom, my adventure begins.

Aboard the Edinburgh Castle steamship, we stopped in Cape Town to refuel and to take on glasses, beer and food. Why glasses and beer one might ask? Well, the ship had 175 girls and 95 young men on board. All heading for the UK and an attempt to flee the restrictions of the pending new Republic of South Africa. The fare was 25 pounds (R50) for the 3-week cruise, and everyone yearned for an overseas adventure, no matter where it took them. The ship departed Durban, where my mother and father came to see me off, father gave me the then princely sum of 30 shillings as a departing gift. The cruise ship sailed via East London, Port Elizabeth and on to Cape Town. This was the jumping-off port across the Atlantic for South Hampton. Cape Town is known for its beauty and cable car to Table Mountain.

After a festive send-off from Cape Town, we embarked on our journey. We all held colonial passports with the phrase 'Union of South Africa' embossed on them, which allowed us to travel freely in the UK, due to South Africa's status as a former colony. Unfortunately, a 'Republic of South Africa' stamp was added to the first page of our passports upon leaving, covering the word 'Union'. The celebrations and joviality on that voyage are cherished memories. We exhausted the ship's drink supplies and depleted the glasses by dropping them or hurling them overboard. I am positive the bottom of the South Atlantic near the African coast is littered with glass from the ships and the merriment of tossing one's glass overboard. The crossing of the equator was a great party with Neptune coming on board. Fancy dress and pool dipping were the order of the day. Fellows stripped to the waist and came as Zulu warriors, and the girls came as sea maidens or anything they could think of. One dress that comes to mind is a three-some. Two guys were dressed in sheets with 'Sheet Abdul' painted on his back, the other guy with 'Sheet Mohamed', and the girl with them had 'Sheet Scared' on her back. Madeira was a refueling and restock stop.

After departing Madeira, we set sail for our destination, Southampton, England. The final docking was done, and farewells were rapidly underway. I had exactly 5 pounds (R10) to my name and had just enough to buy a ticket to Victoria Station. As I walked up to the station, I had time to reflect on where I was and where the hell I was going. Armed with my wonderful old aunt's address, I went to her and Uncle Geoff's home in Richmond.

Aunt Taffy had been a wonderful person. She was my mother's cousin, the daughter of one of the four D'Portal (also spelt De Portal) sisters whose father, my great-grandfather on my mother's side, had left England in the early 1800s to start a tea plantation in Ceylon. With the collapse of Ceylon, he came to South Africa and started a farm in Pietermaritzburg. He was a direct relation to Lord Portal of Hungerford, England, and the D'Portal family of the French aristocracy, who came from a castle in Toulouse. I will get to that part of my life later.

I was greeted by Aunt Taffy and Uncle Geoff, who had held a senior position in the Shell oil company in Cape Town before being transferred to their London head office. They had two daughters. Regrettably, both Geoff and Susan contracted polio in the South African epidemic. Susan died, but Geoff miraculously recovered. Later, they had another daughter, Sally, who, along with her older sister Louise, still lives in Richmond.

They had made a bed for me in their spare room, and I now contemplated my purpose and destiny. Aunt Taffy was a great inspiration to me. Having been labelled a total failure by my father and my self-esteem somewhat diminished by the situation I was in in South Africa, she supported every conversation over the dinner table in the few days I spent with them. She suggested employment possibilities and found no fault in my present, seemingly hopeless situation, due to my lack of education and professional accreditation. As I had been in farming, was well experienced in mechanical devices, and had a heavy-duty driver's license, it seemed I should look to the farming world for a job. While scanning the daily paper, I saw a listing for a farmhand with a driver's license. I made contact with the farmer in Horley and arranged to come down and see him. My Uncle Geoff suggested I go to the local driver's licensing office and inquire about the value of my South African and Rhodesian licenses. So, I did and found that both were valid, and I was subsequently issued a UK heavy-duty license. Gleaming with pride, I departed for Horley, met the farmer, and secured the job.

Unable to tell my aunt and uncle that I now had only about 2 pounds to my name, I had to walk practically back to Victoria Station to catch my train to Richmond. A day or so later, I was once again on my way to Horley to take up my room in the attic of the workhouse, which was run by a rather fierce elderly woman who had stringent conditions and rules for the house. This included a bath once a week at 3 shillings and board for 30 shillings (R3:00) a week, paid in advance.

Now I had a problem and considering the state and warlike manner of the woman, confrontation was not appealing. So, I used all the South African charm I possessed and a smooth talk, regaling her with tales of the bush war coming to South Africa, my desolation, and how my money was en route and would reach me within a week. Thankfully, she bought my story, probably because she did have some relations in Rhodesia who were about to lose all their possessions and had written to her about their decreasing situation in the Federation of Nyasaland and Rhodesia.

It was winter in the UK, and I quickly realized that my 6-foot, 4-and-a-half-inch tanned body, majorly unaccustomed to the cold, was not equipped to handle the new climate. No matter how hard I tried, supported by people laughing at me for working without a jacket, the cold was taking a toll. Little did they know, I did not have the money to purchase a warm jacket or rent.

However, after receiving my first week's pay, a generous sum of 4 pounds (R8:00), I went straight to an army and navy store in Gatwick and bought a surplus army jacket, scratchy warm socks, and some durable green work pants.

The work on the farm involved laborious tasks such as feeding pigs at 7 a.m. with water from a trough I had to break ice off, cleaning sites, and cow barns, and in the afternoon, driving the 5-ton Bedford lorry to obtain feed from a neighboring farm.

Here again, fate showed its hand. While loading feed, the neighboring farmer came over to talk to me. He pointed out some machinery busy excavating land in the distance. He said they were building or renovating an airport there, which he indicated was going to be an international airport for Gatwick and in his opinion, it was never going to work, and the government was wasting taxpayers' money. I learnt very quickly never to objectively reply or enter into a disagreement with an English farmer.

Despite his skepticism, he suggested that it could be a place where I could find good-paying work if I were unsatisfied with farm life. Although he believed London airport was big enough and that the airport wouldn't work, it could present a possible opportunity for me, especially considering I was currently working for a farmer. Little did I know what that airport would mean to me in the future, as I would end up working there intermittently. My lodgings were in a very cold attic that was unheated. To fall asleep at night, I learned to inhale through my nose and exhale from my mouth into the tight gap between my sheet and blanket, thus warming the space around my body. Life was tough on the farm, and our weekly 3-shilling (30c) bath held in front of the fireplace in the lounge felt like a luxury to my tired and physically exhausted body. We spent Friday evenings at the local pub where a pint of warm bitter was 1 shilling and 2 pence. I longed for our famous number 17, spook and diesel, which was common on the North Coast of Natal. Number 17 was a Lion beer, which spells out NO 17 when turned upside down. Spook and Diesel were South Africans for a cane and coke, one of the cheapest drinks one could buy. Cane was a type of white rum extracted from sugar cane and was also used as a motor spirit, being refined into methanol alcohol. I soon concluded that farming in England wasn't for me. Thus, I bid my employer, housemother, and hardworking labourers goodbye, packed my backpack, and headed back to Richmond. A day later, I saw an advertisement for a Singer Sewing machine salesman in Ealing Broadway. The job required a driver's license and included visits and services to housewives around the district to service their sewing machines. It was a warm indoor job that occasionally took me outside the office. I applied and got the job.

Ealing Broadway.

I had the job, but now I had to find a room or some sort of accommodation. Walking up the main street, I saw a sign indicating a room for rent for 30 shillings (R3:00) a week. This was within my depleting budget, so I walked in to see what it consisted of. Well, the room was as big as a large cupboard, with a communal toilet and no bathroom. I had to stand on my bed to dress or undress. It was run by an aged couple desperate for any sort of income they could earn from their home. They lived in the lounge, which was a smoke-filled room, caused by a coal fire which I am sure had been burning since the war. The room was black, they coughed continuously and were almost chair-ridden. It had to do, as there appeared to be nothing else within my meagre price range. I moved in. I found a public bathhouse down the road and was at least able to get a bath once or twice a week at 6 shillings (60c) a time. I later found out that if I was quiet, ran the tap without making any noise and kept the lights off, I could sneak in without paying. The job now included a four-day training program, enlightening me on the ins and outs of how to fool housewives into accepting a demo machine, and then advising them that their machine was not worth fixing. We would then offer a special deal to leave the demo machine with them, taking their machine as a deposit. We would thereby return later to sign a purchase agreement that most could not afford.

The job for me had a lot of perks, as I had the use of a Singer panel van. With the speedometer disconnected and paper, stick-on covers to conceal the Singer adverts on the side of the panels, the vehicle was used to visit most of England and became a taxi for the guys I was later to join in a Communal House. The other prerequisite was meeting many young housewives, which had a tremendous impact on my ego. I remember one incident where I turned from the sewing desk to comment on the condition of the machine, only to find a completely naked, beautiful woman in her mid-twenties standing behind me. There were many other incidents like this before my employment with Singer ended.

This termination occurred because I met a group of Australians, New Zealanders, and a Canadian named Glen Creelman who had rented a large house in Ealing Broadway. I left my small space to join all 28 of them. The main issue we encountered was hot bedding. The first to arrive got the beds, the next got the couches, and the last had the floor. We had a great time visiting Earls Court and many pubs such as the Zambezi Club and the Down Under Club. We also enjoyed meeting newly arriving, financially strapped young colonial backpackers.

It was crucial to stay on your feet while drinking copious amounts of English beer and finding someone whose room you could spend the night in since the underground and trains stopped running after midnight. We also spent a lot of time in coffee shops, particularly in those days when the Beatles were becoming popular in dance halls. Dates for a dance or the movies were readily available as young South Africans were in high demand.

I ran into some old friends, one being Peter Wise, a sugar farmer's son from Compensation Beach in South Africa, with whom I had previously spent time. It was through these backpacking travelers that we learned about working with the Hudson Bay Fur Company. Destiny intersected with me again as Hudson Bay would become a key point in my future. We all went off in search of high-paying jobs sorting furs for buyers, who were known to give generous tips. Despite missing out on that opportunity, I found work as a Roneo printing machine operator with the company, spending my days printing reams of paper alongside a man who believed this was his lifelong job.

The world turned against South Africa, enforcing sanctions. I recall 80 barges of South African butter being dumped into the sea, and Outspan oranges left rotting as stevedores refused to offload South African goods. I remember a disturbing incident during the Notting Hill riots when Enoch Powell was trying to get the UK to repatriate all West Indian, Pakistani, and Indian immigrants, mostly those fleeing Idi Amin's reign of terror in Uganda. Sadly, this is not an uncommon situation for African dictators. Powell wanted them all sent back with first-class tickets and travel money. In retrospect, doing so could have resolved the current immigration and racial problems facing England. Australia had an all-white policy, requiring all people entering or immigrating to prove they were of white Caucasian origin. They also adopted the practice of relocating Aboriginal children to settlement camps, and they used to have the Darwin line, a barrier drawn across Northern Australia, which they allowed the Japanese to approach before declaring an all-out war on them. Our mistake was naming our racial policy "Apartheid," which translates to separate development, a practice the rest of the world had been conducting for years under different names, emphasizing racial or tribal division by colour or creed. Arabs being great slave traders

A humorous incident occurred when some of us South Africans discovered a large board in a churchyard condemning Apartheid. While attempting to shake it loose, laughter erupted from the other end of the board. Printed on the back was a triangular sticker bearing the name "MASONITE" a company based in South Africa. Things progressively worsened for young South African travelers after that, and the South African Passport became unfavourable to hold.

It was then suggested that, given my distant relation to Lord Portal (presumed to be my mother's second cousin), an Air Vice Marshal, I should seek his assistance with the R.A.F. Considering that I might be pilot material, I made inquiries and eventually visited a recruiting station to sit the entrance exam. I was elated when the recruitment officer called me in to go over my question answer paper. He announced, in a crystal-clear English voice, that I was accepted into the Air Force. The position offered was at the hangar, which could potentially lead to a junior mechanic position if I demonstrated mechanical knowledge and a good learning attitude. With time, it could offer a rank, pension, medical benefits, and leave with a reduced rate on British Rail. Thanking him in my distinctive South African accent, I caught the next train back to Ealing Broadway to reunite with my fellow world travelers.

I was resolved to confront the world, sans the assistance of the RAF or any association with Lord Portal or his family. I was convinced that fate had drawn me in a different direction, which surfaced later that night. The Aussie guys had heard that the Channel Island, mainly Jersey, was looking for South African and Australian lifeguards. There was also decent pay in potato packing and most importantly, the island was a Butlins holiday camp Mecca with abundant French, English, and other European girls. Three days later, eight of us piled into the beat-up old VW Kombi that one of the New Zealanders owned and sped off to the Channel Island ferry depot. With almost my last few pounds, I paid for my share of the ticket and Kombi costs, and we merrily set sail for Jersey. It was a beautiful crossing and the islands looked magnificent in the late spring evening sun.

Jersey, Channel Islands

Disembarking we now had to find work and accommodation fast as we had little cash between us. Six of the guys as they were best friends opted to sleep in the kombi, another Aussie and I were out, so it either was on the ground or found some place for the night. The ground became not an option as the police were patrolling and camping near the harbour was out of bounds. As night fell, we walked into St Hellier and found a fish and chip shop on the corner of Duhamel Street. Sitting inside we ordered a fish to be shared and two packets of chips plus two cups of tea. The discussion was over our somewhat poor situation but decided to ask the lady behind the counter if she knew of a YMCA or boarding house, explaining in our funny foreign accent and that we were urgently looking for work. She, as we were to learn was known as Mrs. D, called her husband Bill from the back room. Bill Ducqumin appeared as the epitome of a seafarer, slightly bearded stocky and in a polar neck shirt with boots. He was a fisherman with his son David, his wife, known as Mrs. D, with their young son Billy, together they ran the fish & Chip shop. They turned out to be kind and wonderful people and I remained in contact with them throughout their lives. On explaining our predicament, Bill suggested a boarding house up the road and also revealed that he had rooms upstairs, one of which had a bed available which could be shared with another young man named John. Mrs. D and Bill were kind enough to agree to allow me to stay first and pay later. This was something rarely heard of, but I later recognized it was probably because they had two sons, Dave and Billy, and their lodger John. So, they would have been able to understand the pleading look in a young boy's eyes – mine. I decided to take the room upstairs to share with John, not realizing at the time, that this was going to be a life-changing choice. The next morning was dedicated to looking for work. Bill suggested we try the potato packing warehouses or a trucking company down the road. To my surprise,

I managed to secure a job that very day driving old Thames articulated trucks to deliver hay, animal feed and other goods all over the island. My only problem was that I had no previous experience driving articulated vehicles and the narrow lanes were quite intimidating. Nevertheless, I managed to adapt quickly and was soon earning a living on this beautiful island. Farmers here were friendly, and I would often join them for tea or even breakfast. I gradually familiarized myself with the local culture and environment.

Regrettably, it was while working for this truck company, when I had an accident that nearly cost me my leg. I was tightening a strap at the back of the truck when it snapped, causing me to slide down the load and hit my right leg below the knee on the tailgate. This was the same area where I had sustained similar injuries while in South Africa. Firstly, from my horse and then a car crash in my rebuilt Renault car I had recently sold to a friend who managed to roll it over with me inside the vehicle, an hour after the sale. This accident resulted in me being admitted into Addington Hospital in Durban for surgery to prevent osteomyelitis from infecting the bone – a similar incident happened when my horse slipped in the rain and rolled over me. I spent 10 days in the Marion Hill Monastery Hospital undergoing treatment to prevent a bone infection. The doctors were worried that the osteomyelitis could spread to my hip, which would require amputation of my leg. However, an Australian doctor named Stewart suggested that the bone be aspirated, treated with infrared lamps, and heavy doses of penicillin. During my stay in the hospital, I was served two stout beers every night, and the nurses were pleasing to the eye which made the recovery process slightly more enjoyable.

After being discharged from the hospital four weeks later, I joined my mother on a two-week journey around the UK. This was made possible by a borrowed car from a wealthy French girl I had met on the island. Since I was only 19, parental consent was required by the hospital. The hospital contacted my parents who were my next of kin, after which my mother decided to fly over earlier than her planned overseas trip. She planned to be on hand if surgery was needed as I was still under 21 and considered a minor. She subsequently by prearrangement visited her cousin (my Aunt Taffy), also a descendent of the Portals. After my recovery, I returned to Jersey, and she departed back to South Africa. As the holiday was preplanned it was a welcome trip for her as she had been under a lot of stress.

The arrival of the summer filled the beaches with tourists clad in sandals and socks, handkerchiefs knotted on their heads, sun-burnt skin, and ample amounts of alcohol at every bar. There were even semi-clad gorgeous young women everywhere. Some of my friends who I had travelled with managed to find jobs as lifeguards since they had gotten accustomed to being in the sun and the surf. So, when a job opportunity at the luxurious Blue Waters Hotel came up offering me a chance to be a pool attendant, which included running a speed boat and teaching water skiing, I jumped at it.

With this new job on the other side of the island, I faced a commuting issue which was quickly solved by purchasing a BSA 250cc motorbike. Now equipped with mobility, I could explore the island with my friend Peter Wise. He was the son of a sugar farmer from the North coast of South Africa, the same area where I had spent part of my childhood and worked as a farm overseer. I had been in touch with him earlier and suggested... that this was the place to be. He finally arrived and got a job as a tennis coach then later he got employed as a dishwasher at the same hotel. (Our benefits being two free meals a day and days off), we travelled the length and breadth of the island. Painfully finding out that with a few Jersey beer pints partaken thereof, the narrow lanes were not so navigable causing at one time to end up in the hedgerow. Luckly without much injury bar pride.

This BSA was to travel a long way, much further than I ever expected it to go upon purchasing it. The job was great, I instructed all types of people on the art of water skiing, looked after the pool and kept a close watch on the beach. The chilly water is not conducive to staying in it for long, so the heated pool was popular. The art of skiing requires the boat to pull one up onto a planning position. This was a difficult exercise to teach when one was also running the boat. Out of devilment when a bikini-clad girl was freezing herself in the chilly water I would accelerate rapidly, most times shedding her bikini top, then having to return to collect the said top and delivering it back to her consequently getting half naked onto the boat. Most of the time they thought it hilarious and joined in the fun. True European attitude but it was new for us South Africans. I assisted in a girl's attempt to swim from the neighbour Guernsey Island to Jersey. A 36-mile ice-cold water swim. There was a picture of her in the papers being assisted aboard the hotel boat by myself, taken at such an angle that all one could see of me was my backside. I still claim I made the English papers.

Peter and I in Jersey

A lot of South Africans were leaving the country as the border wars had intensified with all white young boys over 16 years being called up to the armed forces. The Russians supported by the Chinese communists were supplying arms, and ammunition, transporting black soldiers to communist training camps overseas, in general backing the invading northern countries supporting terrorism. Cuba had entered the war, and our boys were fighting to keep South Africa free of communism so a racial war was not altogether the reason as was the opinion of the civilized world.

Church groups and charities were funding opposition groups by chartering aircraft to fly arms and aid the enemies of South Africa. One such emigrating family was the Blaine's sugar farmers from the North Coast of Natal South Africa. Mr Blaine died from a fire caused while working on his car, so Mrs. Margaret Blaine had immigrated to Jersey with her daughters and son. Mrs. Blaine Senior was a friend of my grandmother who when it became known to my mother, asked that I make contact with them in Jersey. I visited now and then to enjoy a delicious meal and chat. It was good to be with North Coast South

Africans again. Much later Rosemary, the oldest daughter and I were to cross paths.

Summer work ended, so I proceeded to look for work elsewhere. It was at this time that I obtained work as a stevedore sweating it out in ship holds, loading sacks of lime onto pallets. Which were then hoisted to the wharf and trucked. It was back-breaking work, and the lime was inclined to split the skin on one's hands. I used to work two shifts to make a handsome 12 pounds (R24:00) a week, very good money compared to my 14 pounds 12 shillings and sixpence (R32:00) a month in South Africa. The treat for the day was a hot cup of tea and a sticky bun served from an old caravan on the dock. One paid a princely price of 3 pence for the tea and 3 pence for the sticky bun. (In South Africa 3 pence was known as a Tickey)

While enjoying my tea a Hovercraft of the Royal Navy came into the harbour. That night discussing it with Bill Ducqumine he figured that the Hovercraft was the vessel of the future and if I wanted a good career, I should get onto being trained on one. He figured out one would need a pilot's license and a seaman ticket.

Flying club, first lesson etc. A day later I went to the Channel Islands aero club situated in an old army Quonset hut at the Jersey airfield. Here I met the instructor, an ex-Wing Commander Pick Pickford who knew Lord Portal then as Vice Air Marshal of the R.A.F. He was delighted to meet me as he was married to a South African lady and had trained in Salisbury Rhodesia. He asked if I could ride a horse and in my reply of yes, convinced me I could learn to fly.

After a beer or two, I returned to my lodging convinced I had found something I wanted to do. I talked it over with Bill and returned to the flying club a day or so later. I was extremely excited at the prospect of flying in so starting lessons with Pick that day. Pick had a small dog called Knobby who had a seat belt and flew with us. His name was

Knobby because he had a small knob on his back, had small legs and walked with a waddle just like Pick. I found getting the hang of flying rather easy and enjoyed the flips around the island. I did not, however, enjoy the aerobatics of Pick and it was put down to being my height and having the centre of gravity closer. Pick explained that fighter pilots were generally small guys with a fighting attitude and were able to withstand higher G force. The aircraft was Auster's, a small 3-seat monoplane with a Gypsy engine, later before my mother returned to South Africa, I was able to take her up on a lesson with Pick and myself for a sight of the island. My mother supported the venture, being convinced that there was something in this flying for me, relating her association to Lord Portal. Remarkably many years later, I found out from a reading that I was spiritually related to a pilot killed over France in the First World War. I was able to make 6 hours and my solo but regrettably the cost was either a matter of starving to death or learning to fly. I opted to give up flying, concentrating on my travel and future endeavours.

Auster

My friend Peter Wise was working as a tennis coach. He later decided it was time to move on and considered going to Australia, which he eventually did. I also thought about that, little did I know how much Australia would come into my life. The old army surplus jacket I had bought in England was now very much in use. I had a job washing cars and did some stevedoring.

EUROPE ON A MOTORBIKE

With what cash I had saved I decided that a motorbike trip was in order, so with Dave, Bill and Mrs. D oldest son of my age, we packed a couple of bags big enough to hang on the BSA, a plastic sheet long enough to create a makeshift tent to go over the bike and along the ground being anchored by the wheels. By placing the bags at the opposite end, it formed our home. We caught the ferry to St Marlo on the French coast and visited the famous Mont St Michel an island monastery accessible only at low tide. We then set off in great spirits for Paris via Alencon. Being a bit late in the summer, we encountered many rain squalls so were wet most of the way. Finding Paris from the outskirts was difficult in the rain as signs were distorted and in French. One horrific incident was when it appeared we had taken a wrong road a huge truck loomed out of the murk. When I was alongside it, Dave with the road map held to my back was able to get the driver's attention. He opened his door and started to give us directions as we sped along the rainy and busy freeway. At one point he was almost out of the truck holding onto the steering wheel with my foot on the step of his cab. Total madness on behalf of the driver and us but as Dave said that's the French for you.

On camping out in fields and byways we arrived in Paris and did the usual hundred turns around the Arc de Triomphe, as a typical foreign driver, we ended up in the centre of the circle. Navigating out of the centre requires nerves of steel, especially on an overloaded wobbling bike caused by the cobbles and in the rain. We found out that the French have no sense of humour and don't give way. Hence, our hundred turns around the circle. The Eiffel Tower was a must to go up so chaining the bike to a lamppost up we went.

The view was great, but a greater need was a public toilet. This we found when as we were relieving ourselves walked a cleaning lady greeting us then proceeded to mop and sweep around our feet. As we were not familiar with this open uni-toilet system, it was a bit of a shock but soon overcome with laughter. The sink was next, and a good face wash was executed. Regretfully the sink became stained with grime of two days on an open bike. Attempting to clean it with a handkerchief only made it worse. On leaving the washroom the same cleaning lady came in followed by a scream of abuse waving her broom with her and then chasing us around the tower. We miraculously found the stairs and disappeared down to the next floor and into the lift. We were honestly sorry for the dirty sink but had no option.

From Paris, we ventured up along the German border, via Nancy, Bonn, through to Holland and back via Brussels. Then down the French coast via Le Havre. The trip was uneventful except when we had camped in a field one very misty night. To do this we left the bike against the fence as there was no room to set up our little camp and climbed under the high wire fence. On waking I was looking at the most unusual face of a bull who had decided to examine what we as two non-motional tube type (sleeping bags) objects were doing in his domain. Very slowly, I woke Dave and we proceeded to slide backwards towards the safety of the now clear high and fortified fence. The bull did not seem to like this and endeavoured to follow with a few warning snorts. Thankfully we squeezed under the wire to safety only to see a very clear sign indicating a dangerous bull breeding area.

On the road to Belgium, we ran across a broken-down Ford Prefect with four Australian girls attempting to push it. It was out of fuel so as gentlemen it was decided that one of us should help them. The question was which one. I came up with a brain wave, why not tow the car with the bike? A rope from their tent was produced and we tied the Bike to the little car. With everyone pushing and me slowly taking up the strain we got mobile. The girls jumped into the car and Dave ran up leaping onto the bike to help hold the rear wheel firmly on the ground. It was hilarious as the heavy traffic passing us gave us the most inquisitive look, some the thumbs up, others shook their heads but eventually, we came to a filling station about 8 kilometres away. The girls camped with us that night but were heading into Brussels and on to Amsterdam We bid farewell and proceeded on down the French coast.

Just before St Marlo on our last night, we stopped at a small village named Agon. There was a narrow door leading to a small bar. As it was our last night, we decided to enjoy the last of our French money. A bottle of wine was ordered, and we sat in among the locals. In the corner was a small group of elderly men, smoking pipes and enjoying their wine, not uncommon in Europe. One of the guys nearest to me enquired in French where we were from as we looked very dirty and unkempt. Dave spoke better French than I explained our road trip as best he could only to find the fellow who spoke English. Embarrassment was obvious to us and caused a motion of laughter from them. He asked what country we were from and was excited when he learnt I was South African. He was a French Foreign Legionnaire who had fought with the South African mercenaries in the Congo War. Well, we became their good friends, much to our disadvantage as copious amounts of local wine appeared with us becoming very intoxicated much to their amusement.

We had to leave and the effort to get ourselves out the door was not as bad as the impact the chilly night weather had on us outside. Dave collapsed in a heap requiring me to attempt to get him on the bike. To do this I had a brilliant idea which was to turn him around and using both our belts secure him to me with his feet over the back kit bag and resting on the number plate. I then tried to start the bike and leave the village as best as possible.

Enduring a huge amount of sway from the overbalanced bike and aided by the wine effect I wobbled onto the road. It became apparent that we had made a lot of friends for as we proceeded along the road people on both sides people waved and were greeting us in what I thought was a French goodbye. Only after my senses cleared did I realize that Dave's legs had fallen off the number plate and I was negotiating the moving road on the wrong side, left for England right lane for Europe had somehow been missed in my attempt to stabilize the bike. Our new roadside good friends had been very obligingly trying to tell me something. Once out of the village I found a small space of green grass, stopped and offloaded Dave who I thought may be dead but was now attempting to speak to me in a very strange language. He was however able to get into his sleeping bag as did I and sleep mercifully came to us both.

Morning arrived with us attempting to recount what and where we had been. Thankfully, no damage except for a very heavy headache and a promise never to drink unlabeled local village wine again. We survived the road trip and except for this incident and one other where we had slept in a pumpkin field, no damage. The pumpkin field incident was a close one. One dark and misty evening we camped out in what we thought was an empty field. With daylight, we realized that we were in a pumpkin field and possibly could have a small pumpkin for dinner, which the farmer would not miss. As we attempted to leave the field a very irate farmer appeared out of nowhere with a gun in hand. We had thankfully not relieved the farmer of one of his small pumpkins but had made some tea on our little primus stove. He approached very aggressively and as he neared, I took hold of the hot dixie of tea and offered him a cup. He realized we were harmless and accepted the tea warning us that we were on private land. I hate to think what he would have done had he known we were going to pick a small pumpkin only minutes before his arrival. As we travelled on, I agreed with Dave that the buckshot in our rear also possibly in our tyres would have had a serious effect on our further travel to the ferry and back to Jersey. I went back to working on the docks. My story will start again when I return to Madeira.

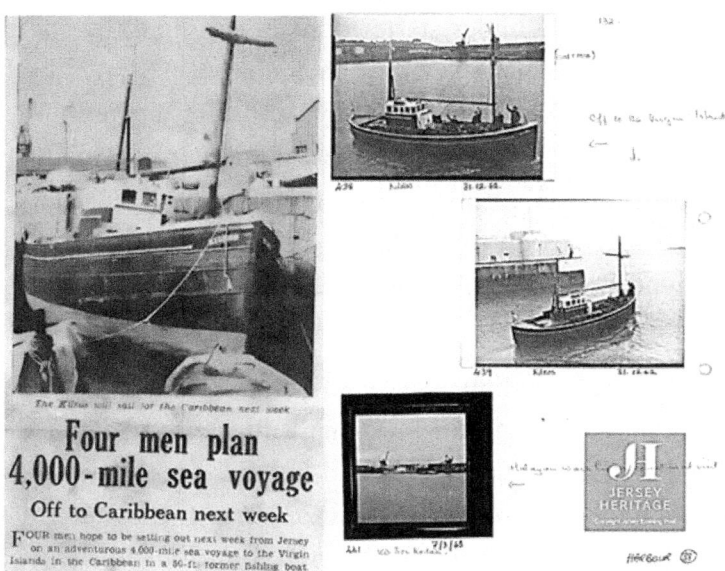

Kilros Adventure, Madera & Atlantic

Four men plan 4,000-mile sea voyage

Off to Caribbean next week

FOUR men hope to be setting out next week from Jersey on an adventurous 4,000-mile sea voyage to the Virgin Islands in the Caribbean in a 50-ft. former fishing boat.

One afternoon, walking up from the docks where I was working as a stevedore, I saw a small vessel that resembled a fishing boat with fuel drums tied to the gunwales. Peering down at it from the dock, a head popped out of the open forhold and acknowledged my presence. I struck up a conversation and found out the vessel had attempted an Atlantic crossing but had developed main engine bearing problems and had limped into St. Helier for repairs. The guy's name was Colin Barnes, and the vessel was owned by Peter Haycraft, a master mariner who had established a small commercial business in Tortola, British Virgin Islands. He was attempting for a second time to get the vessel there to start up an inter-island barge and transport business to boost his small commercial wholesale business venture among the islands. My ears perked up, and I suggested to Colin that the next time he spoke to Peter, who had to return to the Virgin Islands, to tell him that as I had diesel and mechanical experience, I would be interested in joining the venture.

It turned out that Peter accepted my offer, and for the next few weeks, we proceeded to repair "Kilros" and get it ready for sea trials. The Kilros was an old 1942, 48-foot Irish fishing boat, with a 30-ton gross weight wooden canoe hull, and a 4-cylinder 80 H.P National diesel engine which required a one-cylinder starter donkey engine to be started before the main engine would come to life. This engine was started by hand, ran for a brief time, and then a belt was slid across to a fixed pulley on the main engine to start it. This little engine would later prove indispensable, but I'll explain that later. There was also a second auxiliary 30 H.P. engine located forward driving a long wing shaft with a small propeller to add drive when the fishing nets were out.

The vessel also had a small square sail that could be attached to the forward short mast, in addition to a small mizzen sail. Peter discovered her in Chichester harbour and relocated her to Shoreham. This is where he initially attempted to cross the Atlantic, but unfortunately, the attempt failed due to engine trouble that forced him to turn to Jersey. His parents owned a small guesthouse there. The fish hold had been removed, resulting in a small cargo space. An additional fuel tank had been installed to facilitate the crossing. This tank would later cause us serious trouble. This issue was exacerbated by the twelve 45-gallon drums of diesel strapped to the bulwark on either side of the deckhouse. Additional fuel and freshwater tanks were mounted on the deck in front of the wheelhouse. There was room for four bunks below deck, behind the wheelhouse, and a small table. The engine room was a small, cramped 'hell hole', which smelled of diesel, fish, and bilge water and was about 4 meters square. Forward of that was the auxiliary engine. A gas cooker was placed behind the wheel compartment, forming the cooking area. Loads of stores were brought on board, as well as extra cargo for Peter's business consisting of canned vegetables, fruit, and meat pies. Once in the bunks, there wasn't much room to turn over due to the small space between the bunks. Thus, sleeping was primarily on one's back and unsuitable for those suffering from claustrophobia. The ship lacked washing facilities and the toilet, situated in the bow, was a chemical type that required daily emptying. As I progress with this story, I will later attempt to describe the experience of using this toilet in a Force 10 wind against a furious sea. Peter eventually returned from Tortola, and the crew now consisted of Peter the skipper, Colin Barnes, Graham Marks, Johnny Bardon, and me. Except for Peter, none of us had much sailing experience, but sailing was not an issue as the Kilros was a motorboat.

Little did I know that this new adventure was going to turn my life around. Things were glum. I had to leave my room due to financial strain above the fish and chip shop owned by Bill & Mrs. D Ducqumine on Duhamel Street and was sharing a small flat with three other guys and a girl outside the centre of St Hellier. Money was almost zero, and the prospect of returning to England or home as a pauper was possible. Home meant the failure of my around-the-world attempt, so England was the possible solution, but not one I looked forward to. Jersey was a far better place to live, and I had made good friends, preferring the climate and island life.

Eventually, everything was shipshape, and the sea trials proved successful. We carried some small cargo which Peter wanted for his business, food in the form of tinned goods, fresh water in an external tank fitted behind the wheelhouse, and my only worldly possession, my BSA 250cc motorbike. On the eve of our departure, I was walking back to my shared digs, feet wet due to rain, feeling not scared but a little anxious about the outcome of this rapidly approaching new venture. Friends and well-wishers had advised against such a crazy way of getting across the Atlantic, especially without any real sail as a backup means of propulsion. Near my digs was a church where, in the dark, I knelt at its entrance and asked the good Lord, who had always been my friend, to stand by me once more. He would need to be patient as I would call on him again over the years.

The winter of 1962/1963 was particularly severe in the U.K. This had brought light snow to Jersey, something I had no real experience with, so Colin and I built a snowman on the aft deck just for fun. The morning finally arrived, so with a few friends on the dock to bid us farewell and bon voyage, and eager to embark on the adventure, we cast off to chug merrily out into the channel, setting course for the French/Spanish/Portuguese coast. Little did we know that in the next few days our courage, stamina and seaworthiness would be put to the test.

As night fell, we were in merry spirits, and a bottle of wine, which I had hidden in my bunk, was consumed as a good gesture and to celebrate the New Year. We cruised parallel to the French coast heading for the Bay of Biscay expecting to get a good crossing the following morning. By midmorning the following day, we were starting to enter the bay and proceeded on with the expectation of getting across in 24 hours. However, that afternoon Peter and I were standing in the wheelhouse, and what we saw did not make us feel very comfortable. The old saying "Red sky at night sailors' delight. Red sky in the morning, sailor take warning" was very obvious and it was agreed we should turn back to the Isle of Ushant a few hours behind us. Cylinder one had started to give trouble, leaking badly.

Thankfully that night we got safely in the protected bay of the island as a real gale force took hold, with the barometer falling amidst lashing rain. It was 1/1/1963, the sea became a raging fury of spray and heavy swells. We anchored for a day or so until the storm abated and once more, we bravely sailed out into the bay in an attempt to reach Oporto Leixões on the Portuguese coast. It was not to be. Two-thirds of the way across the bay, the twin sister of the earlier storm arrived. It was night, and we were being tossed about like a cork. Later, it got worse as we pitched and rolled down unseen chasms of black water. The Kilros would slide down a wall of water, bury her bow into two or three meters of the sea, and pitch up, forcing the water against the wheelhouse. We would roll over until we were nearly standing on the walls of the wheelhouse, get lifted by the swell, and then hurled off the top of the wave. The propeller would come free, the governor would take over, and we would career down the swell into a valley of churning water where no sky could be seen, just a deep black, bottomless hole, only to start the same gyrations again.

The vessel was taking a pounding; the engine was acting up, and below deck, all we could do was protect ourselves from being bashed about and keep her bow towards the wave, swell, and wind, otherwise, we would capsize. This continued for the whole night and into the day. With no sighting of the sun or stars, Peter could not get a navigation shot to figure out exactly where we were.

Our luck changed as out of the windswept fury, a large cargo vessel, the "M.V. Breta Dan," an Arctic cargo ship also battling the storm, appeared. Peter, via Aldis lamp, was asked if we wanted to abandon the ship. We replied no, looking at the churning ocean, but Peter was able to get a position which alarmingly put us further into the Atlantic than we wanted to be. The Breta Dan gave us valuable port information and compass-wise. That was a heading for Oporto Leixões, a port we now urgently needed for repairs since the engine was still misbehaving, and I attributed it to fuel contamination, plus overheating.

We reduced power, and by that night, the storm seemed to be abating. However, with the good news of a position and the storm easing, we altered course in an attempt to get to Oporto Leixões on the Portuguese coast. The following night, we saw some very welcome shore lights, and by early morning, we had found the port of Oporto. The entrance navigation lights could not be seen in an attempt to enter the harbour.

At the last minute, we nearly took the wrong side of the lighthouse which would have led us directly onto the low submerged concrete shore break, a close call to the wreckage. Navigating this entrance was a serious risk as should the sick engine stop or falter, with the heavy swell, we would have been doomed. By one a.m. that morning we tied up in the main harbour, cleared customs, and all got an hour or two of exhausted sleep.

I was concerned about the engine, and after a careful inspection, I figured out it was the lamina of the inbuilt reserve tank that had come loose, blocking the filters to the main engine. We had, during the voyage so far, been able to rig up a system of bypassing the filter for a few seconds to allow us to wash and clean a second filter. So, rotating the filters every 4 hours on the watch changed, which also required pumping up the header tank to feed the main engine. I also felt that the number 4 cylinder was the cause of the overheating. I pulled the cylinder head off and, with the aid of a carbon strip and grinding paste, was able to sand down a bit of the valve stems, easing the friction, which I was sure was the problem. New Citroën fuel filters were bought, and then I made a conversion to our system to accommodate them. More fuel was taken on; a general cleanup, together with a good night's rest without the hammering and pitching, plus a hot meal, was the order of the day.

With the repairs and rest accomplished, we motored out again into the Atlantic, this time heading for the island of Madeira in the Canaries, our jumping-off point to attempt the Atlantic crossing. It was 12/1/1963.

Oporto Leixões to Madeira is 666 miles.

The weather was good to us, and the passage to Madeira was pleasant. The engine gave trouble a couple of times, requiring us to stop with a stuck number 2 valve. It bent the push rod, so a heave to was required. On 17/1/1963, we sighted Porto Santo, part of the Canary Islands. We were 27 miles from Madeira. The appearance of the island in the setting sun was picturesque, and here I recalled my earlier visit en route to England on the Union Castle Steamship Companies Edinburgh Castle.

Docking in Madeira we were put not far from the yacht club and to our delight, there was a public toilet with showers. At this stage of my story, I am sure one can understand that using a chemical toilet on a pitching rolling floor, inside a tiny almost closet in the bow of a ship was indeed very nearly impossible. The art of straddling a small drum by desperately holding onto the beam above one's head, which most of the time had been crowned by the ship movement, at the same time attempting to shed one's trousers and then timing the upcoming drum at the same time as lowering one's posterior on to it was more than a contortionist could handle. The contents of the drum if aim was successful, would sometimes expel itself into the bilge. The ability to have the use of a clean flushing toilet and to add a shower was absolute heaven.

After cleaning up and looking around, we set to work getting the "Kilros" ship shape. More fuel was ordered, and we topped up our freshwater tank. The drums holding attachments to the gunnels were tightened and secured. One day whilst leaving the showers very fortunately met a lovely young girl. She invited me to meet her father who was the yacht club commodore, and it was to be for dinner at a local hotel. This at first was a problem as I had no clean or presentable clothes but after washing what I had I was able to sort of present myself in respectable attire. Albeit with worn out collar, stained brown pants and a pair of shoes soled by CRAVEN A cigarette cardboard. The evening went very well, with a full 4-course meal I had not seen in months. The conversation was around sailing which I also knew truly little about but stumbled through on a pretense that I was looking at taking it up as a career and the prospects of returning to Madera for a visit. This was tailored by the daughter who had moved closer to my seat. Then I put myself into trouble as I was offered a glass of brandy and a cigar. It went straight to my head forcing me to lose my concentration, balance and ability to communicate on any level besides a mixture of English, Zulu and whatever Spanish I had picked up in one day. Fortunately, I was able to take my leave on whatever excuse I could make myself understood, departing gracefully from the table, out of the Hotel without crashing into anybody or things and attempting to find my ship on to which I was sure I was going to die.

The road had been a two-lane uphill when I arrived but was now a 4-lane downhill swaying highway with all sorts of newfound friends waving en route. How I found the harbour the lord only knows but I did and collapsed on the "Kilros" deck clutching whatever I could hold onto to stop the world from going round. I never saw that gracious young lady or her father again for reasons of which I cannot guess. I do believe she had intentions, especially regarding her interest in my returning to Madeira as a possible yachty.

Peter had been watching the weather and was getting concerned about the delays in attempting to do the jump across the pond. (Atlantic) Therefore, it was not without concern when he suddenly woke us in the morning to say the wind was right and his weather report suggested we depart post haste. All was made ready, and we duly powered out to attempt the crossing. The first day the swell was good with wind reassembly strong and behind us. The canoe hull gave us a wallowing effect, but our speed was good averaging about 8 to 10 knots.

Little did we know that Mother Nature was waiting for us just over the horizon. The night and morning of the second day were good, our spirits were high, and my engine was running well. We sat and watched the breathtaking Atlantic Ocean roll out in front of us. The break and clean up plus a few good meals had done us a world of good. I still felt the effects of my evening out. With the radio working again Peter had sent a message departing Madeira to Tortola Cable and Wireless and his family via London where the London Telegraph was monitoring our progress. The second day out the following waves grew bigger, and the sky became a dark and ominous grey. Soon we were back to pitching, rolling and diving taking water 2 or 3 meters across our bow repeatedly as we surfed off the huge following sea and a wind lashing us as we crested the waves rolling us onto our side.

Night and day we surrendered ourselves to this for 17 days the frightening part was at night when the noise of the growlers grew behind us to an enormous height then sweeping down and underneath us lurching the vessel almost uncontrollably broadside. Using the toilet was almost impossible, so relieving oneself out the rear door without letting the ocean in was an art of its own. We had to go out to the 45-gallon drums and pump fuel into the header tank. The wind ripped at one's body and drove horizontally between the drums, gunnels and wheelhouse. We had only a rope around our waist if this had parted or we lost our grip the crew would have been minus one member with no hope of recovery. Waves crashed against the wheelhouse threatening to tear it off its mountings. (Some 40 years later, I sent Penny Peter's wife a picture on e-mail of a fishing vessel in similar conditions. She asked Peter if it was the same. His answer was worse and more terrifying. (Opinion from a master mariner).

The foremast went sometime during one of the nights and all we could pray for was that the engine kept going. We had to maintain our steering and heading. One terrifying incident happened when a fuel airlock developed transferring fuel, the main engine started to splutter and miss, I made a mad dash with I believe was Graham into the engine room and in an attempt to stop the engine from quitting I started the single-engine starter motor engine which we fondly called the one-armed bandit, opened two of the decompressors on the main and engaged the starter motor running off a belt to the flywheel of the main. While I kept the starter motor going Graham opened the relief valve on the filters and we cleared the airlock. I then closed the decompressors, and the main engine came back to life giving us steerage. I got a bit burnt from having to lean across the main engines' hot cylinders, but we survived.

The days wore on and fatigue was certainly setting in not to mention a certain amount of anxiety. The water was getting low, and the gearbox was overheating so losing a certain amount of drive. In a quiet conversation with Peter, I expressed my concern, and we agreed the Atlantic weather had to abate soon or we were in trouble. On the 19th day out finally, the weather eased, and Peter got a good sextant fix, we were south of track but heading in the right direction hoping to make the Virgin Islands in about 6 days. Water now was down to rations and so was food. Part of our cargo was sealed Steak and kidney pies in metal containers bought from Britain. One had fallen into the bilge and on remembering it I attempted to locate it by fishing around the bilge, which now contained an unthinkable mixture from the toilet with oil and bilge water. Unbelievably I found it but now came the question of how to heat it as our gas for the stove was depleted. From my Boy Scout days, we took an old biscuit tin and tied it to the exhaust manifold turning it into an oven. The sacred pie was opened and heated, consumed rapidly by five very hungry men.

Our living conditions had deteriorated, and our body odour was not related to any known deodorant. It was suggested that we tie a ladder to the side and attempt to get a swim. All agreed with the condition that someone be on watch for sharks that had taken all our fishing gear and at times their length was when alongside longer than our vessel. We all duly had a refreshing swim with no one either missing limb or soul but of the understanding that the nearest land was beneath us at about 6000 meters. Now the other problem was water as our only supply had somehow gotten contaminated with diesel. This had either happened as we unscrewed the drums to attach a wobble pump and the spray from the diesel had been inhaled at the water tank vent behind the wheelhouse. We never knew how this happened but there we were all optimistically saying never mind we will get some rain and we can make 6 days without water or could we? My Boy Scout training came up and I suggested we build a small cement slab made from some of the cement we had as cargo over the stump of where the foremast had been. Then, with the use of an unturned old bucket we had, cut out the bottom and made a stove, thereby allowing us to distil water.

The idea was agreed upon and a piece of the lower cargo pallet was cut up and brought on deck. I took an axe and started to chop a few pieces of kindling. Johnny held the wood on the gunnel as I chopped away. Regrettably, I missed with the rolling vessel and chopped right through my left index finger. Realizing the danger of infection, I got Johnny to get the old farmer's medical cure in the form of methylated spirits from below. As I held the wound open Johnny poured the mentholated spirit into the wound. It stung like hell, but I was satisfied I was clear of infection, as we did this and I opened the wound Johnny was sick, it was not sea sickness. Later that night I got a needle and thread and was able to put a small stitch to hold the flesh together. I still have the scar today as a reminder of the crossing. The distilling project was abandoned and by the grace of God it rained slightly that night allowing us to get some precious water from a small canvas tarpaulin we hastily spread out.

However, our troubles were not over as the gearbox was almost out of commission. In a wild attempt to save oil and keep it going, I had rigged a sack over the overheated box. Pouring seawater over it to cool the system. It eventually gave up and we lay wallowing adrift in the Atlantic. There was a tiny engine in the bow, which had been used to trawl in its fishing days and could give about maybe 2 or 3 knots. We attempted to start it but it caught fire so that was the end of that idea. Peter figured if we spread the canvas tarpaulin out as a sail, which we subsequently did, it could make us maybe 2-3 knots and we could still make the islands in 2 weeks as long as we could have steerage. But the water and food were now a major problem, and we were down to two small rations per day. I had slowly squirrelled away a small amount each night above my bunk and was treating myself to a few crumbs every night. However, by my reckoning, we had about 4 days at the most before dehydration and lack of substance would set in. My mind was working overtime we needed heat to distil water, or we needed to drink a small, controlled amount of seawater.

A night passed and the morning brought a clear blue sky and calm rolling swells. The world looked radiant and yet here we were a floating island slowly dying. Another day came and went making about 5 knots but with sloppy steerage causing us to work the helm continuously. It was the third day that Johnny was at the helm when what looked like a small sliver of something appeared on the horizon. We called all to the deck and attempted to identify it. It was way off to the left or South of us. Slowly it progressed across the horizon, and we guessed it was either another yacht or something unbeknown to us. There was no sail, just this fine moving line fractionally above the horizon. Then it dawned on us as we saw a bow starting to appear ahead of it. It had to be the foremast of a vessel. Peter grabbed the Aldis lamp as the radio, which I think had been previously used by Columbus, was out of commission. Very, very slowly a bridge appeared, and Peter tapped out an SOS. three shorts three longs three shorts. Again, and again but there was no response. Now the vessel was outlined against the horizon it was a huge bulk tanker probably running on autopilot with maybe 8 crew, and a lone helmsman who had not seen us. We had to get its attention. The idea of putting diesel into a can and igniting it was considered to make smoke when all of a sudden, an Aldis lamp (a lamp signaling in Morse code) reply came back to acknowledge our SOS. She was the Royal Dutch Shell Tanker "M.V Crania".

Very slowly, this huge vessel started to turn towards us and in about an hour, she was looming off our starboard bow. A loudhailer sounded and asked what our problem was. Quickly Peter explained our predicament. The master of the ship suggested that as we had no power, he would maneuver downwind allowing us to drift up against his ship. This was agreed and being able to start we got a little gearbox power to make steerage, so in a brief time, we were in his bow wash and bumping alongside. Now we had a problem, we started to bash up against his massive vessel propelled by the huge Atlantic swell and damage was being done to our small old craft opening up the starboard top boards. In desperation, we fended off and were able to get the urgent message across that we needed gearbox oil. A heaving line came down followed by 10 gallons of oil. Then we requested cigarettes and some food. The crew on deck threw down all they had in their pockets littering our deck with fags. Some bread followed and a pile of margarine. By now we were taking water and had to push away from this behemoth of a vessel to save us from breaking up. I topped up the gearbox, got the donkey starter engine up and started the main, we had power.

Very slowly we pulled away and bid farewell to our saviors who advised they would report our position. Now with full power regained and a functional gearbox, we headed straight for Tortola. Albeit for the next 5 days we ate margarine sugar, smoked cigarettes, and drank a little saved rainwater. Occasionally a flying fish would end up on deck so since we had lost all our fishing gear a mad dash was made to secure it. The only other fish we came close to was a whale shark. This fish can be enormous, and this one was about 30 feet in length. It came alongside which was of concern to us as if it had decided to rub itself on our hull it could have possibly capsized us or done damage to our now frail hull after the battering we got alongside the M.V Crania.

A few days later now motoring with the new oil and some food we jiggled the radio to life and contacted the Swedish M.V. Bacherole who in turn radioed our position to Tortola. This, we felt, would be a very welcome message to Peter's wife Penny and the residents of Road Town in Tortola. The 27th day of the crossing from Maderia dawned and all seemed well. Peter was convinced we were getting extremely near, so all eyes were peeled to look for land. It was at 14: 00 hrs. on the 27th day that I asked Johnny to confirm what I saw and convince him from my farming experience, it was land and not cloud. With a great cry of yes! We all confirmed it was land being the island of Anegada to our left and Virgin Gorda to our right. Later that night Sombrero lighthouse was seen confirming our location, Peter with our weak and intermittent radio got a message to Road Town harbour Tortola that we were now in the Anegada channel. The British newspapers had published an article on our voyage so they, the islanders had guessed that were still alive and were close. We then passed into the Sir Frances Drake channel with Ginger Island in sight. At this point, a morse message sent by a car light was seen from the Island asking if we were the Kilros. Peter replied via morse that we were. Soon a launch was seen powering towards us captained by a local character called "Fishy" Soares who when within throwing distance heaved cold beers to us, what a welcome. We steamed up the Sir Frances Drake channel docking at Road Town harbour at 12.15 past midnight.

The island population totaling about 200 Black and 18 white folks were there to meet us, which included a local band. It was also Colin's birthday. After docking with the legal formalities completed it was a wonderful sight to see Peter and Penny embrace and show so much affection after this harrowing crossing. This was a major accomplishment for all. Peter and his partner went on to build his trading empire using the Kilros as a tug and trading vessel for his wholesale business. All of us went our separate ways, Collin stayed in Tortola as an architect, but many years later became ill and had to return to England where he died.

In 1967 coming out of a swimming pool in Edmonton Canada, I was approached by a gentleman asking my name. It was Graham who was in the shop fitting business. Never heard from him again. Johnny later joined me working on the yachts. Years on he stowed away on a cargo ship and returned to England where he became a professional sailor on luxury yachts. He also authored a small article and I believe a book on his ventures and his success as a Captain on large luxury sailing vessels. I did see him briefly again in 1995 in Palma Majorca where he had taken up residence working as a captain for a large family luxury yacht.

For me, it was the start of a new life to challenge the impossible. Here I was thousands of miles from any salvation, with no education, and only a dream to see the world. The crossing was only the beginning of what was to come. It also was a mark of something that would develop in later years.

Tortola

Penny had made arrangements for us to stay at the Treasure Island Hotel owned by the Roy family, so we proceeded up the hill to this beautiful family-run hotel and hot baths, a real meal and a bed. The scum line on the bath took me 10 minutes to clean off as my body had not seen a hot wash, was covered in diesel and oil plus the bilge water smell. Sleep was hard to come by as it was almost dawn, I walked out onto the veranda and was struck by the beauty of the picturesque view looking down onto the Road Town harbour bay, the Sir Francis Drake channel and some of the Virgin Islands sort of forming a necklace for the crystal blue sea. I was overwhelmed by the beauty of something I had never seen or expected to see, taking quite a while to absorb it all.

The hotel is owned by Charles and Rowan Roy with their respective families of English extraction where all islanders have been there for many years. Now the reality of the situation was on us, and work had to be obtained. Not being islanders, this was a problem and it appeared that all we could do for the moment was to work for our keep. I got involved in fixing some water pumps there was also a Willy's Jeep the same as I had in South Africa, which needed some attention. As I was a diver, I was able to get some work on a pier in need of repair plus did some painting for Jeffrey Cobham at his small shipyard. Jeffrey was Sir Allan Cobham's son; Sir Allan was the inventor of refueling in the air. Also, he with his wife was the first to fly a seaplane around South Africa.

Fate was showing me something as later time would align me with him and seaplane flying. Jeffrey had a very beautiful wife who would sunbathe on their motor cruiser deck in the bay, regretfully the boat caught fire and burnt to the water level. Thankfully she was not injured but we sure missed seeing her sunbathing on the deck of her boat. The Rockefeller group had started to build a luxury resort on Virgin Gorda and a small island next to it called Beef Island that had a short dirt airstrip. In exploring the island on horseback, I swam the horse across the estuary and found the deserted airstrip with an old Grumman Duck single-hulled WW2 Navy plane lying abandoned. What or how or why it was there I never found out but today it would be worth a fortune. My only thought was that it might have been used to smuggle drugs.

Grumman Duck abandoned Beef Island

Any work on the Rockefeller resort was not available as it was all contracted to overseas companies. My BSA motorcycle had come with us, so to gain some money I sold it. It had travelled a long way I also took shift work behind the bar at the Treasure Island hotel we were not paid as we were working our board but the tips from mainly American tourists certainly helped.

It was one afternoon as I was serving behind the bar that an amphibious Grumman Goose aircraft landed in the harbour. The Treasure Island Hotel was the only hotel in the area where the passengers came to the bar for refreshments. In talking to them I understood a passenger, Mr Mike Burk, owned the aircraft. He also owned a small fleet of cruising yachts called "Windjammer Cruises" and was bringing a couple down to start cruising from the neighboring American Virgin Island of St. Thomas.

Grumman Goose flying boat.

I got on well with him and asked if there was any chance of getting to work on his yachts. He agreed to speak to the incoming Captain and would refer me to him.

A day later the most beautiful yacht sailed into the Road Town harbour under full sail. She was the "Tondelayo" a New York Bermuda race winner of 97feet converted by Windjammer cruises as a 16-passenger cruising yacht. I fell in love with her immediately seeing my way out of the isolation of Totola and the charity of the kind folk who had made work available for my keep. On meeting the captain, he informed me that the owner Mike Burke had spoken to him. He hired me and I sailed that night as engineer crewing on the first 10-day cruise covering Virgin Gorda, across the Anegada passage to the Windward Islands of St Martin and St Bart's. Then south to Nelsons Dockyard in Antigua, west to Nevis, past St Kitts onto Saba the volcanic island and back through the Anegada channel to St Thomas in the American Virgin Islands.

I was extremely happy, and the entire world seemed to be going my way. Here I was on a magnificent sailing ship, sea spray in my face, beautiful islands with beaches to swim in and beautiful young mostly American 16 – 20-year-old girls to share it all with. They loved my accent, and most could not believe I was a South African, relating to their immature knowledge that Africa did not only have Black (Negro) Africans. Confused by the answer that Arabs from Egypt and White Africans from the South also inhabited Africa and were therefore also Africans. One of the first questions I got was, was I a missionary's son or maybe a child of a foreign diplomat? They found it hard to believe I was the 3rd generation South African. Did not ride to school on an elephant or have a pet lion. However, there were times to win a beer or two when a good story was told to amuse the locals and tourists.

One thing one learns is to be friendly to the captain, and secondly the cook. Ironically the cook was a black guy called Wilma Rowel, and for all my time cruising the Caribbean he and I became good friends getting on very well at sea and in Port. Another black cook was J.D., he too was a character. Good guys to know as food was important and anything extra was a bonus. I quickly learnt to sail the big yachts which included square riggers of pirate ship type. This is a picture of a similar sailing boat we had. Our ship was called the "flying cloud".

A 180-foot four-masted Brigantine similar to the "Flying Cloud"

Caribee a 100-foot top sail schooner

Windjammer cruises had the Cutty Sark, Caribee, Yankee and the Yankee Clipper all over 100 feet and under square rigging. Later the "Flying Cloud" arrived she was originally the German steel magnet Krupp 180-foot square rigger brigantine converted to carry 80 passengers. Working the spreaders and topsails was a feat of its own, at times extremely dangerous. The whip effect of the mast sometimes in the dark with often rain, was a hell of a job to stop not to be sent flying of the yards into the ocean or deck. There were a few frightening experiences. In one case a crewmember fell from the yards and was killed. He was put in a sack and placed in the chain locker until the vessel could dock. Another was a young girl passenger feeling sick came up on deck, she tripped on a sleeping crewmember and went overboard. It was a moonless night, and we had all sails up doing an estimate of about 10 knots. By the grace of God, the cook in his white T-shirt and trousers was sitting having a smoke on the transom. He grabbed the main sheet and jumped in grabbing by her hair as she swept by. The captain at the helm came about and shouted for help. In turn, the crew were able to haul them both alongside and onto the deck. She was alive and incredibly lucky to be so. To have come about, bring down the sails and find her in the black sea would have been almost impossible.

My worst experience was on crossing the Anegada passage a well-used shipping lane, from Saba to St Thomas. I had handed over the watch at midnight and was asleep on the main deck next to the main mast. I woke suddenly for reasons I don't know, rolled over to see a straight vertical line merging through the darkness. Leaping up I ran to the helm to find the crewman manning it asleep. I spun the helm as fast as I could to starboard, turning I saw the massive bow of a ship bearing down on us. I hit the starter, which miraculously sprang to life. The bow of the ship was now on us as we slowly healed over as the engine took. We rode the bow wash and slid down the length of the massive ship at about 20 feet. So close I saw a man's red jacket hanging off the door to a cabin. As the vessel passed us, we took the full force of the generated wind effect and the natural wind. We had been on full sail with everything up on a starboard tack therefore the port backstay was down on the main. The Tondelayo healed right overtaking water into the stateroom overhead vents. The boom swung across hitting the gallows and slamming into the starboard backstay with such force I heard the main mast resound. The jib and foresails slammed across the deck and took force with a thundering boom, floundering in the sea. Everything ended up on the starboard gunnels including passengers and crew. The captain came racing up the stairway and into the cockpit. By then we had done a 180-degree turn and with the crew now very much awake we were able to come about and get things ship shape again. It was a remarkably close call, and one wonders how many yachts are lost this way.

In sailing and weather, the bow sprit would rise and fall up to as much as 20 feet, so when working the jibs, one could be one minute almost airborne, the next floundering underwater as the bow buried itself under the sea. I once lost my grip and fell into the head net under the bowsprit. Thankfully the bow was coming up and I had just enough time to scramble back onto the bowsprit, get my hands on the jib and hang on.

In our duties as crew, we had some amusing situations. Our regular attire was usually cut-off jeans, a Swedish stainless sheathed knife, and no underwear as we were usually wet and needed as little as possible to dry out. Going up to and working the spreaders and yards we were spread-eagled on the stay wires. Consequently, the young girls below had a sight that became interesting to them.

The islands were relatively virgin tourist-wise, with clean untouched beaches and little tourist activity. This changed drastically later, and they are now a tourist haven. English Harbour and Nelson's dockyard in Antigua were being slowly developed. It was a hidden harbour where Nelson could hide his fleet and sail out attacking pirates and Spanish galleons carrying bullion from South America. It was a difficult harbour to see from the sea and sometimes extremely dangerous to get in through the mouth. The yard had warping irons to get ships in using long boats to assist.

The Nicholson family of white West Indian stock had taken on the venture to turn the harbour into a luxury yacht retreat. Nelson's house was refurbished, and his bed was still there. It looked like a doll's bed as the size of the Englishman in those days was not anything like our South African stock. The old warehouses abandoned for decades were turned into a bar and restaurant with living accommodation above. It was a wonderful place to visit and turn around heading back to the Virgin Islands. Nevis was a beautiful island with a lovely hot spring in the centre. St Kitts is only a mile away and the one island of Eustacia which had a significant history in South Africa. It was on this Island that the ships carrying arms to the American Civil War from Cape Town arrived. They would transship their cargo supporting the Southern States as South Africa was a British colony and therefore supported the Southern States who were also supported by the British flag. It was also one of the first islands to have a synagogue. Some of these ships did sail to Cape Town crossing the South Atlantic to collect the arms cargo, food, goods passengers etc. Today the old Afrikaans Cape songs record their arrival. One being "Dar kom die Alabama" (Here comes the Alabama) can still be heard. In some of the Southern States the African word "Piccanin" is still heard describing the small black African children. Further West Northwest was Saba, an island with a very deep-water anchorage. To tie up usually requires a dive and swim with the hawser through to the eye of the anchored buoy. Passengers and cargo were lowered onto a twin type of canoe lashed together. The paddlers had a caller who was a master at riding the waves onto the beach. He would position the vessel and at his command, the paddlers would frantically paddle on the back of the wave. Surfing onto the beach to be met by a gang of islanders who would grab the vessel and haul it up to the beach before the following wave washed them back into the heavy surf. Quite an experience, which they also did with Land Rovers, strapped to the vessel.

St Bart's had quite a record as it was said the headman of the island had sold fuel and liquor to the German submariners who would Heave To near the reefs for crew rest. St Martin being half Dutch and French was also feeling the tourist development with beach bars, restaurants, duty-free stores and hotels being built. One American couple I met on a cruise and became particularly good friends with was Chuck and Jody Shoemaker. They were on a cruise, had sons about my age and were a great couple. At the end of their cruise, we were short of a stewardess for the next cruise. Chuck had to get back to their business in Kennet Square, so Jody volunteered to do the job as a stewardess. It was challenging work, but she had a great time and enjoyed working with us. Years later their son visited my home in South Africa, touring the country on a 50cc motorcycle. They became family friends and in turn, they visited our home in South Africa with my parents visiting them some years later using an airline ticket I had been able to get for them as a present.

My earlier physical shape can be described as if I put my tongue out, I would look like a zipper or a walking xylophone. However, with the physical work, I started to put on muscle and weight. I was 6 feet tall at 13 years of age so now being 6 feet 4 ½ ins I was able to carry the extra muscle, so back in the sun with a good tan, I felt good. The months went by, and I was enjoying the sailing, but I felt I should move on as time was racing by and I could not see a future in yacht sailing. While in London I applied to Bookers Sugar Estates for a possible overseer job in British Guyana. However, was told they did not hire from England only Georgetown in British Guyana. I decided to leave sailing and head for British Guyana. To do this I bought a ticket on the Federal Palm an island freighter given to the islands by the Canadian Government. She and her sister ship the Federal Maple were old liberty ships converted to freighters with a hold consisting of bunk beds in tiers of 3. The sleeping accommodation was hot as hell so most slept on the deck. There was a first-class section below the bridge and a galley below that. The cattle class in which I was in shared a couple of showers and toilets. Drinkable water was obtainable from a water fountain on the deck or a tap in the shower room. An area which was far from hygienic smelling of urine and body odour. I found my bunk hiding my possessions at the bottom of my kit bag with my money and passport in my belly pouch. Sailing from Antigua an island that would become very much part of my life, we stopped at Guadeloupe, Dominicana (another island destined to be a mark in my life) St Lucia, St Vincent, past the beautiful Grenadines to Grenada and on to Trinidad. Food had to be brought on board or purchased from the galley being leftovers from the first class or cheap daily boiled chicken rice and breadfruit sold at a very low price. It was while on the voyage I met some very good Trinidadian first class passengers, they were Fred and Rita Scott who had cousins in Grenada,

Leo and Brenda De-Gale. In learning of my precarious situation and endeavor to travel the world. They kindly got food from their dinners and gave it to me at the handrail separating the steerage (cattle) class from First.

In Grenada, I met the De Gales and had a marvelous lunch with them. I also met a German fighter pilot who had been shot down by an RAF pilot and now living on the island. They fought each other in the war but by accident met in Grenada and became good friends. On arrival in Trinidad Fred and Rita offered the hospitality of their home, which I duly accepted. The immigration officers had never seen a Republic of South Africa Passport, but with Fred's involvement, it was considered that I was of colonial birth therefore British by origin and allowed in. They were incredibly good to me as a total young stranger and showed me around Trinidad. The pleasure of a hot bath and a proper bed, home-cooked food will always go down in my memory as very pleasant. I was extremely grateful to them and kept in touch for years.

Now trouble came from as usual, unexpectedly. My journey was to take me from Trinidad to British Guyana in an attempt to get a job with Bookers Sugar Estates however, the civil war started in Georgetown British Guyana, so travel was restricted. There was no way I could proceed and had to consider somehow returning to the West Indies to get back on a yacht or something to survive. My money was almost depleted and could not stay on with Scott's. Scott ironically would be a name that would come into my life in later years.

Bidding them farewell and getting to the harbour I searched for a yacht or something to get me back hopefully to Antigua where I had yacht contacts but there was nothing. However, the Federal Maple was sailing from Trinidad to Grenada, but I did not have the full fare to enable me to get a ticket to Antigua. That night evading the shore police and immigration, I slept in the hold of a friendly fisherman's island sloop. The following day I found an island sloop heading for Grenada, so with the offer of being an unpaid deckhand I bummed a ride. She was loaded and low in the water; I had to sleep on the rolling wet deck and was offered boiled chicken with rice served from a somewhat dirty pot for dinner. Midafternoon the next day we sailed into Grenada and there to my delight was the Federal Maple. With every penny I had plus now being closer to Antigua, I was able to buy a ticket and a bunch of bananas. At this point, all I owned in my entire life was SIX BANANAS.

The accommodation was the same as the Federal Palm, bunks and just as dirty. With insufficient funds for food, I lived on Bananas and water a foul-tasting stuff from the ship's supply. However, by chance, I found that if I stood by the galley entrance, food left over from the first-class plates such as slices of bread, jam, the odd chop or steak, and potatoes was readily available for my taking from the steward's tray. The only young white man doing this seemed out of place however, most times I think out of sympathy the stewards did not object but were rather amazed or amused. This therefore became my menu supplemented by my bananas on the 4-day sail back to Antigua.

Destiny and family background.

The wash from the ship's screw was churning up phosphorous leaving a trail in the dark waters behind the Federal Palm as we steamed North through the Grenadine Islands, St Vincent, St Lucia, Martinique, Dominica, Guadeloupe heading for Antigua. I pondered my deteriorating situation; would destiny again show her face? My thoughts looking at this propwash brought me back home and my life so far.

I was born in Pietermaritzburg Ex Union of South Africa on the 10th of August 1942. My mother was Gwladys Doreen Portal Evans (Nee Shores), and my father was Charles Evans a building contractor. I was to have two siblings, a sister Beverley Gwladys being 4 years younger and Wallis David an afterthought or mistake being 12 years younger. Beverley was to meet me later in Canada, marry a Canadian bank manager and have two boys Mark and Troy. She resides in Victoria.

British Columbia Canada. Wallis was to complete his education and get a university degree in Geology was drafted into the military, as all white South African boys had to serve. He was to join the Air Force as an electrician and fought the black communists during the ongoing border war in South Africa. He later went into his own business and married Gail who years later by circumstance became my younger son's godparent's daughter. Their marriage bore two boys Chase and Rhett.

At this point just about all our family were boys as I too was to have two sons Scott and Grant. Both our parents were born in South Africa in 1912. Father had had a very tough life as his father, also Charles Evans, had died when he was 16 and left him to care for his ailing stepmother plus two half-brothers, Arthur and Rolly. Grandfather Charles Evans was Welsh coming out to South Africa to fight in the Boer war with a Welsh regiment. After the war, he remained in the new British crown colony then called the Union of South Africa. He became a builder and contracted the length and breadth of the Province of Natal.

At my father's birth, his mother and my father's twin brother died. My grandfather now faced with a newborn baby hired a wet nurse to feed my father. A thing quite often done in those days in so enabling another woman to breastfeed a newborn. Grandfather Charles ended up marrying the lady and bore two sons with her. Arthur and Rolland.

My father was an excellent violin player and became the Durban Orchestra's leading violinist at 16 years old. He also was a lay preacher but with his father's death and as the 30's depression hit he was forced to lay bricks on sweat gangs working for the Durban municipality to enable him to feed his family. Being a musician, he at night ran a band of his own called the "Apollo's" and turned the handle of a sewing machine late into the night so that his stepmother could sew sheets for the hotels. The background of my grandfather's family we therefore knew little about. All we knew was his military history and that he had seven brothers as told to my father by his grandmother whom he by accident later met. Two went to the USA and got into the printing and film industry and another went to Australia. We did not know of any of their whereabouts except that in 1929 my father won a trip to England with the Boy Scouts to an international scout Jamboree. The names were published in British papers of the incoming overseas scouts, his was on the list. When in England he was introduced to his grandmother who had seen the name Charles Evans in the paper and thought it was her long-lost son. Only to find it was my father, her grandson. That was the only family history we knew about my father's side of the family.

My mother's side was quite different. Her grandfather was a D'Portal from the Portal family of Tonge house, Norwood, Berkshire, England. He was Horace Portal the son of Richard Brinsley the second with seven siblings and whose cousin was Lord Charles Portal ex viscount Portal of Hungerford of the Royal Air Force. Lord Charles was also the cousin to Sir Spencer John Portal's father of Oldric, Raymond and Francis Spencer of the Lady Dian elk. The D'Portal family were of French nobility coming from Bagnols, Languedoc France, not far from Toulouse so our family crest had the twin turrets of the Toulouse castle in it. We can trace our family tree back to 1456 with Louis De Portal as the earliest recorded in Burke's book of Peerage, Baronetage and Knightage.

During the French Revolution of 1789 to 1799 two brothers, Jean Francois and Guillaume and a sister escaped execution by fleeing to the French coast. Regrettably, the sister perished in a bakery they were hiding in, being accidentally shut in an oven, and died. The two brothers were hidden in wine casks and secretly shipped to England and distant relatives. These wine casks are in the London Museum. To hide their identity as noblemen they dropped the comer and the D' which was a nobleman's sign such as Lord or Von in German. Many years later I had a copy but since lost, the King of England gave them back the right to use the D' or Lord in some cases Viscount. Horace married the General Sir John Spurrier and Louisa Freeman (1815) family by marrying their

Granddaughter Gwlady Anderson Madeleine nee Lanphier. I still have a painted portrait of General Spurrier, his commission certificate, a lock of his hair and his gilded epaulettes, which were used in the Battle of Waterloo.

The family split up into the older and younger brother lines. One of the brothers developed a paper company which to this day I believe the paper used to print British currency is from the Portal family business. We are related to many great names, some even coming to South Africa like Sir Brigadier General Bertram Portal to fight the Boer war. Another Sir Gerald Portal with his brother Captain Raymond Portal was sent by the British High Commission (1893) to Zanzibar to free the slaves from the Sultan of Oman. He was then sent on to free slaves in Uganda from Arabs, doing an incredible 180-day walk where he lost his brother Raymond to malaria. He later mysteriously died on the ship returning to England from the grueling effects of the march. There is a book written about it called "The Mission to Uganda." Fort Portal in Uganda is named after Raymond. When Lord Montague of car fame brought his motor racing cars out to South Africa. My grandmother and he were of Portal blood and knew each other and I, together with my grandmother, met him in Durban. I was just a young chap but remember him only by his cars, particularly one green racing car that looked like a bullet and the fact that he patted me on my head. The original family crest was the twin turreted castle of Toulouse with a "Fleur-de-Lis" on each side. The motto was "Armet nos ultio regum" Translated - let vengeance for princes arm us. Lord Portal changed his to have an airman and mechanic in service dress on each side of the shield with the twin turreted Toulouse castle overlooking the shield of crown and dragon.

Horace Portal left England to start a tea estate in Ceylon. There is some suggestion he was a remittance man and never went back to England. However, never confirmed. He built an estate called "Darawella" in the highlands a 2-day ride from Colombo past Kandy where the temple of the tooth is and on to Nuwara Eliya. It is still there to this day, and I was to see it in 1984. Photographing myself exactly where he sketched the hills in the front of the house known as Sheba's breasts. This he sent to his bride-to-be in England. After establishing the estate via a long-distance romance, he eventually convinced the granddaughter of General John Spurrier who was married to (nee) Louise Freeman who bore seven children, one being Mary who married William Lanphier Anderson. This union produced a huge family of 12 children. One of the daughters, Mary Louis Anderson became Horace Portal's wife and travelled out to Ceylon to a wedding, marriage and the estate. Something happened and it is understood that the politics and encroaching problems forced Horace to leave Ceylon and the estate. He proceeded to come to South Africa a place he considered similar to Ceylon and searched for a suitable farm. Not finding this in South Africa, he travelled on to South America but returned sometime later. Then settling in Richmond a small farm settlement in the colony of Natal. Natal was named and founded by Vasco De Gama a Portuguese explorer who arrived there on Christmas day, so the name "Natal.' It was almost virgin land with no known permanent native inhabitants. However, some indication of cannibalism was present possibly the remains of marauding Maputo tribes who later joined the Zulu tribe under Chaka the chief who formed the Zulu nation in 1819.

Later Horace moved to Pietermaritzburg, the then capital, and established a successful estate with its own zoo. This estate is now the property of the University of Pietermaritzburg; his old farm homestead is still standing, and I remember as a small boy my father obtained the gates from the farm to place on our own home which was built in Westville Natal. The marriage produced four daughters, Daisy, Gwladys, Amy and Irma. Horace died in 1910 but his wife lived on to 1931. Regretfully his health and years of work in the tropics had finally caught up with him. Malaria, blackwater fever and other ailments were common, with little or no medicines available.

Gwladys Anderson Madeleine born in 1881 and married Alan Tatham Shores an engineering son of John Wallis Shores and Katherine Florence Shores, (nee Goslett). John Wallis Shores was sent out to the Natal Colony in South Africa by the British Government to become the Engineer in chief of the Natal Government Railway project. He was held in high esteem by the colonial office, and he had received the "Companion and Order of St George and St Michael." A rail line of about 5 miles had been established across Durban to the Umgeni River, however, a line was intended to reach Johannesburg as the gold rush and expansion of the British colony was underway. A union of the three countries was formed in 1910.

Problems had been encountered and finance for a rail line was a matter very much in the fore. The Swedish Government had proposed a finance package so John Wallis Shores being the man on site with experience and his pregnant wife were sent to Stockholm to consider or secure the venture. Whilst in Stockholm a son was born Alan Tatham Shores, 1881. He was later to have a brother born in South Africa who unfortunately we believe died as a young man of malaria. In pioneering the wild in South Africa many young men, and women, especially in childbirth, died of unknown tropical infections and diseases. Local and overseas wars, which the young South African men were sent to on behalf of the British Empire, also took a huge toll on eligible males. As I mentioned earlier all South African men over 16 years did military training. Here is a list of some of the confrontations we South Africans fought. Eight Zulu rebellions. Anglo Zulu War, two Boer wars, the First and Second World Wars, Crimean War, aided the U.S.A. in the Korean War. Rhodesian war, Biafran war, mercenaries in the Congo war and some in the Viet Nam war. After twenty years of bush war fighting the communists who used the black population attempted via the African National Congress to destabilize the country. Later they did take the government over peacefully, via the foresight of De Klerk and Mandela. The Russians wanted the Cape Sea route a strategic position regarding shipping and military movement.

John Wallis Shores was to become a major factor in the construction of the railway to Johannesburg. His surveying and engineering skills were above normal and today most of the old rail line bears his signature with accolades paid to him in historic railway books. He was a hardy man spending weeks at a time away in the bush surveying and scouting the land for a favourable route. When the line was finally underway it was handicapped by the Boer war which destroyed many bridges. At Ladysmith, a decision had to be made as to whether the rail line was to go to Johannesburg the Gold Rush or Kimberly and the Diamond rush. A race was on as the line from Mozambique was also underway and another from Cape Town. The Natal line was finally settled to go to Johannesburg and won the race by one day from the Mozambique line. It was on this Natal line that the swing system of ascending the mountains was developed. It consisted of a system where the train climbed up then a switch was operated to swing the train onto an upper line on its reversing. This allowed the train to traverse the mountain chain in a secession of forward and back motions climbing the incline.

He retired in 1904 after 35 years of service and with full honours. I have a plaque with all the senior staff's signatures and names bidding farewell on his retirement. Alan Tatham Shores became an engineer/surveyor who worked with his father and served in the First World War and the Boer War. He married Gwladys Anderson Madeleine Portal in 1910 from which they had one daughter Gwladys Doreen Portal Shores 1912. My mother, born in Durban, grew up very much in the ways of a lady as schooled by her mother, being rather Victorian. She was educated at the best of girls' schools and taught the ways of a young lady. She spoke of being introduced to the eligible young men at the evening dress balls, and social events in Pietermaritzburg and Durban. In her younger days, she spent time with her Grandparents the Portals, on their farm called "Rutlands" now the grounds of the Natal University in Pietermaritzburg. It was a big farm with its own small zoo. When Horace Portal's death it was divided among the family, except the gates which were at our family home in Westville, Natal. Mother talked of going to the theatre and opera where the family had a private box in a lantern light horse-drawn carriage. However, she by heart was a tomboy and just loved to be with her father sometimes at the railhead. She loved the African bush, the wildlife and all Africa had to offer. A waterfall for a shower and no running water was not a problem for her. When young lady friends were out in their fine wear, she would prefer to be in boots out scouting for the game or tramping through the bush to find survey points.

Her father adored her, and she was very close to him. In so spent many of her holidays out in tents roughing it just to be with him as he worked the surveying and engineering section of the railway in its progress across the virgin and wild land. It was on one of these holidays spent with her father that a water shortage at the camp took place. A bush truck driver was needed to fetch water from a river some miles away. Driving was without power steering, antbear holes could and did break your thumbs on the steering wheel if you hit them plus the manual gears needed double-declutching to change. A driver usually had a man sitting on the mudguard to warn of ant bear holes, wildlife was present, and a load of water needed at least four labourers to fill the tanks in a bucket chain action method.

As her father had taught her to drive at 16 in the bush, she volunteered much against her father's wishes. However, as a daughter, he relented and against his better wishes allotted her a truck and five black labourers. Here she was a 16-year-old young and attractive girl crashing through the bush hauling water daily for the camp. This would be unheard of today but so was the trust and respect of our ancestors and black Africans towards each other, nothing unthinkable took place. Grandfather Shores had to write up the account and explain why a truck had been taken off the work schedule plus the engagement of a driver. To do this he named the driver Robert and so from that day on my dear mother lost her lady-like name of Gwladys and was forever known as Bobby a name she cherished and enjoyed all her life, many times being asked to tell the unusual story of how it transpired.

She attended, I believe, Durban Girls High School excelling in athletics and became a fast sprinter. Later she ran for a sports club in Pietermaritzburg and competed around the country. She ran against Marjorie Clark who was the Natal and Springbok level champion beating her in an informal race. From this, she was chosen to compete in the 1929 European Olympics, with the Tock H charity organization sponsoring her travel requirements. Regretfully while on the water en route to the games they cancelled all women from competing. She therefore became a spectator, saw a bit of Europe, and was able to visit her relatives in England, and the ancestral home "Tonge House."

Returning to South Africa her father who was a friend of Lord Baden Powell and involved in Scouting was working on the North coast with a troop of scouts spraying paraffin on rivers, dams, lakes anywhere mosquito lava could be spawning. This was an attempt to kill mosquitoes and control malaria fever the biggest killer in Africa. As a scout himself my father Charles had volunteered to help and was working with my Grandfather Alan in the bush. My mother had decided to visit her father so together with her mother Gwladys these two ladies drove a Model T Ford a full day up the coast on bush roads to find him. They did it alone to surprise him, although he was a little annoyed at the risk they had taken. Grandfather Alan was a stocky powerful man who always wore a large leather belt which if wrapped around his knuckles could down any opponent, was a Bisley shot and an exceptionally good marksman who carried a gun in reach at all times. However, very much a gentleman with a wicked sense of humour and a practical joker.

That was just one of many adventures she had with no fear of the African bush, people, or wildlife. It also sowed the seed for her family all of whom became world travellers like herself and the man she met at my grandfather's camp, her future husbands my father, Charles. They courted and married 4 years later much to my Victorian-minded Grandmother Gwladys objection. She believed my mother was marrying out of her station and to just be a common builder. Bit hypocritical as she loved the African bush spending a lot of her life as a teacher to Boer (Afrikaner) and English farmer's sons. Some of them started lessons at the age of 16 years and were twice her size. She would often have to travel distances on horseback and always had a manservant with her, visiting them once or twice a month. She told stories of fording swollen crocodile-infested rivers, bitten by ticks and gnats. One such story was being attacked by a troop of Baboons which she out rode beating them with her brass riding crop. Others have to blindfold their horses and gallop them through raging grass bush (veldt fires) common in the bush. She too loved the camps and travel however she was very much a lady and thought her tomboy daughter should be the same.

After their marriage, honeymooning in Howick and Underberg they found there were sections of land for sale about 16 kilometres from Durban the seaport. Father was able to obtain site and location plans. One Sunday they set out in their trusty 1936 Chevrolet to find and view the said land. They found out in the bush off the main Durban to Johannesburg Road at a place called Westville. It had no road to it but was accessible by turning off the old Johannesburg Durban Road at a property owned by a resident called Jack Martens. Then by driving through the long grass so locating the land on a hill looking at the back of Durban with the sea in the distance. They bought it to build a house, with my father making a road which he called St James Avenue, for a reason we never knew. He now being in the building and construction business was doing well taking over from his father who died of malaria when he was 16. He became the youngest master builder in Natal and developed a sound company. All was done professionally, honestly and on a gentleman's handshake. This was to become his downfall. In the interim, he built a large four-bedroomed home, double garage, and servant's quarters all with a magnificent view.

Mother terraced the land and grew fruit trees, flowers, and vegetables. There were chickens, ducks, cats, and dogs. The property was I believe

10 acres; it was eventually named after my sister Beverley as Beverley Hills with wild buck, baboons, monkeys, and a lot of snakes. Later we had two huge tortoises which my sister and I as youngsters could ride around the garden. As a young woman mother created a home and laughed as she told us her first dining room table was four upturned sewerage pipes and an old door. There was no electricity or water. Mother would go down to the bottom of our land to a little waterfall with a maidservant. Here she would strip off to her petticoat and shower in the river water.

As the house was built water was trucked up in drums and later Father built a small dam with what was known as a RAM-type pump, to pump water into a large round reservoir built in the front garden. From here it was hand pumped up to a holding tank then gravity fed for house usage. Fathers' business was doing well however all the workshop and office requirements were done in our garage and one converted bedroom. He needed to expand so with a small loan from my grandmother he bought a workshop and office near the centre of the now rapidly growing village of Westville. The loan in my mother's name was to be his saving grace. Social life grew, and he built most of the municipality buildings including extensions to the Town hall. His professional ability was in demand with everything on the up. He was nominated to be the first Justice of the Peace for Westville. Became the Boy Scout Commissioner for all the villages in the nearby counties. Both for the black scouts known as Pathfinders and the disabled scouts whom he assisted in teaching to tie knots with their feet and attend camps, some without limbs. He still played his violin at functions when asked with many musical evenings amongst friends such as pianist Frank Williams in our home. He built the Westville tennis courts and bowling green, becoming a member of the founding club. He went on to purchase the property where the office and workshop were located, later to include the attached trading store. It was renamed "Attercliffe Stores."

With work now taking him away up the North Coast, building bakeries, and power stations he was being drawn away for a week or more at a time. Hauling material now with two trucks and shipping building requirements by train. Four years later I was due, so my mother went to stay with her parents Alan & Gwlady Shores at their retirement home in Mountain Rise, Pietermaritzburg, Now the capital city of the province of Natal. According to my mother, I nearly killed her being a slim and athletic woman having to give birth to a just less than 9-pound first child. I arrived all intact with black hair and in good health on the 10th of August 1942. Father was gaining more work up the North coast and into Zululand requiring him to expand his business with a part of the work being controlled from his Westville office, the other from a rented house in Zululand village called mPhamula. This was a small dusty outback African village, so Mother decided to move there to be near him, leaving our home in Westville as the main base needing a visit every two weeks.

I was bar one other little girl who was the baker's daughter and left a year later the only white child. My father and mother both spoke fluent Zulu. Our servants were Zulu but could not speak English. It was therefore only natural that my first tongue was Zulu which I have spoken all my life. As I had hair on my arms and was a bit of a handful (understatement), being quite sturdy I was given a Zulu name "Phube" (translated meaning tough one) Being known by this among all our Zulu employees and friends until I left South Africa. The work and the need for school plus the expected birth of my sister Beverley being due, directed my folks back to Westville. Mother ran the trading store and started a small tearoom from a converted service station office.

My sister was born on the 19th of January 1946 a beautiful fair-haired baby but suffered from a small, uncommon disease called "Pink's disease' affecting her digestion and food intake. She was put onto a non-solid and basic fruit and vegetable diet. For years, the rest of the family had peaches while she the juice mixed with KLIM powdered milk which then agreed with her dietary problem.

Life was good and all was well. I was told I would soon be going to preschool held at Mrs. Dougals's home across the valley. Little did Mrs. Dougal, or my mother know what they were in for. I hated shoes, wore mainly only a pair of shorts occasionally and a shirt if it got cool. Spoke only Zulu. If I could not be found at wash and bedtime, I was sure to be in the servant's quarters talking with them around the fire and very possibly eating their phutu. (traditional food made from maize meal.) I loved the bush where I spent most of my time playing with my father's African workers' children. The river was our hideout, we made clay animals, slings, and a tree house our secret place. Why did I have to go to school, wear shoes, speak complicated English and play with white kids who knew truly little about how to set bird traps, hunt down rats, catch small rock pythons live off the wild berries, bananas, guavas and did not like or eat European food. My life and desired freedom were in for a major change, which in turn was going to reflect my future in many ways. Not all for the good.

In my fifth (5) year I was, on the appointed day, taken to preschool or Kindergarten in a clean white shirt, pressed short trousers and a new pair of black shoes with grey socks. Grandmother told me to be a good boy and behave myself in front of other people. Being introduced to Mrs. Dougal I refused to speak and hid behind my mother, eyeing about 10 young children of my age in the classroom with suspicious concern. Mother left leaving me in Mrs. Dougals' care, with my last sight of her motoring down the drive. I knew exactly where I was as the building was built like a castle with towers I could see from my domain and a small world across the valley. I was told to sit down and given a slate with some chalk being told in English to draw a picture or something none of which I could clearly understand. Mrs. Dougal approached me with what I considered a face about to give me some sort of reprimand. That was it, I dropped the slate and headed for the door out onto the grass off came my shoes, the fence was no problem, however the barbed wire did some damage to my shirt. My home was in sight across the valley and river, I knew all the paths. It took a brief time before I was in my home territory and in our servant's quarters. The maid was alerted to my presence and informed my grandmother who came down and extracted me by my ear from the quarters marching me up to the main house. Mother duly arrived after some shopping so without cell phones or even a phone knew nothing of my presence until Grandmother turned me in. I by then had hidden under my bed but was with the combined effort of both mother and grandmother supported by the maid pulled out to a tongue lashing about my shirt and losing my shoes never mind the threat of what my father was going to do to me on his arrival home.

My sibling's sister disowned me, so I was left in my room to await my fate or possible death if what I had been told was going to happen to me. I think my prayers helped as we were a religious family, also explaining to the good Lord, Jesus, the profit Mohamed, plus Mary or even an iSangoma (African witch doctor) that surely my life of only 5 years could not end now, saved my hide as instead of a severe hiding I got a smack across the back of my head, asked who the hell was going to pay for the shirt and shoes. (Shoes recovered later). I was told to apologize to both my grandmother and mother. This followed being sent to bed without dinner and told not to come out until told to. All of this with a finger about one inch from my face and the most frightening face I had ever seen on my father. No persuasion would get me now anywhere near a school again. Come hell or high water I was not going to that preschool or any other school, so a year went by in my home territory with my friends both black and white.

Regretfully Government policy came to bear and in my sixth year I was dragged to the new Westville School run from a farmhouse donated by Mrs. Wandsbeck. The house consisted of a centre room where Mrs. Carr the headmistress together with Mrs. Pat Stockhill and other teachers ran the classes. Mrs. Stockhill would come into my life much later on in the most unusual way. The stables had been turned into small classrooms for classes one and two before the standard classes of one to six. Years later the school developed into a big and highly successful school, becoming one of the best in the province. One of its students Chad Le Clos became the world's fastest swimmer, plus the Procter family of good cricketers. I found a few of my local friends who, like me, had been brought up in a free and somewhat wild childhood. We hated wearing shoes as they hurt but eventually, we formed our little groups and settled in.

Some names I remember are Barry Miles whose father had a small farm with horses that we rode and fell off. The Moffat brothers Denny, Douglas Mike. and Chris. The Williams, Lesters, Cuthberts, Serion Robertson, Freddy who was nicknamed Freddy Mazambaan in Zulu meaning Freddy potato unkindly because he seemed to have a bigger head than most of us. Lynton, Cedric

Dalgleish Tim Goodrich, Clive Marnoch, the Chalmers brothers. The Laity twins Diane and John, (John was later killed in a car crash and died in his sisters' arms) Silvia Nunn the daughter of an English chauffer and his wife who was the housekeeper for an English Lord living partly in Westville for the English winter and sailing back to England for their summer. We were informed he always sailed POSH meaning Port Outbound, Starboard Home so that they always had the sun shining on their side of the ship.

I was to meet Silvia again many years later in the most incredible way. I was on my motorbike in Jersey at a stop street. Another bike pulled up alongside me, both extending a small hand greeting.

I asked if he was from Jersey, which he replied he was, and where was I from. In replying to South Africa, he indicated the girl riding the pillion was from there. We pulled over and with great astonishment; it was Silvia Nunn a long way from our little village of Westville. Later again by accident, I met an ex-schoolteacher now living in a flat in St Helier who had caned me for being insubordinate. He had told me that a horse can be taken to water, but you cannot make it drink. My response regarding the caning was, I am not a bloody horse. It was an indication of where my education was going.

World War 2

War came to South Africa being a British colony and the Cape being a strategic point. Battleships appeared off the coast, Sunderland Flying boats, following the British Imperial Airways route from England via Southampton, Calais, Alexandria, Khartoum, and Lake Victoria, Victoria Falls started arriving and landing in Durban harbour ferrying troops to the front. From our house on a hill, we could see a long way out so watched the increase of flights fascinating our imagination. Durban was active in war and peacetime with flying boats. It was the end of the line for Imperial Airways and also for the Sunderland military flying boats coming from Europe and the UK. Watching them land in Durban harbour was rather a spectacular sight. Here again, fate was starting to make its point, which will be seen later. On the opposite hill to St James Avenue and Beverly Hills, a searchlight station was placed. Our house had to be sort of camouflaged and all windows blacked out as it was caught in the searchlight sweep.

A lot of men some of our best friends were being called up, including my Uncle Rolly who went to North Africa. My Uncle Arthur and Father were put on home guard and served in the war effort involved in home defense. The sea routes to the UK and Europe were being heavily attached sinking thousands of tons of urgently needed war supplies, as a whole South Africa was rich in food and materials that were desperately needed in the war machine. German U-boats were prowling off our coast restricting the food and war material from getting to its destination. The Japanese came into the war and now it was established they too were off our coast. Huge defense guns were established along our coastline and on Durban harbour plus submarine nets across the harbour mouth. Catalina Flying boats were brought in to search for the subs flying a patrol circuit to Cape Town and around Madagascar. A large base was built in the St Lucia Lake and estuary about 110 miles North of Durban, hidden by sand dunes and bush from the sea. A Catalina crashed there coming from one of its patrols, so one bay was called Catalina Bay. The amphibious Cat could fly in loiter mode for 28 hrs. at 105 knots, on R1800 Pratt & Whitney engines. It also had an R2000 engine with a clipper hull as compared to the standard hull. The whole wing was a fuel tank, and it had no flaps. Here is an extract from an article written by Jeff Gaisford with more interesting information.

Durban had a big flying boat base serving Imperial Airways flying a 5-day trip from the UK via Egypt and the war with Sunderland's. Our coastline is inundated with wrecked wartime ships and the establishment of a hidden base in St Lucia was a major asset in stopping German and Japanese invasion of our land. It's not commonly known how much we played in the defense of the supply line to Europe and the front, but it was very big in men volunteering for the war and supplies.

Lake St Lucia is one of the oldest game reserves in Africa, having been established in 1895. It also lies within South Africa's first World Heritage Site - the Greater St Lucia Wetland Park. It is the largest estuarine lake system in sub-Saharan Africa, it contains large numbers of hippos and crocodiles, and the 36,000-ha water body is an average of one meter deep. Today it is a prime ecotourism destination - but 60 years ago it was the scene of some spectacular military aviation activity. Admiral Karl Doenitz, Head of the German U-boat arm, in looking for new hunting grounds for his U-boats, sent two groups of them to hunt in Cape waters in early 1942 and also sent individual U-boats to the east coast of South Africa. The U-boats reaped a terrible harvest and operated virtually unopposed at first. The big 1600-ton, type IX U-boats had a sea-going range of over 25 000 miles and were commanded by veteran skippers such as Bartels (U-197), Lassen (U160) Wolfgang Luth (U-181), and Gysae (U-177), who all operated off the east coast at some stage, destroying much Allied shipping. On the 28th of November 1942, Captain Gysea torpedoed the passenger vessel "M.V. Nova Scotia" 48 km off the coast. It was carrying 654 Italian prisoners of war bound for the Pietermaritzburg prison camp 89 km from the port of Durban. The vessel sank in 15 minutes leaving 1,052 passengers and prisoners to their fate in shark-infested waters. It became a shark feeding frenzy with only 196 surviving. The U-boat used machined gunfire to ward off anyone attempting to board the submarine as they were under "Laconia orders"

This was an order from Germany's grand admiral Karel Donitz, stemming from a British passenger ship the "Laconia" that was torpedoed with 2,732 passengers and 1,703 Italian prisoners of war, including woman and children.

The U-boat Captain was Captain Hartenstein a German officer with a heart. He immediately started rescue operations broadcasting his humane intentions to the allied forces. Surfacing he picked up 193 survivors accommodating them on the foredeck. Sadly, after four days on the surface flying the Red Cross flag and towing lifeboats, an American B24 Liberator bombed the U156 which slowly submerged killing most of the survivors. From that, on 17 September 1942, the "Laconia" order was implemented ordering all U boat Captains not to offer any assistance or help to survivors of allied shipping Ironically, the only known U-boat sinking in that area was that of Bartels' U-197 sunk by Catalinas of 262 and 259 Squadron RAF south of Madagascar. The sinking of this U-boat was probably due to information gained from the breaking of the German ENIGMA codes. Access to these codes was one of the most jealously guarded of Allied secrets and enabled Allied High Command to eavesdrop on German operational radio messages throughout most of the war.

In the early 1940s, the first Catalina squadrons of the Royal Air Force began anti-submarine operations off the Cape coast, flying mostly from Langebaan. As the U-boats moved eastwards so did the Catalinas, arriving eventually at their base at Congella in Durban Harbour. They quickly identified the need for a forward base and Lake St Lucia, with its large expanses of water, was chosen after a snap survey. On 1 December 1942, the first ground crews led by Flight Lieutenant S J Wood arrived on the Eastern Shores and built a standard pattern RAF sea-plane base at what is now known as Catalina Bay on the eastern shore. They dynamited the rocks on the seashore at Mission Rocks for concrete and built strip roads connecting various installations at points along the adjoining dunes. To this day the blast marks are clearly visible at Mission Rocks. A massive radar installation was also built on one of the higher dunes, called Mount Tabor by the local missionaries. The main bunker is still used today as a trail base by hikers in the area. The Officer's mess and certain other installations were sited across the Lake at Charter's Creek. The first Catalinas of 262 Squadron arrived on 26 February 1942 and began using the St Lucia base as a springboard for extended 20 to 24-hour patrols along the sea lanes up to Madagascar and down to Durban. These were mostly Catalina 1B aircraft. The flarepath consisted of a double row of bomb scows moored at intervals diagonally with lanterns for use during night landings. Ivan Spring, in his book "Flying Boat", tells an amusing story of a Catalina coming in to land at the height of a storm one night in which some of the vital scows were sunk. One of the base staff hurried out in a launch and took up position where the main scow should have been and signaled to the incoming aircraft "I am a flare...I am a flare..." Some of the U-boat skippers were more than willing to fight it out on the surface and more than once, a Catalina limped back to St Lucia trailing smoke and with shell holes decorating its wing panels.

The base was ideal, being shielded from the sea by a bank of high, forested dunes. Operations from this tropical base were not without incident, despite the idyllic setting. One of the early clashes occurred when gunners decided that basking crocs made good targets for the .50 waist guns as they droned their way up the Lake. The local game warden was very soon banging on the base commander's door! A very long T jetty was also built for refueling and "bombing up". The last of the pilings of this structure were removed by the conservation authorities in the 1980s and the area became known as "The Old Jetty". There is also still a slipway leading to a concrete apron probably used when hauling the Cats out for maintenance. Various other foundations and well points litter the area but are mostly very overgrown. On the night of 7 June 1943 Catalina E (FP 275) of 259 Squadron, piloted by Flight Lieutenant J A B Kennedy RAF, was returning from an operational flight and made its final approach from the south, coming in over very flat terrain of reed beds and meanders of the Lake itself. As the big flying boat passed low towards what is now called Mitchell Island, for no apparent reason it suddenly stalled and plunged into the shallows, killing all but one of its crew. The survivor was Sgt N A Workman. The aircraft was a total loss although the base staff did salvage certain parts of it. During these operations, they sank several sections of concrete pipe into the mud to use as a base for a working platform alongside the wreck. These pipes were in later years usually all that could be seen of the crash site. The wreck was also used as a bombing target later, resulting in it being further broken up. As the years went by the wreck slowly disintegrated as exposure to the elements and salt water took its toll.

At the time of writing Lake St Lucia and its environment are in the grip of a growing drought and with the mouth of the system being closed by a natural sand bar, the level of the Lake has dropped to a meter below sea level. As a result, the great mudflat on which the stark and shattered remainsof Catalina "E" is completely exposed.

I waded to the wreckage in the early 80s, in calf-deep water with two colleagues, wishing at every step that I could lift both feet out of the water. All around us grew thick mats of seagrass in which lived hundreds of large mud crabs the size of dinner plates and armed with fearsome pincers. As we walked, the matted seagrass heaved and moved as these monsters scuttled out of our way. We retrieved an intact section of the tailplane that is now stored in the KZN Wildlife offices at St Lucia. Shortly after the fatal crash of "E", in the dark before dawn of 25 June 1943, Catalina H (FP265) of 262 Squadron RAF, piloted by Flying Officer F N C White, took off in dead calm conditions for an extended patrol. All seaplanes require a degree of chop on the water to "unstick" and apparently, the glassy calmness of the water contributed to subsequent. A launch, with Flying Officer Keely on board, also went out to create a bit of chop on the water. The heavily laden Catalina ran the full length of the flarepath from the Eastern Shores towards Charters Creek and was seen climbing steeply, only to stall and plummet into the Lake where it exploded. A young Zulu herd boy, who later became a field ranger at St Lucia, witnessed the crash and told a colleague that the explosion lit up the entire south basin of the Lake. This account tallies with Keely's eyewitness report of a terrific flash of red followed by an explosion. One crewman, Sgt Benjamin Lee, survived. Navy divers recovered the bodies of the crew by blasting the sunken wreckage, but complained of zero visibility in the cold, muddy waters, having to work entirely by feel. In addition, there were crocodiles and hippos in the lake. The bodies of the crew were buried in the Stellawood Cemetery in Durban. This aircraft crashed into an unusually deep part of the Lake and its exact location is unknown today.

Part of the administrative section of 262 Squadron was located in the home of the Selley family in St Lucia village. They ran the Estuary Hotel, and their one son, the late Mr Jeff Selley, an army engineer on leave from North Africa, heard of the crash and took his small boat, propelled by a stuttering 2 candle-power Seagull engine, 22km up the St Lucia estuary in the dark and assisted the RAF at the scene. He was told to be careful of anything that might look like a dustbin, as it was probably an unexploded depth charge! Lake St Lucia has always been a bit fickle, and its water levels are ever capricious. 262 Squadron had set up their base at a time of high-water levels and as time went on the lake began to get shallower. A Catalina draws 3'6" when afloat and as St Lucia's levels dropped, so the RAF began to cast anxious eyes around for another operational base. The last Catalina flew off St Lucia on 13 October 1944. The RAF chose Lake Umsingazi at Richards Bay as an alternative and the squadron eventually relocated there in November 1944. British tongues could not master the Zulu Umsingazi, and the base was called "Loch Richard".

By this time more than a few South Africans were serving in 262 Squadron and it eventually was handed over to the SAAF to become 35 Squadron, later being equipped with Short Sunderland flying boats. There were two other flying-boat crashes, both at Lake Umsingazi. In 1945 Catalina JX 367 made a bad landing and crashed into the bush fringing the lake. A 35 Sqn SAAF Sunderland RB-N crashed and sank on the night of 1 November 1956 in bad weather. As a boy I saw, the stripped hull of this aircraft being winched out of the lake in about 1958.

It was later allowed to slip back into the water where it remains to this day.

The Catalina operations at St Lucia left an interesting legacy of artefacts on the Eastern Shores, and the shattered wreck of Catalina E will lie exposed on its mudflat until the rains come and the waters of the great Lake St Lucia once more rise to cover its corroding frames. The lost wreck of Catalina H remains an enigma and perhaps one day a fisherman will pull up part of it and establish its last resting place. As happened with a wing float from the Sunderland, some enterprising young men waded out to the wreck of Catalina E in the 1960s and removed an undamaged wing float. This was shortened slightly and fitted with an outboard motor, making a reasonably respectable small ski boat that was regularly taken out to sea at Cape Vidal and Maphelane where it eventually came to grief.

Jeff Gaisford is currently the Media Officer for Ezemvelo KZN Wildlife. He has a deep interest in the flying boats which operated in Zululand, and this led to the writing of this article. It first
appeared on World Air News

Clipper bowed Catalina PBY on landing at St Lucia

Durban flying boats early Imperial and military service

Shorts Sunderland of S/African 35 Squadron Shorts Imperial Airways "The Golden Hind

Shorts Imperial Airways" Coriolalanus" Moored Durban Bay 1950 made ready for the return flight to England (Southampton)

Early Imperial Airways office Salisbury Island Durban. This would be the end of the 5-day flight from England to Durban South Africa.

Last flight of the Imperial flying boat "Cleopatra" service Durban to England 1953

Salisbury Island maintenance base Durban. This base served Air Force Catalina, Sunderland and Imperial flying boats on their 5-day maintenance stop en route from Southampton, via Calais, Alexandria, Lake Victoria, Victoria Falls to Durban. First-class silver service overnighting in luxurious old colonial standard hotels. London to Durban

A Catalina converted to a yacht in Australia.

The Imperial flying boat "Southampton" serviced Durban to England in 1953 on the Zambezi River above Victoria Falls.

The first aircraft to land on Lake Nyasa was a Lioré et Olivier LEO H-194 flying boat of the 'Aeronavale' (French Fleet Air Arm) piloted by 'Lieutenant de Vaisseau' (Lieutenant-Commander) Marc Bernard

Durban Beach post-war in the 1950's

Durban set up military hospitals to cater for the hospital ships arriving in from the brutal war being fought in Burma, Southeast Asia, Singapore and the Indonesian island. With this came terrifying news of the brutality, torture, and imprisonment by the Japanese. Men were dying a cruel death in prison camps or on enslaved Malaysian/Burma railway construction with beheading being the nature of the day. Ships and their escorts were now arriving and departing daily in an attempt to run the gauntlet of the South African coast and the Atlantic in convoys to reach the war zones. Colonial and foreign pilots were being trained at safe airports built across the country and into the Rhodesia's.

Colonial support was desperately needed so the harbour was full of sailors and transient servicemen. My parents would take a truck down to the city and pick up as many servicemen as the vehicle would hold. Bringing them to our house where mother and Grandparents would supply freshly baked scones and tea. It was a breath of fresh air literally, as many of the men had not seen green grass, fresh food and air for months. Not to mention being served by lovely ladies with freshly baked food. Many broke down in tears, mother being a beautiful 32-year-old woman got more compliments than she ever had in her life. Grandmother followed in a respectful hot pursuit.

One very funny incident happened when father was delivering a truckload of men back to the Durban centre. An Australian jumped off the back ran into the Botanical gardens, pulled up a flower plant and ran back dumping it in my mothers' lap kissed her on the cheek and said in broad Aussie slang. "It's for, you Mame." I remember being carried on the shoulders of the men when taking walks down to the river and across our land. Some stayed in touch for years and one very kind soldier by the name of Marshal gave me a gold cross to hang around my neck. With the war dragging on Durban became very susceptible to being attacked. Enemy aircraft were reported overhead so a blackout was very important. In addition, at war end 28 ships had been sunk off our shores mainly by German U-boats but the Japs had also advanced. The Japanese imperial navy had conducted reconnaissance flights on the East African coast operating from a Submarine. A 1-10 type seaplane had flown over Durban on many occasions. At this point, the threat to Durban from the Japanese was believed to be pretty high and the squadrons were preparing to help defend the city. The citizens were put on high alert and food rationing was targeted for the war cause. Father had to buy old cars to get tyres and oil for his company trucks.

Royal visit.

Another interesting point was that in 1947 the King, Queen and two princes Elizabeth and Margaret visited Durban on the Royal Yacht Britannia. On their way to Eshowe a Zululand town to meet the Zulu King, they passed over a rail bridge where I was able to see them in their carriage. We and the family were travelling to Eshowe with my father who, being a Boy Scout commissioner, was involved with the scouts doing a guard of honour. He had the privilege of shaking hands with King George at the parade. Later the King was to inspect the military forces on a parade at the Durban military headquarters on Battery Bay. To do this the military and persons in charge of security used a look-alike to take his place as there was fear that the remaining Boer forces who were German Nazi sympathizers might attempt to assassinate him. This was because of the Anglo-Boer war of 1899 which the Boer forces lost. In the 2nd World War, our troops also fought the Germans out of German Southwest Africa now Namibia and Tanzania which was called German East Africa. Germany was attempting to build a railway across Africa between the two colonies and it was close to being successful. It now lies in ruins destroyed by central African wars. Believe it is called the Benguela Railway. South Africa then became a union in 1910 under British rule. Later a republic in 1960 under the National government.

Lady in white.

In my travels many times I met war veterans who talked of the lady in white singing at our harbour mouth My father knew Pearle Gibson (nee Siedle) called the "Lady In white", from his music days. She would stand on the dock as the troop ships left the harbour and sing to them such as songs from Vera Lynn "Wish me luck as you wave me goodbye." or "I will be seeing you in all the old familiar places" The ships would almost capsize as the men crammed the gunnels and decks to see and hear her. Many cried openly and I recall standing holding onto my father's trousers watching her plus the shouts of encouragement, wolf whistles, frantic waves and marriage proposals coming from the ship. A great many men never did come back with South Africa losing 112,000. She even sang on the day she heard her son had been killed. These ex-servicemen who upon learning I was from Durban always spoke sometimes very tearfully, highly, and fondly of our unselfish hospitality, the food, climate plus always the Lady in White.

Lady in White

Wartime naval aircraft carrier in Durban harbour.

In 1947 my beloved Grandfather Alan Tatham Shores, passed away. Mainly due to a long battle with a blood infection thought to have been caused by Boer war wounds that would not heal. I called him "Dither" and as he loved gardening, I would walk at his side pulling out the plants he so carefully had just planted. Having not had a son he was extremely fond of me, often just sitting in his chair, pipe in hand with me curled up in his lap going to sleep. My mother took his death very badly and I made it worse by continually asking for Dither. Just before his death, the circle of life had come about and that was the year my little sister Beverley was born.

The grandparents Shores home in Pietermaritzburg was sold and grandmother Gwlady Shores moved into a semidetached house on the Berea in Durban, in so being closer to my parents who were now having to care for her. She was a wonderful lady demanding the best of manners from her grandchildren. No such thing as sitting down before she sat or starting to eat before she did. I was always being pulled up to act like a gentleman, walk on the left side of her or my mother or near the pavement. Take her hand at steps, always have a handkerchief to wipe my nose, wipe her seat on buses and if necessary for her to sit on wherever we might be. Manners, manners very much so, speak when you are spoken to, seen, and not heard but with it all a great sense of humour. She cherished her family, God-fearing, very lady like of old school who we fondly called MUM plus being addressed as such by old scouting associates, other friends, our friends, and my parents. At 83 she would love to have a ride on my motorbike, gave me 10 pounds (our currency in that day) to buy a surplus Willys Jeep, and could still ride side saddle, she advised that the art of leaning to ride was the ability of keeping one's body and ground apart. Loved a shot of whisky or brandy in the evening, this gracious lady passed quietly away in her sleep at 84 years of full life.

I am 16. 1958 with my Cane Rat Special WW2 Jeep

The Jeep was to become my main means of transport. Rebuilt I called it the "Cane rat special". In 1957 I as an adventurer successfully drove it with my mother and sister up the Sani pass into the mountain kingdom of Basuto land. Now independent Lesotho, a mountain climb of 10,500 feet. In those days the only means of getting into the mountain kingdom was by mule up the treacherous Sani Pass Mountain trails. Later I will tell how this pass would start a new chapter in my life.

This lady was, due to circumstances, a grandmother who I spent a lot of time with. She told great stories of her and her husband's adventures in Africa which she embraced. Dearly wanted to take me overseas to meet the D'Portal family and longed to go to the Seychelles islands where she felt future development would come about. Here she was right. The islands would become a tourist haven and later on in my life, I would have a relative (sister-in-law Brenda and husband Andrew Marshal) who would purchase an apartment and keep his luxury boat there. With them I years later had the privilege of a visit to these beautiful islands. She predicted trouble in South Africa and warned us of this coming event. With her joining Alan her beloved husband in 1958 and Horace Portal having no sons the D'Portal name ended in South Africa. My grandmother and mother both wanted to change our surname to Portal-Evans, however in respect to our father it was not done. Her name is the last of our family registered in the Burkes Book of Peerage.

Astrologers say that a person has a North and South node. One south node for example reveals your past lives, the gifts you bring with you into this lifetime and the traits or beliefs you're here to overcome. Your north node on the other hand is your future self, it's the "calling" that you're moving towards, the nirvana you hope to achieve. With the island of Antigua approaching, I knew I was a long way from my nirvana.

Long lonely road ahead.

I had to face the reality that I was penniless unemployed and uneducated. Self-esteem, guts and common sense were my weapons to fight on to fulfil my ambitions. So, upon landing, in Antigua using my crew pass, I headed straight for English harbour getting back to my stomping grounds and sailing friends. Upon arriving and walking across the wharf to my delight there was my ship the "Tondelayo" and who was on board but my black friend the cook Wilma Rowl. Getting some food from him, we sat down and had a talk. Apparently, the ship was having engine trouble, the captain had been stabbed after a fight with a crewmember, and the passengers put onto the Caribbee, in so completing the sail back to St. Thomas. We decided to call Captain Mike Burk the company owner and I would offer my services to get the ship back to St Thomas for repairs. He agreed to this, so together with a loaned skipper, a couple of deck hands Wilma and me, we got the engine running well enough to get us out of English harbour, a very difficult harbour to sail out of. We then set sail for the American Virgin Island a three-day voyage.

With the sails up and no passengers, we sailed steadily Northwest past the islands of Nevis, St Kitts, St Eustatius (this island was where British ships transferred arms from south Africa to supply the Southern States,), Saba then across the Anegada passage arriving in St Thomas Bay 4 days later. St Kitts and Nevis are very beautiful islands. They were inhabited by the indigenous Kalinago people. These people referred to St Kitts as Liamuiga, meaning "fertile land and Nevis as Oualie which meant "land of beauty." On arrival at St. Thomas and with the other Windjammer ships out cruising, there was no need for any extra crew, so the agent paid me off. I was back sleeping on the Tondelayo or docks.

St Croix passage.

Looking around for a job, I found a fellow who wanted help to take a 30-foot sloop across to St Croix, a neighbouring Virgin Island about a day's sail. Departing all was going well however the wind died, and night fell. As is not uncommon in the islands, a heavy rainstorm arrived bringing with it high winds and low visibility. Battling in the dark to hold a heading we suddenly realised we were taking water. With no pumps on board was case bail and bail like hell, we pounded our way with no visibility vaguely in the direction of St Croix. Going below I found that a hull board behind the bulkhead had sprung the ocean was endeavouring to sink us. Using a mattress, I rammed it into the developing hole. It reduced the amount of water coming in but as the board was now protruding into the below-deck ocean, we lost forward control and speed. Sunrise eventually arrived and still bailing we found ourselves gratefully only about 10 miles from the St Croix shore. We decided to head for it regardless, to at least a swimming distance. Very slowly with the sun coming up, we edged closer to find that we were actually, almost heading into the yacht harbour. Exhausted, we limped into the harbour at around lunchtime. The below decks were awash with water almost knee-deep. Getting alongside a pump was arranged and pumping started. With nothing more for me to do and no work available in the yacht yard, I was paid off and headed to the ferry to return to St Thomas.

The nightlife in St Thomas can be quite wild. Young American girls out for the first time from the family fold, are quite willing to spend money on young tanned, healthy 20-year-old yacht sailors, so I made sure that this South African got his share of drinks and a dance. With the Tondelayo still there at least, I had a boat to sleep on, so getting me off the streets. Knowing the cook was of course a great help food-wise. St Thomas and St Croix were at one time under Danish rule. The Danish authority was the cruelest and worst rulers of the entire island. However, black slave masters who had no mercy on their subjects also ruled Haiti. Bearing in mind the murderous slave king Henri Christophe with his mountaintop castle. The Citadel was a torture and maiming prison under black

African masters. The most infamous was the U.S.A-backed "Papa Duvalier" His dictatorship lasted from 1957 until he died in 1971. His misrule was taken over by his son Jean- Claude "Baby Doc". He was a 19-year-old pudgy teenager who had a liking for the fast life. With his coming to power the Haitians thought there would be some mercy extended. This was short-lived as the financing by the U.S.A of $3.8 million a year as a reward to keep the country so close to the U.S.A, away from communism, was increased in 1975 by "Baby Doc" to $35.5 million.

Using this U.S.A finance "Baby Doc" bankrolled thousands of soldiers and thousands of Tonton Macoute. This Tonto Macoute was a private military originally raised by his father. "Baby Doc" went further and raised his own personal counterinsurgency and security forces trained by the U.S.A. military. During the three decades of tyranny under the despotic Duvalier's rule, an estimated 30,000 to 60,000 Haitians were killed. Many were by the Tonton Macoutes who raped and brutally tortured countless of citizens. Millions fled to other countries primarily to the U.S.A. France or neighbouring islands such as Dominican Republic or Porto Rico. In 1986 "Baby Doc" was ousted due to an uprising and fled to France. He returned 25 years later and was allowed to live in peace at Petionville as a common citizen.

It must be remembered that their people sold slaves to white shipmasters. The African chiefs from Niger, Nigeria and West Africa would capture and walk the prisoners for miles to coastal ports. The prisoners being tribal enemies or weak persons, no matter if they were women with children, young men and women all had wood and iron yokes attached with chains, were killed immediately if they faltered. They were then mustered in places like Gambia, Guinea Bissau, Conakry, Abidjan, and Lome and sold to the local black and European slave merchants to be shipped across the Atlantic. The slaves on the islands had a better life than that in Africa. As they had been bought, their general health was cared for. They were allowed to marry, have separate accommodations for homes and be kept in physical shape to accomplish the work required of them. British Lord Codrington was sent to supervise a form of a subtle slave breeding colony on the island of Barbuda 17 miles off the coast of Antigua. Well maintained in one might say, true British fashion. It was only when the slave migration got to the USA did atrocities start at the level we are liked to believe.

Real cruelty was by the Muslims operating in West and Central Africa. They had no mercy. In reality, if one were to consider the number of slaves brought to the islands and later to the Americas, it would have required every European or white person to venture into the depths of tropical Africa to capture slaves. They would have been exposed to deadly tropical diseases, aggression, and death from Africans, and had to walk out hundreds of captured men and women, feeding them and supporting them till they got to the slave merchants on the coast. Statistics are clear that European or white men would not have lasted trekking through Africa, facing disease deadly wildlife and warring Africans. Therefore, who enslaved the Africans? It was their people. Common knowledge across Africa, which today still has brutality, mutilation, tribal warring, trafficking of women and children and death to thousands of Africans? Besides the brutal treatment by their own people, the next wave of brutality was from the Arabs. They ventured as far as the Victoria Falls in what was Rhodesia capturing and enslaving Africans by the hundreds. These falls were found by the great adventurer Dr Livingston. An incredible Scotsman coming from a poor background only to conquer the might of Africa. When he died his heart was removed and buried beside the mighty Zambezi River with his body being carried over 1,000 miles by his faithful manservants of 15 years to be shipped back to England. He was buried in Westminster Abbey with full honours. He too, like my earlier mentioned relatives, was adamantly against slavery. Regretfully slavery has been a blight on humanity for thousands of years. White slavery was only abolished in Saudi Arabia in the 1950s, but slaves of European descent were common in and across all of Europe, Asia, and China. Incas enslaved by the Spanish conquistadors were brutal, usually ending in death. Naturally, the word Nigger comes from an American translation of the fact they came mainly from Niger and Nigeria. In addition, the Ivory Coast and Tonga all being West African. Nigeria had the biggest slavery depot for exportation to Europe and the Americas being controlled by wealthy African rulers mainly black monarchs. These proof of them having gold thrones and jewels beyond belief.

The next night I met a young photographer whom I had met before on one of the earlier cruises into St Thomas. He offered the couch in his apartment if I needed a bed for the night. I accepted and we somehow got to his place in the early hours of the morning. It turned out he was doing photo shoots for postcards and suggested that I could make a few dollars being a model on the shoots. I gladly accepted as anything for money was OK with me at this stage of the game. A few days later I had made a few dollars so decided it was time to move on.

With Africa, and Europe. U.K. and the Caribbean behind me it was now the USA with the idea of getting to Canada and on with my circumnavigation of the world. One of the Canadian guests who with his wife were on an earlier sail and lived in Montreal. He said he knew a company that was rebuilding a schooner, and he would get me a job working on it. Therefore, Montreal was on my list as they were going to sail her back to the Virgin Islands. To do this I purchased a ferry ticket to Porto Rico and later when there, having spent a few days looking around the island, I bought a ticket on a Pan AM B707 to Miami. It's at this point that fate comes again to play its game with me. This flight on a B707 will come into my story much later on in my life and for the aviation minded it's an incredible story. It will align itself with the farmer I met in Croyley, the instructor pilot in Jersey and the casual meeting up with the Kilros venture. During my time in the Virgin Islands and Caribbean LIAT (leeward Island Air Transport) and a Virgin Island flying boat service were actively growing to service the islands by air rather than by sea and land. My thoughts were that if I could get some money and a license, an air cargo service would be a successful venture as most interisland cargo came by boat. However, I put it down to a pipe dream! Fate had other ideas. I never let schooling interfere with my education.

One shilling and sixpence.

I probably believe some have found what I have written a bit boring, but I have tried to cover and bring you into most of my early life linked to my past and present relations. I will here give an insight into my life after school, what schooling I had and what started this whirlwind life of adventure.

In 1954 my father had become very successful in business owning a construction business, trading store and gone into partnership with a Mauritian named Leges, in a coastal shipping company. We had two cars, one being chauffer driven the other my father's, a new Buick super 8 which he used to drive to his office in West Street Durban. The shipping company was called Natal America Line and appeared to be expanding sailing the East coast from Cape Town to Durban to Lorenzo Marques, Beira and the Indian Ocean islands such as Madagascar, Mauritius and Comoros. Social life was good with both parents in the tennis club and enjoying the evening out. As mentioned earlier, father had been nominated for the voluntary position of Justice of the peace.

My sister and I were at well to do private schools such as Marist Brothers for me and Marist Stella for her. The Catholic brothers were very strict, relying on the cane as the primary teaching tool. I was over the years well versed with this teaching method. The masters could cane three strokes, Head prefect one and the Principle up to six. More than three spelling errors on a daily test meant a caning across the hand. I was not faring well battling with a retention problem and a bit slow in general.

One thing that did come to light was that the Durban schools were interviewing students to sing in a school supported opera. I tried out and got a part in Il Trovatore singing in the choirs with now fond memories of the "Anvil song" by Verdi. Again, to enter as a candidate was prompted by my grandmother, who would often get me to sing as she played the piano. She was very proud of my seemingly success which would later take me to sing in other stages of my life. At thirteen I was six foot (2 metres), generally known as a dunce. School and I were not working out so to maintain my playground standing I would participate in the roughest playground games played behind the master's back. Dyslexia was an unknown disability with no known assistance for people suffering from it. In later years I realized this was what I had suffered from battling with it most of my life. Maturity helped to control it, so I was able to progress satisfactorily through life.

Bankruptcy.

I was about 12 years of age when a disastrous turn of events hit our family. My father's partner a Mr. LeGes, in the shipping business absconded. Regretfully leaving the company financially in dire straits as he was the accountant and financial manager. There were huge outstanding debts and funds that could not be accounted for. This was only found out after my father ordered a private financial forensic audit, revealing the corrupt actions of his partner. There were unpaid amounts due for ship leasing that had been transferred a day or two before his disappearance. In brief my father had to liquidate the company but as he was the principal shareholder, he was liable for any uncovered debts.

This all came about on a lovely afternoon. My father suddenly arrived home very early without greeting the children. He briskly walked inside followed by my mother. Later in tears she advised me that I was going to stay with my grandmother for a few days. A long story short, although detectives and my mother traced him, LeGes, to Port Elizabeth a coastal city South of Durban, he disappeared to Mauritius his place of birth.

Charges were brought against him, but his father declared him bankrupt and the possibility of reclaiming any lost funds was useless considering the legal cost, time implications and island legalities. What happened was that we lost our home and the business all except the one truck and the workshop which were in my mother's name.

An almost abandoned old house belonging to a lawyer, Mr. Goodrick, was found so with father's attention it was made livable enough for us to move into. Fortunately, mother had removed all our furniture and belongings and stored them in the workshop before the legal authorities possessed our house and contents. The luxury cars together with office furniture were sold with the business assets. Both my sister and I were transferred to Government schools in Pinetown, a small industrial town about 10 kilometres away. My parents' social life collapsed, and father had to go back to the building and construction trade in an attempt to recover what was left of the business. He was 44 years of age, slowly recovering over the years, however this devastating incident caused damage to our family life. He retired in his late sixties feeling that he had let the family down and never got over it.

At the newly refurbished house there was a very large wild oak tree towering about 4 stories high. One afternoon my friend Denny Moffat and I were as boys will be boys attempted to see how high we could climb then swing down on a rope. I fell from about 30 feet (approx. 9 meters) hitting the compact earth on the left side of head. My mother was called immediately from our store. I was bleeding from my left side and unconscious. Loading me onto a mattress in the back of our Willys station wagon she rushed me off to the nearest hospital, Entabeni hospital Durban. I lay in a coma for 4 days with severe head concussion.

After recovering, I spent a further week under observation then returned home to recover. It was during this hospital period that I again saw in my slow regaining of consciousness a sort of fuzzy light slowly coming towards me. I would later in my life when near death see the same light image again. It took a long time for me to totally recover as I suffered a mild form of amnesia in falling so well behind in my school standard. I had made a remarkable recovery but there was a price to pay which amazingly I was to overcome. This I found out years later after a second injury to the same side. Over the next couple of years my education did not improve. I definitely was not going to be a rocket scientist. In an attempt to improve my education, I with my good friend Barry Law started to attend a private small class school in Durban. Most of us could drive at a young age but to attend school required some means of transport. One had to be 18 to get a motor vehicle driver's license. However, at 16 one could get a license to drive a motorized bicycle called a Buzz bike with a 50cc engine. So, as the family had a Goggo motor scooter this became Barry and my means to attend the school. If the truth be known I did not have a license for the motor scooter but as a youngster had got the 50cc license, so if I was stopped by the law at least I would have a license regardless of the fact that the scooter had 250cc engine. On one of our days returning from the school we both decided that we and schooling had had enough and would part with good intentions. This meant that we would have no school leaving certificate in so showing no education whatsoever. It was decided that Barry would go and work for his mother who owned a lady's dress shop with a men's shoe department. I decided that I was going to go to the sea as an engineer. Only to find without any education certificate this was not going to be possible. The next thing for me was to retreat to my love for the bush and see if I could get a position as an overseer on one of the many neighbouring large sugar farms.

About this time on a school holiday five of us decided we would travel to Rhodesia and possibly Nyasaland to see what jobs in the then rich colony had. Only one of us had a driver's license and an old Opel Kadett car. He Joe DeAgostini and his brother plus Barry, David Michel and I set off with very little funds but in high spirits. Sleeping alongside the car we travelled across eastern South Africa known as the Transvaal via Johannesburg and Beit Bridge. At Victoria Falls my folks had a friend in the government who used to rent our cottage. He was able to get us drivers licenses as in Rhodesia one could drive at 16 years, so it was one of our endeavours to get in so allowing us to drive in south Africa below the age of 18. Travelling we slept by the Zambezi River which is now the bottom of the Kariba dam lake. Wildlife was plentiful so caution was necessary.

In Bulawayo we met some girls whose father allowed us to sleep in their garage. They fed us and wished us well on our journey. The return trip was overall an education and Rhodesia was certainly on the list of possibilities. The DeAgostini brother's father had crossed Africa in a Model T ford many years before, so adventure was seeded in our minds for the future.

Once back I was determined that school days were over. Not advising my parents I set off to hitchhike up the North coast road in the direction of the big sugar company estates and private farms. The farmers were comically called sugar barons as it was a very wealthy farming business. I knew a few farmers' children from our beach cottage area which was situated along the coast of the major sugar farms. One being Jill Hulett whose mother had always been very nice to me. She was a member of the large and very wealthy Hulett family of sugar farmers. Bravely I walked across the Umgeni River bridge with one shilling and sixpence (30c) in my pocket to start my life and find employment. I was somewhat nervous as I thumbed a lift but was determined that I would somehow make it and my dream of seeing the world. After a lift or two I got to the Hulett farm turn off where I walked along the beautiful, treed drive to the main house. Here I met Mrs. Hulett where I meekly explained my needs plus asking if I could stay the night as I had nowhere to go that evening. She very kindly agreed and also suggested that she would speak to her son who was the Mill manager at Darnel, a sugar mill village about 80 kilometres further on. That night she advised me that her son had spoken to her and agreed that if I got to the mill, he might offer me an apprentice job in the machine/garage shops. Mrs. Hulett suggested that I use their phone and call my parents. This I did, advising them that I would not be home that night but safe with friends near our cottage, promising an explanation later. The next day I after a sumptuous breakfast I thank Mrs. Hulett for her hospitality and proceeded to hitch hike on to the Darnel Mill still with my sole fortune of one shilling and sixpence.

Arriving at the mill I was introduced to Mr. Hulett who after understanding my need for a job and my good knowledge of mechanics offered me the job in their workshops. I was to start work in a week's time for a princely sum of fourteen pounds a month (R28.00) from which an amount of seven pounds (R14.00) would be deducted for mess food costs including a room. I was delighted so thanking him I departed to hitch back to my home and give my parents the good news that I was leaving school, had a job and would be departing home in a week's time. They, considering my failing background in school, were pleased and offered to drive me back to the mill to start my employment.

Once ensconced in the mill and working I felt finally independent. It was hard hot work working in the heat, sometimes in the upper 30°c being covered in diesel fumes and dirt. Primarily my job was to clean and prepare the tractor and trucks mechanical parts and assist the foremen and senior mechanics in their duties. I found a lot of the work of assembling the engines I could do but being an apprentice the final work was over overseeing by the senior mechanics.

Life was not easy but at the weekend there was a mill club, bar social functions and a movie on Saturday nights plus sports fields. I was lucky as a friend John Taylor from my Westville days was employed as an overseer on Suella estate bordering the Tugela River not far away. I would spend many weekends with him learning and assisting him with the everyday farm work. It was a good learning time as I was not going to stay as a mechanic for long as my intentions was to join the farming business as an overseer. At this time, I had met up with another overseer,

Dave Burns, who was stationed on an estate near Stanger, a town some distance from Darnel. This was good as we became close friends with me often staying weekends at his house on the estate. We were a bit of a wild bunch and only just evaded getting ourselves into serious trouble with some of our shenanigans, which I will not go into. It was my intention to ask the Hulett estate management if I could transfer from the garage side of the company to the overseeing side. This was a much-closed section as it was usually only open to farmers' sons or friends of farmers and management. But fate was to direct me eventually in that direction.

In the years before starting work for Huletts, my father had bought three semi-wrecked Renault 10 cars. He had given them to me and my friends as a project to rebuild. Just before getting the job at Huletts, we had successfully got one going and although without licenses would drive around evading the police. By now though we had got it licensed and I was able to use it to get to work. I bought the aforementioned Jeep for ten Pounds (20 Rand) so decided to sell the Renault

Amusing Willys Jeep advertisement

One of the other apprentice mechanics indicated he wanted to buy it. So, returning to my home he withdrew the money and paid me my price. He decided that as it was his car, he would drive it back to work that Sunday night with me as the passenger. The road back was a twisting undulating road on which there was one hill that had a bad curve to it. Approaching it I expressed my concern about his speed. The inevitable happened we rolled over sliding partially down a bank. Thankfully nobody was badly injured but I had bashed my leg below my right knee which started to swell very badly. However, with the aid of a passing 4x4 pickup we righted the car, then limping into the local town of Verulam we spent a few hours straightening a wheel and the body.

I had started to develop serious pain in my leg, so it was decided to head back to the nearest hospital where I was treated and returned home. This was not the end of it as I had to take sick leave eventually ending up in hospital for two weeks after having an operation to remove an abscess that had formed on the bone so causing possible osteomyelitis. This was unfortunately the second time the same area on my leg had been injured. Early while galloping home my horse slipped, falling into a riverbed. On getting up my leg sustained a bad injury in the form of a bone bruise which put me into the Marion Hill Monastery Hospital for a week of treatment with infra-red lamps. Later on, this same leg will again be injured seemly I was prone to the injuries which actually was almost a way of life for in my younger days. During my convalescence, I heard from my father that a farmer in Umhlali, a small farming village, Mr. Hackland, was looking for an overseer. I knew Doug Hackland, his son from our days at Willard Beach where a lot of teenagers used to meet. This was exactly what I was looking for so applied immediately. Mr. Hackland was a rather hard farmer but very successful farming about 20,000 chickens, cattle, pigs, a section of vegetables and sugar cane.

Being accepted I resigned from Huletts in so taking up and moving onto the farm. I was in my environment although it was long hours, I enjoyed working the land and with the African employees whose language I spoke. Generally, it was all round overseeing, very early 04.30 am mornings, doing the labour roll call, delivering fresh milk and vegetables to the hotels and shops before 06: 00a.m then out in the fields to supervise the tasks for the workers. My WW2 Jeep known as the "Cane rat" special which I bought with a loan from my grandmother for 20 pounds (R40) was essential to me and gave me freedom to go to Durban, our major city and seaport on the odd weekend off. There we, with my friends Dave and John, would meet girls, usually from the nurses' Training academy and keen to go out on a date. The only problem was if juniors had to be back by 10.00 p.m. or seniors allowed to Midnight. There was a very strict sergeant major type nurse on duty and heaven help if they arrived in late. I had met a lovely girl called Maggie Suttie whose parents were also involved in sugar farming and had a trading store in Eshowe, a village in Zululand some miles from where I was. Her father was a bank executive with a very rich and lovely home in Kloof, a town not far from my own parents' home. We dated steadily which included me being invited to some private functions of her father such as the Kloof country club and the prestigious Durban Country Club. Often John Taylor with the same days off would join us with his girlfriend making a good foursome. Maggies father not having a son. enjoyed a chat or two and seemed concerned as to what direction I was taking in my career. Not owning a farm meant the future required either managership or partnership in a sugar farm. Neither of which of which I had the money to invest or family ties. However, again fate directed me into another direction which would eventually take me to a realm I never expected.

South Africa had become a Republic and there was serious doubt if the future was not going to end in a civil war. It eventually did. One evening at the dinner table old man Hackland looked up after a bad news report on the developing situation. He looked at Doug and me saying he thought for young guys this would be a good time to leave South Africa and see a bit of the world. He was seriously concerned about the future and rising civil border war which we had started fighting with A.N.C black powered opposition party supported by the communists. That night my yearn to travel and my roaming spirit hit me. I decide there and then with not much funds to attempt to hitchhike around the world, after all I had done across South Africa. This would satisfy my thirst for travel and see all the places I had wanted to visit as a lifetime adventure. A few days later I advised Mr Hackland of my intentions to travel, which he supported, however Doug did not but being the heir to the farm I understood.

There was a cheap Union Castle line ship fare of 25 pounds (R50) for a one-way ticket to England. Leaving the farm was hard as I had established a good relationship with all concerned including the African staff. The one head boy named Medala (means old one) wanted desperately for me to take him along. Not understanding I was going overseas. I had my younger brother "Wallis" staying with me the weekend I left. Packing my possessions, we loaded the Jeep and started down the farm track followed by African staff running behind and cheering us on. I with all my savings and selling a few things raised the money for the ticket preparing to depart. Maggie thought I was mad and sad, but I promised I would be back. My other friends all agreed and said I would never do the around the world thing, that I would be back in a few months but wished me good luck. My folks, Maggie and a couple of friends came to see me off. It was a bit sad for Maggie, and I had been very close, and I admitted I was very unsure if I was doing the right thing. Here my father gave me the 30 shillings about R3.00 today as a parting gift. enriching my wealth. As the ship pulled away from the wharf there was lots of singing and wishing of good luck with a bon voyage. It was very fitting as mainly the passengers were all young and out to visit the Overseas Visitors Club in England. In so that started my voyage to England which I explained earlier. The one shilling and sixpence was the catalyst to starting a new life of adventure and success

. Let's get back to flying to Miami.

USA - Canada & Flight School.

Upon arriving in Miami, I proceeded straight to the "Windjammer" hotel this is where Mike Burke had his head office and charter business. He was not in at the time and the receptionist advised that he would be back in a couple of days. With very little money and nowhere to go I got friendly with the beach boy serving the deck chairs on the beach. With night coming I needed a place to hide as the police were apt to arrest people of no known address or accommodation. The beach boy showed me where I could hide my kitbag in the deckchair room and suggested that a lot of hotel guest soften slept on the deckchairs at night to enjoy the open and warm air, if he supplied me with a beach towel and chair, I would probably be alright doing the same on the hotel property. He advised the night guard late that evening, so I bedded down on the beach for my first night in the USA.

I survived like that for two days then, to my relief, Captain Burk returned to his office. I arranged a meeting with him late in the afternoon. He remembered me and my efforts getting Tondelayo back to St. Thomas. To my delight Tondelayo was back in Miami harbour having been repaired and sailed from St. Thomas. He offered me an engineering position on her, which I was very glad to accept. Upon my request knowing how difficult it was to meet with him, I asked if he would give me a reference. He did this crediting me with being an engineer and first mate. I immediately departed to the harbour to find my favourite yacht. To my delight on finding her, she looked good, my old black cook Wilmer was onboard. It was great to see him, he immediately gave me some much-needed food. We were not sure who the captain would be, but it later turned out that would be an ex-Coastguard chap whose name I cannot remember.

In the morning, we prepared to sail with 16 passengers on a Bahamas sail of the usual 7 days duration. That evening with all of the passengers on board, we cast off from Miami harbour, running on the main engine to navigate through the departure lights. Suddenly out of nowhere we came to a juddering stop, the engine started to overspeed and I had to shut it down. We were drifting in the mainstream of the harbour moving toward a known sandbar. We established that something had been wrapped around the prop, which would require an underwater examination. In my foolhardiness I volunteered to dive overboard into the black oily harbour water to see what the problem was with the shaft. Feeling my way down the rudder to the prop in darkness it seemed like there was a hawser securely wrapped around the prop and shaft I then surfaced and explained what I thought was the problem. The current was strong and there was a fear of possibly being swept away. Not a pleasant thought as the harbour water was all black, so a rope was lashed to the transom and tied around my waist. I then, armed with a breadknife, continued to dive into the foul water holding my breath as long as I could and hacked away at the hawser which had securely wrapped itself around the prop and shaft. All this in total blindness. Exhausted, I finally cut it clear and was hauled up on deck covered in grimy oily water. With the prop clear, we were able to start the engine, but our troubles were not over as in the dark and semi-powerless we suddenly heeled over as we ran aground on a sandbar.

No matter how hard we tried, including attempting to roll her using the mainsail and our outboard tender we remained firmly stuck. As were now just off the shipping lane, a coast guard cutter came and stood off. They offered assistance after we agreed that we were unable to move on our own. A heaving line was shot over to us, and a towline followed. This was secured through the port gunnel onto the anchor stanchion post near the foremast. Slowly the slack was taken up and then a heaving line was shot over to us, and a towline followed. This was secured through the port gunnel, onto the anchor stanchion post near the foremast. Slowly the slack was taken up, and then they opened up with full power. The line sung as it strained then the transom post tore itself out of the deck and had it not that we all shouted to stop the tow, the gunwale/bulwark would have gone with it. There was some serious damage, but we were off the sand bar. Casting off the tow hawser and contact with the coast guard cutter we powered back to the dock. Mike Burk was called to see the damage and what actually transpired after that I did not know. For me Wilmer and I were placed on the Caribbee and sailed 2 days later. It was great sailing as the Caribbee was square rigged at about 136 feet. The Bahamas as far as I am concerned are too overpopulated and not as lovely as the then new sailing of the Virgin Islands.

After this sail and having nothing immediate, I accepted a position on a smaller private yacht to fill in until my next Windjammer cruise. At "Stirrup Quay" island, I turned 21 so the crew tossed me overboard full of rum and coke. As I swam to the side to heave myself back on board, a crewmember fishing off the transom caught a small shark. Well as I figured it out, I had at least made 21 years. However, trouble was about to come as upon arriving at Bimini as the Captain informed us that the owner had instructed him to have the yacht stay there. The other deckhand and I were to be paid off and we were to find our own way from there on. Well, this was not what I was expecting as I was intending to get back to Miami and Windjammers, so the other chap and I found ourselves on the dock with nowhere to go. In vain we searched for a boat that might get us back but by nightfall we had not succeeded. So, bed for the night was on the docks hidden behind a small sea wall. The next day another yachty befriended us offering his boat which he was caretaking as a refuge. We later understood it had been there for some time needing a lot of repairs. So that night we at least had the comfort of cover albeit on a very old and creaky barely seaworthy Ketch. I heard later that it actually sank about 3 weeks after we were aboard.

Nevertheless, as luck has it, we by chance through the help of a barman heard of a Newport Ketch that was looking for crew to sail her to Fort Lauderdale. There was no pay, but it was a ticket to the mainland, cover and food for the two-day sail. The captain told us that he wanted to get into Fort Lauderdale late in the evening of the second days sail as he was expecting someone to meet him. This did not seem to be a problem as all we wanted was a passage to the mainland. We sailed that evening on a fresh wind with a relatively calm sea. She was a beautiful boat and the accommodation very luxurious. By mid-afternoon the next day we could see landfall so with a following wind we were approaching Fort Lauderdale at a steady 8 -10 knots. About 10 miles off the captain ordered all sails to be belayed and stowed. We then lay becalmed until about 17:00 hours when he started the engines and proceeded to head for the yacht harbour. It was just dusk as we entered the harbour and moored. The captain thanked us and advised we would have to clear immigration in the main building at the end of the dock as he was awaiting customs, but it would be OK for us to proceed. As we walked down the dock a uniformed customs officer appeared at the end of the pier. He asked if we were from the newly arrived yacht and if we had anything to declare. We explained that we did not, had just come from Bimini and were going to clear immigration. He seemed quite happy with that, so allowing us to go on our way. At the immigration office we were cleared on seaman's passes after we explained, together with my letter from Capt. Mike Burk that we were enroute to join a ship of Windjammers in Miami.

The whole procedure after leaving the yacht took about 40 minutes. As we left the building, another yachty in passing us asked if we had come off the boat to which he was pointing. Looking in the direction of the boat, we saw about four police officers aboard the yacht we had just come in on. The yachty then proceeded to tell us that the boat had been impounded and the captain arrested for smuggling whisky in the bilge. Immediately I did not know anything about the boat and the two of us made a hasty disappearing act into the parking bay and out into the traffic. It was now night, so we decided considering what had happened to split up, going our separate ways. Just outside of the parking lot there is a large vehicle roundabout with a rather high bush fence. This I decided was going to be my hide for the night so pushing in between a thicket I found an ideal spot out of sight of the road and public. Immediately I changed my shirt in an attempt to look different and decided that as it was not cold, I would sleep there as best I could in my clothes with my backpack as my backrest. Hidden in the bushes and being very attentive of any sudden action or the possibility of being found, the night seemed very long. With an early warm morning, I slipped out and headed for a supermarket I could see down the road. Here I bought a hot dog and coffee, then proceeded outside to a bus stop bench to consider my plan and future.

In my address book and diary (which regrettably has been lost), I had a large number of phone numbers indexed to cities of people offering assistance. Looking at Fort Lauderdale I found an address of a girl I had met sailing the Caribbean. She had extended a very warm invitation to visit if I was in the area. This now appeared to be my temporary choice as a bolt hole and gave her a call. She was delighted to hear from me so after she confirmed my invitation with her mother, which did seem to take a long time, we agreed to a pickup spot across from the supermarket. To my utter surprise about 30 minutes later she arrived in a yellow Mustang, which she claimed was hers, a gift from her father to complete college. I was very yachty looking, a bit bedraggled in cutoff jeans and thongs. However, I thought of what my South African friends and family would think if they could see me now in a yellow Mustang, driven by a gorgeous 20-year-old blonde-haired sexy girl in Florida. This was a hell of an introduction to rural American life. Unbelievable in years to come I will own a Mustang.

Arriving at her home I was greeted by her mother rather cautiously but after I explained in my soft and very polite South African accent that I had just delivered a yacht to Fort Lauderdale and had been at sea for a long time. I suggested, which was understood, that if I could get a hot shower, I would look a bit more presentable. This was offered and I duly emerged a bit more or less respectably attired increased but clean jeans shorts shirt and slops. The next hurdle was to meet father upon his returning home. This took place in a very cordial way and by the end of the evening, which included a supper, I had enthralled them both in my world adventures, in so winning their present approval. Her father I think had wanted a son so with my background of adventure, purposely and cautiously eliminating some grey areas, we got on well. It was getting late so after a bid of good night to all I was escorted to my room.

I was very tired and fell asleep rather quickly aided by a soft warm bed, hot dinner, something I had not had for a long time. However, some ungodly early hour the daughter joined me. This was a very dangerous situation, it was a something I had thought about, but looking at the delicate situation regarding the law plus caution in the face, I had decided against any further action in that direction. Behaving myself as best I could, just before sunup I was able to entice her to leave my room if we both wanted to be alive for breakfast. All went well thank God and her mother with what I sensed as a jaundice eye served a full breakfast. On the grounds of that I explained I was to be in Miami and asked to be excused for staying just the one night. A favourable goodbye to all was conducted with a rather subdued drop off at the bus station followed by a cold kiss that marked the end of what I took as a nervous stay in Fort Lauderdale. I found an appropriate buss, which took me back to Miami Beach, and what I hoped would be the safety of another Windjammer yacht. Nevertheless, things changed, and fate somehow took over again.

On arrival at the Windjammer Hotel, I met a local guy who also was looking for a job on a cruise. There appeared to be nothing immediate, so we headed off to the local bar for a beer. He was a guy of my age and had been to Europe, so we got on well talking about worldly things like the pending nuclear war, which had reached a very serious state of affairs with Kennedy and the Cuban conflict. A bit too close for comfort, as Cuba was only 100 nautical miles for Key West. The Bay of Pigs issue and so on. The afternoon was being eaten up or should I say drunk up and I needed a place to camp out or rely again on my beach chair at the hotel. He offered the use of his couch at a small apartment he shared. I took up the offer gladly travelling there on the local bus. It was nice little apartment not far from Miami Beach. That evening, I met his roommate who had no objection to my bunking there for a day or two. Finding his roommate was from Kentucky and had been to Lake Okeechobee, which was in the Everglades I became very interested, as it was one of the places I wanted to see. It was also related to the conception that in the early days when South Africa was assisting the South in the civil war supplying support to fight the damn Yankees as they were called. As a point of interest in South African street slang the word Okie means a man or boy or another chap.

The next day instead of heading for the Windjammer hotel, I caught a bus out of town and started hitching for the Everglades. Lifts were good and by afternoon I had reached the glades. But this was where trouble started. My last lift had been with an elderly guy with a strong Southern accent. He questioned why I was wanting to get into the everglades and did I really want to camp there. It was a long lift with him dropping me off about a mile or so from a town he suggested I might find a camp or caravan site. I started walking down the ramped dirt road when true to the glades an alligator crossed over the road. By the end of my walk, it was not alligators I was concerned about but the swarms of mosquitoes that were literally eating me alive. Getting to the small town consisting of a boat ramp, a petrol, station and small country store, I dived into the store for relief from the mozzies. An elderly black guy greeted me asking what I wanted. I remember his name was Blackie, which I found amusing. I briefly explained my idea of camping, which he very seriously advised against. Yes, there was a place for a caravan or two but nobody in their right mind would consider camping on any vacant land as Alligators are inclined to roam about. I was in a dilemma and sort his advice to which he suggested his son was driving back to the outskirts of the Everglades that night and he would give me a lift. It did not take me long to agree and so an hour later I was bumping my way back out of the glades to semi civilization in a Fort Myers direction. More alligators were seen on the road edge which it was explained that they did this in the evening. It did remind me very much of the story of the blond who went hunting alligators to get a pair of alligator shoes. It transpired that she shot 20 and never found any with shoes on. I was dropped off just short of Fort Myers getting another lift luckily at night to the centre of the city. Here I found the Greyhound bus depot where I spent the night.

By morning I headed to the freeway and hitched back to Miami. It was here that I found out the Highway patrol do not take kindly to hitchers who are on the main freeways. I learnt fast from the patrol officer that I must be off the fringe and off the freeway but allowed on the feeder roads. Back in Miami I bunked up again with my new mates getting a good laugh about the mozzies and my two-day sortie into the glades. Having come from Africa and fully aware of the malaria baring Anopheles mosquitoes, which kills half a million annually. I wondered what would happen if these Florida mosquitoes became malaria carriers. They constitute the family Culicidae. Females of most species are ectoparasites, whose tube-like mouthparts (called a proboscis) pierce the hosts' skin to consume blood. The Aedes Aegyptus mosquito carries yellow fever which has killed thousands in South America. It targets small children who develop a brain and head shrinkage either before or after birth. The Aedes Albopictus or Asian Tiger mosquito is another and if these insects got to the USA they could also get to Canada. Both countries with large lake and river areas creating ideal breeding nurseries. Over 200 million people are infected by mosquitoes with half a million in the Americas alone. 50 years after I was there the Ziha mosquito hit Florida with serious consequences. Mosquitoes are the biggest killer in the world, breeding in sewers, rural dumps, vacant land, abandoned tires and ponds all enhanced by over population.

With still no work on the Windjammer yachts, I had to rethink my next move. With my good friends Jody and Chuck Shoemaker who lived in Kennet Square, a girl friend in New York and the offer of a job on a Brigantine being rebuilt in Montreal, to be sailed back to the Caribbean, I started to look North supported by my desire to see Canada and the mounted Police. The Bay of Pigs situation in Cuba had started to accelerate, war with the states appeared possible and here was I with very little money, no work permit and no way of getting home. One has to fight off occasional fits of depression which I was starting to experience. It seemed that the best route was to head North to the freedom of Canada and what I had seen of it via National geographic. I liked the Bahamas but something I found hard to believe was that Americans where knowingly led to understand that Christopher Columbus found the mainland of the U.S.A. This is in fact very wrong. He first landed at San Salvador an island south of the Bahamas. He then established himself on what is now the Dominican Republic Island as shared with Haiti, where today they have a church, which they claim has his remains. In 1492 on founding these islands which he named Hispaniola. The Spanish then proceeded to mine the gold on the island using native islanders called Taino. They so brutally treated them as slaves and forced labour that all died, assisted by European diseases such as smallpox and syphilis. He was an Italian funded by the Spanish crown and died in Spain. Another belief is he is buried in a pauper's grave somewhere in Spain. America was incorrectly named after Amerigo another adventurer whose name was wrongly given to a German monk writing history. First humans into North America were the Eskimos stemming from the Mongolian side of the Berring straits then the Scandinavian Vikings in Newfoundland Eastern Canada moving down to Maine.

The following morning having discussed my considered move my mates buddy phoned to say he knew of a guy who had to drive a car to New York for a car delivery service. Would I be interested in helping him share the driving? Without any idea of the distance, I accepted. A day later, together with Keith the driver and Liz his girlfriend we set off from Miami to New York, an estimated drive of two days. We were a merry bunch together with the fact the Keith was a Southerner and enjoyed moonshine which he sipped on my turn to drive. Jacksonville came and went; Savannah came and sometime north of that we stopped in the middle of the night at a roadside diner. It was here while having a breakfast that the cook serving us the meal detected my accent. First questioning why an Englishman was in the USA then an Australian. When I informed him that I was South African, he wiped his forehead with his cloth, lent over towards me, looked me in the eye, then in a loud Southern accent said that if we South Africans ever wanted help with them there Niggers, to give him a call and they would bring the Southerners to our assistance. I was amused but it was the first time I had detected any animosity between the races. Promising that I would do as he requested, we drove on up through Richmond heading for Washington. I had contacted Jody and Chuck who advised that when I got past Baltimore and heading to Wilmington, I should call, and they would meet me at Wilmington bus depot. After two days of being on the road sharing a car with 2 other mad folks, I was looking forward to getting off.

What eventually transpired was that we got to Wilmington, found Jody and Chuck, bid goodbye and good luck to the other two who had now decided to get married. Jody and Chuck made me very welcome in their lovely home, meeting their three sons, the oldest being about my age. I cannot express more how hospitable they were showing me around Pennsylvania and Washington. Knowing my interest in flying, they also introduced me to lady Louise Sacchi (Sacchi Air Services) who was a transatlantic bomber ferry pilot during the war. She was part of a woman flying group known as the Ninety Niners. Amelia Earhart was the first president.

Consequently, the Schoemakers became lifelong friends and later did visit South Africa. My parents and brother many years later also had the privilege of visiting them and being shown the same wonderful hospitality and warmth of the Shoemaker family. Chuck had an old Chevrolet car which as his eldest son and I were discussing going to New York, he offered to lend us rather than catch a bus. Well so it transpired that we did set off a day or so later to New York and the big city. I had called the girlfriend I had known briefly when she was on a cruise with Windjammers to say we were coming and did the offer to stay with them still exist? Her answer was to the affirmative, so we had a place to stay rather than attempt to find some sort of cheap joint. Driving the old Chevy up there was fun and upon arriving meeting up with Tammy Thomas, we bunked down in her and her mother's flat couch and floor. Tammy had a little girl, so their two-bed roomed flat was a bit crowded but true to New York hospitality, they kindly shared their space with us for the two days we were there. New York was amazing to me as I had never seen such a city that never slept. Tammy and I saw the Empire State Building, the Statue of Liberty and Time Square where we saw and listened to a famous drummer, Gene Krupper. With regret we had to leave so although I promised I would visit again we departed back to Kennet square. I think the trip was a success for Chuck's son who had not met or been with a world traveler. A few years later he travelled out to South Africa doing the same thing back packing. He did buy a motorized bike with all of 50cc power and rode it from Durban to Cape Town a distance of 1600k. I think I may have sowed the travel bug within him.

Time was moving on so if I wanted to get to Canada I had to make a move. Albeit rather reluctantly as the Shoemakers had made me feel at home offered to get some political influence if I wanted to stay and work initially in Chuck's wood factory. It was tempting I had been on the road a long time with no support or means to a future but the hand of the wanderer, fate, and the desire to circumnavigate the world, pointed north. So once again I bid a due to the great Shoemaker family and bussed back to New York. I met up again with Tammy but leaving her I think with a bit of a sad feeling from her towards me moving on catching a bus to Waterbury in Connecticut. Here I contacted another girl whom I had met on the Windjammer cruises. She too had offered a place to stay should I come her way. I duly arrived and as prearranged met her parents. Her father was a small time produce farmer having on his small holding an old WW2 Willys jeep just like my own. I spent a couple of days with them helped him with a bit of bricklaying and general work around the holding to which he paid me and I in turn worked my stay. The money was much appreciated.

They were great country people, but I had to move on so a day later headed for Buffalo and Niagara. Arriving on a late bus at Buffalo I was confronted by the border police who accused me of being a vagrant as I had no known address or place of residence. They were not too nice about it but supported by my South African English accent a letter from my father's bank saying funds could be obtained if any requirement was needed. My explanation and reason to travel was I was a university student writing a thesis on back packing around the world. They released me, escorting me to the Greyhound bus departing for Niagara.

It was dark when I got to Niagara but quickly slipped out the rear entrance of the depot fearful of meeting more police. There was a sign indicating the way to the Peace Bridge crossing into Canada. Following this I started to walk across but found the way inaccessible because there was a customs and immigration post at the bridge. The officer on duty had seen me appear so I boldly walked towards him. I explained I had missed the bus to the Canadian side of the Niagara Falls but was expecting to meet college friends on the other side who were waiting for me. He passed me on to immigration where they mildly looked at my South African passport, all its stamps and my seaman's visa for the USA. It must be remembered that at that time South Africa was still considered a member of the commonwealth so very few borders had been advised of any restrictions being a republic. The USA and Canada borders were very open and crossing in most cases was merely a formality of showing some sort of I.D. The officer had a French accent, which at the time was bit confusing to me. He did not seem to care much at that time of the night, light another cigarette stamped my passport and closing the door biding me in French, good night.

I was able to walk towards the falls another thing I had wanted to see, considering I had seen Victoria Falls. It was dark but I found a spot almost at the crest of the raging waterfall. Bit tired I settled down out of sight and in behind some bushes. Morning came quickly, the sound of roaring water I had gotten used to but the sight in daylight was magnificent. Taking pictures, I strolled along the embankment and into the town. Here I was able to get some food and a hot drink. Not exactly sure how far I was from Montreal I moved out onto the highway in the direction of a notice board to Toronto. Toronto, Montreal and Niagara would without my knowledge be entwined with my future.

Getting onto the highway I got a lift with a farmer travelling to a small town called Stoney Creek with a load of apples. He was very friendly as are all Canadians, so upon arriving at his farm he offered me work for the day off loading and loading produce onto his truck. This I did willingly as funds were a definite need for concern. Later that day, with the work finished, I was duly paid and dropped off at the bus depot. Here I caught the late bus into the Toronto bus terminal where I spent part of the night. Here I was able to board the late red-eye bus to Montreal. Six hours later having slept on the bus I found myself in the centre of Montreal. Cleaning up in the toilet I proceeded to look for the address of the CNR (Canadian National Railway) where the gentleman who I had met in the Caribbean, offering me a job on a Brigantine being rebuilt and to be sailed back to the Caribbean, had his office.

It was difficult as most pedestrians I spoke to replied in French however, after walking for some time I found the desired building and got an office number. I presented myself to a secretary who fortunately spoke English and advised me to wait a moment. A short while later I was ushered into the office of the gentleman who I immediately recognized. He was incredibly surprised to see me but after I explained how I got there and why I was there, his expression changed. He advised me that his friend who was involved with the ship rebuild had been transferred. He himself knew nothing of the working or who was doing the work in so advised that there was nothing he could do about it for me. Here I was on the other side of the world with no job, very little money and not exactly sure of where I was headed for. I immediately made a quick decision explaining to him that I was writing a book on young people travelling the world. Could he possibly arrange a reduced rate train ticket to Vancouver for me? I again was ignorant as to how far Vancouver was but took a long shot. To this day I have no idea why I said that, as it was definitely not true. His reply was to the negative and offering me a cup of coffee, which the secretary would give me, thereby ushering me out of his office on the grounds he had work to attend to. Accepting the coffee gratefully I found myself out on the street with nothing but the pavement to consider.

I was a bit heartbroken, scared, and my sorry position was beginning to creep up on me. I had to maintain a clear head. My plan was to work in Montreal on the ship and sail her back to the Caribbean. Fate again played its hand, and I decided that I would hitchhike to Alaska where I understood land was available for homesteaders. Alaska was about three and a half thousand miles away. However, my footprints on the pavement went in the direction of the bus terminal where I would be able to get a bus. At the bus depot, I caught a bus to take me out of town and onto the Trans Canadian highway, which links east to West across the whole of Canada a distance of about 5,000 plus kilometres. Walking the highway and looking at the never-ending path of black tarmac my mind started to run rampant with ideas and fear started to edge into my thoughts. Where was going, what would happen if I got ill? How and when would I ever get home now thousands of miles and across oceans away? So far, the Caribbean, Florida, Bahamas, the Atlantic crossing, Europe had all been a big adventure but now all I owned was on my back, money was short, work was not available. The road was long to complete my circumnavigation of the world, I was getting lonely and tired, fear started to set in.

Trans Canadian Highway

Night in Quebec, especially in August comes early and there were signs of it plus a bit of cold which dampened my spirits. Lifts were not coming as I plodded on towards North Bay a town on the Trans Canadian highway by the great lakes. Luckily, a chap stopped and offered me lift to North Bay, his home and destination. It was a long 4-hour drive. He had seen the South African flag on my kitbag and was curious. Mark this as my first lift as it will come up later. He was very chatty, interested in my travels and adventures so much so that upon arriving in North Bay later that evening he offered me a place to stay, albeit on the lounge floor not having another bedroom.

I met his wife who was a lovely lady about my age, we settled down to some Rye whisky and seven up drinks, which after dinner led onto some beers.

By about Midnight all had consumed a fare few drinks, the mood was merry, and he decided he had enough so retiring to bed. I laid out my sleeping bag in the corner of the lounge attempting to get a good night's sleep in a warm environment, which I had not had in days. Later in the night, I was disturbed by his wife who it appeared my company was more desirable than her husbands' was. I could hear him snoring and found myself in a very difficult position to say the least. My sleeping bag was my protection, which I thank the lord slowly discouraged her and she very slowly departed for her bed walking into the darkened door. This aroused her husband who I heard him enquire what was up, there was no reply.

At crack of dawn, I packed leaving a thank you note on the table amongst the debris of the night and departed. I walked very briskly out of town heading onto the Trans Canadian Highway not stopping until I was at least a few miles from the town. The road was quiet, so I decided against my usual manner of standing to be seen in full, but to just walk on in hope of a lift. I am not sure of the time; however, I had stopped to make myself some tea and eat some bread I had with me. I missed a few cars doing this but eventually was back on the road heading for Sudbury, Sault St Marie and Thunder Bay.

It was definitely getting cooler, so I had put on my old British army jacket, which I had bought in England from the Army surplus store. Regretfully it was a bit tattered, so my appearance was a bit shabby. However, I pressed on laughing a bit to myself about the events of the past evening. Finally, a very large Mac truck pulled up and offered a lift via Sudbury to the outskirts of Sault Ste Marie. These towns would again appear in my story but in a more dangerous manner. It was good to get off the roadside and although slow at least I was in my imagination heading to Alaska and a homestead to forge my future or even strike gold. Little did I know what was to develop. Passing the nuclear power station, we rumbled on coming into Sudbury early afternoon. Here he made a relief stop for a coffee and donuts which I gratefully accepted. By 01:00 pm we were away again, reaching his final destination. Here he dropped me off, he wished me well and drove on into the enveloping mist. Mark this as my second lift. The mist and oncoming evening caused the road to be exceedingly difficult to see as well as oncoming cars. When hitching it is advisable to have your kitbag well clear of the road as unbelievably some cars almost run you down. I decided that it was useless to attempt hitching any further, so walked down a dip in the road and found a hill being part of the road cutting. Climbing up the cutting I saw a good spot to camp well clear of the road and out of sight. It was misty so the visibility was not good. I made my camp boiled up my water for soup and munched on the bread, cold meat, and mayonnaise I carried.

It was lovely being alone in the bush. No sound of civilization and very quiet. My sleeping bag consisted of a bag inside a waterproof canvass sleeve. The head part had a canvas flap where I put my kitbag. I would then take the shoulder strap and hook it into my belt in the event someone tried to snatch my bag with all my worldly possessions. Passports and money were in my lap bag on my waist with my trusty knife held firmly against my chest. I lay there with the mist and now a drizzle of rain trying to calm my nerves and clear my head as to exactly where I was going. Sleep did not come easily, however at sometime during the night I was violently woken by the ground shuddering. My immediate reaction was to flip off the head cover to my sleeping bag. As I did this, I was confronted by a huge light eliminating the entire bush around me. The ground shook, my heart was pounding as I battled to identify and see what was happening. As it turned out in the dark and mist, I had not seen the railway line just off my campsite. The light shot by me followed by three thundering diesel electric train engines and what seemed like an endless train of freight trucks. I had never seen a train that long before estimating at least 100 trucks. I had learnt a lesson, it was par for the course, but sleep for the rest of the night was hard to come by.

A misty morning eventually arrived so making some tea and a sandwich I packed my kit. The path down to the road was slippery, misty, and wet. The road was dreadful, a hitchhiker's nightmare with low visibility. Cars came out of the mist and shot by. An hour or so went by with no luck. Then out of the mist I detected a different engine tone from the usual American cars. Interested I put out my thumb just in time to confront a small red English sports car, which shot by me. To my delight its red brake lights came on. I hurriedly walked up to the car and on bending down to what I had thought was a young guy but turned out to be a beautiful 20-year-old girl. On explaining I was heading for Alaska and was wondering if she was going to Sault St Marie, she replied she was going to Vancouver. The car was a small British built Sunbeam Alpine and my kit bag would not quite fit in unless it was on my lap. Well by hell or high water by placing my bag on the ground then squeezing it into the gap between my chest and the dashboard, I got it in. I was going to Vancouver. Not to mention I was wet and had dirty boots, so it was a tight fit. I offered her half of my sandwich, which she declined suggesting we stop in Sault St Marie for a coffee break.

Her name was Julie Kniffen, a college student from Vancouver who had driven across the USA visiting friends and was on her way back across Canada to Vancouver. We got on very well and she was enthralled with my travel stories. At Sault St Marie we stopped for a necessary break. Here we rearranged the car and got my bag into the trunk with some of her stuff behind the seat. Over coffee, she expressed that she was happy for me to travel with her, so sharing the driving. Her father paid for the petrol, but we would have come to some sleeping arrangements as she had a limited amount of money to cover motels etc. During this break, we worked out the road distance from Sudbury, which meant that if I went with her to Vancouver, it was 2,675 miles. (4,458 kilometres) The longest lift I have ever known of anyone having. In addition, I would have hitchhiked across Canada in three lifts, as I marked earlier, covering about 3,100 highway miles. (5,166 Kilometres) quite a record, I think.

Trans Canadian.

With everything agreed upon we repacked the car to make more room and set off heading West on the great Trans Canadian highway. It was good and a platonic relationship began which would last for some time to come. The little 4-cylinder sports car pulled well as we drove in the direction of Thunder Bay and Winnipeg. The prairies miles rolled on with their massive wheat fields, small villages, one-horse towns, reminding me so much of the movie "Oklahoma". The great black tar seemed to go on forever. We camped at some places and got motels in others, which Julie kindly paid for.

It was great, we laughed a lot and discussed life as we had lived it. Julie was a great girl, a good driver and lots of fun. Rolling through the prairies of Saskatchewan, Manitoba and Alberta, the road was as straight as a ruler. Miles upon miles of swaying wheat fields as we headed West via Regina for Calgary renowned for its "Calgary stampede", a big rodeo display with cowboys and cattle country. The miles rolled on with the great Rocky Mountains slowly coming into view. Passing Calgary, we headed into the beautiful British Columbia Mountains and to Lake Louise. This had a magnificent clear blue lake bordered by snow-covered mountains reaching for the sky, draped in fresh snow-covered mantels. Here we swam in a lake and camped in a closed down national park, it being it was out of season so we should not have been there. Using the side dirt road, we hid ourselves in amongst the forest near an ablution block, which still had water. Totally ignorant that it was bear country however we did see some Moose and when on the side road driving to the closed park, a lot of deer. The mountains caress you, gigantic in appearance and awe-inspiring picturesque dressed in green with forests as a petticoat. The sky was blue so with the top down we sang and reveled in the audacious, mystic feeling of their presence. We were young and carefree. The sixties and flower children theme were very much in our spirits, boosted I might add by a few bottles of cheap wine. Motoring on we passed the great "Kicking horse pass" heading for the mountain town of Prince George. Here I was going to have to make a decision which could have changed my life. Was I going on with Julie to Vancouver or was I going to leave her and attempt to hitch to Alaska another 600 miles due Northwest and what I was not taking into consideration, the winter. Fate, the good Lords hand, and a soft word from Julie convinced me I should stay with her to complete the Trans Canadian adventure of travelling from Niagara, Montreal to Vancouver a distance of over 3600 miles. In addition, now my sixth sense indicated I should head for a harbour to either get a job on a ship to Alaska or onward to Australia.

Arriving at Prince George, we stopped at a diner to refresh with a coffee and to let me think on my predicament. Walking back to the car from the diner I looked at Julie, the car then looked at the cold high mountains to the West. Could I possibly do it or was it just a mad dream to homestead in a foreign country, icy cold in winter, no money, plus no experience of the Alaskan wild. My gut feeling roused itself as I put my backpack back into the car. Getting back in beside Julie, she smiled and said she was glad I was going to continue accompanying her to Vancouver. Another fork in my life had been overcome; unknown to me at the time the attempt to get to Alaska could have been fatal. The road is rough, hewed out of the mountain and forest. Dirt a good length of the way, following a pipeline with little or no towns enroute.

We sped on down through great mountain ranges and magnificent forest trees. Being almost autumn, the foliage and forests were ablaze in magnificent colour. Light browns, soft greens, pale yellow and blues. Reaching the Town of" Hope" at the foot of the mountains and the beginning of Vancouver valley, we joined the well-used Hope Penticton highway being part of the Trans Canadian. In the great days of the gold rush and pioneering of the Rocky Mountains, believe it or not but camels were used to haul goods up the precarious mountain valley trails.

Now passing a place called Abbotsford which was unbeknown to me at the time, would become synonymous to me and my life. We were on the last leg of the journey so ahead lay the beautiful city of Vancouver, my destination and Julie's home. With Julie now driving, we passed through the city heading to the dockyard and harbour. Julie had explained that she could not really invite me to her home as it would take too much explanation and she would not want the wrong impression to be cast onto her parents. I totally understood and explained that I could not really expect anything more than what we had agreed upon. It had been a great 10-day journey and now our ships had to part comfortably. Not in the night but as good friends of the world.

In the dockyard, a large unattended tall grass covered area looked like possibly it had been an old shunting yard. Here we stopped, I extracted my kit bag placing it next to the car. Julie stood next to me giving me a warm kiss, bidding goodbye and good luck. She then drove away leaving me alone to see what next had to be done to survive with 17 dollars in my pocket, no job, no home, no friends, no food, no travel ticket too anywhere and now thousands of miles from home. Things did not look good, but here I was halfway around the world, so, so far so good.

Rocky Mountains, Abbotsford flying school.

The weather had set in a bit, being misty and damp. At the far end of the vacant shunting yard there appeared to be a small store of some sort. Approaching it, I was able to see a sign advertising food hot drinks, cigarettes, and groceries. The building was rather old, and weather beaten, probably from being so close to the harbour. Entering it, I found an elderly Chinese man standing behind a counter with large assortments of saleable goods. There was also a hot skillet, coffee machine, pay telephone, and cigarette machine. On the skillet counter, there was a sign advertising burgers, hot dogs, and hot soup. The soup was 15c a bowl so with a ham sandwich for 35c and the soup I had found my dinner.

Leaving the Chinaman's shop the weather had worsened so it was time to find a place to sleep, preferably well away from the public eye. Behind an old railway line stop barrier, I found an ideal place and set out my usual sleeping arrangements. It was a long night just lying there wondering what was going to develop in the morning. By morning the weather had cleared. I could now see the ships at the docks and sort of where I was in the proximity of roads, city, and general surrounds. My biggest concern was the notorious Canadian mounted police who I had learnt from the Chinaman did patrol the area. However, my new Canadian residential spot with an ocean view I might add, situated in the far corner of the yard seemed safe for now.

Packing up I quickly moved out and got to the Chinaman's store. Here after a cup of hot coffee boiled yesterday, I set off to get onto the docks. It was about 8: am when I got to the first ship, a large cargo carrier with a gang plank down amidships. After a chat with a sailor at the head of the plank and asking to speak to the captain, he ushered me to a cabin on the second deck. Here a rather small man with a distinctive America accent confronted me. He politely explained although I had a seaman's visa he could not and would not take aboard any person not in the seaman's union plus he was not bound for Alaska. Therefore, would I politely leave his ship? This introduction got me thinking as to whether I was uninformed about getting temporary work on ships.

The next ship a smaller vessel looked like it was carrying timber. Regretfully I did not even get to the gangplank as a burley sailor forbad me to even step on it. Ship after ship was a no go, either not being allowed on board or not being able to meet the captain. On one ship, the sailor smoking a cigarette on the deck allowed me aboard. He advised that he could smuggle me over to Victoria on Vancouver Island but that was the best he could do. The second night was back at my newfound shunting yard residence, followed again by a sleepless night worrying about my not so favourable predicament. Dinner, not silver service being the only meal of the day was served by the Chinaman at his greasy spoon shop, consisting of soup, toast with the usual boiled yesterday coffee.

That evening while standing in the Chainman's shop a chap walked in looking for cigarettes. Having briefly discussed my predicament with the Chinaman about not being able to get a job on a ship, he the Chinaman referred me to the chap. The man was a Canadian fishing boat crewmember who was on shore leave. He explained that there was probably no ship at this time of the year that would even consider hiring crew experienced or not. The reason was that the North passages to Alaska were closing due to the oncoming subzero weather. He left me in a glum mood and rather depressed.

Things were going from bad to worse. I decided I would give it one more try in the morning, if not successful would have to try to get a job of any sort or get help from the Salvation Army. There was, however, one other shot I could take and that was referring to my address book. Morning came and I saw a police cruiser go by, so I realized my time was short. I again tried the ships, which proved fruitless, so it was to my address book I turned. My book had numbers from people I had met on my travels, not by name but by country or city. Looking up Vancouver I had no reference but looking up British Columbia I found an address and phone number for a fellow traveler I had met when living in the house with all the Aussies and New Zealanders at Ealing Broadway in London. He was Glen Creelman a Canadian guy a bit older than I was. Going to the phone at the Chinaman's store, I dialed his number using my precious dwindling funds. A woman answered the phone explaining she was his mother and that he worked for the Pacific Great Eastern (Although in the West) Railway as micro technician in the Columbia range mountains. She gave me a contact number to call on his microwave system. Calling this number, I got hold of him immediately. After the usual greeting and refreshing him as to who I was, I elaborated as to my very serious position, and could he help in any way such as offering a place to stay for a few days. Glen explained that he lived high up in the Columbia Range Mountains at a place called Alta Lake, residing in two trailer camp units. He was sympathetic to my need, as he understood backpacking himself. He went on to explain that he had no problem in helping me out, but I was quite away from his camp. If I wished to get to him, I would have to hitch to Squamish, a coastal and logging town about 80 miles along the west coast up an inlet. Here was a rail terminal and he would arrange with the caboose guard on the midnight logging train to allow me to ride up to Alta Lake being a halt where I would have to jump off the slow-moving train. He indicated I would have to walk from the docks, through the lower city across the park and Lions Gate Bridge. The other side being North Vancouver was where I would find the road to Squamish via Lions Gate. I agreed to do this and would have the stationmaster at Squamish advise him by radio, when on the train. It was midday as I slogged on through the city into the park at Bay head. It was a beautiful park bordered on one side by the sea and the other by the city. This city was a beautiful place, so I stopped to have a sandwich I had bought from the Chinaman's store. Sitting on a log looking out at the Straits of Georgia I pondered my predicament and what was going to happen. Glen's place now seemed my only choice where possibly I could get a job. Unbeknown to me I was to find out this was not possible.

Walking on over the huge bridge cradling the entrance to Vancouver harbour I got to North Vancouver and found the road out to Squamish. Now fate was to play the most remarkable card it had ever played before. As I write I still find it hard to believe what happened. Standing at the crossroad to the road exiting North Vancouver to Lions Gate and Squamish the light just turned red against my crossing. My foot was actually across the pavement about to cross on the green. Waiting for the red to change to green, so allowing my passage across the road I proceeded on the change to green. With traffic coming from my left to right I placed my kitbag down on the pavement stepping out to thumb a lift. The first car to cross pulled over ahead of me. I walked up to the open window explaining I was looking for a lift to Squamish. The driver said he could give me a lift to Lions Gate, a town some miles on. I agreed to put my bag on the back seat I got in next to the driver. We pulled away and for a moment nothing was said. Then I noticed he had looked in the rear mirror and was looking at what I thought was my bag. He asked my name and noted that I had a South African badge on my kitbag. I explained I was from South Africa and was attempting to circumnavigate the world.

He questioned whereabouts I was from in South Africa as he had lived in Durban after the war. I commented that I also was from Westville, a small town outside of Durban. At this point he slowed down looking at me in a strange manner, remarking he had worked for "Chas Evans Construction" in Westville. Well, I went rather cold for a second; he looked back at the road with a puzzled expression on his face. When I told him I was Alan Evans, Chas Evans's son, he pulled over stopping the car. It was incredible and almost frightening that this man a second after I crossed the road where I could have missed him by a light change was an ex-employee of my fathers. Flabbergasted, he insisted I come to his home to meet his wife. This I did so after arriving at his home and meeting his wife, he took out pictures of my younger sister Beverley, and me riding tortoises at our beautiful home in Westville. He also had a photo of my mother, father and himself working with them to build our caravan. It was a very weird feeling as if time and fate had converged for me to meet these people. Once again, the gate to my incredible road of life had opened just in time.

They insisted that I stay the night with them, and he would take me to Squamish in the morning. That was fine with me knowing Glen would only get a call from the Squamish stationmaster when I was aboard the midnight train. Well, they were very gracious people of originally Dutch descent. They had left South Africa after immigrating there from war torn Europe. However, as he was a carpenter and plasterer, they did not find South Africa to their liking so moved on to Canada where they settled and had a family. His wife washed all my clothes and donated a clean shirt to me. After a long talk about my family, my dad going bankrupt by embezzlement from his Mauritian partner, the arrival of my brother 12 years younger than myself, we retired to what for me was a magnificent clean bed and soft mattress. With morning and a hot cup of coffee, we had breakfast. More talks on the South African situation now being a Republic and its future. He suggested that after lunch he would take me to Squamish, as I was only to be there that night. Bidding farewell to his wife we proceeded to Squamish getting there about 4:00pm. He insisted to wait and see if the arrangements with the stationmaster were in order. This I did and confirmed back to him, at which point he said goodbye suggesting that if I needed anything to call him.

He did not realize what a predicament I was in, no cash, no job, and no home. As he walked away shaking his head, I heard him mutter "incredible". Opening and then closing the car door he waved and drove off, leaving me with a very cold and slightly concerned gut feeling of emptiness. It had been a small touch of home. Sitting on the platform bench, I observed the hustle and bustle of a logging train depot. The nerve centre of the P.G.E. Shunters moving back and forth with the clanging and banging of empty logging trucks being positioned to depart to their destination. Filling in time, I found some interesting information on the railway. Quite a history so will enclose it.

Railway History

Named after the Great Eastern Railway of England, the Pacific Great Eastern Railway was incorporated in Vancouver in 1912.

In its early years, the railway was the only means of shipping cattle out of the area. Later on, it became the main carrier of forest products and minerals.

By building and operating a railway between North Vancouver and Prince George, the founders of PGE hoped to open up the interior of the province. The line, which would link with the Grand Trunk Pacific Railroad in Prince George, would provide cheap north/south transportation for freight, passengers and mail. At the time, the only link to BC's vast interior was the Caribou Wagon Road which had seen better days and only went as far as Barkerville.

Obstacles to the PGE Railway

Challenging terrain at the beginning of the proposed line convinced the builders to start the track at Squamish instead of North Vancouver. Union Steam Ships completed the link to North Vancouver until 1956 when the 'first' part of the line was completed.

By the time the rail service reached Clinton in 1916 the company was bankrupt. The trains continued to operate, but there was no further construction. World War I was blamed for the lack of investors. In 1918 Premier John Oliver's government reluctantly assumed responsibility for the railroad. Well aware of the agricultural potential in the Caribou and Peace River, the government hired Northern Construction to finish the line to Prince George. This huge undertaking resulted in an equally huge debt.

On to Williams Lake

Caribou cattlemen greeted the continuation of the rail line with great enthusiasm because the package included the establishment of stockyards in Williams Lake. This meant the end of the long, brutal cattle drives to Ashcroft. With the coming of the PGE, Williams Lake became the prime cattle shipping centre for the province.

Construction to extend the line from Clinton began in the winter of 1919. William Pinchbeck's original wheat field was chosen as the site for the village of Williams Lake. Entrepreneurs rushed to the area, and when the first work train puffed into Williams Lake on September 15, 1919, the community boasted stores, banks and hotels, some housed in rough tarpaper shacks or tents. The steam locomotives pulled mixed trains of passengers, freight, cattle and fuel to the new town.

Extending the PGE North

Williams Lake was the end of the line until 1921 when the rail line was pushed north to Quesnel. Again, rough terrain stopped construction, just north of Quesnel and it was over 30 years before the line was extended to Prince George, arriving there in 1952. The link to Fort Nelson was not complete until 1971 and the PGE became known as "the railway from nowhere to nowhere."

Was the PGE a Success?

Critics from the Lower Mainland said it was neither "Pacific, Great nor Eastern," but to the Caribou, the railway was the economic lifeline. It did indeed "open up the country" bringing with it both people and prosperity – and the city of Williams Lake.

I was sure glad they were successful as the train I was destined to ride on that night was a one-way ticket to my last hope to survive my endeavour to hitch the world. At about half past eleven that night the stationmaster found me sleeping on the bench. He took me to the carriage, being the only carriage (The Caboose) at the rear of the train, the rest were empty logging trucks. Here he introduced me to the guard, and I climbed aboard getting out of the cold and into a sort of cargo carriage with a pot-bellied heater and smokestack. It contained general goods such as post, mining equipment, truck parts, logging equipment, and food, with large packages of unknown items. All head into the mountain range to be deposited at stops and small villages deep in the mountains, which are part of the Rockies.

"Finally, we pulled away with a lot of jerking and shuddering as the trucks interlinked and took the strain. The guard told me that we would pass through the "Cheakamus Canyon" a very beautiful pass then on through Garibaldi Park, estimating Alta Lake at about 02:30 am. There are two seats mounted high on the wall in the rear guard's van, each can observe the train ahead and the rails. I understood from the guard that it was his job to observe the trains' progress and report accordingly to the train engineer. One of the things he had to watch for besides brake fires or truck derailments was sparks from the steel wheels, which could set fire to the brush alongside the rails. A forest fire here is a very serious event, losing millions in timber. Bears were also a problem being on the tracks.

I lifted myself up onto one of these seats so observing the winding trucks and view ahead. Regretfully it was a bit overcast so with no moon all I was able to sense was the beautiful mountains and forests as we climbed though the canyon. A cup of hot black coffee appeared, and light conversation took place. The three big diesel units hauled and heaved their train of steel trucks with their powerful head light slicing into the darkness. Suddenly a blue night sky appeared with rather clear vision ahead. We seemed to have levelled out a bit and picked up speed. The guard informed me that we were through Garibaldi Park and the next stop would be mine. He advised that it was not a regular stop for logging trains so the engineer would slow the train down to walking pace at which point I was to step off the rear plate. I felt the train slowing down so got onto the rear plate being watched by the guard who held my kitbag.

Out of the darkness, a small shed appeared at which point the guard indicated I should jump off. This I did grabbing my kitbag from the guard as my feet touched the sleepers. The train pulled away leaving me totally alone in almost pitch blackness standing on the rails. The units at least a mile ahead were picking up speed. The headlight penetrating the line ahead eliminating the dark, but the forest was shrouded in a murk of the night silhouetted by the background of high snow topped black mountains. The red taillight of the trains guard van (Caboose) disappearing into the darkness was bit nerve racking. I was the captain "of my destiny" but now I was isolated in the cleft of mountains and not exactly sure where fate was taking me. Looking around and getting my eyes conditioned to the night, I made out what looked like a small station on my side of the line. I could also hear the sound of what I considered to be a generator, putt putting away some distance from my position.

Walking towards the sound, I was able to make out a wire of some sorts leading from the top of the station into the forest. Following this along a narrow bush path, I came across a small clearing on which there were two porta-cabins. One had a set of stairs leading up to a door. I ascended the stairs and knocked loudly on the door. For a while nothing happened so I tried again. On this attempt, a light came on and I heard a door opening in the cabin. The night was very still, black and silent. Well, the door opened cautiously and there was Glen Creelman, man was I glad to see him.

Entering we greeted each other and got down to a brief chat on what was going on. Glen suggested we get some sleep showing me a space in one of the cabins, which was the technical and instrument section of the two units. Getting my kit bag sorted out and opening up my sleeping bag, I was asleep almost immediately. Morning came with Glen awakening me advising that he had to leave for a while. There was coffee and toast in the galley in the other unit, which was his living quarter of the two porta-cabins. Awake, I found a bathroom with a shower so was able to shave and clean up. Glen arrived back at midmorning, so we talked until after lunch, I explaining my predicament and all that had happened since we had met in London.

He continued his travels around Europe and returned to his job as a technician enjoying the freedom of his position way up there in the mountains. He had a speeder (a small power trolley) that ran on the rail line. In addition, a Jeep. He suggested that while there we should do some hiking and possibly climb up one of the mountains called Whistler, which was not far from the cabins. In addition, he showed me Alta Lake next to the rail line on which there was a lodge called "The Rainbow Lodge" frequented on weekends by people arriving on the passenger train to spend weekend away from Vancouver.

It was possible he thought that they might be able to give me some sort of work as the summer season was finishing but they did stay open for skiers in winter. He warned that it was bear country so to be always aware, especially if walking around or down to the rail track and the small station. Getting to work was the first thing on my list, so suggested we get to the lodge as soon as possible. That evening we used the canoe, paddled over to the lodge to meet the manager who Glen knew well. Regretfully he explained he had filled all the staff positions needed for the foreseeable time but would bear me in mind if the situation changed. Over the next couple of days, I accompanied Glen on his daily work schedule.

That weekend we attended the lodge function, meeting a lot of the regular visitors, all of whom knew Glen. They were very charitable as I was not in any position to buy drinks or food. One elderly lady with a daughter a bit older than myself suggested that if I came to Vancouver job hunting, I would be welcome to stay a day or so with them. Later I was to use this invitation. On one of Glen's free days off we climbed "Whistler Mountain "never believing it would later become a world-famous ski resort. It was on this climb that I saw what I thought was an

Alsatian dog, to be enlightened that it was a mountain wolf. A magnificent animal who was accompanied, as we saw later, by a small pack. Glen had a rifle over his back but explained that there was no problem as it was very unlikely, they would attack humans. Subsequently I learnt that there is hardly any history of wolves attacking humans.

Alta Lake was a beautiful place, it was generally thought by all I met, that someday it would become a well-known ski and recreation area. Consequently Glen, and some of the regular visitors were attempting to buy land from the province. With no work available at the lake Glen suggested that he would have to go to Pemberton line to get supplies, a very small logging town deep into the mountains and about 20 miles further up the rail line. He thought that if there was any chance of getting work it might be there as there is a mill and small centre to supply goods to the town. Therefore, we agreed to travel there on his little powered rail speeder, following the first train coming through in the morning. The first train came thundering through early the next day, so we lifted the speeder onto the rail line and sped off following the train ahead. It was rather fun sitting on this little flat platform powered by a small engine speeding along the line in the fresh mountain air. About five miles along the way Glen pointed out a brown bear that had been spooked away from the line by the preceding train. This was indeed wild Canadian mountain country that Glen enjoyed working in and I was beginning to love it.

Pemberton was indeed a small mountain town. A dirt main street, a few houses dotted around, a small shopping centre and a large timber mill. The mill was the main reason for Pemberton to be there. It was the junction of the loggers and railhead to transport milled timber to Squamish then to Vancouver for shipment. With the small population being mainly mill workers, the shopping centre we walked into knew glen well. The store consisted of a small checkout and the rest of the building contained every sort of merchandise one could think of. From tobacco, cloth, food. meat, picks, shovels, guns you name it, it was somewhere there. Occupants were few and mixed between housewives in boots, a few Indians, and a couple of rough looking men.

After Glen collected his supplies, we went next door to what appeared to be a small coffee shop, come burger joint, with a few bottles of whisky on the back shelf. It was not the cleanest of places with heavy boot marks and dirt on the floor. There were a couple of stalls at the back, so we proceeded to sit down and order some coffee from a Chinese fellow who had greeted Glen. On serving the coffee, Glen asked the chap about whom to see if one wanted a job in the mill. A name was given which we wrote down on the paper napkin. After coffee, I left Glen in the coffee shop, walked across to the main office visible by the sign hanging at an angle over a door in front of some 4x4 trucks. Entering the office and enquiring as to where I could find the person in question, I was sent to an office further into the factory building. Here I met the manager who after introductions and me explaining why I was there, he suggested that they might be needing a diesel mechanic so I should go and see the workshop supervisor as he was not involved in hiring on site staff. My hopes and morale shot up immediately.

With directions I found the supervisor/foreman and again after introductions explained I did have diesel experience and would be willing to do any work that might be available. He asked when I could start as they would need an extra hand for the winter milling. I advised him that I would have to go back to Alta Lake with Glen to get my belongings. He suggested that in that case I could catch the morning logging train that he would arrange to have it slow down at Alta Lake, so allowing me to jump onto the guards-van plate and board the carriage. Being familiar with this I agreed to be there by midday the following day.

The Irish poet and Nobel prize winner Seamus Heaney once wrote. "If you have a strong first world and a strong set of relationships, then in some part of you, you are always free, you can walk the world because you know where you belong, you have some place to come back to". It bore resemblance in some way to myself and my present predicament, but thousands of miles from my home and any relations. But I was free.

Pemberton.

Returning with Glen, I prepared my belongings, which consisted of a backpack, sleeping bag, small stove, a knife and fork kit, and personal clothing. The morning came and as per the schedule, the logging train slowed down enough for me to grab the handlebar and jump onto the plate. Upon entering the caboose, I met the guard and settled down for the 25-minute ride.

Upon arriving in Pemberton, I located the mill foreman and presented myself for work. He ushered me into his office, which was very close to the mill's gigantic saw blade, and sat me down, offering coffee. He seemed concerned, which caught my attention. He explained that he could not hire me as they had overlooked something; there was nowhere in the small mill town of Pemberton for me to stay. There was no boarding house, no hotel, and the only woman who accommodated boarders was full. As a compromise, he offered to arrange a ride for me back to Alta Lake on the late train. I was shattered, my hopes dashed and with no thoughts about what to do next. Glumly, I told him I understood and accepted the ride back on the late train. He shook my hand and escorted me out to the dirt road running alongside the mill.

Here, he pointed out the place where the train would depart while picking up the empty logging carriages from the mill. This was the second time in Canada that I found myself penniless and had lost a job offer. With my backpack on, I walked across the rail line that came out of the mill and led into the mountains. From across the barren land surrounding the one-horse town, I spotted what looked like a caravan in the not-too-distant horizon. Instinctively, I decided to investigate it.

Upon closer examination, it revealed itself to be a two-wheel, single-bedroom caravan, rather worse for wear and obviously abandoned, someone had left the door unlocked. Inside, I found a bare spring bed, without a mattress, scattered with old newspapers, cans, bits of bush and leaves, and some broken beer bottles littering the galley cabinet. Despite its frail condition, the structure held firm. This sparked a glimmer of hope; could I use it and, if so, who owned it?

I went back to the mill foreman for some answers. I asked him if he knew who the caravan belonged to, and whether he would still hire me if I used it. To my relief, he confirmed his temporary job offer if I could find a place to stay. He recalled that the train had shipped the caravan a few years earlier for a 'Cat Skinner' (a term used for a caterpillar tractor driver). The individual had left a year or so back, abandoning the caravan which hasn't been used or touched since. The mill manager confirmed this, adding that, as far as they knew, the caravan belonged to no one.

Elated, I cleaned the caravan, got myself settled, and by nightfall, it was almost in shipshape. I placed a large piece of cardboard on the bed springs and spread out my sleeping bag on top. Although the galley was stained and covered with cigarette burns, it now housed my small primus stove and utensils. For now, the toilet situation was "Ala Bush," but the mill provided me with a shower and toilet just about 200 meters away. I could get fresh water from the mill toilet in my camper's cooking pot.

After a long day, and with only a quick breakfast with Glen behind me, I was getting a bit hungry. It was growing dark and chilly, so I decided to head to a café to see what I could afford. A slice of toast, a bowl of spaghetti soup, and a cup of coffee later, I felt considerably better. Feeling satisfied, I returned to my mountain lodge, now wheelless and tireless, to get some sleep. The bed wasn't that bad; I had slept on worse things such as harbour docks, rocking boats, beaches, and garden chairs. However, what I didn't realize was how cold it got, especially given the number of wall holes through which the breeze came.

Morning found me at the mill, where I was given a pair of overalls, gloves, a hard hat, and a set of work boots. My job was to help strip down the gearing and gearboxes of some very heavy 4x4 logging trucks. When lunchtime came, I walked across to the shop and bought some bread along with a small jug of milk.

By evening, with the mill whistle sounding, all the workers left. I saw the foreman and asked if it was possible for me to get a daily advance on my wages, as I was regretfully without funds. He said he would see what he could do in the morning, although it wasn't company policy. I didn't want to tell him that, unless I got some money to buy food, they might have a corpse on their hands. The small shop, thankfully, sold small cans of soup, beans, and bully beef. So, with a small can of beans clutched in my hands and after a hot shower at the mill, I retreated to my dark and cold residence. On my way, I picked up some old cardboard boxes which I used to plug up some drafty holes, making my retirement that night a little less cold.

The following day, the foreman advised me that because of my circumstance, they would advance me a day's pay, for which I was most grateful. That night, I was called to the street office and handed a cash envelope containing $7.50, one day's pay. It felt like winning the lottery, so that night I was able to buy some decent food at the coffee shop, which also served as a general dealer's store, post office, meeting place, saloon, and cafe.

The next day, I was called to the office, where it was explained to me that there was a problem with me working at the mill. This was apparently something that had not been discussed during my recruitment by the mill office. To continue working there, I needed a Canadian Social Security card as well as some form of identification, like a driver's license or Canadian I.D., neither of which I had. It was agreed that, for the time being, as the entire mill knew of my poor situation, I could continue working but only on a daily basis, as there was also a requirement to join the workers' union. I could sense trouble coming, so that night was not an easy one.

At some ungodly hour, I was awakened by something scratching and jostling my frail abode. I cautiously looked out the window to see a rather large bear sniffing around the door, possibly smelling my newly cooked food. I immediately decided I was not about to share my food or become its food, so using my flashlight to flash in its face and banging on the trailer wall sent it off in another direction.

A couple of days went by during which I awaited my doom. However, fate and destiny were about to settle on my shoulders as if planned, presenting the biggest card in my life's progress. It was a very cold and misty in the afternoon, all the workers and crew were gearing up for the possibility of snow. The mountains were hidden in curtains of heavy mist, and the valley where Pemberton was nestled turned foggy.

I was working on a tractor which was parked outside the mill garage, removing a diesel fuel rack. Suddenly, I heard a strange noise that sounded like loud pumping or flapping. Searching the sky in the direction of the noise, I noticed a red rotating light. And there, out of the mist, a helicopter materialized and landed in the open space between the mill garage and the cafe/food store.

I saw the pilot disembark and meet a police officer who had arrived on the scene. They walked towards the coffee shop, soon disappearing from my sight. By evening, the mist had thickened. As I was walking towards the coffee shop, I circled the helicopter to take a closer look. The pilot had just finished refueling; there were empty jerry cans on the back of a nearby parked pickup. Curious by nature, I approached the pilot and introduced myself. His name was Ian, but due to a lost diary, I have since forgotten his surname. We talked about our shared fascination with flying and how the adverse weather had forced his unexpected landing. We agreed to meet at the coffee shop/general store across the road. He joined me there after securing his helicopter. We found ourselves a cozy spot at the back of the store, served by the jovial Chinese fellow who personally knew Glen.

Ian was a super person. We compared our experiences in aviation, as I had started learning to fly in the Channel Islands a year earlier, but unfortunately had to quit due to the financial strain. He found my distant relation to Lord Portal amusing and even offered some advice regarding joining the Royal Air Force. He encouraged me to continue flying, sharing his own experience of rigorous training and hard work to acquire a flying license. Ian suggested that there were adult programs in Canada that could offer some government assistance. He jotted down a few flying training schools in Vancouver and even gave me a list of potential jobs around the school. It left me feeling inspired and determined.

After a round of whisky (for which he generously picked up the tab), we said our goodbyes. I walked across the barren field to my caravan, my thoughts spinning with newfound aspirations. It confirmed what I already believed; my place was in the sky or on the water. Like the Sunderland flying boats landing in Durban that captivated me as a boy. Or the wide-open farm life that I had always loved. And the restless call to be one with nature – the wind, the rain, the sun and the storm – that was always surging in my blood.

I realized that traveling through the ocean and lands was only a steppingstone towards the wild plans of my future. The idea of walking on a knife-edge was beginning to grow on me. Would I be able to do it? How could I leave this mountain town and chase the impossible in a city filled with strangers? Would I be seen as a 'dropout' or 'failure' in the eyes of my father and peers? Despite these doubts, I was determined to strive for my dreams. No matter what, I was going to do it. Somehow! I had a restless night but by morning when I heard the helicopter fly out, I had made up my mind. I would follow the helicopter and as John Gillespie Magee wrote, "I have danced in the skies, put out my hand and touched the face of God". I was not going to last through the winter and the job was insecure.

Packing all my gear, I went to the mill and explained my desire to leave. They paid me my due deducting the boots, which I donated to the next employee, as I could not carry them. With permission to travel on the afternoon logging train to Alta Lake and on the morning train to Squamish, I jumped off at Alta Lake so spending the night with Glen. Morning found me jumping again onto the logging train and ending up in Squamish. There I hitched to Vancouver contacted the two lady friends I had met in the Lodge, who had offered me a bed for a night or two, got directions by bus and arrived at the house late afternoon. They were very kind offering me their spare room and use of the phone. A good dinner with them and a soft bed to sleep in found me refreshed and ready to see what flying schools could offer. There were a few, Vancouver flying school, Skyways at a place called Langley and another new school at Abbotsford about 45k from Vancouver. The schools gave me all the details about the requirements for training and cost.

On the phone to Abbotsford Air Service, the owner Herb Porter gave me a very encouraging talk on what my possibilities would be to complete a commercial pilot's license. He seemed keen to get students and agreed there was very possibly some part-time work. He also indicated that he could get me cheap accommodation, as Abbotsford was not as expensive as Vancouver was. I agreed to catch the bus out to see him the next day. This I did and for some unknown reason I took all my kit with me.

Abbotsford Air Services

Herb met me at the Greyhound bus station and then drove to the airport, an old ex-RCAF field, where he had his office and school. Here, I met the instructor, an ex-RAF squadron leader, Tony Cosgrove. He was surprised by my distant relationship to Lord Portal, who was a Vice Air Marshal of the R.A.F. during the war. He looked at my logbook, showing the few hours I had accumulated at the Channel Islands Flying School, indicating that he knew Group Captain Pic Pickford from his air force days.

It appeared that between the three of us, there was a possible way for me to enter the training program. If I could get a letter from my parents stating that funds could be made available if needed, the path would be easier. A meeting with the bank manager, who was a friend of Herb's, could secure an adult training loan. Furthermore, part-time employment, such as at a burger shop or at Herb and his brother's farm where they sometimes needed extra hands, could be possible.

In addition, extra work around the hangar, such as fueling, cleaning aircraft and at times, working in the office, were options. This extra work would support my accommodation costs, which was a huge relief. Herb contacted a family living not far from the field. They were members of a Russian sect, many of whom are present in Canada, like the Mennonites and Amish. They agreed to house me at a reasonable rate in their unfinished basement, accepting payment at the end of the month through Herb's chat. Now all it took was Herb's fax and telephone to send a message to my father, encouraging him to write a supporting letter for the issue. Would he do it for his son, whom he'd called useless, uneducated, and good for nothing? I got Herb to draft the necessary letter explaining my intent and backing the fact that he would ensure the completion of my training, qualifying me as a commercial pilot.

After a week of communication, the required letter arrived. Meanwhile, I was performing odd jobs around the hangar to pay for my board with the Mennonite family that made the most unusual food. But given my appetite, it was all very good. To comply with the above condition, I had to become a resident alien of Canada. I applied at the Canadian immigration office in Vancouver. To my surprise, three weeks later, I had a resident alien stamp in my old South African passport. No questions asked.

I then got an ID card and set up a bank account with the Canadian Imperial Bank of Commerce. This was my first bank account ever, facilitated by the fact that Canada still considered us part of the British Commonwealth. With my paperwork in order, I started ground school and my first lessons under instructor Tony Cosgrove in the cheapest aircraft Herb had—a two-seater Cessna 140.

By this time, I had met other students such as Peter Cowie, Rick Grey, and a new member—Ray Seamore from Australia. Ray, a wild and adventure-loving individual, had worked in Fort Simpson in the wild Northwest and decided to get his license to become a bush pilot. Another friend who arrived was from New Guinea—a tugboat captain who also decided to learn to fly. We were a cheerful bunch of guys who got along well, ribbing each other about who was the better pilot.

Over the months, I completed my solo flight in good time. However, I gave the school a scare by taking a bumpy ride into the mountains, exceeding altitude limits without the necessary mountain training. Ray and I got ourselves in a fix, landing near Harrison Lake, approximately 25 miles deep into the mountains. On landing, our Cessna 150 got stuck in mud. We had to manually turn the aircraft around, with Ray hanging from the side, barely avoiding crashing into the lake. We decided not to disclose this mishap, but upon our return to Abbotsford, Herb, noticing the muddy condition of the aircraft, grounded us both.

Despite the dangers and close calls, my main focus was studying. I needed an aviation calculator for my upcoming exams, but I couldn't afford an expensive one. So, I got a cardboard one from the fuel distributors, which remained with me throughout my training. We did run into trouble a couple of times for flying under the influence of alcohol, even if it was from the night before. But all things considered, we managed to avoid any major accidents and, most importantly, finally became licensed commercial pilots. I didn't have the mind of a scholar, so I needed all the help I could get. Meteorology was a breeze, mechanics and airframe presented no problem, though Navigation gave me a bit of a problem. Nevertheless, Air Law was a double failure. However, by then, having started in October 1963, Christmas was coming up and so were the weather conditions. To build up flight time, I would fly as far as I could, visiting charter and bush companies in the "

Hopes of looking for a future job prompted Ray and I to decide to fly to Fort Simpson to visit his wife and friends. We made the journey via Prince George, flying up the canyons and riverbeds. After leaving Prince George, deeply enveloped in the Canadian forest and northern land mountains, we received information from the meteorology department about having a clear run to Fort Simpson. However, true to mountain weather, Prince George shut down due to mist and ice crystals just as we reached the point of no return. As we continued flying, we were slowly forced lower and lower until we were at tree-top level. The situation was getting a bit dangerous, but we had no way of turning back. With no training on instruments, we had to continue on visual conditions. By now, neither of us could see more than about fifty meters. By flying very slowly and with flaps down, we continued, starting to encounter light snow.

By the grace of God, we cleared a mountain ridge which allowed us to drop down to the forest top slope. We saw a river below us, and we hoped it would lead us into Fort Simpson. Now flying below tree-top level over the river, Ray recognized a clearing up ahead. He was certain it was the town, and the airport would be next to it. He was correct, and we managed to land in almost zero visibility.

Everyone was pleased to see us and wondered how we, two foreign pilots, had managed to land in what was considered experienced bush pilot territory. The local Ministry of Transport office questioned our arrival and declared visibility, but ultimately turned a blind eye on the matter.

The return flight was good, and we were able to fly a good portion of the way in clear sky, thereby enjoying the incredible scenery of British Columbia. Flying down the Fraser valley was a sight to behold. Once back at the field and flying school, the flight was briefly discussed as good, and no mention was made of flying illegally below limits.

Herb and Kathy in the office of Abbotsford flying school.

By now, Herb had got engaged and Kathy his beautiful fiancée was now very often at the school working at the office and staffing the needs for charter, booking flight training hours plus the book work. The school was growing, and Herb needed more aircraft. One evening when I had finished some work I was doing, Herb got the good news that financing had been approved and he would be going down to Wichita to buy two new aircraft. A Cessna 172 for charter and another Cessna 150 for training. He would need another pilot to bring one machine back and asked if I would like to travel with him and Kathy to Wichita to ferry them back.

I jumped at the chance, as it was all flying hours, so I was building my flight time to meet the 150 hours required for the government-approved commercial flight time course. It was decided that we would rent a car and drive, as the flight costs were a bit high, and I, for one, did not have the airfare. With Kathy coming along, there would be two seats in one aircraft and a spare seat in the other. Herb agreed to my inviting a friend, so we could share the cost. I called Glen at his mountain camp, asking if he would like to do the trip flying back with me. He agreed and was up for the small adventure to fly back in a light aircraft. This was put together with us departing in a rented car, driving overnight to avoid overnight costs, via Seattle and on to Salt Lake City, then Wichita. En route in the early morning, we got stopped by a speed cop. I got out, and in my clear English accent, I asked what the problem was. He indicated that he was going to give me a citation for speeding in the 50-mile per hour highway speed restriction. I frankly did not know what a citation was and politely asked him to explain. He questioned where I was from and where I was going, who was asleep in the car. I politely answered, producing a South African driver's license. I also apologized for the speeding infringement since the highway speeds are not restricted in South Africa. He examined the license, exclaiming he had never seen a South African white driver's license. With that, he put away his charge book, gave me a warning about speeding in the USA, and let us go. Herb, half-asleep in the back, said that he would not have gotten away with it and thought it was unfair that we foreigners could get away with so much.

Abbotsford Flying school apron with C180 and C172 trainers plus Avenger fire bomber taxing by.

CESSNA factory in Wichita where the two aircraft were waiting for us. A Cessna 150 and a Cessna 172 with the new omni vision windows. Without any delay, we decided after the formalities to start the return flight straight away. Herb and Cathy took off first with the Cessna 172, followed by Glen and me in the Cessna 150. We agreed to meet up at

Denver via our planned flight route through Goodland. It was April 1964 so the weather was changing to spring but there were still patches of snow-covered land as we pressed on. Overnighting in Denver we flight planned our route to meet up again at Seattle. Our planned route was Denver, Rock Springs, Ogden, Burley, Boise, Baker, and Le Grande landing at Seattle for fuel. Then the final leg to Abbotsford. Herb was away again first and was expected to await my arrival in Seattle. Following our planned route and flying only on VFR (Visual Flight Rules) we pressed on merrily enjoying the scenery. However, by midafternoon heavy cloud formation had come into sight and we were flying low following visual signs such as small towns, roads and railways. At one point traversing the Wasatch Mountain range, following a railway we nearly flew up a valley into a tunnel. We both agreed it was close and felt that Herb would have been very upset at us destroying his new plane. He probably would have made us stay there to repair it.

Our map showed a river leading up to Burley where we needed to refuel. It was very hazy, and both of us were finding it hard to see much ahead. Suddenly, at the bend of the river, we saw what definitely looked like an airfield with marker lights on the runway edge. With a quick turn to the right, I planned a straight-in landing so as not to lose sight of the field. Glen had the map on his lap, but due to the visibility, we were both eagerly searching ahead to confirm the field sighting. With full flap and a short final, I landed in hazy conditions. Once we stopped, I turned to look at Glen, who was now pointing out the window with a strange look on his face. The first words out of his mouth were, "God, those are not runway lights, those are fire hydrants".

Looking out my side window, I first saw a woman on the field perimeter hanging up washed sheets. She was half holding up a sheet, but the look on her face was something I will never forget. We had somehow mistaken the landing field for a large development ground under road construction. I immediately turned the aircraft around, hastily retreated to the far end of the road, and turned to position the aircraft for take-off, only to see a row of trees at the end of the field. They were not all that high, but it was questionable whether we could fly over them. Without time to wait, our decision was to go. I applied full power, held the brakes, and then releasing them, jumped the flap from zero to the take-off position. The small 150 leapt into the air right on the stall and headed straight for the trees. Judging the distance to the trees, I headed straight for the middle, slowly picking up speed. At the last minute, I pulled up realizing I wasn't going to clear them, so I turned the aircraft a bit to the side and slipped the wing between two of the trees. It was a narrow escape, but as we flew over the river, there on the left side was the actual runway.

We needed to land for fuel, so we did a precautionary approach and landed, pulling up by the fuel pumps. A quick look at the map showed that we had mistaken the runway for being on the right side of the river when it was actually on the left side. Soon, a young guy came and started to fill our tanks. He was a quiet sort of chap who nonchalantly asked if we had seen another aircraft in the area. To which our reply was a definite "No". Looking at us rather suspiciously, he mentioned that he had heard a rumour about a light aircraft landing in a new mall parking lot development, on the other side of the river. We paid our fuel bill and made a hasty departure heading for Boise, Idaho.

By now, the weather was really settling in. We could not return to Burley, so we agreed to fly on, following the main road into Boise. The light was fading, and we were flying with our wings just above the freeway road lights. With cars passing underneath, we could see at times some startled drivers. In desperation, our eyes were out on stalks searching for the runway, which was supposed to start visibly very close to the freeway. To make things worse, it had started to snow lightly, decreasing our visibility even more. Suddenly, we both saw the threshold of the runway, a dark bit of tarmac in the gloom. A sharp turn, with full flap selected, a bumpy landing was made. With great relief, we stopped, hardly able to see the sides of the runway. In the murky distance, there was a neon sign which we interpreted as a Clubhouse and Coffee Shop. It was now snowing heavily, so we stopped as close as we dared. I shut down the engine, and we made our way into the warmth of the office/coffee shop. There were a few guys around who seemed surprised to see us. When asked where we had come from, we skipped Burley, saying we had come from Rock Springs. They were quite interested in how we had made it in. Our reply was casual, and being Canadian bush pilots, we were used to this kind of weather. One guy asked how we got over the bridge that spanned the river and freeway? My reply was evasive, indicating it was not a problem. With little funds and the nearest motel being some distance away, we asked if we could get some sleep on the two big couches in the corner, given it was an all-night coffee shop. They did not mind, so we bedded down to get some much-needed sleep.

Early morning came, which found me outside looking at a snow and ice-covered aircraft. Making arrangements to get it prepared to fly, I was with the ground man who was loaning me brooms and scrapers. He pointed to the lifting visibility and the direction from which we had arrived. There, to my horror, was a massive steel-arched bridge spanning the river and freeway. He asked the same question I had been asked the night before in the coffee shop. Shaking my head, I walked away to find Glen and to get us going. We both realized we had flown under the massive bridge in the half dark and snow. Pushing on, we flew to Baker, then to Le Grande, and on to Seattle in good weather, much to our relief. Herb had been concerned but had seen by our cancelled flight plan that we had overnighted in Boise. We just said the overnight was OK, as the club had given us the use of their couches. Nothing more than that, for sure.

From Seattle, we flew up the coast past Mount Baker and on to Abbotsford to meet the customs officers. I had put in more flight time, slowly gaining more experience at no cost to me. My next venture was to get a seaplane and multi-engine rating. Herb had the chance to rent a Piper Apache for a multi-engine rating at a very low cost. Including myself and two other trainee pilots, we did the training with Tony Cosgrove and were officially checked out by the M.O.T inspector Mr. B, Thompson. This endorsement allowed us to fly multi-engine light aircraft.

There was one flight that gave me a scare. A man had purchased a Mooney MK21 aircraft in San Francisco and wanted it ferried back to him for a small fee. Under the mistaken impression that I had piloted a Mooney before, I agreed to do this. In truth, the Mooney was a fast aircraft and I had only flown one once for 40 minutes. He offered to cover my journey to San Francisco and the flight time back. So, I set off, collecting the aircraft from the California agent. Without any checkout time, I departed San Francisco, navigating through the congested airways, a challenge I had never faced before, and headed up the coast following the airways to Abbotsford. The weather was excellent, with a thick cloud layer beneath me. In the USA, you are allowed to fly VFR (Visual Flight Rules) above the cloud.

South of Portland, there was a sudden explosion in the cockpit, followed by choking smoke and decreasing visibility. In desperation, I turned off all my radios, opened the small vent on the side window to get some fresh air, which also cleared the smoke. I regained visibility and began coughing uncontrollably. I swung the aircraft to the left and right, checking for any trailing smoke in my flight path. Finding none, I cautiously switched on the radios one by one; they all worked normally, and there were no signs of trouble. Looking at the dense cloud cover below, not knowing what lay beneath, was terrifying. My lips were parched so I involuntarily licked them and tasted a chemical or soda-like substance. My mind raced, and I reached under the seat to find the remnants of a fire extinguisher. It had exploded, showering its fine powder contents all over the interior of the aircraft. Gradually regaining my composure, I carried on, passing Mount Hood and, with Mount Baker in sight, crossed into British Columbia and landed at Abbotsford.

It was quite an experience, but it marked the beginning of my flying career and was the start of a wealth of experience yet to come.

Flying.

"Things were progressing quite rapidly with my flying. Herb had been able to lease a twin-engine Piper Apache, which enabled us to gain twin-engine experience. Although not much, I was able to pass and acquire the twin rating on my license. Later, I flew over to Victoria, where I received some training on a Luscombe floatplane. This consisted of three hours and fifteen minutes with instructors G. Jeune and N. Copping. I then spent two hours doing touch-and-goes on the harbour, consequently earning my seaplane rating. According to the instructors, I had done well, possibly due to my sailing and ocean work. While there, I had the opportunity to climb onboard a Mars Martin flying boat. There were three of them. During a hurricane, one had been blown ashore, which allowed me to enter the cockpit and explore this mammoth flying boat. Many years later, the Flying Fireman of Vancouver resurrected one and used it as a firefighting aircraft. For their era, they were enormous being able to carry 280 troops or, via a winch suspended from the wing, haul in vehicles such as jeeps and cannons.

It was December 1964, and I had successfully written and obtained my private license. I then needed to accumulate flying time to reach the 150 hours required for my commercial license. To build up my flying time, I got a job flying skydivers. This was an excellent opportunity to gain time, as I would race the divers down to the field situated along the river. This allowed me to do quick turnarounds, making the most of the short daylight, given that it was winter. I could put in a good 2-3 hours a day, usually on weekends. I was persuaded to do a couple of jumps, but asked myself why I would want to jump out of a perfectly sound and functional aircraft. I do agree though, that the first jump is an exciting experience. The second is not as one is aware of the experience ahead of you. The flying was becoming second nature, and I found it exhilarating moving into a full-time career.

Here is something for colleagues, good friends and brothers who have danced with the sky. Once the wings go on, they never come off, whether they can be seen or not. They fuse to the soul through adversity, fear, and adrenaline, and no one who has ever worn them with pride, integrity, and guts can ever sleep through the "call of the wild" that wafts through the bedroom windows in the deep of the night. When a good aircrew man leaves the job and retires, many are jealous, some are pleased, and yet others, who may have already retired, wonder. We wonder if he knows what he is leaving behind because we already know. We know, for example, that after a lifetime of camaraderie that few experience, it will remain as a longing for those past times. We know in the world of flying, there is a fellowship which lasts long after the flight suits are hung up in the back of the closet. We know even if he throws them away, they will be on him with every step and breath that remains in his life. We also know how the very bearing of a man speaks of what he was and, in his heart, still is. Because we flew, we envy no man on earth. Author unknown.

WW 2. Mars Martin flying boat converted to a water bomber in action.

D C 10 converted to water bomber

In early January 1964, I received a welcome surprise when my parents wrote to tell me that my younger sister, Beverley, was coming to join me. South Africa was in flux, and it appeared that trouble was emanating from across the borders. Young white boys were being conscripted for compulsory military service. The battle with the Russian-supported African rebels was intensifying, and lives were being lost. Our forces had pushed back the communist-backed insurgents to the Angola border. Russia and the African National Congress were now importing Cuban troops to fight against us. Russia, using the black African forces, wanted the Cape for its sea route. With the Suez and Panama Canals blocked, no heavy tankers supplying fuel to Europe, or the Eastern seaboard could operate. Rhodesia was embroiled in its bush war, and Ian Smith was being betrayed by British politicians. Eventually, he had to declare a UDI (Unilateral Declaration of Independence). The magnificent countries of Northern and Southern Rhodesia and Nyasaland would eventually collapse into a state of turmoil, poverty, and ruthless brutality executed by the black government troops. I had managed to establish myself in the beautiful and free country of Canada.

The warm welcome from Canadians and the supportive environment reinforced the idea for her to come and see for herself. Beverly, who was four years younger than me, arrived and we set up home in a small basement flat in Abbotsford. She found employment at the Royal Bank and adjusted to Canadian life while I pursued my commercial license.

During our stay in Abbotsford, we befriended a lovely family known as the Hardys. Norris worked in the tire business and had three great kids, Wendy, Jane, and Gordon, with his wife, Merle. My sister ended up marrying and residing permanently in British Columbia with her husband Len Adamson, a bank manager. They have two sons, Mark and Troy. Beverly found a second family in the Hardys. However, she later divorced and now resides on Vancouver Island near Mark, his wife, and her adored grandson, Quinn. Her younger son, Troy, is an actor based in Vancouver. From my Caribbean days, I had become friends with a fellow sailor from Seattle. I would sometimes fly down to spend the weekend with his family.

On one occasion, I brought along Australian Ray. We had a great time visiting the pubs and meeting college girls. However, when it was time to return the aircraft to Herb and Abbottsford, the weather had turned against us., To our horror, Monday morning came but as is the weather pattern of the San Juan sound, it was bad. The metrology office gave us 1,000 feet in mist and broken overcast. Aircraft had reported clear skies at 2,500 feet. Well, we decided to file a visual flight plan to fly visually on top of cloud when able. On take-off we climbed straight into solid cloud. Not being instrument rated the world closed into us. Frantically trying to make head or tail out of the limited flight instruments, we suddenly saw a line of what appeared to be cloud base at a 45-degree angle. Remembering the basic instrument flight training I had, I maintained airspeed and with the grace of God popped out almost in a 60-degree turn. Saved by the moment of seeing the cloud base we proceeded on via observing Mount Hood and Mount Baker as navigation points eventually arriving at Abbotsford on time. That night over a beer or two, we both agreed we were lucky not to be a crumpled mess on the Seattle airport. Regretfully one of the many lessons on learns in obtaining flying experience. The quote "Watch thee thy flying speed, least the earth comes up and smite thee" is very real and saved us from stalling the aircraft possibly losing our lives. By May 1964, I had logged 185 hours of flying in the past five months, enabling me to write my commercial license. Although I had started my training on November 13, 1963, I'd done well, having gained extra flight time from ferry and skydiving flights. After passing the commercial flight test, I was officially a licensed commercial pilot with multi-engine and seaplane ratings at 21 years old. I was grateful to Canada and its people for how far I had come from being an uneducated farmhand and world hitchhiker of two years earlier. My next mission was to find a job.

B747 water bomber

Once the wings go on, they never come off whether they can be seen or not. It fuses to the soul through adversity, fear and adrenaline and no one who has ever worn them with pride, integrity and guts can ever sleep through the "call of the wild" that wafts through the bedroom windows in the deep of the night. When a good aircrew man leaves the "job" and retires, many are jealous, some are pleased and yet others, who may have already retired, wonder. We wonder if he knows what he is leaving behind because we already know. We know, for example, that after a lifetime of camaraderie that few experience, it will remain as a longing for those past times. We know in the world of flying, there is a fellowship which lasts long after the flight suits are hung up in the back of the closet. We know even if he throws them away, they will be on him with every step and breath that remains in his life. We also know how the very bearing of a man speaks of what he was and, in his heart, still is. Because we flew, we envy no man on earth.

Bush pilot country where fire bombers operated.

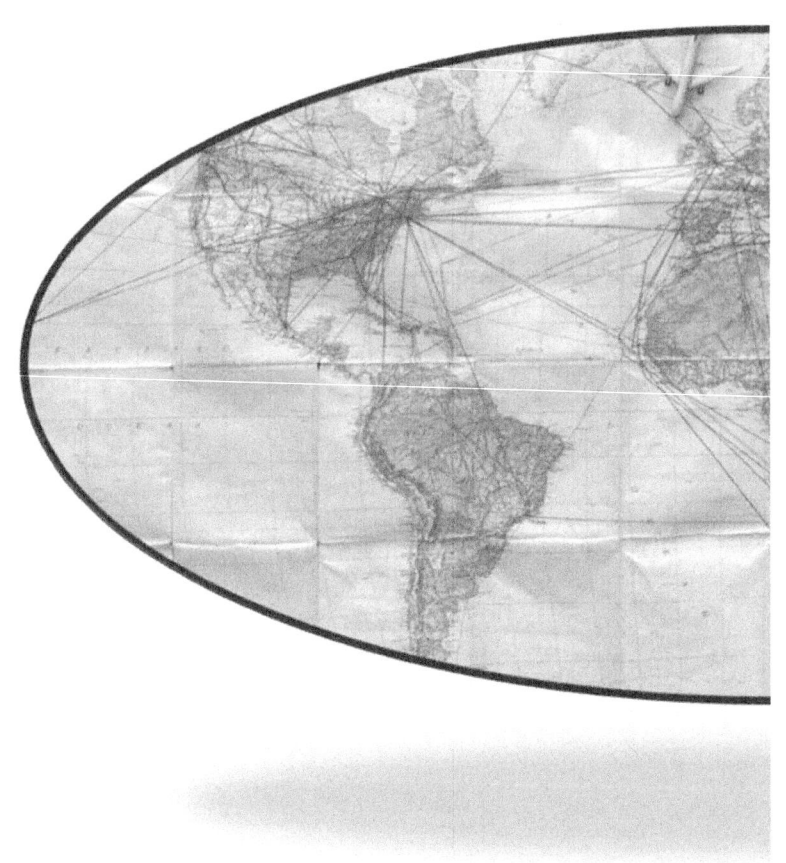

Look out world Alan's flying.

As with all newly licensed pilots, the next step is to get a job. It usually requires working for small fly-by-night charter or crop-dusting companies. Nevertheless, the requirement to build flying experience and flight time is the secret to making a career out of aviation. In building the time I already had filled the 150 hours needed on the Government approved course, I had flown to almost every charter and Bush Company within the radius of Abbotsford. One of these was a small company at a west coast inlet called Sechelt Air services. Sechelt is a coastal logging town situated on the mainland and the waterway called Skookumchuck in Indian or Straits of Georgia, which flows between it and Vancouver Island. The inlet stretches deep into the high Columbia Range Mountains where there are dozens of logging operations being serviced by bush companies and their pilots.

The bush pilot is a vital link to their operation, supplying them with food, mail, equipment, spares and medical evacuations.

A fellow student at the flying school, Rich Grey, had been able to obtain a flying job with an opposition company to Sechelt Air services. He and I had been good friends at school, I watched him bypass me job wise. One afternoon, he called the flying school to inform me that he had heard Sechelt Air Services might be looking for a pilot. He cautioned me that it was a small, family-run operation with limited quality aircraft and mechanics. It was no different from many other bush operations running on a shoestring. I immediately jumped into a Cessna 150 from the school and flew there to see them. They had a copy of my resume (CV) and offered me a job. It entailed cleaning, loading aircraft, and helping to service their three-floatplane aircraft. Flying was to be the occasional charter on the smaller of their planes, a Cessna 170 floatplane, and in general, acting as an all-round helper. I accepted it, as having a job upon completion of one's commercial licenses was not very common. Sometimes jobs did not materialize for months and even years, causing some pilots to give up the idea of flying as a career. My friend Rich was a boarder at a small house owned by a local woman. He made arrangements for me to secure a room there, which included bed and breakfast. I was to start work in two days, so upon returning to Abbotsford, I arranged for another student to fly me back the next day. On May 28, 1963, I embarked on my first commercial flight, flying to Nanaimo on Vancouver Island to collect equipment to be flown up to a logging camp at Secret Cove. It was a magnificent morning; the sun was rising as I took off from the inlet and turned to cross over to Vancouver Island and Nanaimo. Tugboats were everywhere, hauling long lines of logs on their way to the mills. This same waterway hosts whales, porpoises (dolphins), and seals. It is the main waterway to Alaska and the Yukon. The sight was magnificent: clear blue water framed by the majestic Columbia range mountains, and the long, undulating Vancouver Island stretching far to the northwest. Huge forests reaching for the sky, and hundreds of beautiful coves dotted with small islands, lay at its feet. South of Vancouver Island is the Straits of Juan de Fuca, with the city of Victoria at its tip. The Mexican border used to extend up the west coast almost as far as this point until the USA took over. Consequently, many towns and cities such as Los Angeles, San Diego, and San Francisco (named after a Spanish monk who had a mission there) have Spanish names. Incidentally, Los Angeles and Bangkok share the same meaning: City of Angels. I was as proud and happy as any pilot could be in my chosen career. Little did I know what a career it was going to be!

For the next few months, I flew the West coast and far as the Queen Charlotte straits into the mountain inlets servicing logging camps with just about everything one could think of. If I carried a paper and landed at a camp, I was sure to get a good meal in return. A bush pilot is always hungry. One particular flight I had; the company had received an emergency call from the RCMP for an emergency evacuation of an injured logger.

Mountain fjords are deadly dangerous if caught with no way out. I crashed in one like this.

Joining me on the charter was a nurse attending to a severely injured man. We departed and flew up the inlet to a camp called, surprisingly, "Evans Logging". The weather was poor, so I flew very low over the water, with a curtain of mist ahead. Despite the conditions, we found the camp and landed. We learned that the logger had been racing another logger to prove who was the fastest. Regrettably, while bringing the chainsaw up to complete the cut, it slipped, catching his jeans' rivet and slicing into his groin. He urgently needed a hospital. I removed the aircraft's door and slid him in on a stretcher, with the nurse administering a drip next to him. We attempted to depart, but the weather had worsened to nearly zero visibility. We had to turn back as night fell, making departure impossible. With the patient on the kitchen table, the nurse administered morphine and whatever medication she had available. I took over watching him at night to allow her to rest.

Morning came with what seemed like a break in the weather. Loaded up, I attempted to navigate through the narrow mountain pass. The nurse informed me that the patient was weakening and that it was essential to reach the coastal town of Powell River or return to Sechelt. Unable to fly due to almost zero visibility, I landed and performed a steamboat maneuver. By keeping the aircraft on the step and using it as a high-speed boat, we got through the narrows, down the Jarvis Inlet, and made it flying very low to Sechelt. An ambulance awaited us there and quickly took us to the local medical centre.

The story took an unusual turn many years later when, walking along Vancouver Main Street, I was recognized by a man and a woman. It was the logger whose life and leg were saved by the nurse, whom he later married. She agreed that if I hadn't managed to navigate under the mist and motorboat down the inlet, her husband would have died.

On another occasion, I was tasked to pick up a heavily pregnant Native Indian American woman at a large logging camp up the inlet. The urgency of her condition required immediate flight to Sechelt. We accomplished this without any notable issues. My company advised by radio that an ambulance was waiting at the main dock and instructed me to dock there instead of our private dock. Apart from her water breaking, all went smoothly. I landed, taxied to the dock, and tied up. Two ambulance attendants helped her out onto the floats and into a wheelchair. She was then wheeled to the waiting ambulance. I was pumping my floats when I realized that the ambulance had not moved, with the paramedics standing around the open doors. After finishing up, I walked over to see what was going on. One ambulance attendant informed me that the baby was about to be born. I was somewhat shocked as the woman had just got out of my small 4-seater floatplane, having very little room and absolutely no place to go but my destination Sechelt. After the birth, she enquired through the ambulance driver what my name was and decided to name her newborn son after me. Therefore, somewhere in the mountains, I have a little Native American boy named after me, I think.

Bush flying operators often run on a tight budget, skimping on services and maintenance for the aircraft. They only really have the summer to make a profit, as winter flying is costly and requires many diversions, failed charters, and naturally, the inclement weather. My company was no different, running a maintenance operation off the dock and a small shed along the inlet bank. I was regrettably about to find out the hard way of flying as a bush pilot for such an operation.

After finishing for the day, I was told I had an early morning charter to pick up two geologists at Nanaimo on Vancouver Island. They were to be flown up the inlet arm north of Sechelt towards Mount Garibaldi, an inlet with a very narrow point and an island in the middle. This inlet's sides are steep and often misty, especially at that time of the year, being autumn.

Early the next morning, I departed with the Cessna 170 to Nanaimo. This aircraft is low powered and had been giving some trouble on earlier flights. Furthermore, the floats leaked, requiring them to be pumped out after every landing. I had forgotten to pump out the floats at Nanaimo, so I probably had water in some of the float compartments. However, the take-off seemed fine, so I did not concern myself with the issue.

Flying up the inlet, the mountain tops were covered in fresh snow. As I turned into the Northern arm of the inlet, I saw a fog bank appearing to come right down to the water. Encouraged by the geologists, I continued up the inlet, flying lower and lower to avoid the fog. As I neared the narrow pass, I could no longer see the island, a navigation point. The mist off the water was now obscuring the water itself. The engine had coughed a few times, which I attributed to possible carburetor icing, and cleared it with the heat.

The situation worsened, and I suggested we turn back as I was losing forward visibility. The mist over the water had thickened to the point where I had to execute a steep turn between the mountain slopes. Suddenly, my engine backfired and spluttered, forcing me to tighten the turn to avoid collision with the high forest and mountainside. Then, the engine came to a sudden stop, followed by a deathly silence and swearing from one of the passengers.

Now, I was descending into the mist with no knowledge of where the water was. To maintain flying speed and prevent stalling, I had to increase the pitch and tighten the turn, losing all visibility of the mountain edge or the waterline. A fraction of a minute later, I saw the water, but it was too late to recover with diminishing airspeed. All I could do was level the wings, but I hit the water so hard that we collapsed the floats and nose-dived into the freezing inlet.

The tail came up and the cockpit began filling with water. I was able to escape the sinking aircraft via the door on my side that had sprung open upon impact. The passenger on my right was attempting to get out of the same door but was still strapped in by his seat belt. With my trusty sailor's knife, I dived back into the filling cabin, cut the seat belt loose, grabbed him by the coat, and pulled him out the door to the surface. I quickly told him to strip off the coat and boots and, after confirming that he could swim, told him to get to the shore about 100 yards away. The aircraft was now nose-down with the flooding cockpit underwater. One float was alongside the fuselage, so I dived back into the cabin to find the other passenger. He seemed confused so with all my strength I hauled him over the front seats and out the door onto the wing.

Here I realized he was somewhat unconscious, but the cold water was reviving him. I cut off his boots and some clothing, and did the same for myself, leaving only my jeans on. I realized I was bleeding heavily from a gash across my left eyebrow and cheek, which was caused by hitting the cross member above the instrument panel.

I saw that the first passenger had reached the shoreline, so I pushed the second passenger—who was unable to swim—towards the shore. The aircraft had now sunk with just the tail visible. The cold water was biting into me as I side-swam lifesaver style, pulling the passenger along.

As I neared the shore, fatigue overcame me, but I realized that if I pushed the passenger hard, he would make it to the shore where his partner could maybe help him. After doing so, and seeing the passenger on the shore wade in to help him, I sunk with a peaceful and warm feeling washing over me. I looked up at the sun's rays penetrating the water above me, feeling comfortable and warm with sleep overtaking me.

I opened my eyes to a round, cotton wool light. As I tried to make sense of the sight, my feet touched the rocky bottom of the shore. Instinctively, I pushed forward and surfaced a few feet away from the shore. I sank again but because I was tall, my feet once more met the shoreline rocks. I pushed again and found myself standing in shallower water. One passenger was lying on the rocky shore while the other offered me a handout of the freezing water. Accepting his hand, I crawled onto the shore and urged both men to lie in the sunshine against a fallen tree. Then, I fell to my knees. Hypothermia was setting in. I had a severe headache and was trembling badly. Forcing myself to stand, I confirmed by the blood on my face and body that I had sustained a serious cut on my left forehead and cheek. Taking out my handkerchief, I split it in two and tied up the loose eyebrow to keep it off my eyelid.

Remembering the existence of a children's religious camp along the shore, I suggested that the two passengers stay by the tree trunk in the sun to stay as warm as they could. I proposed to tread along the shore of fallen trees and rocks to get to the camp. I wasn't sure if it was occupied but at least it might provide us with shelter and possibly a boat. I set out stumbling over the fallen tree trunks and wading through the water in places to reach the camp. Due to blood loss and cold, I fainted a few times, once falling into the water which revived me. In the process, I cut my hands and knees on the rocks and oysters because this inlet was also sea-fed. The accident occurred around 8:30. Eventually, I found the fence encompassing the camp. Climbing over it, I crawled up a bank. A camp with its huts scattered around the property stood in front of me. Thankfully, I saw a person painting one of the huts roofs. I called out to him in my best English and asked if he could help me. He instantly stood up, shouting, I believe, in total fear. An apparition covered in blood, wearing only tattered, mud and blood-covered jeans, barely able to stand, was in front of him. As the man struggled to find a ladder, a door opened and women ran towards me, also shouting for help. Suddenly, I was surrounded by people rushing me into a hut, throwing a blanket over my shoulders, and giving me a hot cup of tea. I remember swearing and was told not to worry. I then provided a detailed explanation about where the passengers were. It was nearly 12:00 pm; I had been staggering along the shore for about 3 hours.

People were surprised that, covered in blood, I was lucky the bears had not sensed my presence. A speedboat was immediately dispatched to collect the passengers. We returned in time before the cold or bears could harm them. Sechelt and my company had been informed by then, and a boat was sent to pick us up. We thanked the camp residents and departed later that afternoon, arriving back in Sechelt around 5:00 PM. We were all taken to the local clinic where I was cleaned up and received 18 stitches on my face and cheek. The two passengers were deemed fit enough to be discharged to a hotel. My friend, Rick Grey, visited me after I suggested he bring a bottle of rum to help us back at our accommodations. After a hot shower and a few hefty shots of rum, I finally went to sleep. The next day, despite the severe pain in my head, I went straight to the dockside office and collected the logbooks for the aircraft.

With the arrival of the M.O.T. accident investigating officers, I produced the logbooks which showed a history of poor maintenance. The passengers and I filed a report that satisfied the M.O.T. officers. Subsequently, I was not held responsible. The floats may have had some water in them, making the plane possibly heavier than expected, plus the lack of good maintenance, including bad weather conditions which might have caused some icing, were written down as the cause of the failed engine and the crash. Recall earlier in my story, this was the second time in my life I had sustained a serious head injury on my left side. As a boy of 12 years, I had been in a coma for 5 days after falling from a high tree. Naturally, my job with Sechelt Air Services was over. I packed my bags and headed back to rejoin my sister in Abbotsford. However, before I left, Rick Grey and I were invited by some girls we knew to a barbecue at the home of the daughter of a businessman who owned a radio station in Powell River.

Powell River was another town northwest of Sechelt with an airstrip and seaplane base run by Norm Gold called Powell River Airways. His operation was a generally better-run charter company. My face and head had swelled to make me look more like a pumpkin with the stitches now pulling at the skin across my eyebrow and cheek. At the party, I had some explaining to do regarding my appearance. The host had a good-sized pool into which it was decided that the temperature only invited fools. Well, the bet was on, so in I went, followed by Rick. The cold water was just bearable but the effect it had on my face and head was very soothing. I stayed in as long as I could and won the bet. Later, the host's father engaged me in a discussion about South Africa and my adventurous life. He kindly suggested that he knew Norm Gold and would put in a word for me. To this day, I think he was hinting that I should consider seeing his daughter if I worked in the area. Her choice of young men in the immediate area was very scarce, as most were either loggers or rough mill workers.

To cut a long story short, I returned to Abbotsford and did some charter flying for Herb at the flying school. The most amazing thing was that the swelling on my face after the ice-cold swim reduced overnight to almost normal. To this day, I have very little scarring and credit it to the swim.

Powell River Airways

The intro I got to Norm Gold consequently got me a job with Powell River Airways. I started with them almost immediately following a check flight with the resident chief pilot. I was issued a very neat uniform consisting of an airline blue bomber type jacket, Cap, tie, two shirts, and two trousers. For the first time in my life, I was in uniform added to the very fact I had come a long way, so was proud of the uniform and my career as a commercial pilot. I was able to get a room with the lady that ran the airport cafeteria. About the same time, I heard that another pilot was needed so contacting Rick Grey suggesting he join a better operation. Later he also was employed with Powell River Airways, which changed its name to Air West. There was little to no accommodation available, so my landlady agreed that if we shared a large double bed, he could board with her. This we did keeping our respective distances with the aid of sleeping in our sleeping bags. It did not work out too badly as most of the time one of us was away flying into the inlets and up as far as Port Hardy on the northern tip of Vancouver Island.

The seaplane base was separate from the airport where the office and dispatch were. Late one evening while at the seaplane base cleaning and pumping fuel, a question was brought up as to whether one could ski behind an aircraft. In secret we decided to see as one of the aircraft had to be moved to the dock. Well, we did it but I cannot recommend anyone to try it. The reason is as the aircraft is taking off, the spray from the prop wash stung and with the aircraft low flying at about 70 miles an hour on falling off, the water is damned hard. I certainly will not attempt it again. One other incident happened on a charter that Norm did. It was to fly some nuns to a religious camp west of Powell River. Norm had his own private amphibious Cessna 182. This aircraft was able to land and take-off from land and sea so was kept in the maintenance hangar. The charterers duly arrived at the airport and were boarded onto the aircraft. The charter departed heading west.

Sometime later Norm suddenly came walking along the taxiway from the runway. He was fuming storming into the office demanding to see the chief mechanic. They then departed to the hanger where the dolly, (wheeled cradle) which housed the Cessna amphibian, was stored. Connecting it to the service truck, they cleared themselves on the radio to be on the runway.

A little while later around the taxiway came the Cessna 182 being towed on the dolly and heading towards the hanger. Nobody said a word but later the story arose. Apparently, Norm had forgotten to extend the wheels from the seaplane landing and landed on the float skids. However, it also appeared from word-of-mouth rumour that after take-off earlier from the airport on wheels he landed on the water with the wheels still down.

The aircraft pitched over spinning onto the front of the floats, touching the water with a wing tip and bouncing back onto the floats.

Port Hardy

It was understood that this story would never be repeated but it was also understood that Norm disembarked the nuns at their destination with much apology for the rough landing due to water conditions. I am sure the incident did not become an accident with all the Hail Mary's the nuns must have said. He was thanked for the safe flight regardless. One afternoon Norm came to the pilots suggesting that he was going to put an aircraft onto Texada Island doing a regular service to Vancouver. This island was a few miles of the coast of Powell River and had a mine with a small population on it. He asked if any of us would be willing to be transferred there on a semi trial basis. It offered free accommodation and a small salary increase. Well, my hand was the first up almost at the speed of sound. Therefore, at the month's end I moved over to the island and took up board with a family who Norm had made arrangements with. The aircraft was a Cessna 172 operating a set daily flight to Vancouver. Basically, it was to fly down the Straits of Georgia (Skookumchuck in Indian) from the dirt field and into the traffic of Vancouver international. I was very content with the job as I was my own boss and was building flying hours.

The company had a small depot at Vancouver to serve the seaplane operation and to collect cargo, parts, and passengers to be flown by our aircraft including the mine on the island. With the advancing winter, flying was often down at very low-level missing fishing boats and their booms, tankers, plus other low flying bush operators such as B.C. Airways all low flying to get to their destination. The person operating the base and I had a coded word when in radio contact from the island to advise me if he thought I could get in. It was related to seagulls. If he stated, they were on the ground I did not attempt to fly. If they were somewhat airborne, I would make an attempt and see what it looked like. On one of my returning flights from Vancouver with a load of cargo, I killed the first of two animals I would kill with an airplane. The weather was coming down, so I was flying very low in an attempt to land on the island strip. The strip was actually about 150 feet above sea level with the runway stopping on a cliff face. At my altitude of about 100 feet, I had to swoop up into sea mist to land on the threshold. Seeing the face of the cliff coming up I climbed slightly and saw the threshold. As I crossed the threshold, a large deer walked onto the runway. Unable to go around due to the mist I had to land attempting not to hit the animal. On touchdown I felt a hard thump. Successfully landing, I turned the aircraft around followed by the lights of the mine truck awaiting my arrival. There at the end of the runway was the big deer, very dead. On examination, I had hit it on the neck killing it instantly from the impact of the aircrafts wheel. It was early winter, and Christmas was coming. The carcass was butchered and put into cold storage.

I spent Christmas day with my landlords and their children. The venison roast meal was much appreciated and enjoyed. It was also shared between the mine management and some staff so a few of the mine's homes had a good meal. With the Christmas holidays I was able to visit my sister. She advised that she and her boyfriend, a Royal Bank manager Len Adamson wanted to get engaged and married. I would sign the marriage license with them, with this in mind and being away from home for four years, I felt it was time to return to see my ageing parents. Powell River airways now called AIR WEST had an agreement with Canadian Pacific Airlines for rebate tickets. I applied and got a 90% ticket to London returning via Rome. The flying was slow as the winter set in. Norm had no objections to my taking a leave of absence. Packing my bag, bidding adieu to all, I set off for London.

Earlier in my teenage life, I had dated a friend of mine, John Laity's, twin sister Diane. Regretfully he was killed in a car accident witnessed by his sister. I had consequently become close to the family and very respectful of his father who was a Marine in the war. He was aboard the HMS Oxford, which was sunk by German U boat in the Atlantic consequently spending 36 hours in the ocean. I had mailed them over the years hearing via a return letter from her folks that she was in London. They suggested that I should try to meet her and possibly convince her to return home. This I did and found her in London via the overseas Visitors Club. We enjoyed a night or two out in London. One evening we saw Camelot, a live play I thoroughly enjoyed it. After the show we discussed her returning to South Africa. She said she had had enough of the U.K.so would join me journeying back to our homeland and families.

To get to South Africa we found a cheap fare with a company called TREK owned by two men ex pilots, named Meredith and Snelgar. It operated a Super Constellation from Gatwick to Palma Majorca and on to Luanda in Angola. Here it night stopped then proceeding on to

Johannesburg. Departing Gatwick and then Palma Majorca we flew through the night across Africa to Luanda. I introduced myself to the pilots by showing them my commercial license. They allowed me to sit in the copilot's seat and feel the aircraft with its four huge piston engines. I was enthralled and was informed by the pilots that there was shortage of commercial pilots in South Africa. This was mainly because the military was recruiting as many aviators as possible that could pass the stringent flight training. War was flaring up so the air force and military needed as many young white men as they could conscript. The final part of our journey was on to Johannesburg catching a DC6 Sky master to Durban.

Trek Airways Super Constellation

Here Dianne's folks met us with great glee and happiness. They gave me a lift to my folk's home where my father and mother, with open arms, tears of joy, and love met me. It had been a long four years. The prodigal son had returned a man and a son to be proud of. A hell of a long way from the skinny lost soul, almost penniless and school dropout not having any document to say he had been to school.

My folks at their up-country home with guard dogs.

Home & South Africa

Settling into home life and having family around took a bit of getting used to. Looking up old friends I found most had either got married, were pregnant, had the same jobs, and in some cases had not been out of their hometown, never mind the country. Conversation was very limited with any stories from me, looks were either, do not believe it, or not sure what you are talking about. Some had been in the army as it was required that all white boys had to serve time in the army. The country was at war with the black communist supported troops on our borders of Mozambique, Rhodesia, and Angola. At the age of 16, I had signed up as was the requirement of the defense force, however, some years earlier during my absence a military jeep had arrived at my parent's home to arrest me for not reporting to the army. Explanations were exchanged as to my absence with the officers duly departing. Being back in the country, I suspected I would eventually receive my call up papers so waited for some correspondence from the Army. Nothing immediately was forthcoming; however, times were changing. I settled down to the comforts of home and started looking around at the flying prospects, taking into consideration what I had heard from the TREK AIRLINE Captain. My father had a friend with whom they had kept up a boyhood acquaintance. Father had in fact built his previous homes and we as families were good friends. Ken Granger was the M.D. of "Five Roses Tea" in Durban. He had a family of girls, the oldest being about the same age as my sister and myself. The older girl Gillian was employed with a company called "Map Studio Productions" a cartography and map printing company in Johannesburg. She advised that their company was thinking of buying their own aircraft to do mapping, photo, and survey work.

Hearing I was back in town, she put in a word for me. The response was that they would like to meet me regarding possible employment. Ken Granger had become the CEO of "Five Roses" and been transferred to Johannesburg. He offered accommodation should I wish to travel to Johannesburg so being able to attend a meeting with Map Studio. I borrowed my mother's car and travelled six and a half hours to Ken's house, accepting the offer to visit. The meeting with Map Studio went very well. They were pleased with my experience and the fact that I had done a lot of low flying on a Cessna 180, which they had on lease. The one problem was that I did not have a South African License. They suggested that if I could get this the job offer would materialize in a few weeks. I immediately arranged a meeting with e ministry of Transport and found out that I would have to do an air law exam, Radio check, a flight check with a South African inspector and a medical at the Air force medical centre. In the next two weeks I obtained a copy of the air law, arranged a medical and booked a couple of hours on a Tri-pacer at Wonderboom airport. I successfully passed the medical, got an inspector to give me a check ride on the Tri-pacer which I passed and was able to sit the air law exam. Now with a South African Commercial license in my hand I was employed by Map Studio Productions. I found out via the pilot fraternity the Baragwanath flying club at the old Baragwanath airport had rooms to rent. This airport had been a training centre for many years including wartime training. It was on the outskirts of Johannesburg but ideally suited for me with an old school colonial atmosphere having a dining room, laundry, and bar. I moved in purchasing a beautifully kept old Riley 1.5 motor car. I was set, job, car, and accommodation all in two weeks. Exactly three weeks since I had left Canada.

The work for Map Studio Productions got underway rather quickly. At first it was flying a Cessna 180 out of Johannesburg doing oblique photo shots of factories, private properties and then covering a lot of mine sink holes. These were occurring more to the west of Johannesburg and becoming rather dangerous. I would fly with the door off and the cameraman sitting on the ledge. He had a harness with a large camera attached to his chest. In turn he had a belt attached to the vacant right seat mounts. On one occasion I nearly lost the cameraman. He was turning from his position with his legs extended over the door sill into the open air. He unlatched his belt harness to reach back to reload a plate into the camera. I had not seen him do this as I was at low level and concentrated on the site to be photo'd. I turned to the right which caused him to slide out of his seated position. His camera was heavy and being attached to his chest caused him to lurch out of the open door. I was able to grab his harness as he desperately tried to stop himself from becoming airborne without a parachute. Straightening up the aircraft to level flight I heaved him back on board controlling the aircraft with my left hand only, as my right hand was clamped onto the harness of a very frightening looking cameraman. It was a close call but luckily, we got away with it.

Work for the Cessna 180 was taking us further and further afield. These were the prospects of a huge new harbour being built at Richards Bay on the East coast. Just South of Richards Bay is the Tugela River. The Zulus had attacked the British troops at Isandlwana which was their greatest win and defeat of the British army. Durban being south of the Tugela was anticipating another bloody

Zulu attack. The British 91st Highlanders and the 60th rifles under lieutenant Arthur Mynors (age 22) were marched from Durban for two days to the Tugela River where Fort Pearson was on one side with Fort

Tenedos named after the vessel that had brought the troops to the colony, on the other side. From here the troops fought a vicious and bloody battle with the Zulu army to relieve the besieged troops under Colonel Pearson inland at Eshowe (an abandoned mission station). This was April 1879 and became part of the Anglo Zulu war where the Zulu army was eventually defeated in so establishing British troops to protect the pioneer colonies such as Natal. I was sent down there a few times to do high- and low-level photo shots to make up a mosaic of photos to be used in surveying the area. There was only a small grass strip and a few fisherman cottages on the estuary. Later in the year we did more survey photos with a faster and higher-flying aircraft that was now in the pipeline to be purchased. Little did I know that this would become a major seaport servicing most of the North and eastern provinces in Southern Africa? Hindsight is 20/20 vision, but had I had money and bought some of this bush land, I would have become a millionaire in later years.

The general manager's secretary was a girl called Ursula Mansell. She had been married and divorced and had a small one-year-old child called Dale. She was the main link I had with the head office, so we corresponded a lot. A relationship struck which later led to us cohabitating together. I was away a lot so did not need my room at the Baragwaneth Flying Club. Thereby resided with her at her farm cottage in Rosebank situated north of Johannesburg centre. I had a car which she had the use in my absence, we shared the rent; I would often pick up Dale for her if she had to work late, and all worked out well for us. The work now grew to a heavier pace. I was told the company was buying a fast twin-engine Aero Commander aircraft from the sports company Slazenger which was in Cape Town having a new engine fitted. It was duly delivered to Johannesburg where wide-angled Zeise and Wilde wide-angle cameras were fitted into its belly. I was checked out on the aircraft and Bill Henderson an ex-navigator from the Canadian Air Force was hired. Rob Frost a photo lab technician was trained up as the cameraman making up a full flying survey crew. Being the pilot and captain of the crew I was responsible for the aircraft, arranging maintenance and scheduling our survey operation as the company required. With this aircraft, we could do high- and low-level contour surveys traversing the whole of South Africa and Namibia. All the photos were sent back to our photogrammetric laboratories where they were transformed into maps and geo contour variation lines. We were now flying as a team all over the country. The Richards Bay harbour development went ahead with us doing more surveying there. Durban Harbour was another contract including the new freeway to Johannesburg. We moved all over the country staying in hotels and B & B where we could. The Hendrik Verwoerd Dam was another big contract plus all of Cape Town Harbour including the

Cape Town and Table Mountain   *Verwoerd Dam under construction.*

reclaimed coastal land development. Moving up the West Coast into Namibia we did the Skeleton coast, first survey ever to be completed successfully due to the big tidal affected shoreline. Lots of wrecked ships and tales of diamond smuggling. Johannesburg was another low- and high-level photo survey to construct the new entering and exiting freeways in and out of the centre. This required us to fly at one point between the skyscrapers. A special permit was issued by the Ministry of Transport to allow this to be done on a specific day. We had to match this with a noon flight to eliminate shadow with clear and calm weather. One problem was the turbulence from the road and pavement heat. We succeeded with an enlarged copy of one of our prints being placed at the entrance to Anglo Americans office in central Johannesburg. Flying survey is not easy.

The weather must be good, no clouds, no turbulence, no shadow and with every firing of the cameras the wings must be level to stop blurring or overlapping. We initially had some problems with the cameras at high level frosting up. No solution was available so in desperation I drilled a small hole into the camera chassis. I then inserted a thread and attached a flexible line from our aircraft heating outlet. It worked but the general manager nearly had a heart attack when he heard of what I had done to a very expensive camera. We were on the road most of the time but there were many days when we could not fly due to weather or military restrictions on areas we were to fly though. This then left us with the tough job of sitting in hotels or whatever accommodation we could find, drinking fine South African wine and beer. Many a good day was spent at the poolside or an evening of camaraderie awaiting weather or further instructions.

On one of the flights in Cape Town we took off to do the days flying. Before the cameras can be on a survey line they are checked for service and clarity. On this day we did a run past Lions head to a small mountain next to Table Mountain. We passed over the famous Clifton beach with the cameras running in what was called push offs. Sometime later when back in our office a photo lab technician called me aside to come into their department office. Behind the door was a full-length picture of a nude woman. The technicians had seen on one of the push-offs taken at 2000 feet, an image of a girl sunbathing on Clifton beach. With their advanced machines and what was called the baby box brownie, a camera the size of a small room, they had blown up the image to life size, air brushing the Bikini away. It was a great achievement from their department showing its technical ability. I to this day bet that that girl never knew she was printed stark naked and hung behind an office door in Johannesburg.

The aircraft and crew were doing well with more than expected work coming in. The cabin of the aircraft consisted of a pilot seat, a navigator seat which had a bubble window on the right side together with aligning rakes on the fuselage. Behind these seats were the two cameras then the cameraman's seat with magazines stacked on each side of the cabin wall. There was one small exit next to the cameraman. As the aircraft was equipped to do high level work, we also had oxygen masks connected to an onboard oxygen cylinder. There was no toilet, only small relief tubs under our seats. On one such high level flight Rob the cameraman suddenly developed a case of severe cramps and a dire need to use a toilet urgently. Unable to land or break off the survey, something had to be done. We used maps that were made of partial material so in desperation a used map was spread out on the floor space next to the cameras. Not going into detail, poor Rob was able to relieve himself of his painful problem on the map. Now the problem lies in how to remove the little soggy parcel from the aircraft. It was decided to wedge a magazine tray into the partial open door and distribute the map and contents out into the slipstream and over what we considered wild Africa. This was duly done to the relief of all, especially Rob. The details were completed with us returning to Rand airport. Upon landing I was taxied in by one of our ground engineers who when in parked position drew his hand across his neck indicating a shutdown. He walked forward to my small window shoving some wheel chocks in at the same time indicating he had a message. I opened the window enquiring about what was up. He asked if we had had a good flight and was there anything wrong. Thinking about Robs problem I discreetly replied that no, it was a good flight. Indicating I should get out, he then pointed to the rear elevator and rudder. To my horror and Rob's there was the MAP plastered against the tail section complete with its contents smeared across the airframe. Well poor old Rob was never allowed to forget this incident as it was the engineer's duty to clean up the mess. I too was declared the pilot who caused his crew to sh----t themselves. Regretfully years later I heard Rob was killed in a crash doing the same work detail we had done.

Trouble was coming to South Africa. It was 1965 Nyasaland and the Rhodesia's were in political disarray. Ian Smith was fighting hard to get the British to come their senses. Communist forces were supporting an aggressive African movement which was about to erupt in civil war. We in South Africa were preparing for such a war, as all white South African males over 16 had to attend military training, therefore the country had a decisive military strength to oppose such a war if it crossed our borders? I was in the head office one afternoon when I got a message from Ursula that the boss man wanted to see me. Arriving at his upper-level office I was ushered in to be met by the managing director and a military man wearing a lot of brass. Sitting down it was explained to me that the military intelligence had suspicions that gorilla insurgents were mustering on our border with Southern Rhodesia. The air force surveillance aircraft had seen them but as a military machine if seen to cross the border it might be considered an aggressive maneuver. This could not happen as South Africa worldwide was under pressure with trade restrictions and sanctions. Such a report could ignite an unwanted problem with the sensitive situation now standing. What was asked was whether I and my crew would be agreeable to fly over the border at high and low levels to establish with our cameras where and to what strength these reported troops were. On some sections we would get air force cover, but it was all to be a clandestine operation without even preferably my own crew knowing of the military implication.

I asked if I could consider it for a day to which they agreed. In respect to my crew, I explained the true story, the needed secrecy and asked if they had any objection. Rob was bit concerned but as it was for the good of our country agreed to it and its secrecy. Bill did not give a damn being Canadian and asked when we were to start. With that answer from the crew, I advised the boss of our decision. Very soon we were sent to Hoedspruit, a small grass strip not too far from the border. Upon landing the natives rushed out to see the aircraft and nearly ran into the spinning prop blades. We instructed them that we would be coming in and out daily so for them to stay away from the propellers. A small B & B nearby became our home for some weeks. It had a bar and in the high African heat a very welcome swimming pool. Within days a military jeep arrived with maps and outlined areas that they wanted to fly. Daily we flew across and up the borders as well into Rhodesian space. Some areas were very sensitive with notes to us to be cautious as ground fire was possible. Being a civilian aircraft, we went unnoticed but on more than one occasion we did see ground fire which fortunately never hit us. Again, on some of the outlined areas South African Air force SABRES circled above us for what we understood as protection. After every flight a military vehicle would be waiting for us to collect our photo magazines. It appeared our flights were a great success as the military could now see the daily movements of troops, so enabling our troops to be out of the terrorist's range. It was a good feeling to know we were helping to improve intelligence. I received a telegram from the military thanking us for the successful reconnaissance project.

Baragwaneth airport. Self, Cameraman Rob Frost, Navigator Bill Henderson

Finally, Ian Smith declared Unilateral. Declaration. of Independence (UDI going it alone.) Things were hotting up and we were advised to return to Johannesburg. I had at the same time been advised by my parents that the military had contacted them to advise them that I had been called up for army training. It was ironic that I was flying the border doing what was considered civilian work for the military. The managing director called upon the officer who I had met in his office. They agreed that my service to the company and to the military was important. A week later I was exempted from army training continuing to do prime airborne survey for the government and prime sensitive projects such as new harbours dams and railways.

We did another military survey. This was up at Upington a very hot town in a dry area to the north of South Africa. It was we learnt to survey a strip of land to the Caprivi Strip a hot spot for coming military action against the Cuban backed terrorists from Angola. This detail was to survey sites to build underground airports so enabling the air force to operate in safety against the oncoming terrorist Russian and Cuban supported armies. South Africa would go on to fight a bush war for the next twenty or so years. Hundreds of young white boys would be lost. Rhodesia would also go headlong into war calling upon all its pioneers to hear the clarion call. Many would die, farms would be destroyed, men and their families tortured and brutally killed. Woman raped to death of impaled. Livestock and dogs impaled on fences and often burnt alive. Huge farms supporting the indigenous would be destroyed with the locals having to beg for food on the streets. Eventually it would collapse, never ever under Mugabe to come back to its previous productive standard. Starvation from unemployed workers would rise to an unimaginable desperate level causing death to hundreds of Africans. Brutal punishment and death or jailing was the name of the game not to mention incredible torture to children in front of the parents if they did not support the terrorist movement by supplying food or information. Known or unknown.

I was very pleased at the position I was in. A crew of my own, building flight hours on a twin-engine aircraft, paid with perks and now romantically involved with Ursula. Not to mention her lovely little daughter Dale. Life seemed good engagement and marriage possibly on the cards but the target to become an airline pilot was very strong. The year was fast coming to an end. It was about this time that I heard that TREK Airlines was going to buy a B707 and would be looking for crew. I contacted their head office asking if I could see either Capt. Meredith or Snelgar, the two owners of the company. They had started the company many years before using VIKING aircraft the DC3 and later Super Constellations. I had travelled out to South Africa on one of their flights. They were rather unique as an embargo for all South African registered aircraft was in order not allowing them to over Africa. TREK circumvented this by having TREK on one side of their aircraft and Luxavia on the other side. They were registered in both countries so enabling them to fly directly across Africa to Palma, on to Europe and the U.K.

To see either of these gentlemen seemed impossible according to their secretary, however with a bit of smooth talking and some delivered flowers to her I got a date to meet one of them. I explained my desire to be in the airline apologized for my cheeky push to meet but asked them to understand my sincere desire to work for an independent airline. I was told that as I did not have an instrument rating and upgrade to my commercial pilot rating they could not assist. They did advise though that if I could get this rating before the arrival of the B707 they could possibly offer me a pilot position. I then decided to upgrade my license to have the instrument rating only to find that I could not write the exam before the B707 arrived. The South Africa M.O.T. only sat the exam every 3 months. My answer was then to resign taking a chance I would be hired by TREK and return to Canada where I could obtain LINK training and write the exam on my Canadian license. I had some explaining to do with Ursula, but she did understand. Resigning I used my now almost expiring return ticket to get me back to Vancouver where I had contact with Herb and Cathy Porter to start the needed training.

My enroute ticket took me to Rome where I was to transit to Canadian Pacific Airline direct to Vancouver. In the customs hall the man in front of me looked familiar. As he turned around, I asked if he was by chance Rex Harrison. He replied he was, so I invited him to join me for a drink at the bar to await our respective flights. He accepted and we spent a very enjoyable two hours chatting. He was the most open-minded and pleasant gentleman I have ever had the pleasure of meeting. We discussed the regrettable loss of his wife Kay Kendall who he expressed as the love of his life. In discussing my life and the present situation he wished me all the very best signing a card as we parted I expressing the same. I still have it in my diary.

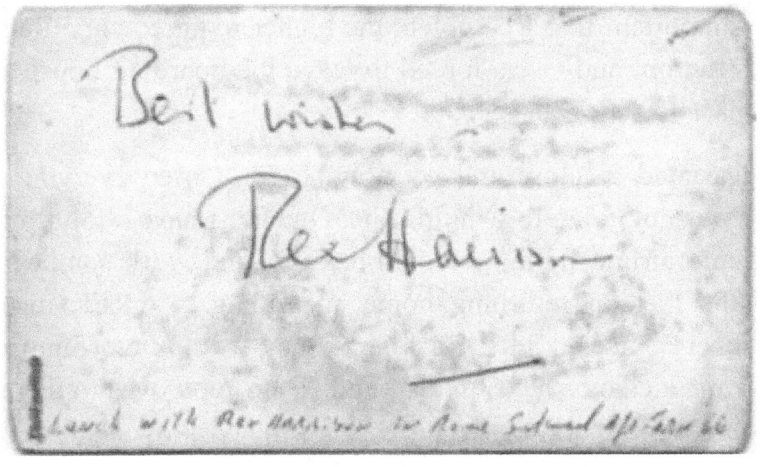

Arriving in Vancouver my old South African friend Keith Chiazzari met me flying us to Abbotsford where he was getting his Commercial license with Herb at Abbotsford Air Services. It was great meeting seeing Kathy and Herb again. I quickly made progress to find a LINK and a school to be trained in instrument flying. The LINK is a crude sort of like a stationary mini aircraft but it's the old-fashioned way of getting the hang of blind flying on instruments. Needle, Ball and airspeed.

I found one at the Canadian Pacific Airline Hangar, arranged for training and was given a private home address down the street where I could board. With all this getting underway I got the syllabus from the Ministry of Transport in Vancouver. For the next two weeks I was studying at night and meeting the training officer at the LINK trainer by day. It was not easy as I was under severe pressure because funds were depleting fast, time was against me to meet the TREK deadline, and I had my career in my hands so could not afford to fail. I found it hard to get to the standard required to pass the LINK exam but did pass the written. Now every time I was shut in the LINK, I started to panic a bit but consoled myself as best I could. I eventually passed the LINK test but still had to rent a twin-engine aircraft to pass the M.O.T flight exam and get the instrument endorsement on my senior commercial license. I would need this to upgrade later to an Airline Transport License, so it was very important that I complete the higher requirements. Regretfully my funds ran out and I was forced to leave the boarding house and find another place to stay.

I was devastated so close and yet now so far. I tried everything but it seemed I was not going to win this one. One must have a lot of money to progress into airline flying. I would have to find work somewhere and give up the idea of returning home and going to TREK airlines. In desperation I contacted TREK asking if they would help fund me or at least give me a chance next time around. Their reply was to the negative and no suggestion that they would wait for me or allow a slot in the next crew intake. It was all over. I was a bit distraught.

Ursula was not happy with the present situation, and it seemed as if the long-distance romance was ending. There was nothing I could do but promise her that if I could change it I would. Maybe even bring her and Dale to Canada. This never happened and our relationship eventually ended.

Almost penniless, I had no alternative but to turn to my close charitable friends for a bed. Herb and Kathy came to my aid with me offering to do any work at the office of Abbotsford Air Services or hanger in return. Proceeding back to Abbotsford where I desperately started looking for a flying job or for that matter any job. I was a bit depressed as I had given up a good job in Johannesburg, left my home country, my girlfriend and family all for the sake of a desire to progress up the aviation ladder. But thanks to the support of my good friends Herb, Kathy, Keith and Alison I sorted things out and looked ahead as there were more flying jobs in Canada than South Africa.

There are rules for pilots mainly there for our own benefit. The best way to learn the rules is best from our own mistakes but it is an aviation omen that one won't live long enough to learn from all the mistakes pilots often make. We derive these rules from pilots who have previously made these mistakes.

Vancouver, Northwest Territories & Arctic.

The job with TREK airlines now being out of the question I had to look for employment in Canada. Luckly I still had a current license now upgraded to senior commercial. The Airline Transport rating exams I had been able to write but without further funds to complete the instrument rating to a first class I had to accept the fact that returning to South Africa was unfeasibly and financially not possible. Abbotsford airport was the base for a firefighting operation flying Grumman WW2 TBM converted aircraft carrier torpedo bombers. These guys were well paid, but it was an extremely dangerous flying job operating in the mountains and flying directly in smoke. The aircraft upon dropping their water load would kick up like a horse often with the engines spluttering to get air. The pilots would be vectored into the fire by a bird dog plane flying above, so directing the firefighting aircraft into the hot spot. One of these pilots was returning to Edmonton in his little MG and offered me a ride. With no hope of work in Vancouver I accepted, arriving in Edmonton travelling once again the long road over the Rockies as I did in 1963.

This was now early spring of 1966 but ironically driving again in a little sports car. Staying at the local YMCA, I started a frantic search for work at the industrial airport. This airport was a major base for the maintenance and operations of charter and bush companies operating in the wild Northwest Territories and the Arctic. With enough money for only a couple of days, I had to do something fast or look for work in the city. To my good fortune on the very first day, I heard of a company wanting a pilot with a floatplane rating to go North. I met the owners of the aircraft a

Cessna 180 on floats. I seemed to fit the bill but failed to tell them I had only about 100 hours on floats but current on the Cessna 180 from Map Studio Productions. They needed someone right away to fly to Hay River on the Great Slave Lake and pick up the Cessna 180, ferrying it across the lake to Yellowknife. They gave me some per diem cash and a ticket on P.W.A. to Hay River. (little did I know again how fate would put me in the scene with P.W.A. (Pacific Western Airlines) What they did not tell me was that the Great Slave Lake was still frozen but Yellowknife being a main float plane base had a small, cleared stretch of water alongside the dock. Having to go North meant I needed a sleeping bag and a rifle which is required by all pilots operating in the wild North. The sleeping bag I got from the Army and navy surplus and a second-hand Winchester 3030 in good condition from a local gun shop. Arriving at Hay River airport I was met by a young guy in charge of the Cessna and taken to sort of motel with wooden cabins. He explained that the aircraft was on the canal alongside the town of Hay River and sort of frozen in. He had worked on the machine indicating it was in good condition and ready to go on lease to Yellowknife. It was apparent they needed it there as soon as possible, as the lease was active, and the owners were losing money. I had at this point to address the situation very closely. Firstly, I was penniless, I was not actually current on the 180 floatplanes, and the canal was only open a very short distance, requiring a short as possible take off. My general floatplane time was limited to just a few 3 hours and 15 minutes hours on a small Luscombe.

To think this over I returned to the motel to check in and get some much-needed food. Collecting my bags plus my gun I walked out on a wooded boardwalk which covered the mush of soil underneath being a permafrost area, allowing me to get to my outdoor cabin. As I reached my cabin, a young Indian squaw came to my side. She wanted to go into the cabin. She offered herself to me in exchange for a few dollars. I rejected her offer at the same time, baring the door from her insistent attempt to enter. She reduced her fee from money to a bottle of Cocoa Cola. I had by this time placed my belonging into the cabin as again she attempted to enter lifting her tatty dress revealing dirty legs and a pair of covered in mud worn Indian boots made from animal hide. My rifle was leaning up against the wall, so I picked it up, pointed it at her and cocked the hammer. She got the picture and disappeared into the dark. On relating this to the young mechanic who worked for Parsons Airways a local bush company, he explained that they do this for the men folk allowing them to buy more liquor or the Coke to use as a mix. They are roughly treated so money for food and children has to come out of the deal as well. It's seemed a shame that a proud nation like the Indian tribes had come to this. As my time up North went along, I was to learn a lot more about their almost unhuman deprived predicament. I wondered about our apartheid system where although separated we were at least giving the black African a chance to be educated, have a birth certificate, learn to read and write, teach a trade and develop some sort of initiative in becoming westernized or civilized which ever suited the progress. At least they did not get cash handout and forced into reservations to rot, as was the North American Indian. Years later this did come about in South Africa with massive unemployment requiring government grants to keep a South African black majority alive. Overpopulation (young teen age mothers) in Africa was and is a major crisis.

The morning came and, in my favour, as it was a clear bright day. The canal was still only open a short distance but with the night's sleep and a fresh look at the situation I decided to give it a go. Loading the Cessna with minimum fuel and only my personal bags, the aircraft was not heavy and although the mechanic was a bit apprehensive, I started the machine, warmed her up and cast her off. I had to all of a sudden remember all I had learnt about float plane flying with no instruction present. The wind was quite strong coming off the main lake, so taxiing back down the canal was not so hard. Attempting to turn I drifted against the canal ice and for a few minutes was stuck broadside.

However, with the water rudders down and a bit of power I broke through a small piece of the floating ice and made the turn. With full power and stick right back I got on the step very early skimming across the water with the canal open water end approaching very rapidly. In the final and only chance of getting airborne, I jumped the flap to a second notch causing the aircraft to leave the water except for a small bit of the chine. I clipped a bit of the far canal ice but was airborne and flying clear. Making radio contact with Hay River tower I reported my take off and headed across the 120 miles of frozen lake to Yellowknife. This ice is meters thick and in deep winter roads are cut across it to facilitate heavy equipment and road transport vehicles to cross an ice bridge. In Russia they actually lay rail lines across similar lakes.

In contact with Yellowknife control, I was advised the open ice channel at the floatplane base was closing and questioned whether I could land there in time. If not, I would have to return to Hay River as the Great Slave Lake was still frozen. What they did not know was that to take off from the Hay River canal I had to reduce my fuel to only enough to get me to yellow knife. Finding the inlet and floatplane base I saw that the cleared and open channel alongside the dock was open but very short. Indicating to the tower that I was going to land, I was told to contact Northwest Territorial Airways a base on the inlet on their radio frequency. This I did advising on an open radio channel to all aircraft of my intention to land on the lake. Turning final from a good distance out I was able to make a long slow and only feet above the ice approach. With the threshold of the open water just under my nose, I cut the power and landed on the open water. Bringing the stick right back I mushed onto the water, chopping the power I settled into the wash and came to a moderate stop about 20 feet from the ice. With a little sweat and a sigh of relief I looked about to see what was next. There appeared a small channel of broken ice leading to the dock where I saw a couple of chaps walking out. I got out and stood on the float catching a line they threw at me. Very slowly, they pulled me alongside the dock where I was able to tie up. The one fellow came over and welcomed me to Yellowknife indicating he was the charterer being a prospecting company called North West Explorations.

This was the beginning of an incredible year for the only known South African pilot this far North. Leaving the dock, I was put up at a local sort of hotel. Yellowknife was a frontier town with dirt streets, a few government offices and some staff. A Hudson Bay trading store a few buildings with flats and a bar. Down on the lake dockside there were a few bush plane operators such as Wardair and Ptarmigan airways. Northwest Territorial Airways with whom to my delight an old friend Peter Cowie was working for. Wardair was the base from which Max Ward started his flying and later airline using a Puss moth. He had well known bush pilots such as Don Braun and a fleet of aircraft consisting of twin Otters. Beavers, single engine Otters and in the past some Bristol freighters. One of which lay crashed not far from the airport. Ptarmigan if I remember correctly was owned by brothers and had a gull winged Stinson. Rather unique for the North plus a few light aircraft such as a Cessna 185 and 180. Northwest Territorial Airways was owner by Bob Engels an American from the west coast. Bob had come North to found and develop his company looking at the growing need for bush operations especially as the D.E.W (Distant Early Warning) radar stations were being set up by the Americans across the whole arctic from the Atlantic to the Pacific, as protection from the considered Russian strike over the pole. This being the nearest North American land mass to Russia. Bush pilots carried the early equipment in, such as bulldozers and support material by dismantling the equipment, tying it to their spreaders and floats. After a runway was built heavier aircraft such a

DC3, C46 and air force freighters got in so building the radar defense line. It was tough and dangerous flying for the earlier bush pilots, however good money was made as the USA contractors paid well. For history's sake early bush flying was credited to great frontier pilots who ventured North into the unknown. Risking life and limb to open up the North and Arctic routes. They knew very little about what they were heading into, many died and were lost in no man's land. One of the most famous was Punch Dixons flying Fokker registered as GC-ASK. One bush pilot very recently got lost and ended up way off track crashing into a forest. He was a chap called Martin Hartwell from Alaric flying a Beech 18. often called a widow maker. Two of his passengers a nurse and pregnant Indian woman died. A young boy passenger and Martin survived the crash. Weeks went by with no food and temperatures at minus 30c to 50c below. In desperation he decided to eat the flesh off the dead nurse, but the young boy refused. He died leaving Martin in a desperate final attempt to live, eating the leg muscles off the dead girl. He was miraculously saved many weeks later by a lone pilot who was able to rescue him and get him back to a Northern outpost. He was never accused of any form of cannibalism and went on to fly again. On a similar note, I was part of another such incredible rescue. A pilot heading south from Cambridge Bay was trying to find Contorto Lake where there was a radio station set up and manned by two men doing six months on six months off. Its location was about halfway from Cambridge Bay to Yellowknife. This was to assist the now developing air transport, airline and used in the DEW line days as a navigation assist point. The weather had diminished to treetop level, and he could not locate the radio station. The guys manning the station thought they heard him flying close by. He disappeared and being mid-winter with temperatures at minus 35was considered lost. Weeks went into months; search parties and bush pilots all were on the lookout for him.

How I came into the picture was when the end of summer was approaching with the prospectors returning home, my contract finishing I was offered the chance to fly for Northwest Territorial Airways as pilot and Co Pilot on the DC3 and Beech18. A golden opportunity to get onto bigger aircraft. The problem with joining them was there was no accommodation. So, for 2 weeks I slept on the workshop floor. We at the time had a DC3 cargo flight to Port Radium now called Echo Bay mining. It was a very cold night being a mid-winter flight. Landing on the ice we offloaded and reloaded outbound cargo some of which was solid silver bars. Just on take-off I heard what sounded like "mayday, mayday" Turning to Darryl I asked if he had heard it. Over the noise of the engines his reply was no. I remained alert to the radio for some while not hearing a repeat of what I thought I had heard. Returning to Yellowknife I approached Bob the boss telling him of what I had heard. The location of where we were was a long way away from the flight planned route the lost pilot was on. Bob agreed with Daryl it was not possible to be associated, from which I received a bit of teasing going back to the "Nigger Kicker". A month or so went by when a pilot flying a new turbo Beaver from Yellowknife to Coppermine, a route well west of the lost pilots' route, saw something flash in the now early summer light. Not immediately taking much notice of it, he did though decide to turn back. He was able to make out the silhouette of an aircraft wing. He then saw a movement of what appeared to be a man. He was rescued having been lost for over 60 days in deep frozen weather. If my attempt to get Bob or Daryl to listen to me he would have been rescued a month earlier as his location to Echo Bay was only about 60 miles, but he was over a hundred miles off course well West of his intended flight path. So, lie many skeletons of the Northern bush pilots and many wrecks of aircraft of every conceivable type, dating way back to old Fokker's. To this day I wished I had been able to convince Bob of my hearing of the mayday. Bob had a small fleet of aircraft but was developing well, giving Max Wards' Wardair a bit of competition. At Maxs dock there was a Cessna 180, a single engine Otter, a beaver and a twin beech all on floats. It was rumoured he was getting a DC3 to operate from the airport. Besides Peter Cowie he had pilots such as Daryl Brown, Joe Sorrenson guys I would get to know well over the coming year.

With the spring thaw now underway I was put to work immediately. My main job was to support prospectors moving into the Arctic flying them from one location to another plus keeping them supplied with food. To do this fuel drops were set up in far-off locations around the North. I was to run the supply line from Yellowknife as far North as could be got with the retreating ice. It was terrific flying being on my operating into small lakes and rivers. Sleeping out under tents, rifle by my side, having the time to build my docks, working late into the night as there was no darkness to see the midnight sun. There were Caribou, Moose, bears and North Grizzly bears, all to be contended with. However, worst of all was the "No see em gnats" and mosquitoes. The "no see ems" nick-named by the Indians, would eat you alive by biting the back of your neck or any exposed area. One flew with boots tied down, long-sleeved shirts, and done-up collars plus caps. In some cases, the mosquitoes were so bad on take-off that the windscreen would be bloodied so badly, that one had to land and after cleaning, try again. On the radial engine aircraft, the oil filters were known to block up. Prospectors wore hats with veils to protect them like beekeepers. One young Australian university prospector named Ryan was so badly bitten he was going insane consequently; I had to fly him out permanently. Moving the equipment entailed tying the

In the Arctic with young prospectors. The chap on the left was Ryan the Aussie and next to him was the future owner of Echo Bay mines son., his friend and me

canoe to the side of the float stays. Bulk equipment was carried on the float spreaders, everything else was in the cabin. Other jobs were to now and then drop into the many fishing camps that entertained wealthy fishermen from southern provinces and the United States. It was often just to get a coffee or a piece of pie. In turn, I would take back to Yellowknife mail and lists of supplies they would need on their next charter run bringing in client fishermen. The arctic char is a great fish, very tasty, popular for fishermen but expensive having to come so far to catch it. Most of the time I flew a fellow whose name I think was MacBeth, a professional prospector. I would leave him at one location and pick him up many miles away days later using fuel caches that had been positioned over the previous winter. Prospectors have to be moved continuously to new sites over the short summer months. MacBeth was positive he would find the mother lode of silver and he did. On one trip into the Arctic Circle MacBeth and I landed at Port Radium on Great Bear Lake.

Also known as Echo Bay Mine. This mine had been abandoned since the war. The whole mine including the clothing, household goods and furniture was left as the personnel were flown out. We slept in the old kitchen which was very much intact. The prospector then went about his explorations with me, returning some days later from Yellowknife to collect him. He later gave me a piece of native silver which he had first extracted from the old mine shaft and was convinced he had found the mother lode. Over the next month or so I flew men and equipment into the Echo Bay. Small-scale mining started immediately with drills and diggings in the old exploratory tunnel down by the bay edge. I found that I could land in the small bay beside the dock, a

Typical bush camp set up for prospectors which I had to move around weekly.

sort of half-moon bay. I would slide in over the trees and make a side slip onto the water decreasing my flying and taxi time to save precious fuel. On one occasion I got an unseen tail wind and ran out of water forcing me to grind upon the stone beach on the opposite side. I damaged a float, so a replacement was flown in on the single engine Otter, a rig was made up and a float change was completed. I got a bit of a dressing down on that but that's bush flying. I should have invested in his exploration company as he was right, and Port Radium on Echo Bay became one of the biggest silver mines in Canada. Today it has been raised including the buildings and runway, big enough at the time for the mine's private B727, everything returned to its natural state after years of silver productivity. Later when married I had two rings made from silver, a good memento of the Arctic.

The point of this story is that it was from this mine, Port Radium, that the uranium used to manufacture the first A Bomb was obtained. It was shipped down the Great Bear Lake on barges then eventually on to the Mackenzie River via Norm Wells, adjacent to U.S Army camp "Canol"), then west to meet army road transport, eventually to the States Many years later via a correspondent Jack Stevens I learnt that the former U.S.

Army Canol Camp across from Norman Wells, was taken over by Imperial Oil and abandoned in 1977. They left a few Quonsets Huts, and the post office building. The nose hangar was demolished. Jack had the opportunity of visiting the camp years later and took these photos. As a follow up to the barges used to ship material for the A bomb. S.R.

Gage in his book, "A Walk on The Canol Road" writes: "Not all the barges that unloaded at Norman Wells and Camp Canol made the trip south empty. Some stopped to pick up loads of black ore that had been mined at the Government's Eldorado property on Great Bear Lake. The cargo was pitchblende, carried out on the Canol supply route and refined into pure uranium 235 for the Manhattan Project. The ore from Great Bear went to the University of Chicago's reactor, where the atomic bomb was being developed. Canol played an unexpected part in the birth of the nuclear age." All top secret.

Jack Stephens beside abandoned 1944, U.S. Army trucks at Camp Canol

More uranium was obtained from the Congo being flown out by an old Pan Am China clipper flying boat. The same old Clipper crashed while attempting to land on the bay in Trinidad. She was a flying wreck but was passed by the CAA to do the secret Congo Leopoldville flight.

Many of the original clippers or their crew who made the original Pacific crossing did not survive. One clipper ditched on a flight to Hawaii and after an unsuccessful attempt to be towed by a Navy cruiser was destroyed by cannon fire to eliminate it being a sea hazard. Others crashed into the California Mountains, and one disappeared altogether attempting to fly the China route.

Prior to WW 2 the Japanese military became very interested in the new Pratt & Whitney radial engine that powered the Pan Am Clipper. On a flight from San Francisco to China a clipper landed on Truk Lagoon to be refueled by Japanese authorities. Later the clipper was assumed lost over the Pacific. Years later it was revealed that the crew and passengers were arrested and executed, the engines were retrieved and sent to Japan and the clipper was sunk in deep water off Turk lagoon.

I was flying further North as far as Coppermine and the Victoria islands. The Arctic is a fascinating and very beautiful place. It has beauty and tranquility that's hard to believe with some of the lake beaches great for swimming with clear blue water. At one point far north, I used the canoe to explore a glazier field. Alone I paddled out into crystal clear water. The ice cliffs had a sort of blue haze chaperoned by total silence. As I paddled, I started to hear what sounded like a small motor pumping away. Stopping it seemed to distance itself. It was only after I paddled again did I realize the sound was my heartbeat? That was the depth of the silence, uncanny.

The mouth of the Coppermine River opens out into the Arctic Ocean. The arctic char (fish) at this point are so numerous that by standing on the wing of the aircraft and looking down at the underwater was clear and a mass of moving fish, so is the quality of the water and food in the North. Illegally one evening I took my rifle and shot one. In camp that night the lone prospector who I was to meet up with and I enjoyed a good fish dinner. Sometimes at the meeting point I would get there first; I would then put all the supplies into the canoe I usually carried and swing it up high into the treetops. This was because bears would find it, devour the contents and destroy the canoe if left on the ground. I would then fire two shots into the air to alert the prospector if in the area that I was on the meeting point. On one occasion, we camped on a small island off the lake edge thinking it to be safe spot. When I returned some hours later the camp was destroyed. Every food can was punctured. Sugar and flour in all directions, clothes torn and sleeping bags ripped. Thankfully the canoe was out with the prospector as we were due to return to Yellowknife that day. The brown bears are not so ferocious, but the big grizzly can stand 8 feet tall and looks like a tractor when coming through the bush. A very mean character and not one to mess with.

Self in a bush camp/mosquitoes and gnats

Beaver. Work horse flown by my old friend Keith Chiazzari another South African a West coast bush pilot and old school friend.

Goa Haven (killer whale) and wrecked ships.

It was early winter now flying the DC3 /Beech 18 for Northwest when a charter to Goa Haven (Goa the name of an early adventures boat) an isolated Eskimo outlet on King William Island inside the Arctic Circle was needed to do a supply run before the big freeze set in. Daryl Brown and I were rostered to do the trip with the Beech 18 on floats departing from Cambridge Bay. King William Island had become famous as on May 19th, 1845, two ships of the Royal Navy, the HMS Erebus and the HMS Terror departed from England in an attempt to navigate a Northern passage from the Atlantic to the Pacific via the Arctic polar route. The expedition under the command of Jon Franklin, an experienced polar explorer departed with 3 years supply of provisions with their hulls reinforced with iron to withstand the crushing ice. The expedition ventured into unknown and dangerous waters. Compasses did not work correctly because their magnetic readings were impaired by the proximity to the North Pole. There was no weather report and sometimes years of no summer ice melt. Consequently, ships can become trapped in cement-like ice. There is a book on this written by John Geiger and Alanna Mitchell which is a very good read and gives more information than I can supply here. Eventually, the expedition got as far as 77 degrees and about 1367km from the North Pole before wintering on a small uninhabited island. In September 1846 the expedition made a fateful decision to sail into the Victoria Straits. Here it is believed a massive winter storm trapped the ships within hours.

Norseman. *In Flin Flon Manitoba, the pilot's name was* **Hank Parsons** *who became the owner of Parsons Airways.*

The men were trapped for two years as the ice did not break. Franklin and some crew died leaving the remaining crew abandoned. In April 1848 the remaining crew attempted to walk to the Canadian mainland. They all perished and reverted in their death walk to cannibalism. They would boil the body parts in their boots. How this information was recorded was that some Inuit had told a search party sent out to find the ships, of what they had seen. It was not until 152 years later that explorations to find the ship were successful. The HMS Erebus was found in September 2014 in the Queen Maud Gulf close to the Canadian mainland. The H.M.S Terror was found in what is now named Terror Bay on King William Island.

Departing Cambridge Bay, we flew on true heading using visual and true compass settings. Arriving at Gjoa Haven we circled the bay to establish the best landing approach. The Eskimos had a camp on the bay so were out to see us land. We decided to land towards the bay and into wind, paralleling the shore on calm still water. In the landing configuration we were about to touch down on the water when suddenly a whale surfaced right in our landing path. We hit the whale squarely across its back with both floats. Bouncing into the air Daryl established control and came down back on the water nose high and causing large water turbulence. Gathering our nerves we completed our landing run turning to see what had happened to the whale. The Eskimos had by now launched their kayaks and were heading for the bleeding whale at great speed. Taxing ashore it was established that small whale was dead with two huge gashes across its back. The Eskimos were very happy as it was going to be a good winter with the extra food. Our aircraft fortunately was not damaged, so completing the offload we returned to Cambridge Bay with a good story. As I indicate earlier in my writing this was the second animal that had been killed during my flying career, the first was the Deer on Texada Island British Columbia back in 1964.

Beech 18 on floats.

Peary island killers.

The Indians and Eskimos' have a tribal tradition that if they are snowed in, isolated, and starving, the oldest member of the tribe will step out into the freezing climate and freeze themselves to death. This is to supply food for the young children and remaining tribal members. There was an incident on Perry Island where in the middle of a long freezing winter, such a tradition took place. To spare death by freezing two of the tribal members went out and shot the freezing elders. In so sparing them of the agony of the biting and freezing weather. The incident came to the attention of the Mounties who investigated the matter and found it to be true. A warrant for their arrest was issued in Cambridge Bay and we were chartered to go with an Indian affairs officer and bring them back to the authorities at Cambridge Bay. Their camp was near a lonely Hudson Bay fur and trading outpost on a small inlet off the queen Maud gulf where the Hudson Bay Company had a small building standing alone to operate their trading business. The matter went to the courts of Canada and the Peary Island killers as they were known, were exonerated as by tribal law verses western civilization law, they were in their right as per custom and tribal dealings.

A small point of interest here is that earlier in my writing I mentioned I had worked for the Hudson Bay Company in London. At one time the Hudson Bay Company had crown rights to all the rivers off Hudson Bay as trapping rights. Peary Island indicated by radio that there was a small strip of water still open alongside their dock on the inlet. But winter was now upon the Arctic and ice was forming across the North. Finding the inlet, we landed with the Beech 18 and the Indian affairs officer plus a Mounty. Locating the tribe was easy as they were in their winter caribou skinned huts preparing to meet the long winter. There was very little daylight now with the coming of total darkness over the winter. The officials did their required apprehension and prepared to depart. Racing the clock to get out we ran into a major problem. The wind had blown the sea ice into the inlet, and it had become totally blocked. We realized with the ice and closing darkness we would not be able to get out and fly back to Cambridge Bay in time to land on the water. Not a good idea in darkness and possible unseen ice floats. Preparation was made to overnight; however, there was no accommodation anywhere. The

Hudson Bay store was locked as the agent had departed to the next point in his trading business. Daryl extracted a bottle of rum which together with the tribal chief, the agent and Mounty we consumed.

This was to stand me in good stead as the chief, now our best friend, would clear me of an uncomfortable incident that was about to happen. We had to bed down in the tribes' huts. I was allocated a floor space in a smaller hut not far away from the main hut. As I was bedding down a young female dressed in tribal skins and boots came in so making her bed next to my sleeping bag. She made all indications that she was going to disrobe and join me. This is not uncommon for tribes in the north to supply woman to travelers, and if rejected can cause a very insulting loss of face situation. The offer was tempting but one must consider that they have not bathed for maybe 4 to 6 months. Their skins are cured with urine, add this to a sweaty body, and discoloured jagged teeth, the idea of a romantic night with an Eskimo is not attractive. I was able to extract myself from the advances politely but spent the rest of the night keeping a watch on my close lady bed friend. The chief had intervened and got me off the hook so to say. The morning came with a strip of ice-free water, so hastily packing we got airborne and flew back to Cambridge Bay.

DC 3 to Resolute.

Back in Yellowknife Bob Engels the boss, had been able to secure me a small one-bedroom apartment in the Government building. It was shared by a lot of individuals who worked for the government as teachers, clerks, and native affairs officers. So, no more sleeping on the floor in the workshop which was as the temperatures dropped to minus 20 a bit cold. As the winter wore on the spin the bottle parties and all sorts of shenanigans took place in this small apartment building between pilots, nurses and government workers all suffering from cabin fever. There was also a small log bar called "Wildcat café". Another place when not flying to break the freezing, total darkness and boredom of the North. I was now flying mainly the DC3 which suited me down to the ground, as I wanted to log some heavier time on bigger aircraft. I flew lot with Daryl Brown, Sorenson and Engels working all the stations far north as Coppermine, Cambridge Bay, Great Bear Lake as far East as Hudson Bay. Earlier I wrote Hudson Bay would come into my life. It was

December 1966 and the DC3 was now on wheel skies. A lot of our work was also hauling drilling rigs onto the sea ice and supplying fuel to mining exploration outposts. At subzero it takes about 3 hours to get an aircraft up and flying. Firstly, when it comes in the batteries have to be dropped and stored in a warm hut. The oil via dilution switches, has to be diluted with fuel to stop it from freezing. Wing tents must be put on with engine tents coupled to Herman Nelson oil-fired heaters. One is working in a land of darkness, no sunlight, at times with temperatures around -60 below. With engine tents and heater (Herman Nelsons) removed on one engine an attempt is made to start it. Then the second engine same procedure.

DC3 on wheel skis

Polar bear on floating sea ice. Extremely dangerous, they can smell food miles away and will attack.

To remove a cargo locking pin requires the removal of one's mitten, one's glove and attempt by placing your fingers on each side of the pin at the same time pushing down on the locking stud. Well, if one is not fast enough, your fingers freeze to the pin. Now it requires you to either attempt to dislodge your fingers and lose a chunk of skin, or get down on your knees, exhaling hot breath onto the pin to help unfreeze your fingers.

Huskies are incredible animals and a primary means of transport often working in subzero weather. Later I had a husky of my own. The lead dog is quite often a bitch. She/he is the one that takes the command from the driver. Also sets the pace. On sharp ice they wear little boots. On treacherous ice they spread the dogs out in a fan shape.

Indian Squaw and son

The propeller blades must be hand-turned to position the piston to the top cylinder and to exhaust any oil which might cause the engine to hydraulic, so breaking a con rod. With the oil diluted a start can be attempted on the electric starter. There is only a short time that it can be used without burning out or killing the battery. If successful, the same procedure is applied to the other engine and wing. Eventually, if a two-engine start has been successful the co-pilot has to come up from behind the engines, under the wing in full blast of the prop wash and climb up onto the wheel only 2 meters from the whirling prop. Once on the slippery ice-covered wheel, the locking pin for the undercarriage has to be removed. This was up inside the wheel well. One slip and you could very easily fall into the prop. If the engine did not start after a few turns the strain on the starter could burn it out. In that case, it was necessary to tie a rope around the hub of the prop, then using a skidoo, 4 x 4 vehicle or a team of huskies pulling on the rope would cause the prop to turn like a top. Once at Norman Wells, this happened to the DC3. We had no skidoo or anything to attempt a start. By turning the propeller to put the cylinder to top dead centre, and priming the cylinders, two of us hand-started the engine. This was done by me being tall and standing with the other guys back to my chest. With both our hands extended as far up the propeller blade, we lunged pulling the blade in the starting direction. It took 4 attempts, but we got the engine started.

One such charter we had to fly Government officials to Resolute Bay on Cornwallis Island. One of the most Northern outposts in the Arctic is only 600 kilometres from the North Pole and very close to the magnetic north pole. It was also a DEW (distant Early warning) American military station protecting the North American continent from a possible invasion by the Russians coming over the Arctic. The flight had to pass via Cambridge Bay, Daryl and I as flight crew with Daryl's wife, Joyce, I think was her name as hostess for the passengers. It was quite a historic flight as the government intended to split the Northwest Territories and for a native province to be formed in the east, north of Quebec. The capital became Yellowknife and old Frobisher Bay is now called "Iqaluit".

The far north was the Eskimo areas which are called Inuit. Canadian Indians mainly the Maiti and Dog Rib tribes shared the remaining northern areas. The Northwest Territories is now called "Nunavut". This all came about many years later, but for me I believed at that time, being December 1966 I was the only South African to be flying the Arctic having travelled so close to the magnetic North Pole and the true North Pole.

After arriving there and having to prepare the DC3 to depart a day or two later, a huge winter storm set in. To find the aircraft and secure it, I had to tie a rope to myself and a building as a safety measure. The whiteout had hit creating almost zero visibility. Feeling my way out into the storm I was blown over, then had to go by feel to find the aircraft now almost invisible in blinding frozen air. The temperature dropped to minus 60 so added with the chill factor, it was minus 75 to 85. With the help of the attached rope, I got back to the building almost frozen to death. Thankfully I was in full Arctic gear, mittens, thermal pants and jacket. Thermal underwear and booties covered by Company Red overalls, face mask, and headgear. Our legs were usually in Mukluks, a sort of boot tied below the knee, made from sealskin by the Indians and Eskimos. Extremely difficult if one wants to relieve oneself. These we then put into rubber all-weather sole type covers to protect the skin on the foot. Eventually after a 2-day layover, we flew back, but as the base had a small bar called the "Aurora" after the Northern light, a few rums and cokes imbibed while there were appreciated.

A funny point was that there were no women on the base. So, Joyce was very popular having drinks bought for her in numbers. She would in turn quietly slide them over to Daryl and me. Very courteous and sporting of her. Aurora was the Roman goddess of the dawn. Aurora Borealis-Northern lights.

Interesting facts about the Arctic.

In 985 a Viking Captain Herjolfsson while sailing from Iceland to Greenland sailed into a sea fog, when it had cleared, he sighted a new land. This was the Canadian East coast, so he was the first European to see the new world. He met the Paleo- Eskimo people who lived there until the 15th century. Trade routes were set up and Viking ships sailed as far. as Point of Roses in Newfoundland. They called it Vinland. They have also found traces of them in Maine. Columbus never even got to the North America mainland

As mentioned earlier he landed at San Salvador and sailed on to the island of Dominica and Haiti. He was an Italian, financed by the Spanish Queen. He died a pauper. A scribe believed to be a German monk, writing the history made a mistake as he was incorrectly informed that Amerigo had found the new world. So, it was named America.

Midnight sun on the North Pole plateau. 24 hours of day light.

Husky dog teams waiting to collect passengers and freight. Husky teams are used by Eskimos extensively as personal transport. Husky means" Strength" in an ancient Siberian language. The Malamute is a bigger dog used for cargo sleds, neither are related to wolves but possibly linked from a very early dog in Northern Russia.

Typical Turbo Beaver float plane docking at the old Yellowknife Bay.

Flying on ski equipped aircraft can be quite hair raising at times. For example, heavy snow on a lake can cause a blow hole in the centre. The water then is forced out onto the frozen ice. The wind can then cause the water to freeze like a wash board or corrugations. When attempting to land the skis can cause the aircraft to slide uncontrollably across the corrugations. Usually, a ground loop will stop the sliding. Another problem on skis is that the ski is hotter than the ice so will freeze down on the surface. To stop this, one can taxi onto some wood or if frozen down break loose by dropping the wheels down through the wheel skis. This can be a big problem if one does not have wheel skis as the ice will freeze like cement to the ski. This then would require the crew to either chip away at the ice of if available apply heat from the Herman Nelson heaters, however not always carried on the aircraft. Here is a picture I have of a DC3 on skies or should I say one ski. Rex Kiteley the captain on this DC3 at Reddit village bounced on right gear so forcing the left gear to then come down after it was frozen up. The aircraft is an old ex-RCAF machine. A lot were sold off as surplus and ended up as work horses across the Arctic during my time there.

It was now deep mid-winter; we were flying in total darkness and subzero temperatures. Landing such as Coppermine were done with cans of diesel lit and a runway laid out on the frozen sea ice. The heavy 48-ton ice truckers were starting to arrive by driving over ice bridges across the big frozen lake. If the temperature got warmer than minus 6 the routes would be closed in fear of breaking through. They had to maintain a top speed of 15k per hour so not to fracture the ice. On one occasion a truck broke down on the ice bridge in the middle of the lake. A bush pilot in a single engines ski plane was sent out with repair material. He landed near the truck and because he could not turn his engine off as the temperature was minus 25c, he staked it and walked to the disabled truck. While there a front moved in with a white out. His aircraft broke loose and disappeared into the white out with him running after it. The trucker got fixed and departed thinking the pilot had left with his aircraft. The pilot was stranded on the ice not knowing where his aircraft in the blinding white out was. Fortunately, the aircraft pitched over and with luck he found it. Using the radio, he was able to give his location and was rescued. He would have frozen to death very quickly had he not got help from Yellowknife with men on skidoos. This applied to us as well and often after landing you could hear the ice crack with the weight of the aircraft. Looking down into the ice is a beautiful sight. It has prisms of crystal-like images, reflecting the colours of the rainbow. Only once did I fall through a crack, luckily only up to my waist. I had to board the aircraft which was warmer and disrobe my wet pants as fast as possible to stop them freezing to my skin.

Often our cargo and passengers were met by husky dog teams hauling sleds and goods to the base camps and Eskimo habitats. It's a good experience to ride in a sled but the dogs often excrete their food via their ass end which flies into your face. Consequently, hide covers are given to passengers to deflect the flying excrement. The CAT trains also started to move. These were Caterpillar tractors with cabins hauling skids of cargo to mines and outlying Inuit stations. The North is tough and very hard on men and equipment. Only the tough survive.

The Indians would get Government hand out monthly ration cheques. It was a form of paying them off and to keep them quiet. They are now a lost race swallowed up by the advancing western life, drink and drugs. These cheques were cashable at the Hudson Bay trading stores. If one wanted say a new pair of boots or shirts whatever, you could negotiate with the Indians outside the store. They would then buy what you wanted at a reduced price reselling the items to you. It was bit of back door dealing but it happened. Regretfully most of the cash went to the bottle store or if allowed into the beer hall. Some places the Indians and Eskimos were not allowed in such places. One such place is Flin Flon, a mining town heavily invested with South African money, beer halls separated

Indians including Eskimos from the White (European) clients. They also had entrances for men and ladies with escorts. So much for apartheid which does exists around the world separating colour and nationality. Trouble was that South Africa gave it a name.

With the long cold winter, including the summer, I had accumulated valuable flying experience. Plus, at the time the only known South

African to have flown in the Arctic area. The occupants of the flats that I resided in had at one of our passage parties, written up a small poem for me. It went like this. "Here's to the famed nigger kicker from the Cape of Good Hope, who flies from Cambridge to Coppermine trying to cope. Usually done in a loud voice after a few Canadian rye whiskeys and Seven-Up."

With summer now approaching I decided it was time to up my game and heard that a company Pacific Western Airlines founded by bush pilots now operating a scheduled passenger and cargo airline out of Edmonton was looking for pilots. Making an application via their office in Yellowknife I was accepted without an interview mainly because I was flying the Arctic and Northwest as an experienced bush pilot. I was informed that I would be trained onto the DC6 so handed in my notice to Bob who very understandingly supported my intention to climb the airline ladder rather than remaining a lifetime as a bush pilot. Peter Cowie my old friend had decided to get married. Daryl had bought a Pianola or sometimes I believe called a pianoforte (a piano that plays by itself running on clipped paper format rolls) from Edmonton, so a very festive party was held for Peter's wedding. Just after that, I decided to depart the North, so flying to Edmonton and my new career with Pacific Western Airlines on the 4-engine R28 /C54, DC6 Douglas Aircraft. My sights were set on being an airline pilot and I was slowly getting there. My days in the land of the beautiful colourful curtains of the aurora borealis were over, the sky filled with the colours of the rainbow is a sight to be seen. The action of these northern lights on radio instruments could be disastrous as navigation instruments did not work well when they were active. The days of flying by the moon, sun, stars and a sextant were now in the past. At the time being the only northern bush pilot of South African descent, I was glad that the experience gained I could put towards my future flying career. Working in subzero and total 24-hour darkness was not something this white African of tropical blood wanted to repeat. I would happily leave it to the Arctic pilot colleagues, Canadian Indians and the Eskimos. Little did I know that at the age of 80 years, I would travel to Antarctica with my younger son (Grant) fate again.

Much later N.W.T got this Electra. Bob Engles eventually sold out and retired.

Pacific Western Airlines

Arriving in Edmonton I met another new pilot named Glen Delany. He too was new to the town, so we decided to share a flat not too far from the airport and central. For me getting back to civilization was a real treat. I had money in my pocket, a job to start with an airline and a good place to stay. The first thing was to get some wheels, and this came about as I was walking down the street our flat was on. There in the show room was new all black, red upholstery convertible Mustang. For a cash price of $3,650 Canadian dollars, it was mine. Next was to get some decent clothes. A tailor made me a good Harris Tweed suit, enough of the bush mukluks (Eskimo snow boots) and boots plus a few accessories from the local shops fitted me out as a city man. Glen and I were both over 6 feet, drove mustangs and were known as the jolly green giants. Fitting out the flat was not hard with a few essentials. Ground school started on the DC6, so the first two weeks were school and no messing around. P.W.A was an old established airline starting as a bush operation and progressing to charter. With the advent of the bigger aircraft such as the

DC6 they obtained airline schedule rights. We had a fleet of machines varying from Beavers, a Grumman amphibian, DC3, C46 and DC6. Unbeknown to any of us the airline was later to be a case of the mouse that roared. Which I will get to later. As a new pilot we were actually pilot engineers manning the flight engineers' station between the captain and first officer (Co-pilot) Most of the captains gave us time at the controls however there were the exception. Our routes were mainly some charters, with scheduled flights up North to Yellowknife and Cambridge Bay. My old stamping ground.

On one of these flights up North I nearly got fired. We loaded a coffin in a wooden container at Cambridge Bay. On the way back the captain called the purser up on the intercom and asked if she could get his dinner. He suggested that the new girl bring it up as she might like to look at the flight deck. A plot was hatched in which I the junior pilot was to go back into the cargo section in front of the passenger area and lie on the container holding the coffin. To understand this on the DC6, cargo is carried in the front section ahead of the wing. Passengers totaling about 80 are seated behind this. There is a door leading from the passenger cabin into the cargo section. One then has to ease around the cargo nets and edge along the side of the fuselage up to the flight deck. All in darkness I might add. All was set and I lying on the container holding the coffin having covered myself with my winter great coat. As the poor girl came along side, I raised myself up uttering a low moan expecting to just startle her. However, things went wrong. She dropped the tray, screamed at the top of her voice, lunged back wrenching open the passenger compartment door and hysterically ran the length of the cabin back to the galley situated at the rear of the aircraft. Next, we had the purser in the cockpit, a longtime employee and what came out of her mouth would shame an army sergeant. She was irate and informed us there would be a report on this and that it was not funny. Sure enough, the next day the captain, first officer and I were on the carpet in the chief pilot, Captain Mackie's, office. The captain attempted to explain that it was meant as a joke, but the chief pilot was not amused. Threats of firing range around the room, however with the offer of a letter of apology to the hostess and purser, promises of never to do something so damn stupid again the situation calmed down and the reprimand was over.

Cockpit pranks were quite common, another incident happened when a new girl was asked up to the cockpit. She was advised that there was a small problem with an electrical switch which releases the undercarriage, so allowing the wheels to drop for landing. She was asked if she would go back into the passenger cabin and slowly count 12 rows of seats back. There she was to face the bulkhead of the cargo come passenger section. When she saw the no smoking light flash 3 times she jumped up and down on the aisle floor to release the switch so allowing the wheels to come down. This she carefully did and with the second officer watching her through the spy hole in the door the no smoking sign was flashed 3 times. The poor innocent girl attempting to do the very best job ever done started to leap up and down at armrest height, way more than expected. The next thing the purser again a senior hostess knew, was that she had a demented new girl leaping up and down between the passengers. In a rush, she restrained the new girl who blurted out her predicament as instructed by the cockpit crew. This much to the horror of passengers seated around her. Apparently, what happened and was said in the cockpit upon the arrival of the purser was not fit for public knowledge. Nothing was said about it after apologies were extended and an explanation to passengers that it was prank, but for the rest of the flight the cockpit crew had to get their own coffee, lunch was not served nor was it heated up for them. On another flight which the same captain and purser were operating, apparently when the captain went to put on his uniform jacket at the end of the flight, both sleeves of his jacket were sewn up and all his buttons missing.

With the World Expo on in Montreal we did a few charters there. With the schedule services picking up across the provinces P.W.A had started what they called the air-bus service between Edmonton and Calgary costing Passengers just $11.00 each way. The new DC6 service offered a minimum of frills for the one-hour flight. Passengers had to carry their own luggage aboard, buy tickets during the flight from a ticket agent/cabin attendant, and move quickly through a 10-minute airport check-in time. PWA flights departed from Edmonton Municipal Airport and not the international airport. Officials said the reduction in driving time and check-in time for travelers would reduce serious complaints from the present air travel procedure. Free parking for passengers was also offered.

The Edmonton municipal airport was situated next to the railway shunting yards. To operate the DC6 R2800 Pratt & Whitney engine machines was difficult due to the field length and altitude. The C54 engine DC6 B had water injections. The engines were brought up to take off power then the water meth switched on. The engine roar changed to almost a scream as the power took so giving the take off a major boost. The engine cowlings also affecting engine temperatures had to be watched carefully often juggling between engine temperature and airspeed affected by the engine cowls.

It's common knowledge that two captains flying together requires a lot of control as to who actually is the captain of the flight. Many arguments have been had in cockpits over the different understanding of rules. I flew with some great captains such as Harvey, Williams, Lightbrown, Clarke, Maclagan, Bray, Cwihun (Eskimo), Mackie and a fellow named Siddle. A terrible situation regarding two captains had occurred with Captain Siddle. On a check flight with another captain after take-off a call for the gear up was made. The captain under the flight check was in the left seat and captain Siddle was in the right (co-pilot) seat. The gear and flap levers are behind the centre console between the two pilots. The flap lever on the left side with the gear lever on the right near the co-pilot seat. In error the flap lever was lifted as it was closer to the right seat, where if the captain had been in his seat to operate the gear lever, he would reach across right seat to lift the gear. In this case Siddle, being used to having to reach across did just that and lifted the flap. The aircraft stalled and crashed into the shunting yards situated at the end of the runway. The death toll was heavy with blame being put on the pilots. It was understood that because Siddle had a slight physical shake it was from the crash and the nervous reaction. He was very nice guy, but the media crucified him, he got calls from some of the relatives of those killed labelling him a murderer. Aviation is not very forgiving and considering pilots hold more lives in their hands than any surgeon or doctor it is a pressured business needing nerves of steel. It's hard on family life with a high divorce rate.

At the time it was Canada's most deadly air crash. Another was when a Trans Canadian Airline North Star 810-9 flew into the top of Mount Slesse (which means Fang in the Halkomelem language) in the Canadian Rockies on a flight from Vancouver to Calgary. This was near Mount Baker a few miles from Abbotsford where I got my commercial license. The aircraft flew straight into the third peak of Mt. Slesse at more than cruising speed – and crashed in remote and dangerously inhospitable territory – very little information could be gleaned from the wreckage itself as to the cause of what was then the worst aircraft calamity in Canadian history. The wreckage and remains of the passengers and crew totaling 62 were discovered by mountaineers Elfrida Pigou, Geoffrey Walker, and David Cathcart, who were left on the mountain at the crash site. (though body parts found during the coroner's inquiry were interred in two common graves on the mountainside), Despite years of erosion and avalanches, the remains of the aircraft can be seen to this day. It was surrounded by mystery partly because the wreckage wasn't found for 5 months after the crash and no definite cause was ever established. In command was John Clarke an experienced TCA Captain.

Pacific Western operated seven Douglas DC-3's and seven Curtiss C 46 Commandos during the 1950's and 1960's, with many of these aircraft used to transport vast amounts of air cargo to the sites during the construction of the Dew Line, (Distant Early Warning) and later during the resupply phase. Both aircraft types were considered workhorses in their day. Pacific Western Airlines also had the two DC6 and two DC4 s, here is one offloading drums of fuel and lumber at Coppermine NWT (now Kugluktuk Nunavut) one of my old bush pilot bases at N67'49" Latitude W115'08' Longitude in the early 1960's, this with the assistance of local Inuvialuit residents and their dog teams.

Douglas DC 6   *Curtis C46*

Amazingly PWA was to build up a large C130 Hercules cargo division. One of the C130 crashed in the Congo when upon arrival at their destination from Beirut the navigation beacon had been turned off, in so they could not find the field and crashed running out of fuel. It was questionable what the cargo was, possibly forcing them not to go to their alternate. They lost another in South America killing some of the crew, the captain was a I believe a character of note Charley Mac Lagan with whom I had had the pleasure of flying with on the DC 6. Long after I left PWA they bought up Canadian Pacific Airlines expanded and PWA in name went out of business merging it became Canadian Airlines. The Hercules C130 operation was cancelled, however it did a lot of clandestine work. One other Captain was Wop May. It was rumoured that Baron Manfred Von Richthofen was shot down while chasing a pilot called May in WW1. They say the Baron was shot down by Capt. Roy Brown. Both Canadians.

Many funny things happen in cockpits one I remember was when a very attractive passenger was invited up to the cockpit, however, she brought with her a small child. The engineer/2nd Officer sits between the two pilots and has on his left a small round TV-like screen which allows him to select any engine and monitor the firing order and ignition condition. The small boy was invited to sit on his lap as his mother was entertained by the captain who was explaining the flight deck. The small boy looked at the flickering screen and asked what it was. The 2nd officer/flight engineer explained in child detail that it was his TV screen. The child asked to see Mickey Mouse and when the engineer explained that he could not do that the child severely bit into his arm. Another case involved me. When the DC6 was reversing thrust upon landing the 2nd officer had to push down on the mixture controls to lean out the engines as the captain powered into the reverse. Upon landing in Calgary, I leaned out the engines as required but too much and all the engines failed. I was lucky as I immediately went back to the rich selection and 3 of the engines fired up. The comments from the captain are not printable but guess who bought the beers that night?

*Pacific Western Airlines DC-4 aircraft **CF-PWJ** at Winter Harbour on Melville Island, NWT, N74'48" Latitude W110' 30" Longitude in April 1962. This aircraft is one of five DC-4's flown by PWA during the 1950s and 1960s and was used primarily for hauling cargo North from Edmonton and Yellowknife into the Arctic circle. In 1967 I was flying the DC6 similar in looks but a bit bigger, a passenger and cargo aircraft on similar Arctic routes such as Cambridge Bay. Temperatures were*

subzero, sometimes as low as minus 60 with wind factor taking it lower. The engines had to be kept warm or heated with Herman Nelsons as seen attached to the number 4 engine. Without these heaters and oil dilution they would never have started.

On one afternoon as I was doing the regular cockpit checks before a flight, two or three new hostesses walked by the aircraft. The captain remarked that one of them was a good looking Australian. Later I was to meet her, and little did I know what effect it would have on my life. The flat Glen and I shared had a pool plus there were a few hostesses in our building. Social parties, after flight parties and pool parties were part of the social life. I had come off a flight and was in the operations room when in walked the blond Australian. After introduction I understood her name to be Josie Forbes a recent arrival from Australia, being of Australian Irish decent. She had been sent to the USA as voted the top Australian hostess from Ansett ANA airlines to a world airline hostess conference in California. Here she met an American Sandy Flood and together they decided to see the USA and Canada. Hearing there were jobs at the World's Fare in Montreal they travelled by bus across the states to Quebec, Canada. On arrival in Montreal, they found there were no jobs but being an air hostess, heard that P.W.A. in Edmonton was hiring cabin attendants with better pay. Packing their bags they merrily jumped on the Greyhound bus and went to Edmonton a thousand miles away where they were hired.

Later they met up with a Canadian Bobbie Williams and the three of them became great friends in so sharing flats and costs. I started dating Josie on a regular basis attending BBQ and social parties. One day while having a swim in our pool I was approached by a chap who I could not immediately recognize. It turned out to be Graham Marks, one of the guys who had crossed the Atlantic in the Kilros. They say it's a small world but what a surprise to meet by accident so far away from the Caribbean and after all the years. He was in the kitchen fitting business I believe but we did not see each other again as he was moving out of town to Vancouver. It was summer and with the top down (topless as we joked) on the Mustang Josie and I travelled to Banff and Jasper. It brought back memories of my first visit hitching around the world. Times had changed. The Rockies and that area are very beautiful, but winter was coming and so was the expected company seasonal lay off. It was a case of last in first out so after six months I and others were laid off for the winter.

Max Ward a pioneer bush pilot had started Wardair flying a Puss moth (Small single-engine Biplane) in the Northern Territories and Arctic. He had expanded to numerous aircraft such as Bristol's, DC3, Twin Otters, and Beavers. His company had operated a leased DC7 doing returning war bride charters to the United Kingdom. It was so successful that he purchased a B727, which became the most utilized B727 per flight time over 24 hours on record. 19 flight hours over 24 hours. It shuttled back and forth at an amazing rate. He was expanding so I applied for the job of

2nd officer as was the norm to man the engineer's seat and relieve the captain and first officer. Much to my delight, I was accepted and prepared to change airlines. At the very last moment, Ward decided to hire fully certified ground engineers and train them up to B727 flight engineers. I was very disappointed as I felt Ward was going places. (I was finding out fast what Aviation is as a business)

WARDAIR B727 1966

I advised Josie that she should consider them as she had far more experience than the girls he was hiring. In addition, she would get to see overseas locations, whereas PWA was not operating overseas.

Amazingly on a P.W.A. Airbus (not the aircraft) flight from Calgary she accidentally spilt coffee over the lap and into a passenger's briefcase. He was a Wardair director, being so impressed by the way she handled the incident offered her a job. This she accepted providing her two roommates Sandy and Bobbie came with her. All three ended up being employed by Wardair with Josie later becoming the assistant chief hostess at the new base in Toronto. Helen Mc Lagan was the chief hostess in Edmonton with Peter Highfield holding the position of chief pilot at the new Toronto base. Over the years Peter and I became long-standing friends and still are. I had been able to secure an airline discount ticket through PWA for my father to come over from South Africa. Since my sister's marriage in 1964 he had not been able to travel much, so it was good that he could get over seeing his grandchild and daughter. He arrived at the start of my lay off, so I packed my bags, bid goodbye to friends and sweethearts deciding to head for Vancouver where my sister lived. With my father I drove in my pride and joy convertible Mustang the beautiful scenic road via Banff, Jasper, and the magnificent Rockies. It was a wonderful trip through the Kicking Horse Mountain pass, which is on the Coquihalla highway and is one of the most treacherous highways in the world. Rising through the steep mountain passes in British Columbia, it is a gauntlet of brutal weather, snow and white knuckle driving in the winter months. The "Coq" is also the main artery between east and west and I was to drive it a few more times to date Josie. With the autumn forests, and snow-capped mountains both of us had a thoroughly enjoyed trip. We had not been very close, so it was good to spend some time together. He was tough father but if anything, he did teach me how to survive.

Arriving in Vancouver there was room for our father at my sister's small house, but I decided to stay at a communal house I knew off known as

KIWI House. Board only but a lot of good colonial chaps to join up with. It was while there that I heard of a fellow in Toronto, a certain Seymour Greene who was attempting to set up an air cargo company in Antigua. I was able to make contact with him explaining that it had been a dream of mine to return to the Caribbean and start an air cargo company. I faxed him my qualifications to which he replied favourably. Next followed a few phone calls and a suggestion by me that I would consider working for him on a reasonably small salary, with initial expenses covered by him i.e. air ticket and one month's accommodation. Followed after two years by a percentage interest in the company. This he agreed to and the next thing I was off to Antigua possibly to build my air cargo dream. I left my cherished Mustang in the hands of a good friend with the promise that I would as soon as possible supply funds to ship it to South Africa. They were great guys and eventually did ship it for me.

On the flight which required me to transit in Montreal I met an Australian estate agent by the name of Allen Curtis. Over some time, he and I became friends during which I ended up buying a 160acre farm in Cobram, in the state of Victoria, Australia. For the next 39 years I share farmed it with a neighbour farmer, John Ryan.

Many years later I bought a one third share in another 38000 acres sheep and cattle farm. I and two pilot partners, Cooper and Row, attempted to farm the large sparrow grass property from afar. Working as pilots but attempting to run a farm was hard going. Regretfully we ended up losing it due to the collapse of our wool board quota and drought. We were unable to sell our stock, feeding costs were out of budget, there was no water, transport costs to costly, and stock was dying. The bank foreclosed. All this established a foothold for me in Australia in the event anything went politically wrong in South Africa. Little did I know how much I would get involved with Australia?

A DC6 turned into a restaurant. (Note square tail as compared to DC4)

Flying the Caribbean.

It was great to be back in the warm Caribbean sun and as I stepped off the Air Canada Vanguard aircraft, the smell of the sea and island came back to me. Here I was only 4 years after being a yacht bum, penniless and without a career about to venture into the flying world as a DC3 Captain and charter pilot.

Seymour Greene known as CY met me and took me off to meet a fellow by the name of Mike Novisky who had rented a house near the airport and offered to share it with me. Mike was an American working at the USA Nassau Apollo space centre on the island as a technician. These stations in conjunction with others around the world known as Apollo stations were the relay stations attempting to get a man on the moon. The base had many assets such as duty-free liquor, an open-air movies stadium. A duty-free shopping centre and a fast-food outlet. A great asset to anyone who was in any way a friend or related to someone working on the base. Mike and I hit it off straight away, so I moved in to share the three-bed roomed house and over the years became good friends. Later I met Margo Cys' wife. Andy Hunter the ground engineer a broad Scot, plus another pilot Joe Shaja who was a Polish Canadian. Joe was an ex Canadian air force pilot who together with his wife had moved down from Canada to work with CY on developing the company. He had earlier joined the new Zambian air force and told a story about when he was to fly a DC 3 over the Livingstone airfield to celebrate their independence and new air force. Men in the rear of the aircraft where to fire vary pistols out of the removed windows so creating a spectacular fly by. Joe instructed them to fire them down, unfortunately this set fire to the newly cut grass around the field and burnt down the tents, bringing the whole show to a sudden end. He claimed it was a matter of speed as to whether he got to the airport boarding a departing aircraft or was escorted out of the country or possibly to jail.

Later I was taken to the office a small little room at the airport, which could be described as an old British colony building where I met Patricia Patrick a local girl who was the secretary. I had to go to Trinidad to write the British Colonial license enabling me to fly West Indian registered aircraft. I had to do a course on performance A, which was something I dreaded as it entailed an exam on a Viscount working the performance figures. I was not very good at this but succeeded to pass the exams and got my West Indian A.T.P. License. While staying in a small B & B near the Trinidad airport, my neighbour had his pants stolen out of the guarded window to his room. It contained his wallet and personal effects. Theft was common and, in this case, the thieves' modus operandi was to use a fishing rod with a barbed hook. They would then reach into the room, hook up the desired clothing and extract it via the open window. If one was to wake and attempted to grab the fishing rob, broken razor blades would have been attached to the rod. The blades would do serious damage to your hand and the likelihood of losing a finger was possible. In so I was warned not to leave clothes in sight and over the following years learnt to be very aware of theft on the islands.

Later to facilitate me flying into St Martin and the tiny island of St Bart's I got a Dutch West Indian endorsement. St Bart's was a hell of a sand strip situated across the small island ending in the sea. On the left side of the approach was a religious cross. One had to have one's wing below the cross arms and then side slip madly down the hill landing on the 700-foot sand strip which ended in the sea. Many did not make it and there was a small collection of aircraft wrecks on the side of the runway. The island had quite a history as it was said that during the war the chief of the island would entertain the German navy submariners at his local bar and sold fuel to them. They would hide their submarines in the reefs and come ashore to be entertained. It was also rumoured that the chief of the island had sired children from his own daughters. Such was island life! The other serious runway was later built along the mountainside of Saba, the volcanic island I had earlier discussed in my sailing days. This was also a hair-raising approach and landing with heavy up and down drafts prior to touching down on an uphill undulating runway. The pilots from Windward Island airways generally operated out of these strips and were great pilots flying Otters, Islanders and even an Aztec.

Life for me settled down to a great period in what would turn out to be my journey of ten men's lives. I was employed so building flight hours in command, had an income, great climate and was flying bigger equipment. Seagreen Air Transport was expanding; we bought a Beech 18 from the United States army surplus sales. Later I went to the Bahamas to fly back a DC3 we had bought from Bahama Airlines. As Cy was not a rated DC3 Pilot, Joe was leaving so I became chief pilot with a growing pilot contingent of four. I had just turned 25.

There were many pretty French, America, English and Canadian girls visiting the islands, so social life was good, I had joined the infamous "New Club" a very old British type of social club in the centre of St Johns the capital town of Antigua. Many a good night was spent at English harbour tavern, a recently resurrected yacht and sailing centre in the old Nelsons dockyard, later becoming a sailing centre of the world. Flying was mainly charter but some of the passengers were quite VIP. among one was Jackie Kennedy who had a Jeweler on Guadeloupe the neighbouring French island. She would visit Antigua a lot staying at the wealthy Mellon's Island home, uncannily especially when Onassis yacht was lying off the South of the island. With the arrival of the DC3, I was now a Captain at 26 years of age and building flight hours. The company in its expansion had hired another pilot and we to became friends until his death in 2013. He was Gary Dalton an ex Canadian air force guy who was if I remember correctly, in Air Traffic control. His wife had departed with their children, leaving him for a good friend. Therefore, as a bachelor the island was good place for him. One day while standing at the check in counter for Caribbean airlines talking to the manager, a fellow walked up and asked when the next flight to Porto Rico was. In the discussion that followed it appeared he was a Canadian pilot who had left Winnipeg to join a company in Tobago Island a neighbour island off Trinidad. Apparently, on arrival there lock stock and barrel which included wife, the job was non-existent, and he was now desperately trying to get back to Canada to look for work. I explained that Seagreen was expanding and as he was DC 3 endorsed, plus Joe Shaja was leaving maybe we could use him. We walked over to our office spoke with Cy and that night Bob Beck joined our merry band of men. Bob and I were to enjoy over the years many good times and to this day we are still in touch.

The company was now moving into concentrating mainly on cargo. The opposition started and owned by Frank de Lisle, was LIAT airlines (Leeward Island Air Transport) mainly passengers using HS748 and twin Otters. It too was expanding mainly on their schedule runs as far South as Trinidad and North to Porto Rico covering almost all the Caribbean, American Virgin Islands later including the British Virgin Islands. Therefore, for us to compete for passengers with LIAT was not a good idea. About this time Frank De Lisle sold 50% of LIAT to B.W.I.A. (British West Indian Airlines) based in Trinidad. They had a schedule operation using B727 running from Trinidad, Barbados, Antigua, Miami and later New York. Competition was increasing also from Porto Rico with charter companies opening up and rivalry starting to appear. On one occasion operating a cargo flight to Porto Rico, San Juan airport, whilst loading my out bound freight, Sexdos Dias owner of a startup cargo company, and an opposition company run by Fucundo decided to have a gunfight across the loading ramp. To my knowledge no was injured but a couple of aircraft received a bullet hole or two.

Some of these charter companies were using old and unkempt DC3 and C46.aircraft. Many did not make it, one or two lay on the beach around the islands, others were never seen again, lost in the surrounding oceans. It was once when departing from San Juan I very nearly came to grief. I had loaded a 6,000lb load onto our Beech 18. I then had to enter the cockpit by climbing through the side window. On take off some of the load moved back putting my trim out, I frantically was able to leave my seat, fly with one hand and haul some sacks of vegetable back into the cockpit and right seat. This corrected the load shift. However, this was not the end of the problem as at the intersection out bound from San Juan International airport there is a VOR radial from St Thomas marking a turn towards St Thomas Island. I was in light cloud so was on instruments. As I turned to the right intercepting the radial my artificial horizon showed I was turning left. I increase my turn applying more right rudder. Suddenly I noticed my turn and bank was all to the left side now counter acting any movement of my controls. Then my airspeed started to increase and the VSI showed a sudden climb. I was totally unable to read my instruments and became confused as to where or what was happening. At this point my altimeter was unwinding and I sort of guessed I was in a spin but still in cloud. I was feeling disorientated, one engine failed, the altimeter read 1500 feet from 6,000 feet I had been at, the other engine failed then suddenly I broke cloud almost inverted. Grabbing the mixture controls I slammed them into full rich at the same time attempting to right the over loaded Beech now having a visual horizon to work with. Thankfully one engine started allowing me to skim about 200 feet off the water. With one engine at full power, I could not hold altitude or climb, and the water was getting closer. Actuating the primer to my relief the second engine burst into life giving the power to start a slow climb away from the waves. All other operations such as the controls and engines were now operational, but the flight instruments were dead.

A big explanation to air traffic control about loss of power was needed explaining my sudden departure from altitude. I somehow got away with it and decided I had had enough excitement for the day so headed across the Anegada passage for Antigua and a stiff rum and coke. Upon arriving in Antigua, I got hold of Andy our Scottish engineer and ground maintenance man, explaining what had happened. His comment was laddie you were lucky. Later after a full maintenance examination, we found that the Beech 18, being an ex-military machine did not have an electrical standby artificial horizon as required on civilian machines. That the main cause of the problem was that a mesh filter on the instrument vacuum system which had a fine wire support, holding and backing a fabric type cloth had disintegrated. The remains then were sucked up into the instruments so causing the sudden and disorientating failure of the blind flying vacuum operated cockpit instruments. Had it been at night I would not be writing this script. An electrical standby instrument was ordered and immediately fitted before the Beech was flown again.

On another charter, I had a very strange meeting take place. I had flown the Beech over to Montserrat Island about 35 miles West of Antigua. This was the island that a Pan Am B727 inbound from Trinidad had declared that they had Antigua in sight and cancelled Visual Flight Rule conditions. They altered course to the left positioning for a long final onto runway 04 in Antigua. There was very little cloud cover, so they were descending visually. Why and what happened next nobody will ever know as they descended through a small cloud right into Montserrat volcanic mountain driving the aircraft so far into the earth that nothing could be recovered. All that is left of the aircraft, crew and 52 passengers is a small plaque of remembrance on the mountainside.

It was early morning as I was loading a load of fish when a chap arrived in a taxi. He approached me and asked when LIAT would arrive. I explained that they had come and left, being the only flight of the day.

He was an ordinary looking man, in shorts with short socks and shoes. Typical of an English appearance and an up-market accent. He shook his head explaining he needed to get to Antigua as he had to connect with B.O.A.C that night to London. I said that if he did not mind the smell and a hard metal cockpit right seat, he could get a lift with me. He accepted so after I had completed loading the fish that he had to climb over to get into the cockpit, we duly departed for Antigua. During the flight and in conversation he said he was involved in some aviation and was looking around the island. I took no notice of it as it was a short flight, and I was already in contact with Bird Island airport control in Antigua. On leaving the aircraft, he thanked me and said he would be at the Sugar Mill Hotel, which was just up the road from the airport if I would care for a drink. I thanked him and went about the unloading. That night, I think with Gary, we stopped off at the Sugar Mill bar, as it was one of our usual after work haunts. There at the bar was the gentleman in question. I introduced Gary and we ordered a drink. He introduced himself as Adrian and offered to buy the drinks. Being lowly paid pilots, we accepted, later after light insignificant conversation about flying in the Caribbean we left him to the book he was reading. On leaving we bid him goodbye, suggesting if he ever came again to look us up. He offered me his card with his name being Adrian Swire, asking if he could ever be of assistance to contact him. Nothing more was ever discussed or seen of him again. We did wonder if he was ever able to maybe get some sort of aviation business going.

Later that year I was up in Nassau buying the DC3, VP-LIX from Bahama Airlines. As I walked down the office passage with the Chief Pilot Captain P Farmington, I saw the very same gentleman walk out of an office in front of me. He glanced at me as I approached. We greeted each other cordially as someone you may have met before. He asked why I might be here in the Bahamas to which I replied I was buying a DC3. He nodded and proceeded on his way. Turning to Farrington, I saw a look of amazement on his face. He asked if I knew who that man was. My reply was he looked vaguely familiar, to which he replied that that was the CEO and managing director of the Hong Kong based Swire group who had just bought Bahamas Airlines in an attempt to start an around the world service for their major airline Cathay Pacific. Swire group are a major company in Hong Kong with investments in numerous successful businesses. I was amazed to think he travelled in a dirty old Beech 18 cargo machine as an insignificant passenger. When I told Farrington the brief story, he could not believe it, but I agreed that Adrian seemed a nice fellow. Much later in my life, I did call on him for some help in the aviation world, and he obliged.

The company was doing well, we had the cargo DC3, the Beech 18 and an Aztec. The Aztec did the passenger charters. We were now considering another DC3 or even a DC4 but for me there was a problem ahead. This related to my agreement with Cy in the early days of discussion, regarding shares.

Point of aviation history here is that on the North mountainside of Guadeloupe, just above the tree line lies a B707 pan caked against the mountain. It was a flight that turned the wrong way and crashed into the mountain after entering clouds. I understood it was a cargo machine carrying steel rods. On impact the rods penetrated the cockpit killing the crew. It would not be the first jet to crash into the island mountains as Pan Am did exactly the same thing into Montserrat.

The islands were expanding, and tourism was beginning to grow rapidly. A casino had been built on the South shore, which was to be one of our charterers. It started with late night call from the casino manager asking if we could do a quick charter to Porto Rico. It was agreed and the Piper Aztec was readied for the return flight of 4 hours. A vehicle met me at the airport and a single man carrying a black brief type of attaché case boarded the aircraft. Without any further ado we flew to San Juan, Porto Rico, landed and taxied over to the customs area. I presented the usual paper requirements while the passenger departed into the terminal. Returning almost immediately, still carrying what appeared to be the same black attaché bag. Filing the necessary flight plans we flew back to

Antigua arriving almost at sunrise where the same black vehicle met us and departed with the passenger.

It turned out that it was a money transfer flight and over time I did a few of these becoming well known to the casino bosses so much so that I did the flights without a passenger. The confidence they had in me was great as every time I went to the casino to visit Josie, who was to become my wife was given cash to play on the house. A funny incident happened when in later years I got tickets for my folks to visit Antigua and so we went to the casino. My mother was again given token cash to play and won a small jackpot on the slot machines. As the machine paid out in buckets of coins, she thought she had broken the machine and was further shocked that she could keep the payout. Having never been in a casino or won something like this in her life, she insisted she take the winnings back to my house and count it out on the coffee table.

The casino management were very nice people and certainly very courteous. In fact, I kept in touch with one of the directors, Mr Jaffee from New York and much later in my career I met up with him and his family, who entertained me and four of the crew members very well. He had asked me to buy him some Kruger Rands, so on one of the New York stopovers I advised him I had brought them with me. He sent two Cadillac's to fetch any of the crew who would care for a night out. Two stewardesses the First Officer and I accepted. He and his wife then entertained us at his beautiful home in New Jersey. Later we were taken to a night club called "Cloud 9" all at his expense. Upon being delivered back to our New York hotel to our surprise the drivers gave each of us a present explaining it was Christmas and these where from the Jaffee family. The two girls got gold bracelets, the other pilot got gold cufflinks and I got a stereo radio, record player.

Beech 18

Charter flying was not always dull, for instance we got a charter from the Royal Bank of Canada shared with I think it was the Bank of Nova Scotia to take two representatives to the island of Anguilla to collect the bank funds. This was because a mini revolution had started up involving St Kitts and the other islands of Anegada. Upon arrival on the dirt strip in Anguilla a car was waiting to quickly take the passengers to the respective banks. I had placed the aircraft in a position to be able to do a quick take-off. Out of nowhere suddenly two cars approached the aircraft and parked in front of the engines. A group of local men jumped out and ordered me out of the aircraft. They then decided to rough me up and started to search the interior of the plane. They accused me and the company of flying arms into St Kitts, demanding with a gun under my nose, to tell them what I was doing there. One man with a pistol in his hand attempted to slap me but just caught my lip. Not finding anything in the aircraft, they accepted the fact I was only on a charter with two businessmen. I had been cautious not to mention who or what they were there for. Eventually after about a hair raising 20 minutes they left, warning me not to come back. Almost as they were out of sight the car with the two bank representatives approached from the opposite side of the runway. I explained what had happened and suggested we depart ASAP. The car driver with this information then made a hasty departure leaving a cloud of dust. I was able to quickly start up and move into a take-off position when across the airfield I saw the two cars, which had the aggressors in, approaching at speed. I just applied full power halfway down the runway which the cars were now approaching me on a collision course apparently to stop me getting airborne, I was just able to complete the take-off skimming over the cars.

Another incident took place at French/Dutch island of St Martin. As we did not have a clear schedule license to operate into USA territory, we arranged for a USA charter company to meet our DC3 with their C46 at St Martin. We had a load of 8000 pounds to transship. I arrived early at 8am to wait for the C46, however it by 10am had not turned up. My load of live lobster had to be alive on arrival at Porto Rico and we were now in trouble as the tropical heat was intensifying in the aircraft. To save the load I and the co-pilot stripped down to our underwear and off loaded the sacks of lobster into the sea. The co-pilot Ron Thibou was not very happy about the predicament he found himself in. Thankfully by 14:00 the C46 arrived so allowing us to extract the sacks of lobster from the sea alive and reloaded on to the C46 destined to the market in Porto Rico.

C-46

As a struggling charter company, the loss of a load at $5:00 a pound would have been a catastrophe. Our business with the lobster (panula argus) was growing rapidly. I was able to fly over to Barbuda, an island 35 miles from the Antigua coast. It was slave breeding colony years back governed by Lord Codrington. It had a very short strip for a Beech 18 being only 1200 meters, so with a load of lobster and sometimes turtle a take-off over the beach was hair raising. An engine failure of even a cough would have put me into the sea. We had started out at about 700 pounds a week but now we were at about 8000 pounds. Regretfully on looking back we had caused the fisherman to almost destroy the island lobster stock. They were using every considerable means to catch lobster, some grossly underweight and size, plus dynamite to stun them. The reefs were dying, I could see a disastrous end to the stock. It played heavily on my mind.

The return flights usually were filed with meat and dairy products, bound for the merchants in St John the city of Antigua. A lot of the meat was marked time expired, but this did not worry the merchants. It certainly was not our problem. At this point if it could put into our aircraft, we flew it. Dynamite to British Guyana which required special loading and flight clearance from Porto Rico. Cement, telephone units to Aruba and Curacao, one of the Dutch ABC Island which also staked claim to having the biggest brothel in the world.100 rooms. Machinery to the other islands, yacht masts so long, the door had to be removed and the mast tied out and down extending beyond the rear of the aircraft. Bob Beck and I were the two DC3 Captains. Being short of crew another South African who I had met in Canada and had good bush Northern territory experience was hired. Don Burnett duly arrived moving in with Mike and myself. Being South African he too was very pleased to get back to the tropics and away from the cold northern Canada flying. Being both high spirited parties and things we got up to will not be disclosed at this point of my writing. We increased our DC3 pilots by also hiring Joe Reed from Canada and Chris Benton as a co-pilot. If my memory is correct, I believe Joe's wife had been a nun. Flying in the Caribbean and

West Indies was paradise compared to the Arctic or for that matter any place I had flown. I was flying as hard as I could building up constructive medium heavy DC3 twin engine command hours.

On one flight which required the Aztec and the Beech 18 to go to Porto Rico Don was flying the Aztec and I the Beech 18. Returning over the 95-mile open water Anegada passage, I got an indication that I had an engine fire on the right engine. It was at night miles over open water; I could see the glow of what looked like flames on the cowl of the engine. The load was heavy, usually overloaded. The ability to stay up on one engine was not available to me. Don flew up alongside and clearly confirmed that the right engine looked to be on fire. To ditch in the ocean at the position I was at was a definite case of controlled suicide. I had to make the island of St Kitts distantly visible ahead. I attempted to throttle back but immediately started to lose altitude. To attempt to dive and maybe blow the fire out was not a good idea. Don advised that from what he could see it appeared the flames were diminishing. I then decided as there was no runway lights or firefighting equipment available at this time of night in St Kitts, now additionally covered in sea mist, it was best to press on to Antigua 65 miles further on. Eventually we arrived at Antigua and landed at Bird airport with the fire department on standby. Coming to a complete stop I cut the fuel flow and ignition to the right engine immediately the fire went out having been fanned by the prop wash. Towing the aircraft into the maintenance bay it was discovered that it was not the engine but the rubber flange under the cowl that being saturated with old oil had caught fire. It went down in my flying history as another one of those not so good days.

More expansion was being considered in the form of a DC4. One small problem was starting to rear it head and that was the possibility of drugs being smuggled to the USA in our cargo. With this now on our minds more stringent checks and security was increased. Nobody wanted to go to jail. However much later I was told Seagreen had been hit by this smuggling problem. During this time, I had remained in contact with

Josie. To do this required me to go up to the cable and wireless station and bribe the night operator to get me a telephone line through to Toronto. There was no international phone connection to our small local network. We did have telex and telegrams, so business was slow relating to correspondence.

The point of marriage was now also coming into my life. I was 28 years old and felt inclined to consider a family, which was one thing I still had to do. My adventurous life was again knocking at the door. The Viet Nam war was now on, and air cargo movement was in heavy demand. I heard by the grape vine that a company called Air America Airways was looking for pilots of fortune to fly night dropping into North Viet Nam in a clandestine dangerous operation. The aircraft were Otters, Dornier's, Beavers, Helio couriers offloading arms and munitions to the supportive mercenary Vietnam fighters. The pilots flew without uniforms or any identification. No name tags on their clothing or anything that might identify them as foreigners. If caught or shot down death was imminent. This I found out later was horrific. The money was very good by any standard, so with no responsibilities I decided to go have a look see. I would then have a bank roll to consider marriage as my present wage was not doing it.

I was due for some leave so without telling anyone of my intension, I used an agreement we had with Pan Am to buy a 90% discount ticket on an around the world itinerary. Travelling to New York I went on to Honolulu. I had always dreamed of seeing these romantic islands. From there I travelled on to Bangkok where I made contact with Air America which was C.A.T, (civil air transport) representatives. Air America was a chartered subsidiary of the C.I.A. which did clandestine operations for them. Bangkok was the rest and recuperation city for all American troops. It was teaming with soldiers and Pat Pong Street was a sex area I had never in my life thought existed. If in your wildest thoughts one thought of a sex act, these two streets had it. One night while sitting at a bar with a couple of American soldiers, the fellow next to asked if I had ever had oral sex in a bar, my reply was no. He pushed his bar stool back and there between him and the bar was a small young girl offering oral sex to us as she was undoing his zipper. The act cost him $2:00, a huge sum to the little girl. I definitely declined.

Waiting to make more inroads to see if I could or wanted to fly for this mercenary operation, I heard some horror stories of the operation with helicopter pilots and some of the fixed wing crew that had gone down in North Viet Nam. Death was almost immediate by the most lingering or torturous manner. As an example, being strung up inverted with wire and skinned alive was one of the norms. Bamboo impaling on human excretion covered stakes was another. The North Vietnamese were merciless and cruel. My experience as a bush pilot counted a lot and I was accepted to do a trial trip. To go forward on this part of my story is of no interest and becomes a bit involved. I will say that I decided this war was not my war. I could not come to the realization because young Americans were being killed against the advice of world leaders. There appeared to be political involvement which also included ammunition factories near the Clark Air Force base in the Philippines, owned by American politicians. General De Gaulle had strongly advised the USA to stay out of the skirmish indicating that they the French had pulled out as it was a local issue. Churchill also supported this. Eventually if my memory is correct, after I believe 20 years, American troops were beaten with a loss of over 50 thousand young men.

While there I had met an Australian who was buying used and damaged USA army engineering equipment. This was shipped to Sydney where he refurbished the machinery and sold it to corporations who required such used equipment. He was a good entrepreneur, nice guy who invited me to visit him in Sydney. He was leaving in a day's time. I decided there and then to proceed on and return to Antigua hoping in the prospect of getting married. The two days stay with his family in Sydney was great. I so enjoyed the Aussies being sort of kissing cousins to us South

Africans, then known as Yarpies. They sure could drink beer but had some strange drinking hours. It was called swill time when at about 6.00 pm the bars were closed to allow the men to take themselves home and to give the wives their wage money. The bars were cleaned with a fire hose and opened again at 7.00 pm. Josie's folks lived in Adelaide, so I contacted them to suggest we meet. This I did asking her father if I could have her hand in marriage all agreed and it was to be kept a secret until I could get back to Toronto. Being full Irish, this also was a great idea to have some whiskey.

The next morning with a hangover I was not quite sure if I had gone ahead with the marriage proposal idea. Seeing me off they all confirmed the matter, suggesting we have a drink on it. I gracefully turned them down and bid goodbye with hugs and kisses boarding my flight to Sydney and on to Hong Kong for a quick stay. At that time the old runway at Kia Tak was in use which ran along the shoreline. Later I would get to know Hong Kong and the checkerboard approach very well. I headed to Beirut, a wonderful Mediterranean city at the time but later raised by war. A quick trip to Istanbul, then on to Johannesburg and Durban. My folks were very pleased to see me, but I fell ill due mainly I think to travel fatigue. The wonderful thing was that Josie through the interairline agreement had been able to get a rebate ticket to Durban. She joined me for the few days I had at home and thereby met my folks. Upon her return to Toronto, she showed some pictures of her trip. One was of her and our African housemaid. One of the girls remarked that it must have been nice to meet her future mother-in-law. She explained otherwise but even then, in 1969 it was hard to believe how naive the world was to South Africa. The general opinion was that Africa was African. The fact that there are Egyptians, Algerians and white-born people also living there for decades is not understood caused by blatant education and media ignorance. My grandchildren would become 6th generation South Africans,

Three days later we departed to New York via Johannesburg and Dakar. Interesting note here was that BOAC had been commandeered there a few years earlier by revolutionary troops. The crew and passengers were told to stand under the wing. Then instructed to run to a perimeter fence out in the hot sun. The captain refused to run so was shot in the leg. I never knew what the final outcome was. Arriving in New York required a quick transit at the Pan Am world centre back to Antigua. My dream of circumventing the World was now complete.

Time was moving along, a year and a half had already gone by. I decided it was time to approach Josie who now had visited a few times to see if she could take on island life is so consider marrying me. I might add in respect to her being a faithful catholic, she never stayed with me. She always stayed at our neighbour's house. If any marriage was on the book of life, it was going to be a white wedding. I had got my father to buy a 1.25 carat diamond in South Africa. Plus got a design drawn up which consisted of the diamond embraced by a set of aviation wings in white gold. After it was made, he hid it in the centre of a cassette thereby mailing it to me declaring it only as a family recording. With the ring finally in my hands I jump seated (an agreement between airlines to allow uniformed aircrew to travel on the spare cockpit seat) a ride with B.W.I.A. (British West Indian Airlines) to Toronto. After a dinner on the town and back at the girl's apartment, I formally on my knee asked her to marry me. She agreed in so starting a new chapter in both our lives at the ripe old age of 28 years. Departing, I left behind the girls Sandy Flood and Bobbie Williams to start making wedding arrangements. It was big step for Josie as she was the second in command as assistant chief hostess of WARDAIR, a secure job in a fast-developing company and a good city life, supported by many admirers. I returned to Antigua via the same jump seat approval and announced to Cy and friend my intention to marry. It did not take long on the small island for the word to get around, plus I would like to think of a few broken-hearted young ladies whom I knew quite well.

The wedding was duly organized by the girls and set for 26 October1969. It was to be a full catholic affair which required me to do some schooling by a priest. A church was booked with the use of a friend's Rolls Royce to bring in the bride. Mattie Mace an old family friend of Josie's from Edmonton was called upon to give away the bride as Australia was too far for her father to travel. On my side my mother insisted she would be there, so she had booked a ticket from South Africa to witness the wedding celebration of her long-lost son. Two friends from Antigua one a co-pilot from Trinidad Teddy Greel and the other my house mate Mike Novischy who agreed to be best man, with Dan Callaghan and Bill Cosgrave grooms' ushers. Teddy was one of the young bachelors of the island group, a bit of a wild guy but played a beautiful quarto four stringed guitar. With that and copious amounts of rum many a good night on the beaches had passed. With the wedding now all organized and underway the three of us flew up to Toronto a day before the ceremony. This allowed me to have a stag night with my mates and a few guys who I knew in Toronto. One being Joe Shaja ex Seagreen and a few of Wardair pilots, Peter Highfield and Jerry Fatheringham being two of them.

Topless bars were the incoming thing in Toronto at the time, so it was to one of these that we descended upon. A very liquid and merry night was had by all, including the festive celebration which somehow a topless waitress got involved in. Thankfully it was agreed that any pictures taken would be destroyed. Miraculously we all got back to the hotel in one piece, waking early to dress, sobering up etc. departing in time for the church and the full nuptial ceremony.

The church was beautifully decorated with me, Mike and the best men in white tuxedoes. At this point an accident nearly happened. With the effects of the night before a toilet was urgently needed. Being in the back of the church none could be seen. There was a water font mounted in the wall which became a serious point of discussion. Was it blasphemy and how many hail Mary's we would have to pay. Teddy seeing a small door off the passage saved the day as it was much to our relief a toilet. The Rolls arrived with Josie who then was walked down the aisle by Mattie in a grey suit. She was a beautiful girl in her white flowing dress looked magnificent, with the bride's maids Sandy Flood, Bobbie Williams, and Janie Grimwood following dressed in turquoise gowns. Most of the congregation were airline friends, so it followed that it would be an airline party. With the vows and ceremony underway a problem developed which brought the congregation to muffled laugh. Mike, who was on my left, was as we all were, kneeling on a small stand like a podium on the step to the main alter level. Suddenly there was a crash as Mike and stand fell backwards down the steps. This was definitely the effect of the night before; however, a quick recovery was made, and the ceremony completed. Walking out as man and wife we were met by the contingent of fellow pilots and hostesses plus family.

The reception was held at a large private home belonging to a friend. It was the 26 October and the first snow had fallen so it was a great background for some beautiful photos of us and the wedding party. The party went on into the night, but Josie and I were able to slip away to a hotel near the airport. The boys had fixed my car, so as I drove away bits of sardine, powder and flakes of paper cascaded out of the air conditioner. Not to forget the traditional cans tied to the rear bumper. All this forced me to stop and remove the noisy cans before entering the freeway. We had a bottle of champagne delivered to the honeymoon suite which was consumed liberally.

The morning required us to dress and be at the airport by 10:00am. Max Ward, the owner of the airline had given Josie two return tickets to Hawaii allowing us to spend our honeymoon at Honolulu. Flying there on one of Wardair's B707 was great as the crew were either part of the wedding party or knew us well. The rest of the passengers were all mainly woman on a barbershop quartets venture. At one point I was asked by one of the girls to carry up to the front section a small box of wine. As I moved up the aisle two very merry women decided it was time to harass me as the new husband. To do this they grabbed me around the waist placing their hands on my groin and privates, this brought the remaining passengers to hysterics and a lot of teasing and suggestive comments. It was all in good fun with the flight proceeding to Hawaii.

We spent a great week travelling around and seeing the sites. I put a deposit on a piece of ground being developed as an investment. Regretfully later I was forced to sell it as funds were needed for other more important matters. Returning to Toronto we picked up Josie's possessions and flew back to Antigua. Accommodation in Antigua was scarce, but I had been able to rent a small cabana about 100 meters from the sea on the Northeast side in a relatively nice location. The cabana consisted of a main room big enough to have a fold out double bed. A shower bathroom and a kitchenette. We were very cramped, but it was a startup home. Just up the road was a very interesting couple with whom we became good friends. They were group Captain David Torrens and his Swedish wife Tova. David had been the Air vice Marshal for the Royal Air force in Washington. He knew my relation Air Marshal Portal from his military day's part of which he was in charge of Eastly in Kenya. David was with bomber command being shot down over Germany. He spent 4 years in a prison camp and was therefore known as a "Creaky", a name given to ex-prisoners of war. He was also I believe a member of the silent committee behind the great escape. Being released by the allies he found a baby's pram into which he stowed his meagre possessions and walked out of Germany to be evacuated back to England. While transferred to Washington where he held a high position in the RAF, he was struck by a vehicle while crossing a road. Being severely injured he was medically retired and moved to Antigua for a place to spend his days in peace and quiet.

Tova was a character of note. There were always the 5:00pm sundowners which at times were hysterical with the libation being well overdone. Some of David's stories of the war and post war together with the shenanigans the two had got up to in their travels both in the diplomatic core and privately were a laugh a minute. They had no children, so we sort of stood in for that missing part of their life. It was good for Josie as a newcomer to the island was not easy.

Occasionally I would go over to Guadeloupe to fly some interisland charters for Air France. These were to the small islands of Grand Bourg (Maria Galante) and Iles de Santes, situated between Guadeloupe and the island of Dominica. Both have very short and rough airstrips close to the water's edge. Josie came with me so we would spend a weekend savouring the French island atmosphere wine and cuisine. The Beech 18 had a very short and stubby undercarriage. Something like the C46 was known as a widow maker requiring an experienced pilot to fly. The only time in my life I ground looped an aircraft was landing on one of these islands. I might add much to the amusement of watching native islanders but not I am afraid to the 10 passengers about to embark for Guadeloupe. Not being able to explain in island French I did get some very suspicious looks from the boarding passengers who had just seen the aircraft gyrate down the runway almost ending up on the beach.

The island of St Lucia had one domestic airport at "Castries "and an abandoned war time airstrip on the south end near "Vieux Fort". It was also a submarine service base supported by the Americans. These island bases were given over to the USA under President Roosevelt in 1940, in exchange for 52 destroyers naval ships to help the British navy, as their ships were being destroyed by the German U boats. The two interisland ships the Federal Palm and Federal Maple that I had travelled on were the liberty ships donated by the Canadian government build by Kaiser in ferrous cement. Kaiser was also famous for building the Willys Jeep. The abandoned airstrip was called BEANE field by the locals. It was understood because when the American forces departed there was a mountain "Jim Beane" empty whisky bottles the remains of which were still there. But it was a rumour, I think. I was charted by a Canadian government group of engineers and environment men to fly them to the old field which at the time was covered in grass and hardly visible. My enquiries indicated that there was a road down the centre of what was left of the old main runway. Flying over it I felt comfortable attempting a landing. The Beech was higher of the ground than the Aztec, so it was used, also able to carry the 8 men and equipment. The Beech upon touchdown cut away some very small trees and bushes coming to a successful stop at the end of the road, come runway. After a full few hours of investigation and research the departure was completed successfully so we returned to Antigua. The reason for the trip was that the Canadian government was going to refurbish the old field into an international airport. My successful landing on the road being the first there since the war, was the christening of what is now Hewanorra International airport with two active runways making the island an international terminal fortifying a growing tourist need.

It was mid-1969 and NASA had built Apollo bases around the world to attempt the moon landing. Antigua had one on which Mike worked. NASA final attempt succeeded, and Neil Armstrong landed on the moon. One small step for man, one giant leap for mankind. The base erupted with every NASA employee and military personal joining in a huge celebration. Mike brought back pictures of the landing which was to go down in history and change man's future for good. Later it was on international TV allowing the world to see the success of the United States in the race for the moon with Russia.

Regrettably political unrest was starting to spread across the islands. Anegada had had serious upheavals with their relation to St Kitts. Antigua was having problems with an aggressive opposition to the Premier Bird and his party. Guadeloupe was also having domestic trouble plus in South America Guyana was still having a mild civil war. Suddenly Guadeloupe flared up with riots and demonstrations. Overnight the French air force flew in two B707 full of French Gendarmes' and their famous cloaks. By morning there were a few dead, some prisoners, the island was stormed and searched from North to South, uprising over and the police departed. There was never any more trouble. Typical of the French way of dealing with things. Next was Antigua.

The company had to on occasions fly chemicals in 45-gallon drums into St Vincent. It was a difficult approach with one way in and one way out. Drums were to be stood upright and tied down. I had been able to train Don onto the DC3 as a Captain working most of our routes. On a flight into St Vincent the drums broke lose as they had not been tied down as instructed. Rolling back, they put the aircraft out of trim and in danger of crashing as there was no way of going around. Don got away with it but sometime later resigned and left the company. Recreation on the island was mainly a lot of partying with at times 180% proof Guyana rum and coke, diving, and boating. I did not have a boat, however on one afternoon as Josie and I were relaxing at a beach shack bar things changed.

Out on anchor was Madame Renaults 4 masted private yacht. From it came a motorboat towing what looked like a wrecked, very battered old fibre glass Boston whaler. Arriving on the beach he asked where the dump was as he had been instructed to dump the towed boat as scrap. It had been used mainly as a painting and maintenance vessel. I took a quick look at it and offered him a bottle of rum for it. This he took departing back to Madame Renault yacht. I was then driving an old Land rover which I had bought cheap and sort of resurrected. It did not always start so we used to park it where able on a hill. But on this occasion, it started allowing me to drive it to the water edge and with the aid of a fellow drinker, load the scrap boat onto the roof. A lot of jokes and failed senses of humour were expressed including a comment from Josie saying. "What the hell are we going to do with that?" A long story short is that after 2 months of hard spare time work, and a lot of swearing and itching from fibre glass dust, I had completely rebuilt the boat. I extended the rear at the transom by two 12 inches sections, bought a used 35 H.P Evinrude motor which fitted between the extensions and painted it in a lovely sky blue with white trim. In addition, I named it after my wife "THE FLYING J". Over the time that we owned her she brought us a lot of fun as later she will come into my story.

Myself, Josie & Sally Buckley

I knew that Seagreen had financial backing from a Canadian company as I had met one of the directors whose name if my memory is correct, was a Mr. Don Patterson. What I was about to find out was that Cy Green did not have a controlling voice in the progress of the company. It was a hot Saturday afternoon 2 years later when I approached Cy about how much longer it would be before the agreed upon shares in the company would come my way. Upon being told that he was not able to honour the verbal agreement now two years old, and that said shares would therefore not be forthcoming. A big argument followed in the airport office between us which could be overheard in the terminal veranda. I was furious as I had worked hard to build the company from the flying side. Bending the rules at times and working long hours. The secretary Barbara left the office post haste allowing us to face off. I stormed out of the office and down the veranda towards the parking lot.

Standing at a pillar of the veranda was Frank Delisle the founder and 50% owner of Leeward Island Air Transport airlines (LIAT). He stepped towards me asking what the issue was. In brief, I explained I had been cheated out of two years of work. He immediately indicated that he had bought two more H.S.748 Hawker Siddeley 50-passenger aircraft and offered me a direct captaincy on them. He knew I was South African and had voiced before his respect towards the work I was doing for SEAGREEN. I also think that earlier another reason was that he had a beautiful daughter named Janet, who I think would have enjoyed us having a relationship. The islands don't offer much choice for young white island girls in the way of husband material. Joining his airline would give me the break onto turbine aircraft, a young captaincy, access to rebate travel, pension and a secure position in a growing company owned 50% by British West Indies Airlines (BWIA). I accepted immediately, so with a handshake I departed to tell Josie what had taken place. She supported my decision.

In the years that passed Seagreen expanded to a DC4 aircraft. Was sold with an international operator license. Years later I ran into a DC8 crew in Seagreen uniforms and was surprised that they were still operating albeit under new ownership. From what I understood a director's son from the old Seagreen was put in charge. The aircraft and crew were impounded in the USA for carrying drugs. The son I understood went to jail for 7 years. So ended the saga of old Seagreen air Transport.

Leeward Island Air Transport

In the morning, I advised Cy of my resignation and that I was joining LIAT at the end of the month being December 1969. He flew into a rage and threatened to sue me for a million West Indian dollars. Frank Delisle on hearing this advised me not to worry as he being an islander and a successful businessman had the upper hand. The subject, with the aid of Frank's lawyer was never brought up again. I switched over to the airline easily as I was very familiar with the whole West Indian flight routes. Training was brief and I was checked out in two weeks by Capt. Ferdi DeGannes the chief training pilot and signed off by Captain Joe Mahmood the chief pilot. At 26 I was captain on a DC3 freighter and now at 28 I was a captain on HS748 50-seatat airliner. I was moving up, no more dirty loading, cleaning, and working long hours. But things were to happen most unexpectedly. Fate was still playing its game. LIAT now had 4 HS748, I was number 8 on the captaincy list with two other British pilots joining after me. One was John Smith with his wife Anne with whom we became good friends. LIAT now had a need for more pilots so with me leaving SEAGREEN my friends Bob Beck and Gary Dalton resigned as well with job offers from Frank. Gary not having any medium size aircraft experience such as the DC3 was sent down to St Vincent to operate a Britain Norman Islander shuttle service from St Vincent to the tiny island of Mustique and occasional to St Lucia, Barbados and Grenada. Bob, having the DC3 and C46 experience joined the HS 748 section.

Frank DeLisle had started the airline with a single engine Piper Tri Pacer building it with Doves, Heralds, Twin Otters and the HS 748. The LIAT service worked like clockwork with scheduled to Porto Rico via St Kitts, St Martin in the Windward Islands, St Thomas, and St Croix in the Virgin Islands. South bound we operated to Dominica, St Lucia, Barbados, St Vincent, Grenada and Trinidad. Bases got split with resident crews in Barbados and Antigua being the head office. Earlier we flew the full network south from Antigua overnighting in Trinidad at the old BOAC guest house. Except for the 6 expatriate captains most of the pilots were West Indian working their way up to command. Two of us had been cleared to fly a VIP guest Princess Margaret, Des Blanchette (we would meet much later in the aviation world), or I would position down to Barbados to connect with the Atlantic Airline flight from the UK. We would then captain the regular flight flying her over to St Vincent where it was rumoured, she had a lover with a private house on Mustique Island.

A very embarrassing incident happened to me on one of the flights. It was usual for the governor to meet her and escort her over to our flight. I would stand at the bottom of the stairway up to the entrance of the aircraft. On this day she approached the governor introducing me as her usual pilot. However, she was taking great interest in my lower body around my groin. A quick look down revealed that with the strong wind blowing against me, my trouser fly had broken revealing a bright red pair of tropical bikini underwear. I am not sure whether she was amused or not, but I did get a rather unusually cold look. Possibly I had just embarrassed Lord Snowden her ex-husband. She was a bit of a handful, demanding and often insisted on smoking before we were airborne or during the flight. Something that was not allowed Princess or not. Her lady in waiting/secretary and her British police security officer accompanying her, usually talked her out of it.

It was also about this time when on a flight to Porto Rico that the PANAM B747 did its inaugural flight from Miami. The B747 came into the airlines system via Pan Am on 21 January 1970. It was an incredible sight, this huge aircraft stood over all other aircraft on the airport terminal. It towered above the buildings with the diameter of its one engine being bigger than our HS748 fuselage. Bill Allen was then the president of Boeing. The idea of me ever flying such a monster was out of the question, but as usual fate had other ideas.

Avro 748

Court Lines take over.

It had been two years since I joined LIAT when out of the blue the airline was taken over by Court Line of England. They were an economy type charter airline who had a Helicopter (COURT) operation plus owned Appleton shipyard and Halcyon shipping. The charter division operated BAC 1-11 aircraft on cheap bucket and spade tours across the UK and Europe. They were expanding and had purchased two L-1011aircraft so as to operate the Caribbean service where LIAT would transfer the passengers to other islands. The takeover was a bit of a shock to all concerned, never believing Frank Delisle or B.W.I.A would sell out. Court Line was to give us a couple of Trident Jets so by in large it was to be a good upgrade for LIAT pilots on to jets. There was an influx of new management, new cars bought for them and extensions to our offices. British pilots and cabin staff were brought in to train us on the new equipment. They were a great crowd with whom we got on well in so having them on the boat and attending many parties at the White Sands hotel which became their base. The large TRISTAR 1011 started to feed the tourists into Antigua and St Lucia from Europe and the UK. Antigua authorities were very pleased with the increase now to their growing tourist trade.

We the pilots were to be scheduled to go to Court's head office in Luton for ground school and flight orientation onto the BAC 1-11. At about the same time there was a need for one of the HS748 aircraft to be ferried back to Luton in the UK. I was selected together with another Captain Sproel plus a ground engineer Lackman to do the 3 day North Atlantic crossing. We first flew to Nassau which was very nearly the last flight of the aircraft. It was to refuel for the next leg to Quebec. With refueling underway I went to find some coffee. Walking back to the aircraft I noticed fumes coming off the wing around the refuelling port. I found out only to my horror that the refueller had refueled the aircraft with 100/130 high octane petrol. We were a turboprop and on take-off would have most likely exploded. The mistake was the fueling company, so all the fuel was de-tanked and given to the fire department to be used on firefighting exercises. From there we flew on to Montreal and on again to Goosebay which was covered in 6 feet of snow with an icy runway.

Snow covered Sondre Stromfjord ferry route North Atlantic from Antigua to Luton.

After a night stop, we flew on to Sondre Stromfjord also now known as Nuuk or Godthab in Greenland the biggest island in the world. It's a one way in, one way out on a 9000-foot runway bounded on one side by the military and the other by civilian terminals. The approach is visibly marked by a wrecked ship as a reference point, then landing with terrain along the fjord walls rising up to in some areas over 2000 feet. The only alternate was Reykjavik Iceland or back to Frobisher Bay now called Iqaluit. Refueled we then flew over the icecap to Reykjavik the Keflavik airport in Iceland. Here we had another night stop then on to Luton, England. The icecap crossing was very interesting as it was the same route the air forces used to ferry aircraft across the Atlantic to the war frontiers. A lot of these aircraft were piloted by woman of the famous 99's (ninety niners) an aviatrix organization of whom I had met one years before in Washington. Luton was a welcome journeys' end with a wonderful flying club attached to the head office and a very good experience for me having never thought I would ever do a Northern Atlantic crossing in late winter.

I returned to Antigua preparing myself hopefully that according to seniority I would be on my way later to Luton to do the Trident jet training. At this stage it was very important for my career to get onto jets. There appeared to be growing concern about the merger, but all seemed to be going well. The large contingent of management and support staff was a bit worrying as all of a sudden, we were no longer a punctual regular interisland airline. There appeared to be a lot of excessive expenditure. At the time Capt. Peter Dibbly was the Court line chief pilot with whom Josie and I would spend a couple of days with him and his wife when on a holiday visiting Iceland, Copenhagen and London. The Chief pilot for the Court side of our merged airline was Capt. Ball with the general manager being a Mr Mike Clark. On our side we had Capt. Joe Mahmod and Capt. Ferdie DeGanes.

Some Canadian associates who knew Josie from her flying days with Wardair approached her to go to Barbados and train some girls for a startup airline called Air Calypso. This she did and succeeded in getting a good group of girls together for the startup airline. However, this company did not last because of a very serious incident on the Barbados runway. The Air Calypso aircraft had landed and was taxying off the runway which is curved slightly uphill. A friend of mine Jerry Fathingham was the captain on a departing Wardair B707. He had held at the take off point to allow the Air Calypso Convair 440 to clear the runway. Due to the curve Jerry could not see the Convair but was cleared by the tower for take-off. As he approached the top of the curve, too late to abort the take-off, he saw the Convair had not completely cleared the runway. Jerry attempted a take-off trying to miss the Convair. He hit the tail of the Convair severing it completely from the fuselage and opening up a gash down the centre of the B707 belly. Thankfully there is a drop off at the departing sea end of the runway so giving Jerry some more airspace. He realized that the fire and accident facilities at Barbados were not of a high standard, plus the maintenance needed and cost of accommodation allotted to carry on to Toronto unpressurised. Doing this saved Wardair thousands, never mind the inconvenience to the passengers. There upon landing in Toronto they braced the aircraft and removed it to the maintenance area. Miraculously there was no injury or loss of life, but Air Calypso did not operate again. Wardair was lucky that Jerry, a very experienced all-round pilot, was the captain in so saving the day in getting aircraft and passengers back safely.

With the company expanding more stewardesses were needed so Sally Buckley was hired being an ex-BOAC hostess who had taken the ten-year handshake to come and train the cabin staff. We became good friends with Sally, and it was through her learning that Josie was an ex-hostess with training experience, that she was asked to come on board and help Sally This was great as when I was away life on the island was a bit boring although over the years, we had a lot of visitors from mainly Wardair friends and Canada wanting a Caribbean holiday. We did not mind as we now had a two-bedroomed house close to the beach. Rum was cheap at $2 bottle ($4 BWI dollars), and they usually put in for food. There were some hilarious parties consuming copious amounts of rum and many hangovers for them to take back to Canada or wherever. We also had a small island just off the coast where we would take them. We would then hang a cooler filled with bloody Mary's on the only tree. Often, we would be caught by the tide and not be able to get to the mainland due to a fire coral reef. This meant a fire for warmth and to cook lobster we had sort of borrowed from the offshore lobster pots and almost definitely skinny dipping.

Time ticked by and after a year I bought Josie a powder blue Austin Healy Sprite for her birthday. To add one day while on my way to the town I found an Alsatian puppy ambling along the road. Picking him up I over the next few days attempted to find the owner. Nobody ever claimed. By this time, we had become very fond of him so called him "Simba". We found that he enjoyed riding on the bow of the boat, barking at the seagulls and stray dogs on the roadside. He loved riding around with Josie lying in the back space behind the seats of her car. He was a deterrent to rather over friendly locals who often attempted to befriend this beautiful blond, white girl. Regretfully I will explain later how this fear of the locals became a reality, especially for blond, white girls.

Most of our free time was spent on the boat enjoying the warm water and sunshine. Two particular trips come to mind. One, we were skirting the island around the South end when I by accident hit a reef shearing the prop shear pin to the shaft on the motor. The South end of Antigua has very high pounding cliffs which were very close to us. I was afraid of being swept along with the swell and smashed into the cliffs. On board was Josie, my friend Gary and Simba who had now produced puppies. Jumping overboard I with the aid of some wire I had in my tool kit, managed to wire the prop back onto the shaft. Very slowly we were able to go forward without breaking the wire so slipping around the cliff face and into Nelsons harbour. A close call. The other trip was when we had our friend Janie visiting us from Toronto. We decided we would pack the boat and speed over to Barbuda some 30 miles away over open Atlantic water. Lord Codrington had established this island as a slave breeding colony. It was a picturesque Caribbean day with blue sky and sea. Simba was included so camping the night on the isolated beach we had security. Later I realized it had been a bit of a chance with open water and only one 35HP outboard. Had we broken down we would have ended up being swept out into the Atlantic. But we had a great couple of days on the isolated part of the island and life was still an adventure.

Political trouble started again with Prime Minister Bird's party under attack from the opposition led by I think his name was Hallstead. Riots broke out with roving gangs burning down schools and damaging the electrical power facilities. St Johns became unsafe, and we started evacuation of the small hotels to other islands. The New Club shut down for the first time in its history. With our friend Gary Dalton flying the islander service and based in St Vincent, Bob and I sent our wives to stay with him. This unrest became turmoil, and the tourist trade was hit.

After about a week the aggression calmed down, so our wives returned home. I think Gary was thankful as being a bachelor and having two women in his flat for a week was enough. This upheaval would flare up again with more trouble between Anegada and St Kitts. Overnight the Royal Air Force arrived with a contingent of British police support troops, vehicles and supplies with a camp being set up on the old, abandoned runway. The troops put in place around the island portable generators to supplement the power failures. The police were flown over to Anegada to subdue the uprising and political problems. The set-up base was near the Sands Hotel, so it became the favourite drinking place and definitely the place for us to go to have great Friday evening. The guys were great and with our young tanned and beautiful wives, we were popular.

Regrettably on one Friday evening a bit of horse play took part in which a lot of people were tossed into the pool. When the evening closed a body was found at the bottom of the pool. A very unfortunate incident and put a major dampener on future evenings. However, one thing I got out of their visit was that I had met the quartermaster who was in charge of distributing tyres for their military Land Rovers. My tyres were almost bald and a very expensive item on the island. Miraculously over a few too many rums and a trip on my boat for him and his mates, I swopped mine for a new set courtesy of the British Army.

A chap called Tony Gartner had a converted World War 2 Fairmile submarine chaser named "The Warrior Geraint) operating as a day tour cruiser off the island. Occasionally Josie would help him out by working as a hostess to cater for about 30 or 40 people. Tony was a fine cook and supplied a very appetizing lunch on the cruise. I on one occasion was out with my boat when I came alongside his boat lying at Anchor near the airport. He had served the lunch and Josie's assistance was no longer needed. She slipped off the stern and onto my boat. I pulled away heading for the shore when there was an all-mighty explosion. Turning I saw the Warrior Geraint exploding and rearing up breaking in the centre throwing people clear into the air and landing in the water. Racing back, we got as many people on board as I could take, with other boats doing the same. Tony and some passengers ended up in the local hospital, Tony with severe burns to his arm, face and chest. Tony had gone below deck into the galley to light the propane gas fridge that had seemingly gone out. This had filled the bilges with gas so as he lit the burner the boat exploded. Today the sunken wreck is still slightly visible on take-off from the airport. Josie was very lucky as she would have been in the galley.

Old English Harbour Lord Nelsons dockyard.

The pub in Nelsons Dockyard at English harbour was one of our favourite places. Gary my friend was up from St Vincent, so we decided to pay it a visit. Josie agreed to come later in her car. The evening was great and around 10 p.m. we had decided to head home across the island about 15 kilometres in distance. Josie set off first with a small delay on our side to pay the bill. Halfway across the island we came upon Josie's car parked on the side of the dirt road. Lights out and no immediate sign of her. Thinking maybe the call of nature had come requiring a quick pit stop. Pulling up behind her car and having good night vision, I searched the surrounding sugar cane for any sign of her. I immediately saw a movement and heard a sound in amongst the tall cane. At the same time a saw another car parked on the opposite side of the road but ahead of hers. I leapt out of my car racing into the cane. Breaking through into a small break in the rows of cane I came across Josie spread eagled out on the ground. She was being held down by two locals. She had been stripped of her pant suit with her blouse and bra ripped exposing her breast. A third local was kneeling between her thrashing legs attempting to rape her. I charged forward picking up a rock enroute hitting the guy between her legs with my full 6-foot 41/2 inches and a body weighing 102 kilos sending him crashing backwards into the cane. Picking myself up I faced the other two who were now standing to confront me. For reasons I don't know they fled, leaving me time to pick Josie up in my arms and run through the cane to my car where Gary was waiting. I pulled off my shirt wrapping it around her and telling Gary to drive away as fast as he could. Seeing the other car, I associated it with the men. Running to it I opened the fuel tank and stuffed some grass in it. Josie was a smoker, so I often had a lighter in my pocket. I then lit the grass retreating back to her car where I prayed the keys would be in it. The molesting owner's car burst into flames sending bits into the air. The area now being illuminated I carefully searched for Josies keys hoping for a fast safe getaway. Finding them I jumped into her car racing off after Gary.

Getting home we analyzed the situation. Josie had sustained some bad bruising to her legs, her one hand was cut with scratch marks over her lower body and breast, but nothing serious. She had apparently stopped to wait for us as she did not have good night vision and was not sure in the dark quite where she was. They had stopped offering assistance then abducted her out of her open sports car and into the cane. We felt that having destroyed the car it might not be a good idea to report the matter to the local police considering we were white outsiders. Regrettably during our years there two more of our lady friends were raped, one in Antigua the other in Tobago. Joe Shaja the pilot who had left Seagreen earlier, had a similar incident with his attractive wife, He shot the intruder with a spear gun in the legs as he entered their bedroom. The intruder then hastily departed running through a barbed wire fence into the surrounding bush. Although reported to the police, nothing ever came of it. When we eventually left the Antigua almost every white woman living on the island had had a bad incident of rape or molesting. Including the base commander's wife. Another case of someone being shot was when an Australian friend called Peter was building a boat on the beach. He had rented a small beach shack nearby to live in and store equipment. One night coming home very full of rum he caught a thief trying to get out of the window. Peter, grabbing his spear gun, shot him through the side of his stomach, pinning him to the wooden wall. With the poor fellow pleading poverty and mercy Peter felt sorry for him. He proceeded to offer him a drink to kill any pain followed by them sitting on the floor exchanging stories. In the morning, they were both found very drunk and asleep on the floor. Peter actually employed him working together until his boat was finished. One Sunday afternoon when down at Nelsons dockyard there was a beautiful but old RIVA power boat lying on the dock. After some enquiries, I found out it had a seized motor and belonged to Madame Renault. It was up for sale as is. So, with my wife saying "Here we go again" I bought it. She was 28 feet long with double mahogany hull with a Cadillac cockpit. I borrowed a 4-wheel trailer and hauled her to my back yard.

RIVA having new engine fitted.

Three months later with every day I had off, I had sanded down the woodwork, re- stained and painted the hull, rebuilt the motor from a used V8 Chrysler 300 I had bought from St Thomas and was ready to launch her. She was a magnificent craft, very fast but heavy on fuel. I sold the

"Flying J" now boating on this elegant new vessel which we never renamed. This boat was not the only new thing coming into my life.

In February 1973 much to our joy we found out Josie was pregnant, expecting in November. Life was to change but so far, we had had a great 3 years as a young married couple. Travelling as much as we could and preparing to buy a plot of land on a bay South of the airport to build a house on the shoreline with a boat house underneath. It nearly all did not happen as one bright moon light night coming back from the outer reef, suddenly the engine caught fire. I had another couple on board, Josie and Simba. We were about 3 miles offshore heading for the harbour. Over on my right was a sandy beach to which I immediately headed fearful that the 40 gallons of fuel would not explode before I beached the vessel on the shore. Fortunately, the man I had on board was an engineer with the airline. He forced open the engine room doors at the same time grabbing some wet towels from the cockpit. The doors opened directly over the engine; flames were active along the right side. He beat and smothered the flames which amazingly went out. Leaving the doors open I headed directly into the harbour and my mooring. We found out that an electric ignition wire from the one cylinder had become detached. It in turn fell across the oil exhaust breather which ignited. He later became our expected child's godfather with our old friend Anne Smith as his godmother.

With our expected child coming, Simba our dog and a stray cat called "Toeto" meaning kitchen boy in Swahili we thought our family was complete. But one evening when docking the RIVA as I reversed to tie it up there in the wash of my prop was what appeared to be a very large seabird, supposedly dead. So as not to get it caught in my prop, I dragged the body out of the water and threw it up onto the dock. I completed the usual securing of the vessel and proceeded on to the dock. Not wanting to leave the carcass on the wharf I threw it into the box that had contained rubbish. It was a rather big bird which I identified as a Frigate Bird. Driving home to my horror I looked back into rear view mirror to see the bird perched on my back seat. Arriving home I had some difficulty in examining the bird but established it had an almost severed wing possibly from hitting a ship's rigging or something that had cut almost through the wing. I, with the aid of my wife much to her dislike, amputated the wing treating it with an antiseptic to stop the maggot infection which had started to eat the flesh. With the remaining wing I estimated its wingspan to be about 6 or more feet (2+ meters), being a bird that is very seldom on land living on the wing.

A perch was built on my veranda, we named it Nelson due to it being minus a wing. One problem was teaching it to grip the perch and to allow us to feed it by hand with small sprats which we got from the fish market. He had a very sharp beak which cut up my hand a bit until I started feeding him wearing a gardening glove. Nelson became a character who would squawk whenever I drove into the garden, disliked Simba who he would peck and became a subject of interest to passing tour buses. He learnt to ride on the boat and the back seat of my convertible car often spreading out his stumped wing to caress the wind He would allow me to walk with him on my hand down to the beach where he would gaze out at the horizon often turning to face the sea when we walked back. It was very sad, and my heart felt for him, as I could see him trying to understand why and what had happened. It was quite comical in some ways a parade as I would walk with him on my hand like a Hawk, behind me was Simba and behind Simba was Toeto the cat. Once I took him to the bar at Nelsons Dockyard where he sat on the bar edge dipping his beak into my beer, much to the amusement of the bar folk. Unfortunately, I had to leave the island when the airline went bankrupt.

The original airline owner Frank De Lisle took him, but he refused to eat and died.

Nelson

The Caribbean has over the years claimed many aircraft for numerous reasons. Fuel, loss of direction, engine failure and so on. One late afternoon I was waiting to take off from St Martin on our regular service to Porto Rico. We were advised by the tower that a DC 9 of ALM airlines based in the A. B.C Dutch islands was inbound from New York. He attempted to land but missed the approach over shooting for a second attempt. Changing his mind, he advised that he was diverting to St Croix in the USA Virgin Islands about 90 miles away. We were cleared for take-off heading also for St Croix. In radio contact with St Croix control, we heard the ALM aircraft declaring an emergency. I could see him ahead of my flight and it appeared he was descending. The control requested the nature of the emergency with the ALM aircraft indicating he was running out of fuel. The distance from New York to St Martin for a DC9 twin engine jet is very limiting on fuel but to miss an approach and divert to an alternate is very dangerous if running out of fuel. He repeated his mayday call and advised he was going to ditch. We watched as he hit the water leaving cocks tails of water then breaking into three pieces. Circling him I was able to report that it appeared passengers were getting out and into life rafts. By this time the Air Sea rescue had noted my position and was racing to get there. I heard afterwards that only one person drowned, being washed away from the wreckage. Another aircraft was a DC3 that I saw floating off the island of Saba reporting it to the St. Martin control who arranged a rescue. The American pilot later contacted me, and we remained friends for many years.

Initial S.A.A (1972)

About this time, I while flying, overheard a South African aircraft in contact with Trinidad air traffic control He was North bound from Rio to New York. On the general frequency I made contact and introduced myself as a South African flying for the local airline. The chap I spoke to was the first officer by the name of Dick Henry. In the short conversation he questioned why I was not with South African as they were short of pilots. I indicated that I could be interested but did not know how to make contact with their recruiting division. He very quickly gave me a telephone number before going out of radio range. I decided to give the South African Airways number a call and see what was going on regarding the hiring flight crew. They confirmed that they would be hiring and would send me an application form. It duly arrived but it had educational requirements that I could not possibly reach. I did fill it out using a matriculation (grade 12) certificate got from an old South African girlfriend Joy Clark whose name I changed to mine. A few weeks later I received a letter indicating that I was eligible for an interview. I had a few days off so, in addition to a flight swap with my friend Bob and John, I could get away for about a week. A telephone conversation with the operations department put me in touch with the hiring division and explained my position in that I was very interested but could only make a quick visit owing to my present position. A date was offered for a special interview which I accepted.

A couple of days before the date I jump seated on B.W.I.A. to New York. There at the gate I met the captain of the outgoing PANAM B707 departing for Dakar and Johannesburg. I explained my predicament and my need to get to South Africa for an interview He was sympathetic but indicated that the flight had an extra crewmember occupying the jump seat and that the flight was full. He suggested I should wait by the entrance door to see if a seat became available. As the door was closing my hopes faded but suddenly the captain, who I could see from my position via the side cockpit window, waved me to jump aboard. This I did rapidly as I had a meter gap to the edge of the entrance door. I was ushered up to the cockpit where he suggested I sit in the lounge seat for the flight to Dakar where from there to Johannesburg there was a seat available. This was in the good old days of camaraderie amongst flight crew. Regretfully terrorism has removed all of that. After a meal I fell asleep due mainly I think from anticipation of what was ahead and fatigue. Transiting Dakar the new captain was advised of my presence and allowed me to stay in the lounge for the ongoing flight to Johannesburg.

On arriving in Johannesburg my mother had driven up from Durban, taking the short opportunity of seeing her son. Understanding the situation and the very short visit she had checked us into a hotel near the airport. From there I made contact with the flight operations division and was given an interview for the next day. Somewhat jet lagged I tried to get a good sleep proceeding in the morning to the SAA offices. Here I was given an identity card and led into an office occupied by a secretary. She advised me that they were calling the hiring captain and the operations manager plus two other pilots. I was ushered into an office with six men facing me across the floor seated at desks. There was one seat in front of them to which they indicated I should sit. They told me that this was an exceptional interview due to my distant situation, effort on my behalf and the time factor. Questions were asked involving my getting there, my bush pilot days in Canada and the Arctic, my present command position, command time on Turbo prop and DC3 plus my time on DC6. They were intrigued by my progress through aviation, with questions on my education and asked if I spoke Afrikaans. To those who don't know Afrikaans is a Dutch dialect spoken by the Afrikaans pioneers and very much spoken in the military. A large number of SAA pilots had come through the air force, so the language was common on the flight deck plus the airline was under the railway umbrella which was very Afrikaans.

My forged matriculation certificate indicated I had passed Afrikaans in my final year, so they asked me in Afrikaans if I was fluent in the language. Being born in the province of Natal which was very colonial and known as "the last outpost of the British Empire", plus having not learnt Afrikaans at school this could have been an exit ticket. I mustered up as much of the language that I could remember and replied that I was a Banana Boy, (Natal being very big in Banana and sugar plantations) that Zulu was my second language, had been overseas for years, but felt sure I would pick it up. They all laughed at the Banana Boy description with Zulu as a second language. I believe a major bearing on the interview was the letter from the Military thanking me and my crew for the work we did relating to the border photo reconnaissance work done in 1965. With that and wishing me a good trip back, the interview was ended. I then was rushed over to the military medical centre for a medical and the next day into Johannesburg for a stanine test. This was followed by a check flight with a check airman Captain Van Zyl on a SAA aircraft ZS-SBV. I had just one day left to end my precarious visit to SAA and the possibility of being hired. With all the requirements completed I was advised that they would send me their decision in the future. Little did I realize this would come almost two years later. Returning back to the hotel I bid farewell to my mother and got to the airport the following evening to secure, if possible, a jump seat on PANAM back to New York. In my favour and delight the captain was the same chap I had come with from Dakar. I got the jump seat, and he advised the same captain taking over from him in Dakar to New York that I was on board. Consequently, I got back to New York and was able to get the jump seat on BWIA from there to Antigua.

There were two Captains Evans in the Caribbean, me and Junior Evans a Trinidadian who had the accolade of being one of the youngest B727 captains at 23years of age. He was the captain on the flight to Antigua so in the cockpit the discussion was around my venture to South Africa. From information he had received he agreed that the Court Line situation was a bit unpredictable. There seemed to be an awful lot of expenditure. Arriving home I explained the whole situation to Josie, and we deliberated as to what was going to be the outcome if I was ever accepted. Secondly what would we do as we had established ourselves very comfortably in Antigua? Plus, we had considered making a bid on a lovely piece of land on the shoreline of a bay near the airport. Time went by and we did not hear from SAA again. I presumed I had fallen out of their hiring program.

Treasure ship.

Having spent some years in the Caribbean both sailing and flying there were many stories of sunken treasure, Pirate ships and privateers in the wild old days of the pirate and Spanish ships carrying bullion and treasure across the Atlantic. One such story stuck in my mind and that was of a Priest and a few locals on the island of Dominica just South of Guadalupe who had actually found gold doubloons.

According to the story 3 Spanish ships attempting to sail from Central America to Europe were attacked by some British ships probably sailing on the skull and cross bones flag as privateers for the British crown. Then they in an attempt to evade capture, attempted to hide off the northern tip of Dominica. It was understood that a hurricane capsized them, and they were never seen again.

Over the years gold Spanish doubloons had been washed up on the east side of the island. It intrigued me and I started to make enquiries. Two brothers, one a captain with LIAT the other a first officer was from the island so when I flew with the first officer I would enquire more about the story. Their father had a farm on the island which was the last of the Caribbean islands to have the original Arawak and Carib Indians living on it. The Caribs related to the Taino Indians from South America were understood to be cannibals and drove most of the Arawaks off the islands. I was invited to visit so on a couple of days off I flew down on our scheduled flight arranging to spend a night there. The one brother met me and took me to visit the priest who showed me the Spanish doubloon he had acquired from one of the natives. He also showed me a cannon mounted by the church which he claimed came from one of the ships.

My adventurous spirit got me going so on my return I started looking up whatever information I could get about the island. I learnt that the area where the ships disappeared was said to have been a finger of land with a small island at its tip. The finger was mainly a sand bar with mangroves. The island of Dominica is very mountainous being in parts an extinct volcano with deep water at its shoreline. On a couple of empty flights, I diverted over the area of the supposed sinking and noticed that from an altitude I could make out that very possibly the small island mentioned earlier and was now joined to the main island by the mangrove bridge. It in turn had made a sand bar with relatively clear water as the main current swept south down the outer part of the newly formed bay and towards "Roseau" the port town where the bullion and coins had been found. I was now convinced that there in the new bay were very possibly the remains of the 3 ships.

There was another South African named Derrick working in Antigua who was also a diver. We met and started to put together an exploration to see what we could find. Firstly, we got hold of the local pilot's family to see if we could get accommodation and a boat near the area I wanted to explore. They were very kind and said that they had a small wood and iron cottage we could use provided we carried our own supplies. They advised that a fisherman friend would supply a boat. The hard part was being able to fill our tanks with oxygen as we did not have a portable unit. However, at the last moment a chap on the island offered to drive any empty tanks to "Roseau" to be refilled. This was a good 2-hour mountain drive. Finally with all arrangements made the day came to get down to Dominica and start an exciting venture. We were met by a chap with a pickup and drove over the rough road to what I would call a shack overlooking the bay. Here we made camp and awaited the next morning for the boat to arrive. This it did, so carrying our gear down to the water we fitted up and set out to the point I wanted to start at. For the next two hours we took it in turn trawling the bay submerged at about 10 meters, on a trapeze being pulled slowly backward sand forwards traversing the bay. The reason we used a trapeze was to extend our down time so allowing us a larger area to inspect. We found nothing on the first day, but both observed that although the water was very deep, we did see what could have been a large rock or reef appearing below us at about 40 meters, too deep for our bottom time.

After a good meal of chicken and plantain (native banana) we had a reasonably good sleep on the wooden floor, noting the hut had no doors or windows. The next day I decided to concentrate on the dark images we had seen. Sure enough, we identified three darkened images on the side of the steep volcanic face. In our service boat with only one SCUBA tank left, it was decided that Derrick, being more experienced, would skip breath in an attempt on a direct dive to the images. His down time would be about 5 minutes at the most. This he did surfacing to report that the images looked like large stone blocks but there were a few sharks also in the area. The following day we had to wait for the tanks to arrive, so it was a late start which actually was to our benefit. The reason why was that the sun was high and the ocean clear. Locating our dive site, we agreed that Derrick would dive on the stone, and I would keep watch with a spear gun on the shark issue. Down we went, Derrick straight for the stones. Now on the side of the stones I could see what looked like flat rows of lines protruding from the area around the stone. Derrick tried to dig into the sand around the stone's blocks, only to be covered in ash and disappear in the watery murk. The three rows of stone blocks were all pointing up the volcanic slope of the island and the more we tried to dig into the surrounding soil, so it erupted into a murk. Retiring that day, we agreed that for sure these were the ships but almost impossible work at that depth without possibly killing ourselves. Using ordinary SCUBA gear, it is not advisable to attempt a dive at the depth we got to. It was 35 meters and both of us were feeling the effect. With no hospital or decompression chambers near we were asking for trouble. Secondly the boat driver advised that he could only come for one more day. Again, on the next day we waited for our tanks to arrive so again a late start. Working from 25 meters we surveyed ahead of the pointing rocks which we were sure were ballast stone and the lines on each side were the remains of the ribs. We could not see much else such as any superstructure or deck remains, it was too deep. Taking into consideration that they had been sunk by a hurricane they were probably upside down, so all being visible was the rib remains and the ballast. It was not uncommon for pirates to load cannon with bullion and jewels, seal it then dumps it at secret available or convenient place.

In the shallows of the bay, we found an old cannon with just its rusted nose pointing out. This we considered might have been buried there as a marker of some sort. To our surprise when we aligned it with the tip of what was now the point of the bay which had joined the little island to the mainland via the mangroves, the alignment line ran over the exact spot where we had located the ballast and ribs. Our time was up so rather elated and happy we finally returned to Antigua with high hopes of one day returning supported with deeper and more commercial diving equipment. Looking into it money was a big problem as it would require a coffer dam to support the wreck, then some sort of suction vacuum cleaner to suck away the muck and ash. Far too dangerous for amateur divers. To this day I thank the folk on the island who helped us. It was a disappointment with the later collapse of the airline that I never followed up on the adventure. But only Derrick who I believe has died and I know where the ships are. About this time Rosemary Blaine as previously mentioned from the ex-South African Blaine family in Jersey Channel Islands, arrived in Antigua married to a yacht Captain. Later moving to the USA.

Scott (19 Nov 1973)

Our baby was due, so preparations were being made to fly Josie down to Barbados which had a better hospital, together with our friend Anne Smith as company. I had rented a small apartment in Bridgetown Barbados for Josie and Anne. On the day we expected our baby to arrive I had landed to be told by an excited agent that Anne had called Josie was in labour. I rushed to the hospital to be a minute away from the birth of our son, Scott. All went well so 3 days later we started to arrange for all concerned to return to Antigua.

Here we came across a problem. Scott could not be put on Josie's passport as at the time both parents had to be British. We for the same reason could not get him a British passport. There was no South African consulate in Barbados. We were not allowed to leave Barbados or enter Antigua without the correct passport documents for our child. The answer was to make him a Barbados subject and get him a Barbados passport. This required a passport photo of a 3-day-old baby and signed legal documents which we proceeded to get. When the photographer came to the hospital to get a passport photo of Scott, there were about 20 babies in the nursery. All local black except for a very blonde, white baby. He looked at me and asked which one was my child. A rather amusing question to say the least. There was at one point a consideration that due to the legal complications I might have had to smuggle Scott out in my pilot's flight bag but getting him into Antigua would have been a major obstacle. Eventually, a Barbados passport was issued to the three-day-old baby. I was the captain on the flight which safely brought all of them home to Antigua, so it was Scott's first flight of many more.

South African Visit (1973)

It was nearing the Christmas season so with a bit of leave due to me I decided to take the family to South Africa so as to allow my parents to see their new grandchild. There was thankfully a change in the law and with the help of the British high commissioner we were able to have Scott put on his mother's passport. However, he was not eligible for British citizenship. We travelled with British Airways via London and on to Johannesburg connecting with Comair a local subsidiary of British Airways. All went well with my parents and some close relations plus our black maid who was part of the family, being thrilled to see the now five-week-old baby. I was able to register him as a South African citizen so enabling him to have dual passports. Travelling back, we had to stop over in London so waiting for our connecting flight to New York we went to a familiar pub called the "Three monkeys". Scott travelled most of the time in his carry cot with his nappies and food requirements tucked under or on the side of the mattress. There was also often a bottle of Scotch. In the pub I stepped forward to get between the crowd for a drinks order. Josie put the crib behind the couch and stood up to await my return. With my hands full she stepped into the crowd to get the drinks I was attempting to hand her. On getting back to the couch a mere six feet away, Scott was gone. Almost in a panic I ran outside to see if anyone had picked him up, returning back to the crowded bar we searched for and questioned anyone in the vicinity of the couch. Desperation was setting in when a young man said that there was a ladies Christmas party causing some boisterous activity in the conference room next door. Racing into the room we found Scott being handed from lady to lady being smothered in kisses. Apparently, a lady coming back from the bar saw Scott so in her Christmas spirited state of mind, just picked him up to show the other woman. This was an experience we did not wish on anyone, albeit with a happy ending. Travelling via New York we had another amusing experience with Scott. Upon arrival Josie and I were allowed through being British and a Canadian citizen. However, as the transit visa for Josie did not include the baby Scott, he would not be allowed through. A ridiculous situation developed. We got around this by offering the immigration officer the opportunity of keeping the baby for the night or allowing us to transit catching British West Indies flight in the morning to Antigua. After some discussion with his superior and possibly the expectation of babysitting, we were allowed through. After our return to Antigua British Airways sent Scott a small silver mug with a certificate to congratulate him. on doing 16,000 air miles before the age of six weeks. I was able to register him as a South African citizen so enabling him to have dual passports.

UFO

Getting back into the swing of things I still felt that something was not turning out the way Court line was expecting. I was now only two positions away from being trained onto the BAC 1-11 jets so was keen to see things progress. It was about this time that I was operating the evening North bound service from Barbados via St Lucia and then over Guadeloupe to Antigua. Passing over Guadeloupe we were cleared to contact Antigua control and proceed as there was no conflicting traffic. On switching radio frequencies over to Antigua control, the first officer and I both saw what looked from a distance to be a very small light above the evening horizon. In as much time as it takes me to write these few lines the light came straight at us travelling at an incredible speed growing in size. As it came onto us and then under our aircraft it looked like a large fur ball of light. It was saucer shaped and did seem to have a darkened centre, however at the speed it was travelling we were unable to get any recognizable identification of it. Contacting Antigua, they advised confirming the information from Guadeloupe that they had no traffic in the area. They then contacted San Juan control who confirmed again that there was no activity from the military or and aircraft in our sector. To this day with 43 years in the business I have never seen anything like this again. U.F.O does become a possibility as in aviation many strange things are seen. My sixth sense started telling me something was not right with the company, now two years being 1974, into ownership.

Bankruptcy

The bombshell hit out of the blue COURT LINE airlines went into receivership taking with it Halcyon shipping Appleton shipyard, COURT Helicopters and LIAT. We did not know about it as the UK was 5 hours ahead. It was a regular day in Antigua with all the flights operating. Suddenly we were all called to the White Sands Hotel where the managing director came out onto the veranda telling us we were bankrupt, and all flights would end. Everyone was astounded and some of the staff burst into tears. We the foreign pilots and engineers were given 7 weeks to leave the island as no work permits would be issued. A sudden coldness went through the crowd as it was explained that our pensions would be paid off at a fraction of their value. We dispersed to our respective homes to try and figure out what to do. Josie was in tears as I broke the news to her, here we were with a newborn baby, no job and very little money considering the pension collapse. One of the Halcyon ships in port in Canada got the news before the authorities could be advised to hold the ship pending owner lease agreement. The captain mustered his crew and did a runner into international waters. We were stuck now having to sell all we could and make arrangements to leave the island. I sold my RIVA and my Mercedes Benz for $5,000. Josies car for $300, all our household good for $1,700. Initially we decided to get back to Canada, but fate played its hand again, very much in my favour.

There were still a few English pilots and management on the island closing down the offices and operations department. Word got through to me that South Africa Airways was going to hire 18 expatriate COURT LINE pilots for two years to make up a gap in their aircraft upgrade training program. It was short term contract and had been offered to the COURT LINE pilots association. I immediately got onto the phone and made contact with the person concerned with the South African pilot intake. I advised him that I was a COURT LINE crew member being a Captain in the Caribbean division. A South African holding a South African license. In addition, I explained that I had already been interviewed two years before and requested that he check my records which I presumed were on file. Within a few days I received a return fax saying I was hired if I could make my way to London where I would be issued a ticket to Johannesburg to start the training on the B707.

The Trident Court aircraft were being readied to be ferried back to the U.K. by the Court Line crew. I had about two weeks to get myself organized and ship what possessions I could out to South Africa. I was able to put on board one of the returning aircraft a couple of trunks containing what was left of our possessions. Simba now was a problem as we did not want to leave her on the island. The frigate bird Frank Delisle took flying it over to his cottage on Barbuda Island in his Beech Bonanza. Regretfully Nelson refused to eat and died a week later. Toeto the cat went to a resident friend. Making frantic arrangements, I was able to secure a flight from London to Johannesburg a day after the ferrying aircraft with our trunks got to Luton the Court Line base. The crew ferrying the aircraft agreed to take Simba in the cabin with them as long as I took care of the SPCA requirements to transship her to London Airport. With the shortage of time, it was decided that Josie would stay on in Antigua at the White Sands hotel until I could establish a place in Johannesburg. So, with my trunks and Simba enroute to the U.K., I was able to bid all farewell, leaving my newborn and wife on the island and headed to London. Here I rented a van transshipping the trunks and Samba to London Airport and the Cargo section. Tranquillizing Simba I joined the same flight arriving in Johannesburg early the next morning. Thankfully again my parents had come to my rescue. They had a sleeper couch, a small table with two chairs, and a cupboard which the loaded onto their pickup and drove to Johannesburg. Here they found a small one bed roomed flat near the airport, put the deposit down and secured me a roof over my head. My father and I then went over to the cargo to fetch Simba who was more than happy to see us after her caged and possible terrifying flight twice in four days. I still had my Mustang in South Africa, so my mother had driven it to Johannesburg. I therefore now had a car and a roof plus I hoped for a job. I had only one day to climatize and get over the strain of the last month. I was a bit shattered when presenting myself to the operations department to start my training on the B707, however for me it was a lifeline and a major advancement to my career.

I had to leave Josie and Scott in Antigua for 6 weeks as I just could not allow myself to be pressured by the high level of training at the training centre. With exams every week requiring an 80% pass mark it was a case of one failure and you were out. SAA had very high standards and were considered one of the best airlines in the world. It was a huge battle for me, and I could not take the chance of returning nightly to a small flat, a baby, a wife and dog so disturbing the required homework. Simba and I would take a quick walk every morning and evening. It was hard on her as she had never been cooped up and never without our daily company. Eventually the training was over, I had successfully passed and now could concentrate on getting Josie and Scott to South Africa. The crowning fact was I now getting the B707 jet time on my South African license. I was with a major international airline and moving up the ladder to my objective.

South African Airways

Eventually after nearly 2 months I was able to secure travel arrangements for Josie and Scott. They arrived very pleased, and jet lagged as they had travelled nonstop from Antigua to London then a transit of 8 hours and finally on to South Africa. A day after they arrived, I left for a 10-day flight via Rio, New York, Sal Island and Johannesburg. While walking Simba one evening, I met a chap who also lived in the apartment building called Ray Jones, walking his poodles. He and his wife Mel befriended Josie and were a great help to her in my absence. Little did I know how they would become involved in my family matters. Soon after the arrival of Josie and Scott we started looking for a bigger place to set up home. We after about three months finally found a lovely three bed roomed bungalow on a plot of land with a double garage very near our flat in a new area called Highway gardens. Most of the funds we had as the conversion to South Africa Rand was to our favour. The house was being sold at R22,000 South Africa rand. We needed to borrow R4,000. My wages as a pilot married man with a child was R700 per month. It was about the same as a stocker on the railway which controlled the airline. It was hard to get the bond on such a low income, but my father counter signed so helped out and we were able to buy our first home. We called it "Carib cottage" which was ideal for us with room for Simba and the Mustang.

Visiting Carib cottage 6 years later.

A lot of the Court Line pilots who arrived to accept the offered pilot contract I knew from the court line days in the Caribbean. One was Terry McGee, a Tri-Star first officer. Ironically many years later his parents would save the day for me and family in England. As we had a spare bedroom, we offered it to him in, so it helped out on our bond. Another pilot we assisted by hiring a caravan and allowing him to put it on our property was Tom Gilligan. It initially helped him get started with his family who were arriving out from England. The collapse of Court Line had severe effects on a pilot fraternity and a lot of the guys were facing financial problems. The South African contract although very low paid was therefore a godsend. Being on the overseas routes meant a lot of time away. But by not spending much of my per diem allowance I could save a bit by eating off the street so to say and not at the expensive hotels.

South Africa was, due sanctions, not allowed to fly over Africa, so our routes North and South bound diverting into Europe and England were usually via Sal a Portuguese island off the Northwest coast of Africa. Here South African Airways extended the runway turning it into a major refueling airfield with a small hostel like building to house in transit crews. Sometimes a crew would end up spending as much as 2 or 3 days there. Incoming crews would bring in booze and braai (BBQ) meat, so there were many a time when a party would start late at night with the incoming crews ending with the morning sunrise. There was nothing there except a small peer, a few local inhabitants and the S.A.A hostel situated in desert like surroundings by the beach which had shark infested waters and near an old, deserted lighthouse. It was not a tourist spot in any way, however on one flight I did get a visa for Josie to accompany me, and she had the experience of the isolated island crew overnight.

I had a house and knew a few of the 18 contracted first officers from Court Line, so we used to get together quite often over a braai (BBQ). As there was no T.V. in South Africa, we would rent a projector and enjoy a film with folks spread out on the floor and couches. Later, as my father had a speed boat which he had built years earlier and not used much, we borrowed it from his home in Durban 600 kilometres away. This helped to expand our off days to skiing and speed boating on the Vaal River.

Many of the chaps joined in for a day picnic and fun. We all felt a bit alien to the permanent S.A.A crews who looked at us as sort of intruding pilots on their basically military pilot intake system, rather than freelance pilots with not much of a chance to get a permanent position with S.A.A. Secondly, we were in general older than the other second officers, comically called "Boy Pilots". The fact that the pension was very small for incoming short-term crew of our sort, meant we would not get the benefit of an extended say 30 year working life with S.A.A. so making long term prospects a bit questionable. There was the added civil unrest developing throughout the country and civil war was possible. There were a few captains who were very friendly one in mention was Captain Guy Patterson an ex-air force pilot who flew with the South African air force that went to help the American air force in Korea. He was also the captain of a B747 that was hit by shrapnel when attempting a landing in Angola during that war.

At that time S.A.A and other airlines were evacuating Portuguese citizens out of the Portuguese colonies as civil war had broken out with the South African armed forces protecting our borders. As I have mentioned earlier South Africa was fighting Russians backed Cuban soldiers who by infiltrating our black ANC opposition party, were attempting to gain control of South Africa and the strategic Cape Sea route. Patterson was able to fly back to Johannesburg unpressurised with a few holes in the belly of the aircraft. It was said that one piece of shrapnel was embedded in the bottom of a passenger seat. My time flying on the B707 was short lived as only 6 months after being checked out I was informed that I was to start B747 training. This entailed another long ground school program as S.A.A did not train their pilots on a need-to-know basis. We had to learn and pass exams on every nut and bolt of the aircraft which usually took up to three months including simulator sessions. Failing any of it meant you were looking for another job.

Needless to say, I was very excited about this as now I had moved up again onto heavy airline equipment all within one year. The training period also gave me a bit more time at home where regretfully Josie was overdoing the 5pm sundowners. Liquor in South Africa was relatively cheap so coming from the Caribbean and having an Irish family plus being a housewife in a foreign country, whose husband was away a lot, it was a strong social attraction. Things on this matter got progressively worse, which entailed me often having to come home at lunchtime to sort out Scott's feeding and hygiene. Leaving in the morning with Josie still sleeping off the night before, I would have to lock the passage and leave Scott playing in the safe corridor area. The stress was starting to show and my ability to concentrate on the B747 homework requirement was being affected. The course was finally completed, and we were escorted out to the hanger by Captain Trotter, a senior training captain. He stood in front of the massive nose of the B747 looking up at the cockpit 56 feet above him. Turning to us, he remarked that many of us had a love for certain aircraft such as DC3, DC6/7, Viscount, B707 etc. But he said that we would have an affair with the B747. He was absolutely right and in years to come I was to recall his comments clearly as fate had it, I was to have a life ahead of me involving this great aircraft. I was checked out on the aircraft so started into the long-haul Jumbo flights with regretfully more days away. There was a small wage increase so the per diems were increased in line with days away. Ironically if anyone had said to me only a few years earlier I would be a pilot officer on a B747, I would not have believed them.

The house we bought had a double garage, so with my father's help, I converted one garage into a small flat and an office. I had a dream of starting a travel business consisting of a club in which the members were the owners of the aircraft. It would be a privately owned ex-airline machine such as a B707 to escape the high costs of an airline operation. It would start out flying to the UK and back offering club members a very economical seat as overheads would be reduced. I would look at the crew who wanted to do a bit of moonlighting and publish a magazine showing the departure times. I would then look at destinations such as my favourite holiday places or islands.

within the South African area. To start it off I leased a Cessna 402 on paying time used only. I then sold time to business in the Johannesburg area. They paid in advance for the flight time in so had the aircraft at their disposal for that pre-booked time. At first, I flew the aircraft myself with Tom Gilligan helping me. I then hired a Canadian chap who I had met on a short trip I had done back to Toronto to renew my Canadian Instrument rating and license. He arrived with his wife and started work. To get him a car we painted my mother's old Datsun black with a roller and named it the Rolls Royce. The business picked up under the name of "REPHOLD" a closed corporation my lawyer friend Tony Maisels had registered for me. Anthony and his wife Helen later immigrated to Israel, I was to meet them again in 1995, 20 years later. The idea was to progress onto a larger aircraft, but it was a dream that had a long way to go.

SAA. B747 landing in HONG KONG

A picture of one of South African Airways (Union Airways) original AVRO York, a converted bomber registration ZS-ATR named Impala.

About this time my father decided at 75 to retire. He had been in the construction business since he was 16 years of age. Working his way up to a master builder, shipping company, trading store owner plus numerous properties. He with my mother moved to a place called Inchanga. This was an up country very small location on the edge of an area called "The valley of a thousand hills". He had a Nissan 1400 that was his foreman's so as Josie found it hard to drive the Mustang, he gave us the little pickup. It had a canopy so it became our travelling nursery by placing a mattress in the back and parking the vehicle as close as possible to say a house party where Scott could sleep peacefully with his nighttime toys. With the petrol restriction it was far more economical than the Mustang with its big V8 engine.

My old friend Gary who was with us in the Caribbean came out for a visit, so we took him to the Kruger National game park. Convertibles are not allowed but somehow the Mustang did not look like a convertible, so we got away with it. We were able to see the big 5 staying at the lovely lodge cabins. It was a great trip with lots of laughs about our wild days in the Caribbean. Just after this trip Josie found a lump in her left breast causing some concern. She attended the Airline appointed hospital and had it removed. Regretfully the gay male nurse fancied her wedding ring which was made for us by a jeweler in Toronto. They were very beautiful leaves wrapped over each other and often admired by friends. The sister in charge suggested that she wrap the ring in Elastoplast for the operation. However, the male nurse when preparing her for the theatre insisted that it be taken of and left in her bedside locker. After the operation the ring disappeared. It was reported but the hospital indicated they were not responsible. The nurse denied he had instructed her to leave it in the locker. She was heartbroken but by using mine I had an exact copy made for her.

A visit from Josie's parents came as a bit of a surprise. They had made arrangements to visit good old Ireland so did a detour through Johannesburg. I had a flight going to Durban on the Cessna 402, so I flew them to the coast to meet my parents. It was bit hectic as the price of our whisky and they being Irish, caused a few interesting evenings. Regretfully we did not see her father again as he died a year later in Australia. Margaret and Bill Gardner, our English neighbours were a great help to me as they in my absence would keep an eye on Josie, but they to enjoy their G & T at sundown which at times did not help the matter. Just after all this and a visit to the doctor to our delight we found out Josie was pregnant with our second child due in April.

The B747 was operating throughout the S.A.A network concentrating on the long-haul overseas flights. On one occasion the crew I was on hand to meet the incoming flight from Germany at Las Palmas in the Canary Islands. It was a very wet rainy evening; the passengers had boarded, and we were preparing to push back to depart for Johannesburg. Suddenly the captain was informed that a passenger had been found asleep behind a couch in the departure lounge. At this point all the air stairs and ground equipment had been removed. It appeared urgent that we attempt to board the passenger as the next flight was a week later. Facing the urgency of the matter the captain decided that we could possibly board the passenger via what was called the ENE department below the first-class section. This required someone to go and lift the floor panel up, descend down a ladder to the room below containing the electrical equipment. Then via another hatch lowers a ladder down to the ground. I being the junior officer was detailed to do this. Completing the venture, I found myself on the ground next to the nose wheel. Approaching me a small Mini Moke arrived with the female passenger and her baskets. I now to her horror had to persuade her to climb up the ladder. Taking into consideration it was dark, raining, and very noisy as there were four huge engines running, it took supreme convincing to get her to attempt the climb. Finally convinced that she would be left behind, she handed me her basket and started up the ladder. The wind and engine wash took her skirt and turned her into an upside-down umbrella. I immediately downed the basket and attempted to hold down the rouge skirt, with my face against her backside. Eventually interjected with screams and shoving from me, we between us made it to the top and into the first-class lounge. The look on passenger's faces peering down into the compartment hole as the bedraggled duo appeared through the floor was something else. Never mind the fact that one was in uniform and proceeded directly to the cockpit. I am not sure if the passenger entertained the idea of using S.A.A for her return flight. My comment was she had been by mistake put in steerage class. The cabin attendants proceeded to convince the passengers that I was not one of the flying pilots on this leg of their journey.

Pilots on overseas flights have been known to get up to some real naughty antics. I could write a book on things that have happened with some of the airlines I have worked with. Naturally out of respect I could never name them. An example of this was an overnighting crew decided in fun to sprinkle some water on the incoming crew from their hotel veranda. They filled a tin wastepaper basket with water and placed it on the veranda wall. It slipped and crashed below onto the bonnet/hood of a very expensive car owned by the manager. There was hell to pay for that. Another was a crew overnighting in Gatwick. There was a large party going on in the main conference hall. This hall had a small pool filled with some floating arrangements. Two of the crew proceeded down the emergency exit to the door nearest to the pool. Stripping off, in the nude burst through the door, jumped into the pool and retreated in the same way, disappearing up the emergency stairwell. The horror, and ladies screams that erupted was heard from the manager's office. The culprits were identified as airline crew members. The captain of the culprits was immediately summoned to the manager's office. He denied any responsibility supporting his crew by saying they were in a crew briefing and therefore could not have been his crew. He indicated there was another opposition airline crew from the same country in the hotel which he suspected were the rude inconsiderate and shameful culprits. The other crew was evicted from the hotel.

Another company, for instance with days to spare, would arrive in Lisbon with three days to wait. A few of us would rent a Kombi, take the sheets and the emergency candles from the hotel and drive down to the Algarve coast to swim and camp on the beach picking up wine, cheese and food enrooted. On the beach we would dig a small hole inserting the candle so as not to have it blown out. Some of the crew would bring guitars, so entertaining us during the night. On one memorable drive the engineer was driving with me in the right-hand seat. Two male gay attendants had joined the trip and were sitting behind us discussing their romance problems. One guy said that his lover was giving him pain where it should have been pleasure. Well, the engineer nearly drove the kombi off the road.

Scott, now a bouncing bubbly little boy suddenly went down with what we thought was a cold or flu. Every time a lay him down he started to cry, plus his eyes were bulging and looked bruised. This was putting a lot of pressure on me having to handle his mother who was having a sort of prenatal depression fueled with whiskey. My days at the training centre were being adversely affected by having to rush home to check out the home situation. On the second visit to the doctor, I was taken outside and asked how fast I could get Scott to the children's hospital in Johannesburg centre. I advised the doctor I had a fast Mustang how long did he suggest I had. His reply was as soon as possible. I raced through the traffic in so arriving at the hospital to find a nurse waiting for me at the casualty section with a cot. Scott was rushed into an admittance bay whereas I held him across my lap he was administered a lumbar puncture to the spine. Close examination indicated an infection of the ethmoidal passages of the brain affecting the olfactory nerves so causing swelling putting pressure on the brain and consequently the swollen and bruised eyes.

It was life or death matter with him being taken straight into children's ward drains being inserted to relieve the pressure. He was incubated and I had to leave to return home and deal with my wife. I was due out on another overseas flight but by arrangement with the operations department I was relieved of it and put on a later flight. I was told not to visit him, but I did and what I saw horrified me. Here was this frail skeletonized baby lying with tubes in what looked like ever orifice, a limp skin and bone child in an incubator. Time dragged as Scott fought for his life but after 10 days we were called to collect him. The baby bouncing boy was no longer. Now a thin limp child with us being warned there could be some motor system damage.

The stress of this, another child on the way and trying to stay on top of my flying career was getting to me. In need of help at home I asked my mother to fly up from Durban and assist. Which she immediately did, bringing with her some old mothers' remedies and home cooking to try and help in the matter? The cause of this infection was eventually put down to the dust off the Johannesburg mines. This waste is contaminated with arsenic from the gold extraction process. It now appeared that Johannesburg was not the place for Scott to live if he wanted to improve and get back his health. The outcome of this handicapping infection would be with him and us for many years, as the motor system of his brain had been affected. He appeared not to be able to talk and insisted on pointing or drawing anything he wanted. His balance was also affected often just falling over. It was recommended that it would be healthier for him to go down to my folks' home being a lower altitude with a higher humidity. So, this was done, and my mother flew back to Durban with him.

At this time, we seemed to be going through a rough period exerting a lot of pressure on me. Scott sick, Josie about to have our 2nd child, very low income which would not be increased for many years due to seniority, the general political situation appeared to be heading for an all-out political/racial war. I was now on another B727 course being my third in eighteen months. Things were not going well, and a decision was made to return back to Canada at the end of the two-year contract. Grant was duly born so we started making arrangement to leave for Canada in two months' time. This decision was made supported by the political situation, Scott's health and the children's future. Living at the coast Scott had improved a great deal which was a godsend to us but fortified our decision to return to Toronto. An old friend Bob Beck from Seagreen days and LIAT had established that should I return and want an immediate job he could arrange this with a DC3 cargo company called Millard Air. So that was in my back pocket. With everything underway to depart I got a call from a Canadian geological airborne survey company. They had heard I was in South Africa holding a Canadian license with survey experience. One of their survey Catalina aircraft was scheduled to be in Johannesburg. Their Canadian pilot was not able to do the contract in South Africa so would I be interested in taking on the captains' position to complete the survey detail. With South African

Airlines being one of the lowest paid airlines in the world, I was being paid a measly R700:00 ($1,400) per month. Funds to make a move to Canada were very low especially after the cost of Grants birth and Scott's medical needs. The wages to fly the Catalina was double and partly paid in Canada dollars. This finalized the decision, so I arranged to meet the S.A.A chief pilot handing in my resignation effective at the end of my two-year contract in two months' time. They were very annoyed and immediately withdrew my incomplete endorsement on the B727 program. The Geoterix Catalina arrived with a French delivery pilot named Piallat. We did a fast check out flight and a brief ground school on the aircraft after which he then signed the necessary Canadian papers to qualify me on the aircraft.

The Catalina with my father at Phalaborwa in what was called the Eastern Transvaal. They were visiting the Kruger National Game Park.

The aircraft registration was CF-MIR having the R2000 Pratt and Whitney engines with the standard bow. The clipper bow had a higher foredeck with gun position used during the war. This aircraft, after finishing the survey work was literally abandoned at the Rand airport as I was led to understand Geoterix went out of business. Later many, many years later an American bought it, refurbished it to a very good standard and flew it back to California in the U.S.A. Its historic background was that it was this aircraft that sighted the German battleship in the Atlantic so sounding the alarm of a pending major ocean battle. At the time it was flown by an America pilot flying for the Royal Air Force. I believe his name was Smith. An interesting footnote is that the U.S.A did not have an air force till 1947. They had the Army Air Corps.

Having earlier had experience on airborne survey I found getting back into the swing of things very easy. I was now back in command of an aircraft, being a medium size machine with rather a unique rating as there were not many amphibious flying boats still flying. The only difference was that on this heavier aircraft the geological drone was not fixed in the tail but flying on a 100-meter cable below the aircraft. The art of doing the survey lines and steep turning was not to kink the cable so snapping it which would send the drone flying off and crashing. Something one did not want to do considering the cost of the ground recovery required. We usually flew at about 200 feet off the ground contour flying, so accuracy to map read was very important plus missing hydro lines and mountain faces. On one occasion I took Josie and our newborn son Grant with me for an overnight flight to Phalaborwa next to the Kruger game park. Grant, like his brother did his first flight with me in command and on a historic world war aircraft. This job put me financially back in the picture plus later we rented our house to a Geoterix operations chap being based in Johannesburg. I flew on doing all the necessary contracted work, most of it over the same parts of the country I had surveyed back in 1965 for Map Studio productions. We were now ready to return to Canada, but I had to go first leaving Josie and the kids to follow once I got established in Toronto.

SAA to Millard Canada

Leaving a rather tearful family I travelled via London to Toronto where my old friend Bob met me. Taking me back to his home I met his wife Millie whom I had not seen in years. They had an adopted son Kevin and moved back to Toronto when LIAT went bankrupt with Court Line. Gary Dalton had also moved back to Montreal and was flying Shorts sky van for NORDAIR in the far north. After a good meal and a beer or two it was decided that a sound sleep was necessary and then in the morning a visit to Millard air to meet Carl Millard who Bob had seen to secure me a job on the DC3 freighters. The meeting went well so Carl suggested that as my medical and instrument rating were current, Bob should give me a check ride on the DC3 to become current that afternoon. It had been 6 years since I had flown a DC3, but it all came back very quickly. Returning to the office, it was found that the company was short of a captain on the late-night flight to Willow Run in the states. I agreed to do the flight if they gave me an experienced co-pilot who knew all the ropes.

My career with Millard Air had started. In 56 hours, I had left South Africa travelled to Canada, got a job and was flying again. Now the problem was to find a place to stay for me immediately and later the family. Bob kindly loaned me his car to do the night freight flight. While at Millard's office I found out that the building had in fact belonged to the Air Force and was originally across the field. Carl had bought it, moved it on road hauling trailers to its present position. Here he established his business with the two large hangers for his team of engineers to work in servicing the fleet of DC3s, Beech 18 and Hansa jet. Later two DC4s. One half of the building had a hanger and offices which had been rented out to the M.O.T. (ministry of transport.) These were now empty, all with secure doors, toilets and showers. One office had an old bed without a mattress and an ancient TV in it. It did not take me long to size up the situation. Here was in-house accommodation, water, light toilets, fast food across the road and if Carl would allow it at no charge. I immediately confronted Carl with my proposal that I would like to accept occupancy of the indicated office so I would be on call for any flights. Favourable he agreed but was a bit surprised that I would consider living in a partially derelict office. He also had a Cortina car that belonged to his niece and would be selling it for $600.00. I indicated that I did not have $600.00 but when the car was available, I would like to buy it if he deducted the money from my wages, this he agreed to. This car had an interesting life as after every flight to save money on fuel, I would siphon 2 or 3 gallons of aviation fuel from the DC3 and fill my car, it ran like a top. Bob said he had a spare mattress he would give me so within two days I had moved in.

By now I had met some of the copilots, one being Lorne Davidson who was a farmer's son living on his father's farm very near the airport. This also put him on short notice for flights, so we had to fly a lot together. He kindly loaned me his car to renew my Canadian driver license. We were to remain longtime friends. The flying became hectic with flights going out daily and nightly supporting the auto industries assembly lines across the U.S.A. Plus now and then passenger charters nationwide. Being a resident in the building I was first on call and took as many as the office could give me. My first months' pay cheque came in at $1250.00. Flying at $10.00 per flight day plus 10c a mile I had flown 100 hours. This was equal to about R1875.00 rand double my S.A.A wages. I was tired but was there to make the money.

Beech 18 passing Toronto International Airfield

One afternoon Lorne invited me to visit his farm. He and his family were very hospitable where I enjoyed being on a farm, afternoon coffee and a good chat with his folks. Their farm was in the country, but housing complexes and road expansions were rapidly encroaching on their property. Expropriation was inevitable so his father was slowly diminishing farming activities. On the way Lorne pointed out a new town house complex that was under construction. It was a nice location and not far from the airport supported by highway 402 to London Ontario. I made a point of reminding myself to go and check it out. Josie and Grant were waiting for me to advise them on when to travel. Also, as Scott was living in Durban with his grandparents, they too had to be co-ordinate to meet up with Josie and Grant in Johannesburg to travel to Canada. I had been away a month, and things were getting rather urgent in so much as our house in Johannesburg was rented out at the month end. Josie was having a hard time with the new baby however I was concerned about the evening cocktails getting a bit heavy. Alone with only friends' post-natal depression was also a factor. Margaret, our neighbour on more than one occasion had to enter our house only to find Josie asleep with a crying wet and unfed baby.

I was now desperate to find family accommodation so returned to the new town house complex I had seen when visiting Lorne's farm. They looked very nice, consisting of 3 bedrooms on suite bathroom with a second bathroom and a visitor's toilet. Large garage, lounge with fireplace, dining room, medium kitchen plus a small terrace. There was to be a large park with tennis courts and play area and very near a shopping centre. It was perfect for what I needed but the price was the question. They wanted $49,000 per unit on the park. My gut feeling was, "get this now as it was ideal". My conversation with the agent went well as it appeared I would have to put down $1,000 to secure pending a bank loan. My next step was to approach the bank about getting a bond. I met with the Canadian Imperial Bank of Commerce bank manager Mrs. McIntyre at the airport branch. After what I would say was one of the smoothest talks I ever made, she agreed on the grounds that I was gainfully employed by Millard to give me the loan. I must add here that Mrs. Macintyre and I remained friends for many years. I did a lot more business with her and based my financial success on her advice. I left the bank in 7th heaven I was now about to buy my second house this one in Canada. Immediately I got back to the agent who secured a townhouse at the end of the block and in the park but there was a problem. It would not be ready for the family. After explaining my predicament very smoothly and politely she contacted the developer who agreed to rent me a unit until mine was completed. With this all signed and sealed I contacted both families and arranged the travel itinerary. Then it was back to my hanger and tried to fly myself into liquidity. A few weeks later the family arrived extremely tired and worn out after the long travelling time. I met them at the airport then checked us in to the Airport hotel for the night. I had to explain that things were going to be a bit like camping at first but that at least we had a roof over our head which we would eventually own.

After a much-needed night's sleep for all concerned I packed the car and put everything on the roof, which included a baby cot for Grant. Driving out we realized that everything we owned was in and on the car. The unit they had rented us was clean and ready but absolutely stark empty. Quickly I set up the cot, the mattress I had delivered from the hanger the day before. Millie Beck had lent me some sheets to be used as sheeting and curtains. Pillows and towels she also lent us with some spare pots, pans and eating utensils. The old TV also came along as did a DC3 passenger seat I scrounged from the hanger. I visited the shops and filled our food cupboards, a cooler box with ice served as a fridge for the interim. The town house complex was only a few miles from a quaint little village called Streetsville. Here we found a great second-hand shop where we were able to obtain some furnishings and needed stuff to set up home. Within a week we were set and proceeded to enjoy the country life.

Within 2 months our house was completed so a move was made at the same time and with little more funds we furnished it to our satisfaction. Kids had toys, and bikes, and had made friends to play in the lovely park. It was summer so the sun never set until about 22:00. This gave us time to meet neighbours and arrange BBQ get-togethers. Having quite a few friends from the Ward Air days, Josie had the opportunity of meeting up with them again. This sort of expanded our circle of new and old friends. Regretfully a cancer was detected in Josie's uterus, and she had to undergo a hysterectomy. This was now the second showing of cancer considering the earlier lump in her breast. To try and keep flying nightly plus taking care of the children put a strain on us. Our good friends Jean Mackie and Lin Mutiger stepped in to help.

With winter now starting to approach we had to start preparing ourselves for the cold. Children's winter clothing, winter tires and snow shovels were just some of the requirements never mind us needing warm clothing we had not had to have for years. In the winter flying slows down so I was always on the lookout for extra work.

There was on the airfield a new technical exploration company called Barrenger research plus a Hudson Bay Exploration company all working on geometrical survey exploration equipment using test aircraft. As I was now known for having experience in survey flying, I was able to do some flying for the Hudson Bay Company on a DC3 with a large nose loop which I will explain later. Earlier in my story I covered working for the Hudson Bay Company in London operating a printing press. I wonder what that poor fellow who I worked with would think now of where I was in life compared to his mundane 8 to 5 job. Barringer research had a British Norman Trilander test aircraft converted to also do Geometrical airborne survey work but with more advanced air sniffing computerized equipment. This too I will cover later with an interesting outcome.

Millard Air DC 3

I was flying for three companies, one being MILLARD Air at night on the DC3 freighter and the others when needed during the day. They were Barringer Research doing test flying on a modified B/N Trilander with dust sniffing scoops in the nose, and a magnetic anomaly detector in the tail plus Hudson Bays DC3 geo survey experimental aircraft.

Most of the flying for Millard was at night and this particular night me and f/o Mike Merklinger were scheduled to fly a load of auto parts from Toronto to Pittsburgh then on to Philadelphia, Charlot and back to Toronto. We estimated a 6 to 8 hours flight through the night and as usual no autopilot. The weather was deteriorating across the whole of the

Eastern seaboard, but we hoped we would miss most of it by routing via a more inland airway. By about 01 a.m. we were clear of Charlotte so now an empty flight planned back. By the time we had reached the Catskill Mountains the turbulence was bad, and we were picking up a lot of ice. This was standard for the area and considering it was November icing conditions were expected. As we flew towards the lake area, I was getting concerned about our fuel situation as the ice and head wind were taking a heavy toll on our progress. Clearing New York, we made contact with Toronto arrival to be told the airport was going down to minimums with snow and strong winds. We had an alternate at Oshawa or if need be, we could turn for Buffalo City in the USA. Mike got busy attempting to get the most recent MET, but it turned out we were actually being boxed in. The ice was coming off the props like gun fire and our weight was definitely not what we had expected due to ice on the belly. The landing lights showed the leading edges icing but not too seriously. Being over the lake and now on minimum fuel with Toronto going down was not a place I wished to be. Finally, we were able to pick up Toronto ADF and started to position for final. Toronto advised they were at minimums, Oshawa down, Buffalo down all we had was Trenton military field which could give us a G.S.R approach, (Ground Surveillance Radar. A talk down sort of blind landing service) but fuel-wise it was now almost out of range. It was one of those nights, black as pitch, heavy icing, freezing cold cockpit and turbulence over a freezing lake. On intercepting the localizer Toronto advised they were down but as we were established to continue. The glide slope came in and I called for the landing check list. It was the standard old GBUMFFS (Gas, Brakes, Undercarriage, Mixture, Fuel, Flaps, and Switches) which Mike started on. Toronto approach handed us over to Toronto tower for landing clearance with a sort of good luck additive.

With no alternative field, very low on fuel due ice and restricted airspeed we continued. At 10,000 feet landing lights were on but I switched them off as it was blinding with the horizontal snowstorm causing visual deflection, so taking away any hope of seeing a runway or VARSI landing light. With the gear down Mike switched over to the dregs of fuel in the main tanks, immediately at this point both engines started to surge and splutter. I reached down for carb ice when both engines started to backfire, and we slid below the glide slope. With a freezing lake now only 1,200 feet below us a frantic search started to see what was wrong. It took a few seconds, but they were the longest seconds of my life. On reaching over to switch the fuel selectors back to reserve hoping that it was a fuel problem which could be fixed by selecting a reserve with maybe some fuel, I realized that Mike had mistaken the fuel selector handle and turned it the wrong way. On the DC3 the fuel selector is sort of wedge shaped, being a half circle on one end and an arrowhead on the other. Mike had selected the half circle end to the main tanks which in fact shut them off. As we sunk well below the glide scope and now destined for a water landing and death, suddenly the right engine took giving us a few minutes of time to stop the sink and try to get some altitude being only about 500 feet above the water.

At full power we were able to level off at the same time the left engine roared back to power allowing us to start a desperate attempt to get back onto the glide slope. Toronto approach had seen our sudden drop below the glide slope and was feverishly attempting to make contact and advise accordingly. Out of the blackness of the night appeared what I recognized as the smudge of a shoreline, behind it I saw the 401 freeway then the threshold lights dimly visible in the drifting snow. I was off to the left of the runway but by turning across the threshold so attempting to line up with a runway I could not actually see but was able to miraculously land. During this somewhere in the background a clearance to land was heard but we did not respond as it was taking all we had to put the old empty DAK down on a wind torn, snow covered runway which appeared to be moving beneath us. On coming to a halt, I realized we were somewhere halfway down the runway and with lack of vision unable to taxi. A follow me vehicle came out of the night and finally led us to our cargo parking at the Millard Air hangers. I had to file a report with ATC on landing below minimums, which thankfully they accepted recognizing our plight together with the sudden severe weather change.

It was a night Mike and I would never forget, but had it not been for the old DC3 I think the lake would have been our resting spot. This kind of flying was long hours up to 6 or 10 hours, all night some going into day. Many young pilots cut their teeth on this type of flying in an attempt to get flying experience (hours) and went on to become excellent major airline captains. Mike was one.

Carl Millard was a self-made character of note. Almost everyone had at one time or other flown freelance or moonlighted with him to pick up extra cash. The younger commercial pilots desperate to build hours had contract agreements with him to get a DC 3 endorsement and fly as many hours as they could stay awake. Most of the young guys who I flew with over my period of working for Carl as said became major airline pilots. The DC3 was a great aircraft to cut one's teeth on, but not always good for the nerves. I could tell of many stories and incidents I had while flying for Millard Air. One of these was the time I flew an empty DC3 into Oshawa airport as usual late at night to pick up a load of auto parts to be delivered to Chicago. The wind was blowing at between 30 gusting 45 knots. The approach was good breaking cloud at 1500feet. If one knew the DAK it was not hard to make a very short landing provided the aircraft was light and there was a reasonable wind. I approached the threshold in the full landing configuration, selecting full flap as we crossed the fence. The tower advised wind was gusting 45k which I could feel as the DAK was wallowing a bit and trying to dance around. At about touch down the wind gusted 60K on the nose, our landing speed was around 50k or so. We sort of hung there trying to feel the runway but as I was doing this the F/O checked the hanger on the left side bringing it to my quick attention. We were actually flying backwards as the hanger was slowly passing from the rear to the nose. We estimated the touchdown speed had been with full flap around 35k, so taking into consideration a head wind gusting 45k-60k it was feasible and certainly good for joke over a beer. The DC3 I had in the Caribbean operated into a 1000-foot runway, landing at 40 or below knots not being uncommon.

The name of the game with Millard was to make money. He paid $10 a day and 10c a mile. The more miles one could put in the better. This happened when the strike of 1976 hit the Canadian airlines and airports. Main line carriers were almost grounded. Every charter company that could operate was put into service. It was time to make money, so Millard put his DC3s into an across Canada service flying from Toronto to Winnipeg, Calgary over the Rockies to Vancouver. One pilot would fly as the other cat napped on the floor between the cockpit seats. Some of the aircraft did not have autopilots so it was a case of hand flying the whole route. Night and day we flew the circuit carrying banker's documents, Urgent material and human body parts. It was case again of must fly and must get in. To operate the Calgary section over the Rockies to Prince George an intersection, then down to Vancouver required the aircraft to fly at 24,000 feet so requiring oxygen for the crew. On one occasion the oxygen mask failed so we put the tubes in our mouths and pressed on. A couple of the DC3s had long-range Pacific tanks so upon arrival at Vancouver a 13-hour flight, we could turn around and fly direct to Toronto via the Southern route across the Northern USA. Round trip time was 25 hours. To stay awake while one pilot catnapped on the floor, autopilot on, the other pilot would sit on his armrest so if he fell asleep, he would fall off.

Once enroute from Toronto to Winnipeg I smelt smoke. The F/O was flying so I decided to investigate the cargo. Upon opening the door into the cargo area, I saw smoke filling the rear of the aircraft. Being winter with a few airports open due snow covering and late at night Winnipeg was the only field we could land at but 2 hours flying away. Scrambling over the cargo with a fire extinguisher in hand I started to haul the cargo forward searching for the source. The smoke was getting worse as I dug into the bags almost unable to breathe. Shouting forward I instructed the F/O to advise Winnipeg of our position.

Considering a forced landing at night into snow covered unknown terrain was not a happy thought and pressured me on to find the smoke source. Finally, I had moved all the cargo as far forward as I could without identifying the trouble. With the aid of my flashlight, I then established the smoke was coming from the rear toilet compartment which on cargo DC3 is vacant but does have an electrical bay. Upon opening the door, the compartment was saturated in smoke, however I could see a small flame amongst the electrical equipment. Chocking I covered my face and with the aid of the flashlight identified the flame was coming from the DC/AC inverter. Hitting it with the fire extinguisher it went out briefly only to flare up again. We were in serious trouble as if the flame could not be contained it could ignite the wiring and spread into cargo and cockpit section. I realized we might not be able to continue and clambered back to the cockpit. There I switched off all the AC/driven equipment going onto DC battery power only. Thankfully with the inverted being switched off, the flame and smoke ceased. We had about one hour to go so without any electrical power I relied entirely on the batteries to operate our navigation and radio systems. In a quick call to Winnipeg control, I advised we were OK but would only use the VHF radio in 30 minutes time.

This enabled us to maintain as much battery power as available, giving us enough power for the expected instrument approach into Winnipeg. As per our instruction we called again in 30 minutes. Winnipeg advised that the airport was open, no traffic and we were cleared for the approach to call on final. This we successfully made a very welcome landing in a snow-covered wintery night.

Hours later with the arrival of morning and numerous cups of coffee a replacement inverter was located from the local Nordair Company, and we pressed on to Calgary. Ironically on this very route there is a Millardair DC3 lying underwater in a lake between Thunder Bay and Winnipeg clearly seen in summer. Ditched, but the story about it I never did find out.

The DC 3 was a famous aircraft. It was a real work horse and ended up being modified a lot. Some were on floats, some had turbine engines, some ended up as roofs for roadside cafés. A criminal undignified shame for a lady of the skies to die this way. For this one on the roof of a roadhouse in South Africa December 13 proved to be an unlucky day for 6845. Capt. W.L Chiazzari was scheduled to do an air test on 6845. He took with him A/Cpl's FO Burger, JL du Toit and P Harrall. The camouflage paint on the wings of the Dakota did not easily reveal the position of the fuel filler caps and the fact that the port filler cap was not locked tightly in place was not noticed during the pre-flight. After take-off from Zwart Kop Air Station the crew noticed fuel streaming from the port fuel tank. The hot exhaust gases ignited the fumes and despite a hurried landing, the centre section, port motor, port main plane and port elevator were all damaged by the fire before the fire tender could put it out. 18, 000 were built and were noted as "The aircraft that changed the world". There is a book written about it by that name.

Flying the old DC3 was a lot of fun but they were old, and one had to be ready for the unexpected. On another occasion we had completed loading auto parts to be flown to Willowrun in the States, this field was famous for building the B24 bomber during WW2.

As I started number 2 engine the engine seemed to catch fire. The possibility that it was a carburetor fire was possible, so the action is to open the throttle wide and swallow the flame. This I did and the fire extinguished, however as I throttled back the fire reappeared. Something was seriously wrong so with the first officer in the cockpit keeping the engine idling just above where the flame rebirthed, I went and found that the carburetor had come loose from the manifold. Rather than be stuck in freezing winter weather and no place to go, I decided that as long as we could hold power the carburetor would stay in place. This we did flying the aircraft back to Toronto arriving at 6 a.m. and changing planes to continue on to Willow run. It was a bit tough to keep power up on one engine during the approach, but it was not a nice sight to see the flames erupt from under the cowling every time I powered back to below the limit that the carburetor would hold under intake pressure. Finally, we got back to the base in Toronto where the engineers were astounded that we had been able to make it without further incident.

My flying with Millard was to end as I signed a contract with "Barringer Research" as mentioned earlier. At the same time, I also did development work for Hudson Bay mining on another experimental aircraft being a modified DC3 with a huge loop antenna on the nose. They were financially involved with Gold Fields of South Africa so being South Africa and with survey experience, I was suited for the work. This would take us flying into the far North which would become quite hazardous as we pushed the envelope to complete contracts working into a winter. Something I said I would not do again after the year with Northwest Territorial in the Arctic. However, some of the co-pilots who flew with me such as Mike Merklinger, Ray Cook, and Lorne Davidson later became senior captains with Air Canada. Here is an extract from a letter I received from one of them 35 years later. Lorne had remained in contact during his entire flying career. When he retired from Air Canada, he and his wife Sue where able to visit me three times in South Africa during my retired years. We enjoyed taking them to visit the game parks and sights of the country.

'Hi Al.

When I think back to Millard Air days, the only training we got was from you! It's correct that it was partly your efforts that gave Air Canada three career pilots! Mike did his 35 years and punched out. Ray did the same but moved on to freelance flying with ironically QATAR AIRLINES. They changed the rules as of Jan 01 /2014 so that pilots can stay until 71 and Captains until 65. Many or most are staying, we will see how long as it just started.

Take Care.

Lorne."

I took this as a compliment as for all of my career I always attempted to do what I could to help aviators up no matter what level on the ladder of the industry they were at.

Barringer research.

Flying the experimental B/N Trilander for Barringer research as a test aircraft meant a lot of low and medium level flying. The idea was that the intake sniffer in the nose would collect the dust and analyze it on an onboard computer. We also had laser stabilizers across the wing for stability and a magnetic detector sticking out on a tail from the rear of the aircraft to identify below ground mineral anomalies. Most of the time we flew contour at 50 to 100 feet. Late one evening, trying to finish a test detail I started to develop wing and carburetor icing causing the aircraft to ice up. I was forced to do a forced landing on a frozen lake. It was well below zero on the ice and our chances of surviving the night in the aircraft were not good. It was one of those crystal-clear nights with the northern lights showing beautifully far north of us. We were too far from the nearest town for any radio reception on VHF to be heard. I did put out a mayday call but received no response. We discussed if we would survive by trying to walk out to the nearest camp or village, which I might add was some distance according to our charts. Then fate played its hand again. Out of the dark eastern sky we heard a helicopter. I immediately got onto the emergency frequency 121.5 and got a response. The chopper altered course saw the flares we had ignited in so located us. He was able to uplift the three of us as fortunately he was empty and heading for Sudbury, a town to the west. It was good to see the lights of the town as we were very cold and would not have been alive if we had tried to walk out. A grateful thanks to the chopper pilot followed by a taxi to a warm motel, and telephone calls to the company in Toronto. I also filed a note with the Mounties explaining what had happened, indicating no loss of life or damage to the aircraft.

In contact with the company, I indicated that if we could get a generator and some heaters, I could fly the aircraft off the lake. It was approved so we set about hiring a truck, a couple of skidoos with a freight sled, a generator, four heaters plus survival gear and food.

Driving back, we located a spot near the lake. Offloading the skidoos with one towing the sled filled with the generator, heaters and survival gear, we set off cross country to find the lake which was named Night Hawk Lake. As we came to the shoreline we could see the aircraft out in the middle. To our horror as we approached it, it was not what we wanted to see, the plane had slipped beneath the ice and was half filled with frozen water.

I now had to go to plan B and decided to get local hardened foresters from a nearby camp to help. In the days that followed travelling back and forward from Sudbury we build cribbage's under the wings and took the engines off trucking them back to a hanger in Sudbury. We were able to figure out what had happened. The aircraft was very low to the ground, in this case the ice. The warm morning sun reflecting off the ice had thawed the ice close to the fuselage. The weight of the aircraft had pushed down the left side where the ice had thinned. It then slipped into the weakened ice allowing the aircraft to go down onto its wing. There was no damage except for the water that had got into the interior and onto our computers. Otherwise, the machine was in good state but not flyable. A big Sikorsky 206 helicopter was charted, coming in later and lifted the fuselage up with branches tied to the wings to stop them from flying during the positioning flight to Sudbury where it was reassembled. Months later after a complete overhaul I flew it out but again had to land on a lake outside Toronto. Same problem with icing up of the carburetors and no wing de-icing. This time I flew it off in the morning having got a Herman Nelson heater to heat her engines up. I gave up flying it and told the owners it was not meant for winter work 50 feet of the ground. I said someone will get hurt. Sure, enough a young pilot whose name I think was McCurdy, crashed it. I believe he was killed.

With the winter now arriving the flying industry slowed down. There was not much freelance work around. As I had left Millard Air to work full time for Barringer I was no longer on the seniority list. The work for Hudson Bay explorations was not very often as they were still developing the technical side of the project. It looked like a cold unpaid winter. We started to get out ice skating, tobogganing with the kids and in general trying to not get to depressed with cold and our depreciating financial situation.

In late January I heard Cathay Pacific were starting to hire B707 pilots. I in part desperation decided to pull an ACE card and call the gentleman who I had given a lift from Montserrat to Antigua back in the Caribbean days. The same chap I had walked into when buying the DC3 from Bahama Air. Mr. Adrian Swire. He was the CEO of the Swire group who owned Cathay Pacific Airlines. He had indicated that if he could be of help sometime, I should give him a call on the card number he had given me. This I did getting through to his home in England. I apologized for the impulsive call but wondered if his offer to assist was still available. He was extremely polite and did remember me. Following which he said he would see what he could do. True to his word as that of a gentleman, two weeks later I was contacted by Cathay operation to say there was a return ticket for me to come for an interview and simulator check ride in Hong Kong. I was ecstatic as this seemed like the opportunity I had been waiting for. I was almost financially embarrassed with the bond over my head, winter and no income.

Cathay Pacific Airlines

On the appointed day I left for the airport to catch my flight via Vancouver to Hong Kong. As I left my home the weather turned into one of the worst storms Toronto had so far experienced. The temperature dropped down into minus 40°c with heavy snow and then freezing rain. The whole airport came to a stop. No buses, taxis, trains or emergency vehicles could move. Toronto international was closed, iced up. There were no flights in or out and those aircraft out of the hanger looked like they had been dressed in white veils of ice. With no chance of getting out of the airport everyone had to find a spot to sleep. I located a corner lying down for a sleepless night on the hard floor. Midday the next day brought some hope as the sun had come out starting to melt the ice and snow. Aircraft were de-iced with the Air Canada flight to Vancouver connecting with Cathay Pacific expected to depart late that night, 24 hours late. I did not have the cash to make a long-distance call to a number I was not sure of for Cathay operations. So had to wait it out. Eventually I got airborne arriving in Vancouver six hours later in the midmorning.

As I walked into the transit terminal heading for my connecting gate who would I bump into but Bill Henderson my navigator from back in 1965 flying for Map Studio and the military? Bill had become a helicopter pilot now flying for a British Colombian Helicopter Company which I think was Okanagan Helicopters. It was a brief chat where we quickly discussed the past 12 years and what we had been up to. Little did I know that it would be the last time I would see him as he and my other old American friend Richard Dryfus, both killed themselves in helicopters flying the dangerous Columbia range Canadian mountains being part of the Northern Rockies. Richard was the friend when hearing of his death I had telegrammed his parents with my quote for his eulogy. Which was "He is on a flight to far horizons with God as his navigator". Their reply was that they used it. I hope someone will use it for my eulogy.

Departing Vancouver for Hong Kong I tried to get some much-needed sleep. The fatigue and anticipation of what was ahead caused me to not to get much. Arriving at Hong Kong I found that my hotel room had been cancelled due to my non arrival. There was no room but across the road was cheaper hotel within my credit card budget. Contacting the operations department, they were a bit surprised and explained that the simulator sessions were over. I was able to speak to a Capt. McCookweir who was sympathetic after hearing me out and the problems I had had to get there. An hour later he returned my call to say that there was an open secession in two hours' time if I could make it to the training school. He also said that as there were no check instructors available so he would function as the check airman and put me through the paces.

I think the fact that I had been associated to Mr. Swires connection might have opened a time envelope for my check flight. I was exhausted with barely 6 hours sleep in the past 36 hours plus the time change. I took a cold shower, got some hot coffee and departed by taxi for the training school. There I met Capt. McCookweir and explained we had to be quick as the simulator availability was only for an hour. He proceeded to put me through the check test after which I agreed it was not the best, but I was fatigued and finding it hard to concentrate. He arranged for another hour test the next morning in so completing the two-hour required simulator check ride. I returned to the hotel desperately trying to get some rest and sleep. The noise and general day sounds kept me awake for hours but eventually fell into a deep sleep.

I awoke with a wakeup call at 07:00am proceeding after a strange Chinese breakfast to the simulator building. Capt. McCookweir gave me the remaining hour check ride indicating it was a lot better. But it was obvious I had been off the B707 for some time relating to my experience with South Africa Airways three years earlier back in 1974.

I then had an interview with Capt. McCookweir, and I believe a senior flight engineer instructor

Patrick Dunn together with Captain Len Cowper from operations. Captain Cowper also explained that they had hired quite a few South African Airways pilots giving a couple of names. I knew a few, one being (if I remember correctly) was Jack Smith who had been on the same two-year contract as me in SAA. So, I made contact with him and asked if I could bunk down maybe in his spare room, couch or even floor. He advised that their home was not like South Africa with the flats being small. He and his good wife gave me a blow-up mattress on the stair well for a night easing my poor financial state plus a home cooked meal. I was informed by the operations office that I was to depart on the evening flight of the third day and would be advised of my situation regarding being hired. Finally, I returned to Toronto after a hellish 6 day merry go round exhausted with a big-time warp. Captain Cowper contacted me and told me that I had not done to well. He explained that they appreciated the situation I got into referring to time, jet lag etc., but added that if they had had more time available to them, they would have after I had got a day's rest given me another hour in the simulator. He indicated that I was on the hiring list but to be rechecked at a later date when the ground school dates had been set up. It was a matter of wait and see. It was a lot to expect having been flying the DC3 for the last year, and the B747 for the year before that. So, I was out of touch with the B707 for three years.

Hudson Bay Explorations.

Hudson Bay exploration was a subsidiary of Hudson Bay mining and smelting. Up until now I had been doing the entire test flying to develop a flying magnetometer to record the mineral anomalies below the surface. This was done by transmitting a signal from the loop extended in front of the aircraft, it then bounced down below the surface and was picked up by the magnetometer which we called the bird, flying below the aircraft at about 50 -100 feet off the ground. The lower one could fly the bird the more accurate the signal. The bird flying at the end of 100 meters of cable attached to a winch drum in the aircraft, was then flown back into a cradle extending from the rear of the aircraft. All this was very experimental and had only been subjected to test flights north of Toronto. The dangerous part was the actual docking of the bird as if it got out of control due to slip stream effect, it could swing up and collide with the elevators and rudder. Worse still wrap itself around the tail of the aircraft possibly rendering the aircraft uncontrollable.

About a week or two after getting back from Cathay I got a telephone call from a chap named Bevan who was in charge of the experimental section of the company. He indicated that they were happy now to proceed onto a year's program with the experimental aircraft and equipment. Would I be interested in a full-time job with them to develop the equipment on the field? He proposed a salary and in general the terms of employment under the Hudson Bay umbrella. I accepted and got heavily involved on a full-time basis flying of their experimental DC 3. One of the Millard copilots Mike Merklinger came on board as he preferred the full time flying rather than the night cargo work. We continued to perfect the docking of the bird and got all the onboard equipment up to speed and ready to go into production. For this I was informed that we would be based at an isolated place called Flin Flon way north of Winnipeg. Flin Flon was named after a couple of old prospector years back found a comic book with a cartoon about a chap called Flintaboty Flonagan. When iron and silver ore was found there, and a mine established it was comically named after the cartoon character. The mine had big investments from Gold Fields the South African mining investors together with Hudson Bay Mining. Being based this far north was so we could get access to the unexplored areas of the Northern territory and Arctic, plus there was an airfield, fuel with a mining town for supplies. The whole operation was to be moved which included the Aircraft, flight crew, systems operator and a ground engineer. The aircraft was subsequently loaded which included ground generators, Herman Nelsons (winter engine heating tents) camping equipment, tent and outdoor kitchen requirements. The plan was to fly there, set up a camp, find crew accommodation and start a 6-month airborne survey detail covering a large area of the prescribed wild north. I was rather excited about the venture as it was steady good money, my own crew, camping and flying only in good weather. The other good part about it was that summer was arriving; hot weather and I hoped to maybe have my family join me. Finally departing Toronto, we duly arrived at Flin Flon where we hastily started to set up a camp, renting a station wagon and finding accommodation.

The schedule was to fly as many of the programmed flight lines, surveying as far possible over wild Northern territory. Prospectors had identified areas of possible mineral underground deposits. So many anomalous references had been marked out for us to fly and record the necessary data.

Much earlier in my story I mentioned fate would have me with Hudson Bay again.

Hudson Bay explorations survey DC3

Once established I started to see how I could get my family up to spend the summer with me. I found a fold up caravan for sale which had all the utensils I would need to camp out. On the main road near the airport was a sort of general dealers / trading store run by a family of Ukrainians. They lived on the premises with a storeroom below the store. The storeroom had a separate bathroom and toilet accessible to a nice plot of lakeside land which included a small pier and beach. I made arrangements to move the caravan there and must add they were very obliging. In brief I flew my family up and ensconced them at the caravan site where they spent a lovely 3month swimming and playing on the lake beach. I set up a tent which made an outdoor veranda. When not flying the crew would come and spend the evening BBQing and in general enjoying the outdoors. We did some fishing but mainly supplied ourselves from the trading store. The kids loved the water, chased the ducks and made tracks in the sand for their toys. Swimming was good but one had to check the kids and us for leaches, common in Canadian waters.

The survey work was going well with the company being pleased by the lines we were flying. Copilot Mike Merklinger had gone back to Toronto to be replaced by Dave McCurdy. On one such detail we were flying towards what looked like a thunderstorm build-up. Hoping to finish the line and turn back onto the next line we approached the activity with caution. All of a sudden, a fireball erupted near the winching gear at the rear of the aircraft. It raced up past the operator and exploded in the cockpit. All I can say was that both the pilots and the operator needed to visit the laundry after the flight. We put it down to the fact that we were trailing a 100-meter cable attached to the geo drone. It we believed conducted static electricity possibly from the thunderhead, then ran up the cable into the cable drum running on the winch and discharged into the cockpit.

All the flying was at a low level, contouring the land and map reading of geographic maps. We were working further north so sensing the coming winter. Autumn came and it was getting too cold to keep the family in the camp. Duly they departed back to Toronto. Remaining we attempted to complete all the requested flying details. An early winter came upon us with the aircraft needing engine tents and Herman Nelson heaters. I was still living in the caravan but in fear of the gas heater going out while I slept which could then asphyxiate me, I would turn it off. At times waking in the morning with my sleeping bag frozen to the mattress. This was caused by my body heat making a thin layer of dampness which froze. We reached a point where we could continue no further with the survey details as the winter snow and ice was more than we could handle. Especially with the huge loop now collecting rim ice causing vibration and instability in the loop receivers.

Advising the company of our situation we started to pack up preparing to return to Toronto. I sold the caravan to the Ukraine store owners thankful to be out of the area as the fear of meeting bears enroute to the toilet and shower had become a concern. Sometimes I would hear them outside the caravan with the occasional bump or rub against the outer caravan structure. Just before leaving I got a call from the store owner to say I had a telephone call awaiting me in his office. It was from Dusty Thompson, the chief pilot now of Quebec Air in Montreal. He advised that the airline was looking for a temporary B707 first officer to assist with their winter schedule operating out of Montreal. He understood I had the B707 rating acquired from South African Airways. If I was available, he would contact me when back in Toronto. I was delighted and very eager to get back to my home and our Toronto base. This we did putting the aircraft away for the winter season. Equipment and operating gear were serviced and stowed for next year's operation. A lay-off was inevitable now being the 10th December with winter now upon us very little survey work could be completed.

The thought of no work for the winter bothered me but the call from Dusty with the aid of fate changed that. His call came offering me a six-month contract to fly as a first officer on their B707. He understood I was not current and would set up a refresher training program for me and another English chap with American Airlines training academy in Dallas. It was set for the 17th of December. Seven days after flying the DC3 in freezing conditions I was on the B707 refresher course consisting of a week's fast ground school. Then a four-day two-hour section in the simulator training with Capt. Seffert. Finally, a simulator checkout with the M.O.T inspector Jack Bailey.

A day later on the 22nd of December I did a flight check out with Captain Stan Suffer the America Airlines check airman on the American B707 so being current and certified to the flight line. I was also able to get the rating onto my U.S.A license by having completed the requirements for both the Canadian and the USA, M.O.T standards. It had been a hard but a good year and now with a B707 job I was back on the jets so expanding my international license qualifications. Able to spend Christmas at home was also good.

Quebec Air

Quebec Air was based in Montreal which meant I had to find some accommodation to be available for the flights. A call to my old friend Garry Dalton from Seagreen and LIAT days who was now flying for Nordair was made. He and his wife Gail were very pleased to offer me the use of their spare room. Spending Christmas with the family was good but on the 27th I caught the Turbo train to Montreal where Gary met me taking me back to his apartment to meet Gail followed by a good dinner. The next day I reported to the offices of Quebec Air, met Dusty Thompson and did all the necessary paperwork. This completed I was informed by their operations department that I would be operating the following days flight to St Lucia. It was a surprise as it was 10 years earlier that I had flown in with the engineers who were going to convert the old, abandoned war time field to a new international airport to serve the growing tourist industry. Dusty Thompson was the captain on the flight as it was a line check for me as well as indoctrination to their procedures. The B707 they operated was a 720 series which had the dorsal fin at the rear below the rudder. They were relatively fast, old and did not have the passenger capacity of the upgraded series.

Boeing 707 -720

It was mid-winter and very cold as Montreal is between rivers which creates a damp cold. Using taxis to get to work I decided I needed a car to use while in Montreal. I found a used Mazda station wagon at a good price so now had some wheels. On days off commuting on the Turbo or Rapido train a six-hour trip was my only way of getting to my home in Mississauga Toronto. This was quite a spectacular experience on winter nights as the locomotive travelling at high speed ploughed through the high snowbanks sending a wave of snow from the lead engine illuminated by the head light. The New Year came and went but with it came some problems. Josie had been complaining of lower body pains so visited a doctor to see what the problem might be. Following some extensive examinations and x-rays it was established she had cancer of the uterus. It came as a shock with the cure to save her life being a hysterectomy. The pressure was now on as I had to keep flying out of Montreal but was needed to look after the kids and her, during her post operation recovery period. To do this I was able to arrange for an elderly Swedish lady to came and move into our basement unit to keep an eye on things. She was a great help and kept the kids amused with her stories. She would watch our basement TV and have her own running on a different channel. After the surgery Josie seemed to go into menopause and the drinking increased followed by periods of depression. Things were not working out and Josie seemed to object to the woman being in our house and caring for the kids as an au pair. It was a bit nerve racking to leave the kids in the unstable situation not knowing what the situation would be upon my return. Eventually I would leave the lady to care for Grant who was nearly two and travel with Scott to Montreal where Gail would care for him when I went on flights. To try and ease the depression I was able to arrange for two free tickets on Quebec Air for Josie and a friend Janie, to travel to Mexico on a week's holiday. On her return things eased up a bit as she seemed to come to terms with her medical situation.

The contract rolled on with winter excursion flights to the Caribbean, Mexico, Southern States and Nassau. On one of the flights, I think it was via Nassau or Bermuda, we could not start one of the engines. With three engines running the engineer and I took out the starter on a live engine and put it into the dead engine so getting all four engines running enabled us to continue the flight back to Montreal. The noise of standing next to a running jet engine is something one does not want to repeat.

The contract was going well, I was building my flight time on the B707 which would enhance my qualifications for further contracts. Now able to follow up possible work I started to send out resumes (CV) to as many companies I could find who may want a B707 pilot. One was WARDAIR who I had been hounding ever since leaving South Africa. It was of course Josie's old company, so we knew a few of the senior personnel such as Captains Peter Highfield, Garth Martin, Jerry Fartheringham, and John Strickland and a lot of the cabin attendants.

Without my knowledge my father in South Africa decided that my Mustang was taking up too much room in his garage. So out of the blue he shipped it to Montreal. I was then able to drive it back to Toronto but with one car already in the garage a second was a problem. We got over it by careful parking and as summer came it was good to have the conversable back in Canada. My kids loved it, but a problem was coming.

My much-travelled Mustang. Western Canada, South Africa. Eastern Canada. Sold for $4,000. If kept in South Africa in 2019 would have got $100,000

Eventually the last flight was coming up so as I had Scott with me, I prepared to drive back to Toronto in the old Mazda. On a couple of days off I and an engineer whose surname was Ruth sprayed painted the car in his garage to give it a better appearance. Bidding farewell to the company, Gary, Gail and a few friends we left to drive through the night, but the temperature had dropped to minus 30°f with a lot of cross wind, icy highways and snowbanks. Hellish cold drive with heater on full and blanket over my legs. Scott fell asleep in a sleeping bag on the back seat, we eventually we arrived back in Mississauga in the early hours of the morning. Thankfully the old Mazda held out for if it had broken down, I would have had to abandon it to catch a lift with the first passing car or we would have frozen to death.

It was now time to see what was on the aviation market, so far it had been a good year but as they say the hound was but pup. Regretfully I heard years later that Quebec Air had an accident and that the B707 -720 fuselage was scrapped at the St Lucia airport. I believe the company eventually went out of business but that was not uncommon in Canada as over the years I lived there 17 companies failed. Dusty Thompson would not forget me so in years to come we were to meet again. Searching the freelance market was now my main objective but fate was about to play a double headed card. I got a call from Ward Air setting up an interview date. This I thought would be my utopia if I could get a position with them, I would be set for the remaining years of my aviation career.

Ward Air

The interview date came with what I understood to be successful in getting a First Officer position on their B707 fleet. They also had B747s so pilots from the B707 were being trained to meet the required aircrew for the B747 fleet. I had the B707 endorsement, was current on type having done the license qualification in Dallas for Quebec Air, plus I had the B747 experience as supported by the letter of reference from South

African Airways. This letter was later to cause me severe grief. A month later with all the usual indoctrination, paperwork, uniform issue, medical, refresher training a successful final line check was completed with Captain Jim Goodhand, so releasing me to the fleet. It was good to be back flying the routes with a few pilots and cabin staff that knew me from the early days in the Caribbean and when I married Josie. On one of the flights to England we heard that Richard Branson's balloon was ditching in the ocean. We happened to be right over the location in so watched as the balloon basket touched the water leaving a long tail of disturbed water as the canopy settled onto the sea. Thankfully he was rescued.

At this point, I will refer back to the time when I was working as a labourer in Horley U.K. I targeted the conversation with the farmer who said I should go and get a labourer's job at the new airport as they made good money. As I touched down one evening at Gatwick airport, which was the airport he was referring to, I wondered what he would say if I could find him and tell him I was now working at the airport as a pilot flying B707 jets. With steady work, things were looking up. I was paying off our house, we fell under the medical scheme plus paying into the pension system. The kids were well with Scott preparing to start preschool classes. The six-month probationary period was approaching with a possible upgrade to the B747. Then the trouble started. It went like this. A couple of the Ward Air pilots were sitting in a bar at Gatwick when a South African friend who I had helped when with Seagreen to get a job as a DC3 Captain joined them asking if I now was flying for their company. He was fired for failing to secure cargo, especially fuel drums, consequently caused a load of drums and cargo to shift while attempting to land at the island of St Vincent. A precarious situation developed which almost caused a crash. He (let's call him Ron) later joined South African Airways about a year or two before me. He seemed resentful that I had left S.A.A and had now finally joined a very sort after Canadian Company. He had spent some time as a bush pilot in Northern Canada flying for Ptarmigan Airways. His stories were very interesting but my presence, knowing his background, sort of dampened his claim to fame.

When the two Ward Air pilots confirmed that I was flying for them he questioned how I had been able to get the B707 endorsement. He suggested that I had possibly forged a document to qualify for the rating. He added that he knew my matriculation or grade 12 certificates were not authentic. This was true as it was the same one, I had used to get into South African Airways. He was not aware of my American Airline training for Quebec Air or that I had legally done all required exams to qualify for the rating. This was reported back to the Ward Air chief pilot. I was immediately taken off the flight line and summoned to the office for a disciplinary hearing. The letter in question was the topic as I explained that my position with S.A.A was a Second officer and not a senior first officer. I pointed out that the letter of reference from S.A. Airways indicated originally that I was a first officer. To keep the records straight I have changed this letter to read my position as

Ward Air B707

The girl in the right-hand corner became my wife.

second officer, a lower rating. However, although I had thought I was doing the right thing by correcting the rating status they felt I had not been truthful to them. Regardless of the fact I had completed a fully accepted B707 rating training to meet the American F.A.A and the Canadian M.O.T standards. I had the support of a couple of the Captains plus Ward Air did follow up my reference with South African Airways who confirmed my position. Because of bar talk, and a jealous so-called friend, my probation of six months ended with no chance of a permanent position. I was devastated. It seemed my whole world had crashed under me. I repeatedly asked myself why, by being honest were my credentials unacceptable now with a bad mark against my name. The freelance flying business is a tight operation with word of mouth as a major way of getting in or out of work contracts. A bad name will destroy one's qualifications and career no matter how much experience you have. But as things went a few years later Ward Air went out of business with the critics and so-called troublemakers on the street looking for a job or were integrated with the takeover company of Canadian on junior officer levels. It was a massive upheaval for all concerned with many of the pilots and technical staff scouring the contract or freelance market. Mostly only with a Canadian pilot's license and no experience outside of the two main aircraft

Ward Air had at the time the B707 and B747. A major airline has a set program to train their pilots. To work in the freelance market, one has to be willing to do most things oneself, not assisted by a full operations department and set cockpit operations procedures. Changing overnight to a new company and even a new country requires a set amount of self-confidence and a major amount of experience. To me it was one of the worst periods of my life, all I had hoped for was destroyed. I now was morally distraught and just could not seem to get myself off the ground so to say. The idea of having to once again pack a bag pick a uniform Black or Blue from my collection to suit a company and once again set out to work with and go through the difficult program of joining a contract with totally different procedures and rules. Generally, one had to do a simulator check, a medical and write the air law of the hiring contractor's aviation rules. Then it was weeks of work before a break would come to allow you to get home. I was at times away for 3 to 6 months so can advise that a hotel room in another culture is not the way to spend one's time off. With that in mind it was better to fly as much as one could, I on occasion exceeded the flight time limitations allowed. As further on in my story I had flown 100 hours in 8 days. Then again 108 in 10 days covering my tracks by not logging my flight times. A contract pilot flies for money paid by the hour, he is a pilot of fortune.

With the collapse of Ward Air contract maybe I was pushed in the right direction but only fate knew that. My job now was to find another contract. Winter was coming so I had to pull myself together and get something fast.

During an earlier summer a new complex was being built on neighbouring land. All the discarded and scrap wood plus aluminum trimming and Rhino board was being dumped in a skip for removal each morning. In the evening, I would go over and choose pieces of what I could find. I completely rebuilt my basement with a fireplace, small bar and a hideaway bed. I also made a small deck with a BBQ stand. One afternoon I was standing at the BBQ talking to my neighbour who had a visiting friend. His friend informed me that he had a relative flying for Air Jamaica and possibly they were looking for pilots. Realizing I was out of work, he advised me that he would look into it. This he did coming back to say that Air Jamaica was not, but he was told Iran Air was going to hire some pilots. From this grape vine information, I was able to contact the Iran Air office getting a confirmation a few days later that yes, they would be hiring pilots preferentially from Canada. Following up on this and submitting my resume (CV) I a few days later was informed that a Senior Captain who was Iranian lived in Toronto and arrangements could be made to meet. Agreeing to this I was told to be at the Toronto International airport at a set time and date. He would be waiting for me, so I was to look for the captain, whose appearance I did not know amongst the crowded passengers. I walked into the congested terminal saw a chap standing sort of alone and as fate would have it amongst all the people, he was the man I was to meet. A brief discussion confirmed that yes, they were hiring, and could I come to Tehran to meet the operations manager and as he was the chief pilot my interview was almost complete. I left there finding it hard to believe that I was now all but hired by Iran Air.

But surprises do come unexpectedly. Two days later I got told a ticket was waiting for me at the airport and I should depart for Tehran in four days' time. All went well with me travelling on the scheduled flight to Iran. Arriving there I was given an address of a place to stay, with instructions to be at the operations office at 08:00am in the morning. I felt comfortable as everyone had been helpful and courteous. Duly arriving at the office building I was ushered into a very large office and told by an English-speaking lady who I presumed was a secretary to wait as Caption Fotoohi would see me soon. In a few minutes, I was again ushered into a large room with an elaborate desk occupied by a very official-looking man. He suggested I sit down and asked me what I was there for. I went silent for a moment staring at him face to face completely flabbergasted. When I got myself together, I explained what had transpired from the early correspondence and my reason for being there. He shook his head and advised that as far as he knew they did not have any place for foreign pilots. He suggested that I return to Canada and if things changed, I would be advised. He then bid me goodbye showing me the door. I was stunned, got back to my lodgings and prepared to return to Toronto on the ticket the secretary handed me as I left the office.

Back in Toronto my wife and I could not believe what had taken place. I had just gone halfway around the world for a senseless 15-minute meeting, it was my first introduction into the Middle East and their attitude towards employees. In so settled down to find a job anywhere before midwinter. A few of the Ward Air crew such as captains Highfield, Fatheringham. Strickland, Kirby and Martin took my case to Abe Freeman who was the chief of operations. There seemed to be something very wrong, and they attempted to correct it. Therefore, giving me a small bit of hope that I would be re-instated, but no matter I was not and that seemed to be the end of the matter. Today I think it was the admittance that I had a forged G12 (matriculation) certificate that sunk me, regardless of my experience. The exposure of it by my friend Don could not be circumvented so I did not hold any anger with Ward Air, but all the same it was a shock to my system as I seemed at last to be secure and happy with my job offering a better life for my family. If I was having my nerves and patience tested what happens next is another story which puts my life on the line.

Iran Air.

With things once again looking a bit bleak, supported by the oncoming winter which would put most of the jobs on hold till early spring. But then it happened with a telephone call from the Iran Air office. They advised me that they had been given instructions to contact me and explain that there had been a mistake, and I was to proceed back to Tehran to start work for the airline as soon as possible. They indicated that there was a ticket waiting for me at the airport for the next flight out in 3 days' time. In so I followed the same procedures and returned back to Tehran. Once there I was escorted through then to be fitted with uniforms, signed all the required documents, given a copy of their air law and a small booklet on aviation weather. I was told I could stay at the accommodation which they supplied for a week, and I was booked in to have a medical examination plus an exam on their Air Law and meteorology. This was to qualify for an Iranian Airline Transport License. During this period, I met a few more airline officials and pilots. Some of them I knew from the COURT LINE days involving LIAT in the Caribbean. One chap I met was Doug Eden a B737 captain who indicated that he and his wife had a spare room which they would be happy to rent out to me for temporary accommodation. Things were looking up; I was then sent to the flight line to be line checked by Captain Madani which I completed successfully and was assigned to the operations department for flight line duty. I was in contact with my wife and family explaining to them that Tehran was actually a nice place slowly developing into a western way of thinking. Iran was previously called Persia up to 1936. With Christmas approaching I would make arrangements for them to come, and we could possibly look at apartments, schools etc. in expectation of doing a few years there to maintain a steady aviation career.

Farsi was the main language with the Shah Mohammad Reza of the Pahlavi dynasty being very western orientated, controlling what was called the Peacock throne. This throne or Shahhood became a den of trouble and was at one time a serious threat to the world. It becomes confusing as it goes back a long time. Much more than I can explain. I will start before the First World War of 1914 when Churchill had beaten the Germans to the Iran oil reserves, WW2 started three months later. This was done using funds from the British government to buy 51 percent in the now Anglo– Persian Oil company. It was a brilliant move and Briton used the oil to eventually win the war. After WW1 the Shah at the time was Ahmad Shah Qajar who had a Persian Cossack Brigade who became indispensable to the Shah in suppressing rebels, driving out Russian and British occupants so establishing order. In 1925 he had become very powerful deposing the Shah and set up a parliament so initiating himself as the head of the constitutional monarchy. He then pronounced himself as the new Shah, so adopting the surname of Pahlavi. He set about in 1935 renaming Persia to the name of Imperial state of IRAN.

The Pahlavi family would rule for 54 years. During these years there was a lot of conflict involving the control of oil, the Trans–Iranian Railway, the near bankruptcy of the country, heavy disputes of financial investments and numerous close wars by foreign powers such as the U.S.A. Russia. France and Britain. By the early part of the pending World War 2 Germany had an earnest desire for oil. Russia was now an ally of Britain who together needed the railway to move supplies from the Persian Gulf to the Soviet Union and the Eastern war front. The Shah was demanding increasing royalties which Britain had been paying. Doubt now set in that the Shah might not honour agreements in place with the allied countries. Reza Khan was sympathetic to the Nazis but had proclaimed neutrality for Iran. In August 1941 Britain now proclaimed that the German engineers and Technicians were spies or saboteurs, a threat to the oil facilities. A demand was issued that they be sent back to Germany. However, the Shah refused to expel the nationals causing Britain and Russia to invade Iran.

The Shah was arrested and exiled to South Africa. The U.S.A sent in the military to guard the Trans-Iranian Railway. Later the British and Russians joined the U.S.A in controlling the railway and oil industry. That year Reza Khans 22-year-old son, Mohammad Reza Pahlavi was allowed to claim the throne. Appointing a government contingent to the British and Americans. There was still more trouble to come as he was like his father wanting to use the oil to modernize the country. Opposition to this was a parliamentarian named Mohammad Mosaddegh. He was very popular with the people so in 1951 chose him as the prime minster. He set about nationalizing and causing disputes with the agreements in place. He was interested in more than the oil dollar and cents. The cold war was on and his attempt to rule by decree pictured a possible proto- communist alignment with Russia. Although the new Shah opposed him, he feared the west would orchestrate an oil embargo which would put Iran into economic ruin. Although the new shah tried to replace him much of the public seeing a possible foreign hand in the politics started riots. Fearing a mutiny from the army after ordering them to suppress the riots he fled the country. After much dispute and possible take over's eventually it was decided for political and economic reasons Mosaddegh had to go. The USA via the C.I.A assured the Shahs safety if he would return. This he did and attempted to stabilize the country. The C.I.A organized and paid politicians, clergy, army officers and street thugs to join in a campaign of protest exciting them into riots. This also included a gang of Tehran mobsters to incite pro Shah riots. The coupe came about in 1953 after which Moasddegh was arrested and sentenced to three years imprisonment. Some of his supporters were imprisoned and several executed. The forces that supported Mosaddegh did not dissipate as resentment of the Shah rule continued to build. In 1997 it all boiled over as an Islamic revolution with the takeover by the Shiite clergy. The USA judged it futile to reinstate a pro-western government and turned it back on the Shah encouraging an invasion of Iran by Iraq. This was where I came into the picture. But Iraq invaded Iran in 1980 fighting over a border dispute as an excuse to get their hands on the oil, but the real reason was that Saddam was fearful that the Iran Islamic revolutions would incite an attack the Iraq shite concentrated in the South bordering Iran and cause them to rise up against him. It became a bloody conflict ending only 8 years later with millions of dead as Saddam used chemical weapons on the military and civilians alike. There is a lot more to this but too much to write about.

Shah Reza   *Ayatollah Khomeini*

Ironically the story of the peacock throne a priceless chair of jewels and gold was lost at sea off the South African coast enroute to Iran (Persia) many years before. Numerous treasure hunters have attempted to find it but to date the ocean has not revealed its Neptune treasure. The Shah had opposition from the Islamic republic leader Ayatollah who had been deported but obtained sanctuary in France for 17 years. He and his religious followers opposed western thinking plus objected to incoming industrial modern investments. Nobody at this time suspected any major upheavals but as we found out we were wrong.

I was now flying the B707 online to most of the airline's destinations. There were a lot of foreign pilots as the airline was expanding attempting to get onto more international routes with B747s. I had met a group of pilots and cabin attendants who had rented a large manor house with a swimming pool and space to have some good parties. They were English, Australian, South

African, European a mixed bunch but good to get to know as expatriates. Guys such as Brian Saunders ex Court Line, Allan Berg ex QANTAS, (deceased). Sitting having a beer one evening in the Tropical Hotel the fellow next to was introduced himself a Peter Evans an ex-British Airways pilot. Having the same surnames we got into a long conversation. It turned out he was the youngest British Airways captain on the B707 at 28 years of age. He joined B.A. at 16 years of age got his commercial at 18 years of age so took early retirement at 36 years of age now working in the freelance market. We became good friends and to date are still in contact. I had now moved into Doug Eden's spare room which was comfortable for my needs as I was away considerably. Flying with some of the senior captains such as Grayelli, Ansari, Garig, and Timsaw I was informed that there was going to be an upgrade of B707 first officers to captains of which I was being considered. My resume when I left the company indicated this. I was therefore rather keen on such a development, thus supporting a possible family move. Life for families was not too bad. Good shopping centres reasonable social life, beautiful El Burz Mountains where incidentally the Russians had a radar listening base, and there was the big USA military base. There were also good restaurants such as the Italian club and the French cafe. Locals were pleasant but reserved.

Plans were set for the arrival of my family coming via London. I was scheduled to do the connecting flight thereby meeting them at Heathrow Hotel. The captain on my flight was Captain Barry Hakiemin a check pilot for the company. He indicated that this flight could be counted as a check for my considered upgrade to captain. Prior to our departure from Tehran a political demonstration broke out and from what we understood it was possibly going to spread into the rural areas. It was the Islamic republic followers against the Shah, Bhai and Parsi Indians of Persian Zoroastrian origin, had been attacked by the Islam movement opposing their non-Islamic religious beliefs.

With that we continued to operate the flight which was a night stop at London. My family was there so it was a great feeling to be with the wife and boys again after two months. In the morning, we arranged to meet up with my crew so we could depart for the airport together. The incoming flight was on time so the operating crew would be on the bus that would collect our crew. As they got off the bus the incoming captain called us aside. He had a very concerned look on his face following which he explained that there was big trouble in Tehran. The insurgent Islamic movement had gone hostile burning Bhai /Farsi Indians in their locked homes. The Bakhtiari tribes where another tribe within the Iranian territory. They were pro Shah so also under the threat of being murdered by the coming insurrection. The rebellious mobs were rioting on the outskirts of Tehran and things did not look good. He advised us to delay the flight until more information could be collected or not return at all. This we decided to do but now I had a concern about my family. The decision was finally made that the flight would return to Tehran as it was a full load with now desperate Iranians wanting to get back to their homes. I was asked if I would operate the flight as the incoming first officer had refused due to duty time plus not being Iranian therefore not wishing to go back to unknown problems.

Iran Air B707

Barry and the flight engineer both urgently wanted to get back to their families, so I had no option but to sympathize with them so agreed on doing the return flight. Here my old friend and ex-South African, COURT line pilot Terry McGee came to the rescue. He had boarded with us when with South African Airways. His folks had visited us when living in Johannesburg, so we knew them well enough. I had decided I could not take the family back with me but had decided that I would return a day or so later and collect them if all was safe in Iran. I booked them into the Heathrow hotel again for two nights, called Terry's folks who lived outside of London, explaining the predicament and asked if they could keep an eye on things until I got back. They were very warm friendly people so openly offered their kind assistance; little did I know I would be indebted to them for what was to transpire?

Bidding a tearful family goodbye, I flew the service back to Tehran not knowing what to expect. I had not received my much-needed pay for December and my personal effects were there. During the flight, Barry picked up some more information regarding the situation in Tehran and

Iran in general. It was not good with more riots. Once in Iranian airspace, air traffic control advised us that the control of Tehran airport was erratic, they cleared us directly to the airport control centre. Once in contact, we were cleared to report on final for the active runway. At that position, we were cleared to land and given a parking bay to proceed at our discretion.

A rather unusual clearance which we followed. There was no further contact with the tower or the ground control. Once parked no grounds man appeared to chock the aircraft. From a nearby building a grounds man appeared pushing the airstair cart and connected it to the front exit door. He came running up to say there was no ground assistance or any customs, immigration officers. He advised us and passengers to leave the aircraft as quickly as possible. At that point another man arrived opening the cargo doors the two men dumped baggage onto the ground for passengers to help themselves. The captain and flight engineer disappeared between the buildings which appeared to be empty. I picked up my flight bag and followed coming out between the buildings onto a parking area. All that could be heard was the idling of car engines from abandoned cars with some vehicles racing into the USA military area. The military had evacuated their base with personnel and family rushing to board the departing aircraft. At about that same time an Iran Air B747 departed with as we found out later, with as many of the foreign personnel on board that could be contacted. Out of the far corner I saw a Willys station wagon vehicle approaching. These were used as crew transport and from what I could see there was a couple of hostesses in the vehicle. I was able to stop it so getting aboard and asked the driver to take me to my address. The girls reported that the driver was too scared but would get us as close to town as possible. They also informed me that there was big trouble all around and that we should not be seen in uniform as it aligned us to the liberal Shah side of the conflict. I had my big winter coat on so hiding my uniform but placed my hat under the folds of the coat.

Travelling at some speed we passed a convoy of cars and military vehicles heading for the airport. The road from the airport goes up a reasonably steep hill opposite the Hilton hotel. As the vehicle crested the hill there was a sandbagged wall in the middle of the road with two armed soldiers standing alongside it. At gun point the driver was made to stop. We were ordered out of the vehicle and all our bags removed. They made us open everything exposing all its contents which they frisked through. They were about to start on us when a Paycan being a small local pickup, came over the crest of the hill in the opposite direction to us. The soldiers turned shouting and waving their guns indicating that the vehicle must stop, it did not and raced on by us. At that moment one of the soldiers opened fire with the vehicle careening off the left side of the road and ended up in the ditch on its left side. From our position it appeared that the driver was dead with a head wound, but unfortunately there was also a child lying against the dashboard motionless. The soldier nearest to us ordered the driver and ourselves to move on immediately, which we did.

Getting very near the centre of town the driver refused to go any further mainly because of shouting and people attempting to obstruct his way. The girls left and disappeared into the alleyways, I got out and started to walk as fast as I could towards my apartment. To do this I had to walk through the centre of town which was now filling with a large number of shouting and demonstrating people. I kept my head down and made sure my uniform was not seen. Gunfire suddenly broke out on the left side of my intended direction, so I turned to go through Takdijumpshut (cannot remember the correct spelling) which is the centre of the car distribution and sales area. More gun fire opened up in front of me, so I had to turn back in my original direction heading towards the initial gunfire area. Running up a walled alleyway I saw there were two bodies lying in the gutter (gauche) at the same time gunfire behind me was heard followed by a ricochet of bullets off the walls above my head. Looking back, I saw a howling mob of people descending into the square intermingled with a few army jeeps and young men hanging onto their sides. One young man had a pair of headphones on banishing an electric drill. Another had a scarf around his head wearing an Iran Air jacket.

I realized I had to get out of there as fast as possible so increased my now panting stride to a fast walk finally making my way across the hill to Darban Street and to the apartment. The apartment was empty Doug and his wife had managed to get out on the last evacuation flight. So had my friend Peter Evans. From the apartment window I saw a huge cloud of smoke erupting from the Takdijumshut Centre. There was a roar of shouting voices and then a number of loud explosions. The crowd in its frenzy had set fire to the BMW showrooms which had a dozen or more cars containing fuel which had erupted into fire and a dense cloud of smoke. This seemed to arouse the growing crowd more so they decided to destroy as much as they could of the centre. News broke out that there was a civil war underway. Climbing onto the apartment roof I saw and heard nightly the tanks rumbling up the streets with mortar and rocket fire streaking across the city.

Executions were being done at random. The Shah was to be deposed or executed. The Ayatollah Khomeini Islamic Republic leader was returning from 17 years of exile in France. Eventually he took over so destroying the Shahs industrial and economic advancement. All hell was breaking loose around the country. My main concern was how to get out in one piece and preferably with my monthly wages. A sort of bush telegraph became apparent as long as we had telephones; I was able to call my wife to tell her what had happened. She advised that the McGee's had been to see her and invited her to their home. I could give them no indication of when, where or how I would get to England but would keep them advised when possible. I was very glad they had not joined me in Iran as it would have been a far worse situation for me to handle. With the country now in a shutdown mode the chance of getting out by air was impossible. Secondly there were no Iran Air flights and no movement at the airport. The Americans had all been evacuated erroneously leaving behind I might add a number of F16s which were later pilfered by the Russians. Food and supplies became the priority but without money it was not an easy task.

Via the bush telegraph it was established 28 of us were left behind. As aircrew come in on general declarations, we would need a VISA to depart as a passenger should an aircraft become available. We soon established that there was nobody manning the Iran Air offices so obtaining such a VISA was out of the question. We banded together and contingency plans were being considered. Walking out via the Black Sea was one but not recommended as it was about 300k to Rashi on the Caspian Sea. A car had been found with about 30 litres of fuel in it, so a drive-out was also another consideration. But news came that driving out the bandits were taking out the first cars and last car of any convoy attempting to use the mountain road. Then attacking, raping, thieving and destroying all the cars in the middle. At about this time out of the blue we understood that a B707 charter that had come in from the UK was still grounded on the airport apron. Regrettably the crews were in the Tropical hotel also stranded. Over the next few days, the violence got worse. The Islamic crowds were scouring the town for foreigners. One girl had her hair set on fire another was physically molested in the street; There were deaths but numbers unknown.

It was not safe to be out alone never mind being a foreigner. The government ordered a curfew from 7pm to 7am, water was getting scarce and the lights intermittent. A sudden alarm went out that the cabin attendant girls and crew at the Tropical Hotel were being attacked. The insurgents were trying to burn them out of the building. We, when I say we, had set up a sort of escape committee working at getting them out. With phone contact our advice to them was to keep moving one story at a time from the rioting mob so that maybe someone could get to them. As it turned out a South African was able to get two vehicles alongside the back wall allowing the girls and crew to escape over the wall and into the vehicles. We split up the crew, taking a few to each apartment that could handle an extra person. Speaking to Buin Bostard the captain of the grounded charter flight, we understood there was fuel enough on board if we could start the aircraft. So, a plan was put forward to steal the machine and get across the border. The B707 has air start bottles in the nose area so a start without a ground power unit was possible. But could it be done without the launch of Mig fighters that would have no problem in shooting a stolen aircraft down. The idea was put on hold, and it was a good thing as later, being a foreign aircraft, it got diplomatic clearance to depart with its crew only. However, on attempting to start, the air bottles were found to be empty. If we had attempted it, we would have been shot on sight. A military air start unit was found, and it eventually departed only to get to Tabriz being forced back by Mig fighters.

It eventually was cleared to go and on arrival at London airport the TV news filmed their arrival. The news showed a tired and very bedraggled crew of girls getting off the aircraft. It read that they had had a hell of a time and were very pleased to be on English soil. In actual fact the reason why they looked so tired and bedraggled was that there were two complete sets of liqueur trolleys on board. In reality they had had a very good time on the flight back. With the extra people to feed food became the problem. I heard that the Airbus personnel had got out so therefore their apartments were empty. I decided to pay a visit to them and see what they had left behind in the food department. Forcing my way into an apartment I found a very good supply of tinned and some packaged food. Collecting as much as I could, I departed walking down an empty walled road. Reaching a corner, I was apprehended by three young men pointing an Uzi machine gun at my back and head. They demanded who I was and was I American. I repeatedly said I was not American which they did not seem to accept. I indicated my passport was in my upper pocket which I would show them if allowed to put my bags down without annoying them any further. I again repeatedly said I was Canadian when I remembered there was a small Canadian flag stitched on the back pocket of my jeans. Very slowly I turned around, feeling the pressure of the Uzi against my neck. When I pointed to the flag they then understood and relaxed the tension. Seeing this and my passport they indicated that being Canadian I must be French which pleased them as the Ayatollah had been given sanctions by the French for 17 years. I was released to go but walking down the road with my back to them. Nerves were on edge as I kept waiting for the click of the safety release on the Uzi machine gun.

It was close as the same Islamic mobs had gone to the Airlines general managers' home at dinnertime. They then dragged his family out onto the street and executed him in front of them. The situation was getting very bad, and the way out was not going to be easy. Fortunately for me I found out that the chap in the apartments a couple of stories above mine was an American with a lot of information. He had radios and arms in his room, plus high-powered binoculars and seemed to be in contact with the outside world. Befriending him I believed he was a CIA agent who I will at this point call "Bill". His information was very valuable and through him I understood that there was movement afoot to get some evacuation planes in from Europe. Later, however he was involved with the drama involving the crash of a helicopter that was attempting to evacuate the USA embassy staff. It was he who informed me that there was two Air Canada DC8 aircraft being prepared to fly in to evacuate women and children only. This was a military order, no men or boys over 16 years of age allowed. Unfortunately, with the breakdown of telephone communication between the destitute pilots I could not advise everyone. I did contact a fellow pilot who was nearby, so we made plans to somehow get to the airport without being detected.

It was decided we would wake early and start walking at the break of curfew as far as possible out of the city. The idea of wearing an airline uniform was considered as possibly dangerous even if covered by our big winter coats. The decision was to wear the uniform and hope we could somehow get through the airport immigration without exit visas. Bad news came at this point from Bill. He told us the incoming Air

Canada flights had diverted to Syria as the Tehran airport was closed due to heavy fog. The good news was that a couple of SWISS Air aircraft were preparing to depart Geneva bound for Tehran. This prompted us to continue with our plans, which worked out as we were able to get a taxi to the main gates of the airport. There were hundreds of people, both local and of unknown nationality cramming through the gates and far into the courtyard in front of the main buildings huge glass doors. Military police were attempting to drive the shouting and pushing crowds back. I saw a gap along the fence which would take me up to and possibly behind an officer near the doors. I was followed by my companion and got to the officer where we immediately put our caps on. He took a quick look at us possibly thinking we were on duty and made a passage for us into the main hall. The hall and counters were packed with woman and kids all attempting to get to the desk and obtain a pass to allow them into the departure area. Armed guards were protecting the doors and the counter from the pressure of the shouting crowd. We realized we could not get past this without revealing we were part of the Shahs supporters being the airline company. Most likely we would be arrested and jailed.

Patiently we waited hidden amongst the crowd waiting to see what was happening. After some time from the action and sound of the crowd, we understood an aircraft had landed. With this information, it was decided that if we could get over the baggage rails on the side of the building, we could get out onto the departure side at the back of the trolley bay. Being quick, we were able to stealthily walk past a couple of guards that were out on the turning bay smoking. To our delight, there were two SWISS Air DC8 aircraft on the ramp. Watching carefully, we observed the air stairs being positioned against the doors. Some crew came out and stood by the air stairs awaiting someone from the main building. At this point, two people carrying clip boards escorted by a guard, walked to the first aircraft and boarded it. A minute or two later another person with a guard left the building and proceeded to the second aircraft also boarding it. We waited silently watching the two guards who had now walked across the small area ahead of us to stand under the veranda as mist with light rain was starting to come down.

We both felt this was the time to take a chance and get to the aircraft. It would mean we would have to walk past the two guards now standing on the veranda corner. Putting our caps on and pulling our collars up to hide our identity, we silently opened the door leading onto the ramp, walking rather briskly we headed straight for the two SWISS Air aircraft. Ignoring some comments made we presumed were aimed at us, we just walked on as if we were officials and meant to be there. Nothing happened so approaching the first machine I bid farewell and good luck with a handshake visible by the guards at the bottom of the airstair to my colleague. He then in an official manner proceeded onto the next aircraft. At this point, not taking any notice of the guard I sort of ran up the airstair into the entrance door. The agent and a cabin staff were a bit surprised to see me. Standing at the cockpit door was the captain. I greeted him and proceeded to explain my predicament supported by the fact we were foreign pilots in fear of being jailed or shot. I also produced my Canadian and American pilot's license plus my valid passport asking for a lift back to Europe. He as an aviator graciously accepted my situation but indicated that there was a problem as the guards would search the aircraft expelling anyone not on the crew general declaration and any male over the age of 16 years. He said he would take a chance by concealing me in the cockpit when the body count started.

When all the passengers had boarded guards came on board searching under the woman's dresses and any place that might conceal a boy or man. Getting to the cockpit they entered counting the 4 crew members. The captain had stationed himself against the cockpit door behind which I was being pressed against the fuselage. He blocked them from seeing me with the door so with the crew and body count complete and correct the guards left the aircraft much to my and the captains relief. Departure was complete and via the intercompany frequency I understood my colleague was also aboard the second aircraft. Arriving at Damascus in

Syria to refuel and change crew was the plan and completed. But now trouble hit. The taking over captain refused to allow me on board without company authority or a ticket. I was ordered off the aircraft now stranding me in Syria without a visa or much money.

With the doors closing and the flight preparing to depart I got a signal from the rear door to come quickly up the air stairs by what looked like the purser. He understood what had happened, explaining this captain was very strict on company matters. To which he said he would hide me in the clothes closet until after take-off when I could sit on an unseen from the cockpit crew seat by the last bulkhead. This all-transpired departing for Geneva with me in the closet for take-off and landing. Arriving at Geneva I bid a grateful goodbye with many thanks to the purser and cabin crew. Leaving the aircraft in the dark via the rear door I found myself on the air side of Geneva airport. Here I searched for an aircraft going to England fortunately finding a British Airways one on which the captain agreed to help me get back to the UK and my family. This was after he heard my escape story and I identified myself as an aviation colleague in need of help. He then called the steward up telling him to get me a seat, a meal and a scotch. True pilot minded to which I was very grateful. He cleared my being on the aircraft with the agent following which we departed for Heathrow airport. Arriving there I thanked him profusely and using my last few pounds called the family at the McGee's home then bought a ticket on the train to be with them. It was wonderful meeting with my wife and boys in tears. I had made it out and was lucky to be alive from what was being shown on the TV. Civil war appeared to now be underway. The next step now was we had to get back to Canada. I am and was humbly grateful for what the McGee's had done to keep my family there at their expense and patience. My profound thanks will always be with them.

The very next day I, getting some money from my wife, travelled to London. There I approached all the airlines explaining my predicament and what had happened to Iran Air asking for a rebate ticket to get me back to Toronto. KLM offered free tickets via Amsterdam for me and the family. With much thanks I returned back to McGee's home to prepare my family and myself to travel to Toronto as soon as possible. This we did, being very glad to be back in our own home and town. The debts had piled up, the house needed cleaning and I had to find money or a job quickly.

The return to Iran.

Getting in touch with as many people that I had contact numbers on we set up a line of communication. Some pilots were still in Tehran, but telecommunication had been spasmodically established and news was being relayed to their families. From this it was established that a group of both pilots and cabin staff were assembling in London in an attempt to open up a sort of help and information line. They also were in a position to canvas airlines in regard to future jobs. It was also understood that the Saudi Arabian Airlines were planning a major expansion in an attempt to become the biggest Middle Eastern airline so capturing the developing trade routes.

Work in Canada was at a standstill, I had got information that maybe I should consider getting to London as this appeared to be the active area regarding aviation work. Contacting the group there, I arranged to travel back to England on the return part of my KLM ticket which I had convinced the agent when issuing the ticket to make it return. Arriving in England I found that the aforementioned group were all bunked up in one of the stewardess apartments. Sleeping wherever there was a space and sharing food costs. I had to join them as funds were almost non-existent. We were a jolly group with good camaraderie supporting our forlorn predicament. Pressure was put on the small, declined London

Iran air office but not much was forthcoming. It was established that for those still in Iran the paymaster had issued orders for them to be paid and they were about to get exit visas plus a ticket out to their hometown. But a big but, this was only allowed to those who had remained in Tehran. This convinced me that I had to get back into Iran as that would be a Godsend as far as income was concerned. Gulf Air had now been allowed to operate a flight into Tehran from Bahrain so relieving the pressure of persons attempting to leave Iran. When I mentioned this to my colleagues, they pondered how I was going to do this and maybe not such a good idea. Going to Gulf Air offices I was able to convince them to issue me with a ticket via Bahrain back to Tehran. This all went well until I got to Bahrain where the agent would not allow me to continue without an entry Visa for Iran. With good fortune, the captain on the flight was an ex-Court line pilot and knew me from the Caribbean days. He using his authority got me put on the crew declaration list so enabling me to travel in uniform to Tehran. He took a hell of a chance as he was going to have to remove me from the list on departing from Tehran. After landing it was obvious that the terminal and arrival buildings were all but empty. I quickly moved across to the nearest building and then slipped between a neighbouring building to find myself in what I thought was the employee's parking area.

Across from this was the main Iran Air building with offices for the general running of the airline. It was surrounded by a fence which included a main gate. It all looked abandoned, but it was a place I felt I should start to establish in which direction I should head regarding my sudden presence. Entering the main building everything looked as if it was left in a hurry. The offices were empty with papers lying around over vacant desks. Windows were open and doors swung in the breeze. I felt very nervous, concerned that I would be caught there with no reason or excuse for being there. As I started to leave, I suddenly heard the tapping of what seemed to maybe a typewriter. The direction appeared to be coming from the upper level. Proceeding cautiously, I found a lone typist working away at a pile of documents stacked on his desk. I introduced myself, showing him my company I.D. He was initially alarmed but told me he was typing the forms necessary for all the remaining pilots to claim their wages and to enable them to get exit visas plus a ticket to their home country. I could not believe the luck I was having, it seemed impossibly that I had walked into the very spot to initiate the need to be paid and get home.

My I.D. gave him my name and company number. He miraculously had typed my forms, so I was able to get them immediately with instructions from him where to collect the necessary money and travel documents. He advised that things had quieted down but warned about being seen in uniform. I proceeded to find a taxi out on the main road so travelled nervously back to my apartment. I quickly made contact with some of the other pilots giving them the information I had received. In the morning, I went to the appointed office where I found a skeleton staff organizing the necessary travel, exit visa documents and wages. On receiving what was due to me and my travel visa plus the airline ticket I found out that customs would not allow any USA dollars out of the country. Another American pilot was doing the same thing, his name was John Irving a B737 first officer. We sort of palled up making arrangements to meet at the airport. That night I slipped into the market where I bought some jewelry and black-market American dollars, a highly dangerous thing to do considering the militant atmosphere supported by anti-foreign aggression.

A day or so later I got to the airport at the appointed time meeting John. All went well with a seat on the departing aircraft and immigration. However, at customs we were thoroughly checked. I had hidden some jewelry inside my alarm clock plus I had taped inside my guitar all the American dollars. During the customs search John was found to have a hunting knife which they immediately confiscated. He verbally objected, causing a bit of a disturbance but took my advice to let it go. Getting to me the officers made me open my guitar case. I extracted the instrument and sort of handed it to them asking if they could play a guitar. Their reply was not so with my hand firmly clutching my instrument I offered to play them a tune. They were amused, ruffled through my bag and sent me on my way. The relief on my nerves was welcome as all I had was inside that guitar. To the relief of John and myself we boarded departing for England. John and I separated him for the USA, we would meet again. I immediately called my family to say I was on my way home with the funds all in one piece. Making contact with the English group I mentioned earlier, I meet up with them and filled them in on my past experiences.

I found out that Saudi Arabian Airlines was now recruiting in London. A few of the pilots had been to see them advising that I should do the same. Saudia was expecting a huge expansion so experience on the B707 and B747 would certainly get me an interview. This I successfully did but it was explained that as I was residing in Canada, I would come under the USA appointment program. It was a benefit to me as the starting salary was in US dollars and a bit higher than the British or European wage. The interviewers were understanding of Iran Air pilots and their predicament. I was advised to return to Toronto where I would be contacted by the American hiring personnel. Later I wished the English group well and returned to a worried family in Toronto. It was very good to be home where I explained my whole venture and the Saudia situation.

In January 1979, the Shah's government collapsed, and he and his family fled into exile. He died from Cancer years later. He had got sanctuary in the USA but died In Cairo. Born on 24 September 1902 and died in Tehran 3rd June 1989. By getting USA sanctuary Khomeini held hostage the US embassy staff for 444 days demanding he be released to them. Execution would have followed. Ayatollah Khomeini led a bloody and merciless revolution.

Saudia Interview.

Within a short period of time, about a week or two, I heard from the Saudia office in Dallas. They explained that I was eligible to be hired and with an airline ticket plus accommodation I should proceed to the recruitment office in Dallas. This I did going through the whole recruiting procedure which took about a week. I was then instructed to return home to await further correspondence as to whether I was acceptable or not. I was notified that I had been accepted on the B707 as a first officer following which I would be advised on the date and interview for my wife and children. Within about two weeks arrangements arrived for her to travel to Dallas where she was interview and questioned about our marriage and what she expected if relocated to Jeddah in Saudi Arabia. All went well so we were advised that transportation of ourselves, children and household goods should be arranged. I was instructed that I would go ahead of the family to Jeddah and the training school during which time housing would be allocated for the family.

We immediately started preparing the across world home and family transfer. It was a bit exciting but also a bit nervous as it was to a new life in a Middle Eastern country with some very different customs and lifestyles. Children to be taken out of their school leaving friends, we leaving friends and a social Western lifestyle. Over and above it all it was a good job with excellent pay and perks. Free house, furniture, water, light, schooling, good leave, discount airline tickets, tax free, good leave and well paid. This was what we had been waiting for four years, so even if it was an uncertain lifestyle we were going and would make the best of it.

Saudi Arabian Airlines

I departed first as arranged, travelling via London to Jeddah to be billeted at the Kandora Hotel. The flight from London carried a lot of new recruits including cabin attendants, technicians and ground support personnel. Sitting next to me was a cabin attendant from Liverpool named Jackie, travelling out of England for the first time. I will make reference to her later. Checking into the Kandora Hotel about a 3-star rated establishment at the best, I was surprisingly approached by Allen Berg an Australian ex Iran Air captain and a friend I had made while with Iran. He and a lot of aircrews from Iran where already residing in the hotel. I was given a room at the back which appeared to be a prefabricated part of the hotel. Getting together that night we all chatted about where we had been and what had taken place in the interim. Most had been out of work, so we were very pleased to have obtained employment. Accommodation we had but meals were at our expense.

A reconnoiter had been done with the report being that there was not much around except at a couple of expensive hotels including our 3-star hotel. There were a few pavement-type eating shops with racks of grilled chicken on sale plus a pâté type bread and general merchandise. Nothing looked very hygienic or appealing so added to the fact most of us were low on cash, we set up a kitchen from an electric frying pan I had brought with me on my flight allowance. It was amusing to see ex-airline captains peeling potatoes, carrots and onions and breaking up a grilled chicken then squatting on the floor to eat Arab style with their hands. It was to say the least very embarrassing but most of us were very low on cash so made do until we got our allowance.

Saudi Arabia seemed to be awakening from years of isolation, almost medieval. It was starting to gear itself up to participating in the modern world. There were a lot of restrictions and western woman were not looked at with respect. The airline was expanding at a great rate with crews coming in from all corners of the world. In earlier days pilots were often in danger as they after landing mainly using DC3 aircraft, had been attacked by Bedouin tribes. Also, if caught in a sandstorm and having to force land they were at the mercy of the tribes and bandits who looked at them as infidels so were to be executed. If not executed, they would be castrated with the testicles put into their mouths and stitched up. The authorities decided that they would all be given what became known as goolie coins. The coin would be gold and cut in half. The air crew would wear the one half as a necklace, so if captured the other half would be given to the person bringing back the crewman in a whole condition.

Jeddah is the Arabic name for Grandmother. The Arabs believe that Eve is buried there and Adam in Pakistan. It was a relatively small city with limited telephones and fresh water. The old airport was a bit of a mess having to contest with masses of Hadji worshippers annually. Mecca is only about 70 miles away. Our training was set up in the old airport office building. I say old as the new airport was just getting underway being built if I remember correctly by a German company. Its location was well out of Jeddah city. By this time the ground school training had been completed under training by T.W.A. instructors. We were then sent to Karachi to complete the simulator training on the Pakistan Airlines B707 simulator. It was a rather old machine but served the purpose of the rapidly expanding Saudi airline. An amusing part of this was that we were billeted in the old British Overseas Airways crew house. This consisted of two long single-bedroomed buildings with an ablution block at the end. Each room opened onto an open veranda allowing the occupant to get to the toilets. Rather a venture in the middle of the night dressed supposedly in pajamas. The two blocks were divided separating the men from the women. For the ladies to step out in the night to use the toilets was not a very pleasant experience. Each room had a wash hand basin, a small side table, a light and a wardrobe. On the men's side, most of the basins were intact but on the ladies' side, most of the basins were cracked or perilously hanging onto the wall. One can only imagine why the basins were in such a state.

Returning back to Jeddah we started the long process of being allocated family housing, getting a motor vehicle and preparing for the arrival of families. I was located in a small two bedroomed house in a moderate type of compound on the perimeter of the city. My friend and colleague from COURT line and Iran Air Brian Saunders a captain, had been allocated a house in a new area out in the desert comprising of a split level with one three bed roomed, lounge, dining room, kitchen and toilet on top of each other. I learnt from Brian that the chap who was allocated the lower house was not going to continue with Saudi. Brian explained that the location of these houses albeit out in the sand was going to be the site of Saudi City a relatively western company city housing 12,000 people. I immediately consulted the Pakistan officer who was allocating houses and was able to convince him to allow me to transfer my allotment to the new house below Brian's. I explained that I was not American and did not want to live in an American compound supported by the fact that Brian and I were old friends so would enjoy sharing the same house structure. It was a gamble as most of the new incoming crew wanted a location in a compound where there was a social group preferably of the same nationality, but in the end, it paid off being the start of a five-year life in Saudi Arabia.

The houses were comfortably furnished with free light and water. For a long time, we hauled by car 25-litre containers of drinkable water from a water dispensary in the city. The piped water was desalinized water good only for washing and bathing. There were no phones, so any calls meant a trip into the city where there was a bank of public phones on a wall out in the open. With my first month's salary, I had been able to buy a reasonably good Chevrolet V8 Blazer. It was a practical vehicle for the conditions regarding the roads and traffic. To get a driver's license meant a conversion of whatever license you had but one had to get and present a $25,000 blood money insurance policy. The reason was that if you hit anyone, being a foreigner or an infidel, it was immediately your fault. This meant that the family would get a claim against you for about the $25,000 figure. Driving was hectic, traffic rules did not exist. Four lanes meant six lanes plus the sidewalk. A red light was on most occasions a race to beat as it changed from green to red. Traffic jams were common with a lot of shouting, hooting and pushing. If you parked on the curb, it was common to come back and find your vehicle blocked in. This could mean a wait for hours for the drivers to come back, most especially at prayer time as they were in the mosque. In my case, I would engage in a four-wheel drive and bash my way out by forcing cars front and back clearing an escape route.

We called the Blazer Big Red and it was to become our recreation vehicle so getting us out of the confinements of the city. Big Red comes into my story a great deal. With the ground school and simulator training completed we were appointed a B707 check airman to see if we up to standard. Some of these check airmen were young Saudi pilots from an earlier intake and trained by T.W.A.

One or two of them were known to be very short tempered and extremely vain having a dislike for foreigners. They had been first officers with a typical Arab superiority attitude plus a dislike for taking orders. As captains, some as young as 26 exercised their newfound authority on us more experienced foreign pilots. It was thought that the hiring of foreign experienced pilots to fly with them was a safety factor hidden by the management. They were very hard on us and seemed to delight themselves by advising the cabin attendants and invited cockpit guests on how smart they were and us first officers as an evil necessity. A few of the new intake of pilots resigned within 3 months because of this and the fact that their families would not be able to live in Jeddah and the restrictions of life. One such Arab captain was known as the "screaming skull" who came very close to being punched due to his cockpit screaming and on one occasion actually getting out of his seat to reprimand a pilot finger to face.

On completion of my line training, I did a few trips with Arab captains but successful passed and was sent out on the regular line flights with a majority of foreign captains. On one such trip to Chad with a Captain Davies we had a passenger compliment of Hadj refugees. At the end of the Hadj a sweep is done of Jeddah collecting all the left behind Hadj pilgrims. They are then flown back to their respective countries, usually in poor physical condition. Upon arriving at Fort Lamy, now known as Ndjamena, we found ourselves in the middle of a pending war.

Disembarking the passengers as fast as we could we were approached by an official advising us that more landing fees were to be paid. The funds we had paid were insufficient. At this time tanks plus, armored vehicles started to assemble on the airfield. We were advised that we should immediately depart, or we might not be able to take off. Between what the cabin crew and ourselves had in personal cash seemed to eventually satisfy the official. On lining up for take-off we were stopped as some tanks and armored vehicles had assembled on the runway. Eventually the runway was cleared allowing us to depart. The war appeared to have started so we decided to fly low for some miles keeping well clear of the artillery fire which we had seen north of us, or possibly being a target for someone deciding that government officials were escaping on our aircraft. As we departed the war opened up in full swing. We missed being captured or having the aircraft commandeered or even worse hit by rocket fire.

By now, with a fully furnished house allocated, water connected (undrinkable) and securely ensconced into the airline, I awaited my family's arrival. It had been three months of a tough time for all. Stress was one for had I not succeeded in meeting the required standards of the airlines

Saudia Boeing 707

ground school and flying, we would have been on the street. My funds were completely exhausted. All reserves were used up, fearful of not succeeding in the transition to Saudi, the Iran issue was a big strain, and I was mentally and physically tired.

Our house in Jeddah

The family finally arrived very tired but pleased to be with me and our new home. We set about trying to make things as comfortable as possible. The house was out in the desert construction site where houses, flats and sports facilities were being built. It was dusty, no tar roads, no tree or parks, just dust, heat and construction vehicles. I immediately built a wooded fence around the plot as roaming Pakistanis and foreign workers often suddenly appeared at our windows gazing in on our wives and contents. One worker was caught masturbating. They were a pitiful lot as the majority were working two-year contracts away from their families. They were low paid living in despicable accommodations with their passports removed until the completion of their contract. It was only a step away from what I would call slave labour. There was no TV or phones. To make a call meant again going into the town and using an ATNT phone from a bank of phones hanging on a wall. As time passed things got better. An enterprising American strung wires from house to house and played TV recording brought in from the USA. Our homes had four air conditioners that ran night and day plus to ease the dust getting into the house we taped all the windows shut. As social groups built up, often on a cool evening we would meet around a fire in the vacant space and enjoy socializing and in some cases a bit of guitar music.

The contract was for an initial 5 years so we settled down to make the most of our new lives. Scott went off to the Parents Cooperative School followed two years later by Grant. The area around our house bloomed into a city with houses, apartments, and tarred roads for about 12,000 people coming from all walks of life. There were artisans, pilots, ground and flight engineers, maintenance staff, engineers employed in numerous trades and from the four corners of the world. Our complex had tennis courts, swimming pools and even an outdoor theatre. This was never used as men and woman could not sit beside each other as it opposed the Muslim law. Wives were allowed to have their hair uncovered but sometimes received insults and verbal abuse. It was best to wear the traditional black Abaya, a black frock covering all but the face. If their ankles were exposed the religious police using a thin cane would whip them on the exposed ankle. Our Jeddah house in what became known as Saudia City. The bottom half was our section. Brian Saunders lived in the upper level.

In the centre of Jeddah there is a mosque where they do the beheading and severing of hands. It was best not to be around there on Friday afternoon which is sort of their Sunday. The police would suddenly appear cordon off the area forcing everyone to face the Mosque to witness the act. Once I was nearly caught with both the kids at my side. I by sheer force dragging the kids and was able to escape by disappearing down an alleyway, getting well clear of the spectacle and police. It is said that the prisoner is brought up to the ramped mosque terrace removed swiftly from the vehicle head extended and beheaded. It's all done very quickly with a Muslim reciting a pray. I also learnt that if the prisoner was a rapist, drug dealer or a violent criminal, his severed head was turned to face his body. There is apparently enough blood and oxygen in the brain for it to function momentarily so his eyes would visibly blink and look at his beheaded body. There have been known times when the swordsman missed taking a piece off the shoulder or partially decapitating the scull. There is not much crime in Saudi Arabia, but this sort of punishment takes place in the major cities. There are many laws which have to be adhered to. It was best that one got to know them to avoid any problems. One incident happened to Josie, my wife. She was shopping in the vegetable market. A young sounding woman bent down next to her asking my wife not to look around as they were being watched. She asked my wife to phone her mother in the UK and tell her she was alive and living in Jeddah. She indicated that there was a note that she had slipped under a vegetable with the appropriate number. She then stood up and walked away with a group of other women. We did phone her mother who was in tears to hear the news asking us to please help her make contact with her daughter. This was impossible as being dressed the way the young girl was in the Abaya there was no way of identifying her ever again. We gathered from her mother she had met and married a Saudi Arabian at university in England. She returned with him for a holiday and to meet his family. She never returned. We later learnt this was not uncommon from Europe and the USA. Their passports being withdrawn.

Life in general moved on and we made our lives as pleasant as possible. This was helped by driving up the Red Sea coast getting away from any interference from the local Arabs. I had bought the Chevy Blazer which I modified to become a camping vehicle. I had built a false roof for heat protection, raised the front end giving more ground clearance and equipped it with extra fuel and water containers mounted on the rear spare wheel carrier.

Chevy Blazer, we called "Big Red' crossing a river mouth by going into the surf.

We would travel together with another couple of vehicles for protection and form a barrier as close to the water as we could get. This way our wives could enjoy a swim in their bikinis out of sight of any prying eyes. Peter Evans (ex B.A Capt) who I had met in Iran, and I had become good friends, so he joined up doing the same with his vehicle. Brain Saunders ex-Court Line saw how we were enjoying our trips so bought a similar vehicle thereby joining us on what now was scuba diving camps on the magnificent Red Sea coast. Peter's wife Bunty would intermittently come out from their U.K. home to Saudi Arabia, so we became a good group. The coastline is magnificent with some of the best diving in the world. Regrettably not accessible to the tourists. The reef is in most cases about 50 meters from the beach at a varying depth up to one or two meters. Then it drops vertically straight down to an unknown depth. The face of the reef is a haven for every conceivable kind of fish life with massive and multi coloured coral adorned with beautiful sea ferns. The coast goes up to the Gulf of Aqaba joining the Jordanian border. South it goes down to the Yemen coast with many small islands butting up to the eventual exit into the Indian Ocean near Aden. With the vehicles specially modified we were able to traverse the coast as far as we could without being stopped by the desert patrols or the coast guard. This often meant driving out onto the sea reef to get around river mouths. I would sometimes have to walk ahead of the Blazer to seek out a safe passage between the sharp coral, leaving my wife to drive following me. This was totally against Saudi law, but we were usually miles away from any people. It was bit dangerous as should we have broken down and got stuck on the reef or in the desert sand, there would be nobody to help us for miles. Consequently, we always advised someone, Peter or Brian, who had knowledge of the desert, approximately were we would be and for how many days. On one occasion I returned from a flight to hear that Peter had gone out to a place called 29 Palms for a quick swim and to relax on his day off. By nightfall he had not returned so knowing his possible position I set off to find him. As my lights pierced the desert, I ran across him quietly camping next to his deeply stuck Blazer. Digging and with a tow rope we got his vehicle free from what we called a cross axle dig in. This was when the front wheels cause a bank of sand in front of the tires, then they dug in causing the back wheels to do the same. The axle is then twisted and resting on the sand. It takes a lot of digging and pulling sometimes to get out at the same time trying not to get the tow vehicle also stuck.

Desert driving is an art and on one occasion when I was the lead vehicle, it sank into what can be called an unseen quagmire hidden by the sand. Subsurface water becomes mud. Peter was behind me and hooked up for a pull-out as we dug the wheels free. He too went down. It took us two days to get free, having to build cribbage's from driftwood to get the jacks under the vehicles. Then getting Peter free we were able with extended tow ropes to get me free. Another trick was to bury the spare wheel and pull on it with a winch or come along, enabling the vehicle to get its undercarriage off the sand. I had made my tent poles from hard timber which I was able to join together longwise so being able a lay track enabled the wheels to get a grip. There have been deaths from being lost in sandstorms and vehicles getting stuck. Occupants have been found days later dead from dehydration and sunstroke. I carried a lot of extras such as twin spare wheels, water, oil, fuel, fan belts and wheel bearings plus my tent covered the extremities of my vehicle giving me a lot of shade. Temperatures during the day can go to upper 40°c degrees and at night freezing cold. With the lack of firewood, I also carried a gas bottle on the roof for cooking if necessary. Carburetors were covered in mutton cloth to keep out dust with the thermostats removed and 80% antifreeze to keep the radiator water cool.

Our excursions were a breath of fresh air away from the heat and congestion of Jeddah. We had fun camping on virgin beaches, crackling campfires, good camaraderie often with home brew, music, our children and families enjoying the outdoors complimented by great diving. Many of our acquaintances were envious of our almost fortnightly trips. We still had to be careful of possible interference from roving Arabs seeing us as alien infidels plus taking into account there were woman and children with us. In so we between the men stood nightly watches. We did at times have the odd camel or fox come to see what we were. Occasional out of nowhere Arabs in their Land Cruisers sometimes with a camel or goat in the back, would drive by then stop at a distance. They were more inquisitive but seeing we were of no threat to them; they would drive on to where nobody knew.

Seeking shade at 29 Palms Beach.

Death and a Catalina Flying Boat

Regrettably some years back an American on 23 March 1960 flying a Catalina which had been converted into an airborne caravan landed up the north coast towards the Gulf of Aqaba to overnight on the deserted beach, The Thomas Kendel family and friends came ashore to rest, cook a meal and enjoy a swim. A roaming Bedouin group saw them as a foreign infidel enemy so attacked and captured the whole group. Later released by USA intervention. The Catalina was abandoned on the beach and today is just a deteriorating wreck. Any valuable parts were either stolen or destroyed by the harsh environment and washed out to sea on the tide. A tragic end.

This is the remains of a Catalina flying boat that an American family was flying around the world as a fully equipped flying caravan. It was used in the film SOS Pacific

Later I will cover an expedition we did that took 18 months to organize, travelling deep into the great Nafud desert.

There is an interesting thought that Moses did not part the Red Sea but actually crossed at the reef on the mouth of Aqaba then being in safe land headed north to the Promised Land. Mount Sinai is to the west of the Aqaba gulf and today there is a Catholic monastery there which can be toured by getting a plane from Cairo. It's called Mount Saint Catherine. Unusual for a Catholic church to be in a Muslim country. In Jeddah we used to get a visiting priest to do a service in a private home and confirm the children. I don't believe the authorities knew of his presence as he came as a businessman.

The airline was now getting very busy with new routes to many countries. I being on the B707 was operating to Europe, North and East Africa, Pakistan, India plus Morocco in West Africa. The company had put in an order for B747s, so we waited in anticipation of being upgraded to the new machines in so operating to the USA and Far East. I had been able to organize some tickets for my folks to visit much to their excitement. On the night of arrival, I was waiting outside the old terminal which was very dilapidated, hot jammed with multi sweating races and nationalities. My mother came through but was in an alarmed state as it seemed my father had been arrested. On seeing her state, a young Arab offered his help. We accepted gladly as my father was in his eighties, well but not too able to be too stressed. The young Arab was informed of what had happened. He disappeared, returning later with my father. What had transpired was that my folks had bought us a box of chocolates which unknown to them had written on the cover that the chocolates were imitation flavoured with alcohol. This was definitely taboo in Saudi Arabia, but the young Arab had been able to explain the matter to the authorities and my father was released. But it shook him a bit. Going in and out of customs was a major problem. Women were directed to one entrance alcove where they were felt from top to bottom by woman customs officials. Men into another alcove and also physically searched. My wife hated it as she was not sure where the female officers' hands had been, but they left nothing untouched. Many things were not allowed. Some for example was Coco Cola, Decker records, Ford, with a list too long to write. Sex books were another jailing item including Playboy and such like. On one returning trip to Jeddah my wife bought some garden magazines. The female officer pointed at the magazines uttering the word sex. My wife horrified quickly replied no "Gardening." The woman insisted to point saying the word sex. Josie appealing to the woman opened one to show her it was gardening information. The woman then grabbed the magazines and counted out in broken English 1-2-3-4-5-6. Repeating the word that sounded like sex but meaning six. Josie came out sweating and very annoyed. She certainly did not fancy a night in jail.

As many items could not be bought in Saudi lots of requirements were smuggled in with returning families and crew members from leave. There was always the chance of being caught but it was miraculous how the items were smuggled in concealed packages. Liquor was not available to the public however the hierarchy had home bars that would put a hotel bar to shame. We could make our own beer and wine. Generally, with items bought at the regular shops. Special additives were smuggled in such as essence to convert Sidiky to taste like whisky, gin and so on. Sidiky is the Arab word for "My friend". It was illegally produced at the time of the construction crews building the new airport. Basically, it's a refined alcohol, moonshine, white lightning which a 5-gallon jerry can be bought for $2. 000.It was very potent and had to be cut 50/50 with water. Mixing it then with other essence and regular Pepsi (Coke was not allowed) or whatever. It had a kick but being pure the hangovers were not bad. Wine was made from Grolsch grape juice fermented into alcohol. The bottles were resealable, so we used them to store the wine. Beer made in 25 litre garbage drums containing water sugar yeast and tea. Also, some of the chaps made very potent beer. Peter Evans and I, now good friends, would always share a drum. There was many a good night at my house or his flat. One American pilot got caught and jailed. He was sentenced to a long term but over a period of time was allowed to exercise around the jail. He made a plan with friends to escape by jumping into a van and disappearing towards the airport. Here a waiting cargo aircraft was loading enabling him to hide in the cargo bay and escape to the USA. All very carefully planned with his associates.

Tri-Star fire.

One evening while preparing to depart Riyadh a terrible accident took place. A Saudia Tri-Star flight 163 on the 19th of August 1980 departed for Jeddah an hour's flight time away in good weather. During the climb to altitude the hostess advised the Arab Captain Khowyter that there was smoke pouring out of the floor in the rear. He advised her to use the fire extinguisher on it. She returned saying it was flaming and she had used all the extinguishers. He suggested that they move the passengers forward. Then again, the hostess returned very alarmed indicating that the floor was on fire. The captain asked the flight engineer to look up in the emergency procedures as to what action should be taken. The flight engineer Curtis Bradley advised the captain that there was no such emergency list and suggested they turn back. The captain accused the American flight engineer of being a donkey and begrudgingly asked the Arab first officer Hasanain to get permission to turn back to Riyadh. They were at 35000 feet taking into consideration the captain had been advised twice during the climb of the dire situation. During training the captain did not have a good record.

Later from information received from the Firemen, they reported that as the aircraft was landing flames could be seen clearly through the windows. Now here is where it all went wrong. The captain landed on the main runway. However, it is believed that the Kings VIP B747 was waiting to depart on the same runway. The rumour was that the captain was told to taxi onto the nearest exit taxiway ahead of him and clear the runway. This he did not do but taxied to the end of the runway. Fire trucks could not rapidly get to him, but the firemen saw a door attempting to open. This meant the aircraft was depressurized but took in oxygen. The plane erupted into a ball of flame, burning alive all the 287 passengers and 13 crew. By landing and then moving forward the captain stopped any possible attempt to evacuate the passengers. He had not advised the cabin attendants to prepare for an evacuation. When the fire was eventually extinguished the firemen boarded the burnt-out remains. They found the cabin attendants in their seats, still harnessed with the charred bodies of passengers jamming them from getting up to release the doors and slides. There were 8 bodies in the cockpit all jammed against the windscreen which had melted onto their remains. They had been attempting to escape via the windscreen, in so blocking the cockpit crew from escaping. Therefore, the cockpit crew were also still in their seats unable to assist in any way. The firemen said as they attempted to lift the cabin crew's bodies out of their seats the bodies came apart like an overcooked chicken. Rib cages and heads separate from the spine. Saudia and the government attempted to hide this terrible accident from the media. If the captain had stopped on the runway most of the passengers would have escaped. The blame for this accident was entirely on the captains. The aircraft remains were dragged to the end of the runway and buried to hide any evidence of the catastrophe. I was flying the B707 and very secretly took a photo of the burnt-out wreck as we passed by. I never showed the photo to anyone while employed with Saudia.

Official accident conclusion.

PROBABLE CAUSE: "The initiation of a fire in the C-3 cargo compartment. The source of the ignition of the fire is undetermined. Factors contributing to the fatal results of this accident were **1)** the failure of the captain to prepare the cabin crew for immediate evacuation upon landing and his failure in not making a maximum stop landing on the runway, with immediate evacuation, **2)** the failure of the captain to properly utilize his flight crew throughout the emergency **3)** the failure of

C/F/R headquarters management personnel to ensure that its personnel had adequate equipment and training to function as required during an emergency."

Saudi Arabia was not without crashes. There was a B707 that crashed about 100 miles east of Jeddah, the cause being unknown, but it was suspected that the passengers raced forward in the fuselage and upset the aircraft putting it out of control in a dive. All were killed. Another was DC8 leaving Medina with a full load of Hadj pilgrims when it had a wheel well fire. The DC 8 does not have an alarm system to detect wheel-well fires. The overheated brakes set fire to the tire which then set fire to the aluminum of the wheel well. This area in an old, leased aircraft like this DC 8 is usually dirty, has hydraulic leaks and is vulnerable to burning. This happened with the captain attempting to return to the runway. Regretfully the whole rear section of the fuselage was alight burning through the control cables and melting. On final passengers and seats started to fall out of the burning aircraft. Regretfully the aircraft crashed killing all about 1 mile from the threshold of the active runway. A Canadian DC8 belonging to Nationair crashed at Jeddah with the same problem. Wheel well fire from a burst tire.

In the years I was flying the B747, a flight heading for New York lost an engine. The flight was diverted to Goose Bay Canada. The flight I was on followed departing Jeddah with a 5th pod carrying a replacement engine which looks rather unusual as it appears as if there were 5 engines Arriving in Goose Bay the engine was detached and fitted to the other crippled B747. Our aircraft then proceeded on to New York with the repaired aircraft following 2 days later.

Another incident was a wheel tyre exploded in the wheel well of a Lockheed 1011 Tri-Star out of Dhahran. The explosion split the floor above the wheel housing. It was understood that a child was sucked out of the crack due to the pressurization. There were all sorts of stories that the child lived and was found by fisherman but all of this I put down to rumours.

Years later SAUDIA did have a B747 overrun the runway in Hong Kong

The flight crews grew rapidly as the airline expanded. Pilots were being employed from all corners of the earth. One afternoon I bumped into Des Blanchette a fellow captain from L.I.A.T in the Caribbean. It was great to see an old colleague from the West Indies. Des was actually from St Bart's a sister island to St Martin. He I believe stayed for years with Saudia but had to leave and immigrated to Canada when his daughters became 16 years of age. Girls at that age had to leave Saudi Arabia.

With the airline expanding, B747 s were on order. I was in line to be promoted preparing to go to Seattle Boeing field to do the ground school and simulator training. Having to leave the family for this length of time was not going to be easy as Josie was not handling the lifestyle there very well. Social homebrew drinks were too easy to get.

The due dates came for the six-week conversion training so about 20 of us departed for Seattle and Boeing. I immediately felt comfortable being back on the B747 as I had already done a training course with South African Airways. The Boeing training program is very thorough with very knowledgeable instructors in the classrooms and in the simulators. It was a matter of need to know rather than the older version from S.A.A having to know every nut and bolt. We had been billeted at a motel near the training centre. An amusing point here was that the prostitutes found out we were an Arab company so must have a lot of money. They used to circle the motel advertising their wares nightly. With the conversion successfully completed we had our Saudia licenses endorsed so returning to Jeddah to start flying the new extended B747 routes. This meant there were more overnights and with it more per diem pay. My wages were now looking a lot better, so I increased the payments on my Canadian home. I eventually paid it off in the first year and a half then proceeded to buy a second one in the same block.

The B747 routes now covered the USA, Europe, the Far East, the Philippians, India, Thailand, Korea and Sri Lanka. I would always bid for the Southeast Asia and Far East as the American pilots wanted the New York flights enabling them on the days off to get home or make contact with their families. I would often take my sons with me to get some dad time, especially to places where they could enjoy themselves being a vast difference to the desert of Saudi Arabia. One of our favourite places was Manila as the hotel had a very large pool and slide. At night we would walk down to the centre to watch the shows, one being the bamboo dance. One evening the dancing girls saw the boys and then got them up on the stage to dance with them. This consisted of bamboo poles being crossed at a steady speed to which one had to step dance between them. On the very long flights, they would come into the cockpit and sleep in the vacant crew bunks. On one trip to Thailand, we accidentally walked down the famous Pat Pong sex street while attempting to get to a recommended restaurant we had heard of. There were plenty of nude dancing acts behind show fronts. The passage was busy, so I had stopped when all of a sudden, the boys were whisked away and taken up onto the stage where the topless dancer act was on. I should have been annoyed but the girls dancing were very kind, hugging and kissing the two blond, blue-eyed kids. They were a woman after all, and it was a harmless thing but good to remember. Later I was asked why the ladies had no tops, my reply was that's the way they dance here. The subject never came up again.

By and in large with the interline discounts available to the whole family we were able to get away and visit places we had wanted to see, such as Disney World plus Disney Land, relatives and friends at least once a year. During the very hot months of June, July, August most of the wives and children left for their homes or as in my case I booked holiday places such as Bear Lake in California where we had friends. Scott was battling a bit with the school so on one summer break I sent him to a Special Swiss school to give him some assistance. Grant on another occasion went to summer school in Toronto. Other times we travelled to Australia to visit the farm I owned at Cobram in Victoria state and Josie's parents.

Saudia City was almost complete with swimming pools, tennis courts and a small playground. The boys had joined the Sharks swimming team with inter-club competitions from other compounds. They both did reasonably well but Grant came out the better of the two. He had more of a competitive character which would show most of his life. There was a competition against the military. Grant at the age of 8 years with his team was flown to the military camp. Amazingly he won being given a medallion by Prince Sultan as his reward. I think in all fairness if it was against Camel riders he would have lost. Arab soldiers are not prone to be good swimmers. I had found a dilapidated old go-cart frame which I rebuilt with a small engine. The kids and their friends had a great time driving around the desert playground. It was very important to keep the children busy and amused. Social life had picked up with regular evening parties. However, one of these parties became a dangerous chapter in my life.

I was scheduled to fly the night flight to London so was not able to attend the neighbour's party which did include homebrew. Josie, my wife, attended with me preparing to leave and the boys asleep in our house next door. Dressed and ready to go, suddenly Josie raced in saying someone had been shot at the party. I immediately advised them to stay in the house and not say a word. Proceeding next door, I found a woman from the neighbouring compound in the bathroom with blood all over the bath. Lifting her hair up I observed a nick across the back of her neck. Asking for a bandage and any disinfectant, I proceeded to wash the wound in cold water attempting to stem the now small bleeding. The story was that her husband, a pilot, had suspected her of having an affair in his absence. Furious with her denial he produced an illegal handgun threatening to kill her. Regretfully but thankfully for him, the gun went off just nicking her neck. I advised all at the party to disperse back to their homes and say nothing to anyone. Leaving her comfortable I had to depart to sign in for my flight. Once in my home again I told Josie not to say a word and to stay well out of it all. I then departed for my 3-day flight. Returning I found a different situation. The friends of the woman concerned had stayed on to comfort her and to commiserate on the affair. At this point, just after my departure, the police arrived to investigate a reported shooting. They arrested all the remaining friends plus the house owner and his wife. This was a deadly serious situation as there were charges of attempted murder, possession of a handgun, illegal liquor, and women alone with men not being their husbands. This was about the house owner, the other wives and male friends, plus the affair accusation. The affair is a stoning, the attempted shooting is a beheading and the rest which would include the possession of liquor is a long-term jail sentence. All 6 women were in the women's prison close to the city centre. The men nobody had been able to establish where they were.

During this period that we had lived in Saudi, I made very good friends with the Australian Embassy mainly because we obtained visas to travel to Australia my wife being Australian plus my farming involvements. All the embassies have an allowance of liquor which is supplied to their embassy bars within the embassy building supporting invited guests only. No Arabs. For the Australians, they had a great bar called the "Dead Dingo". Importation of the liquor was not always through the usual diplomatic channels. On one occasion the embassy got a call to say that the piano they had imported now on the docks was leaking. They were a great group to be associated with plus the invitation to the pub was a breath of fresh air being served regular beers, wines and spirits.

I was fortunate to be invited to some embassy functions so meeting a few diplomats and ambassadors. These contacts I now attempted to make use of whichever way possible to assist the imprisoned friends. Another contact I had was an Arab businessman who had the General Motors distributorship for all of Saudi Arabia. He, Ali bin Balbaid and I met by accident at his show rooms and became good friends. He had visited my Saudia City home with his first wife. She in turn had sent a chauffeured driven car on two or three occasions to fetch Josie, inviting her to a lady's fashion parade at her house. Josie had then had the privilege of seeing his two wives in the privacy of their individual homes plus a look at their unveiled people in very expensive attire. She said they were very beautiful, elegant ladies who made her feel welcome. Each wife gets the same attention as often in their own homes. The matriarch is very powerful, basically controlling the family. Contrary it being understood that it's a male dominated world. Josie understood that the first wife is appointed by the mother. The second by the mother and the first wife. Ali was in line for a third wife which they would pick.

I did get an invitation to a wedding which is quite an affair. Arab wedding is a long procedure including male dances, marriage ceremony in two different tents as often they have not met. The consummation of the marriage in the presence of her mother where in some cases the bride is shaven clean and covered with a sheet except for the appropriate area. Then after consummation, a towel is shown to all indicating the virginal blood. No blood means she was not a virgin, and all hell could break loose. It is told that some woman got a small pouch of dove's blood and then concealed it in their vagina. After the nuptial act, they would break it with one of their sharpened nails to cover any questionable doubts. It's a very complicated and deadly matter. In many cases, the woman has been stoned to death which also applies to adultery.

A lot of tribal and existing laws were introduced by the woman. As an example, there was a bus service in Jeddah. But the woman had to travel in a caged area at the back. This was installed by them to protect themselves from being in contact with any men. A fate worse than death if seen by the religious police who patrolled the streets and alleyways. If one's wife or daughter was walking and her ankles were exposed, the police would as mention before whip the exposed ankle from behind. Also, there is a bank in Jeddah for women only.

Having returned I to my horror got the story of the arrest and the present situation. I was very thankful that I had got my wife out before the police arrived. The boys would have been abandoned waking in the morning to an empty house. I quickly established that not much had been done. Apparently, the American embassy had in accordance with U.S.A. law, advised the families plus the husbands and wives who were incarcerated that their only responsibility was to ensure that the prisoners were fed, and not mistreated. Such as torture. Otherwise, their hands were tied as it was Sharia law controlled by the Muslim imams.

Nobody had been to see the prisoners as they awaited the paperwork to be approved. Getting the families of the prisoners together I decided that I would try through my contacts to firstly find out where the men were and try to get to get in to see the woman at the city jail. To do this I would need some sort of authority as I was not a lawyer nor had any reference from the authorities to allow me through the jail gate. What I did have was a very official looking Canadian citizen identification card. It had the Canadian crest and looked very official.

Arriving at the gate I dressed in business like shirt and tie and presented my card to the guard. I explained that I was on official business to see one of the women. I also had a file showing my official Canadian citizen certificate with official looking seals and a copy of one of the woman's passports. Albeit the conversation between us was in broken English and Arabic. It worked so I was allowed into the visitor section of the jail. The visitor's section is separated from the main hall type prison which houses up to about 80 prisoners. There are no beds as all sleep on mats on the floor with a few open-door toilets at the back. Food is supplied in large half drum type containers consisting of what the ladies told me of mixed stew, chicken, rice and bread. Water was available from some outlets somewhere in the hall.

There was a large open viewing area of about 2 metres by 4 metres covered in heavy jackal wire which faced the visitor's section. This section was separated by a space of about 6 metres with an access door on one side. The visitors section had a steel grilled viewing space also of about 2 by 4 allowed visitors to see and shout at the imprisoned woman. Being able to make contact by shouting over and above the other woman and some children visitors, my presence brought on some tears with our woman. I was thereby able to give them some news and explained I would try and return when possible. I got urgent requests from them for toiletries and a change of clothes as apparently, they had not been able to ablute themselves since being imprisoned. I noticed that a child or two was allowed into the space separating the visitor's room from the prisoners viewing point. The children kissed through the spaces in the jackal wire what I presumed were their mothers. I also learnt that the children had in their mouths small balled up notes which they transferred in the kiss. Another thing I saw was a woman on the visitor's side discretely removing their bras and using the bra as a sling fired notes across to the prisoner's section. This gave me an idea that if I could get another visit, I would try to bring one of my sons with me. I was extremely concerned that I would be caught out which would without a doubt put me also into jail. I immediately contacted the families of the imprisoned woman and advised them of the situation. I felt I could possibly get away with another visit so could see if I could get the needed change of clothes and urgent ladies' toiletries to them. I was not too sure but felt we should try. I now had to find the men so turned to my Aussie contact who in turn was able to establish that he was informed that they were in prison outside of Jeddah on the road to Medina. A day or so later I found the jail rather isolated out in the desert.

Using the same documents but replaced by a passport photo of one of the men I was ushered into the commandant's office. My Arabic was not that good but by using the Arabic pleasantries in greeting etc, plus courteous manners so convinced the young officer to at least allow me to see their condition. He escorted me to the centre of the jail. Here in a very large hall like room were steel cages holding about 6 men per cage. The cages made of steel bars did not touch the floor. The men sat on a sort of woven mat. There was no toilet or ablution area to be seen. In the corners of some of the cages were signs of human excrement with some men shackled to the bars by their feet or hands.

I was not allowed more than a few minutes but was able to see the men I had come to find. The officer now demanded in a very official tone of voice I presumed to show his authority, that I leave immediately not allowing any communication with the men. One of the men saw me and shouted my name, so I was satisfied they now knew we had been able to establish their whereabouts. As I left, I noticed a fire hose being used to wash the floor under the men's feet causing them to climb onto the lower bars to keep from getting soaked. This was the jails hygiene procedure.

Getting back to Saudi City a meeting was held between the remaining families and I to establish what could be done, Sharia law is violent, and death could be imminent. It was decided that as I had been successful in establishing the whereabouts and got access to the prisoners, I should try again to see them. I brought with me my oldest son. At the gate, my Canadian Identification card worked plus Arabs are very fond of small male kids so Scott was an asset appealing to the socially poor guard who must have had children somewhere. I was allowed to deposit the clothes and toiletries in a separate room to be searched and then handed to the woman. By lip-reading due to the shouting of visitors to prisoners I got the message that the food was uneatable, causing upset stomachs. My reply was that I would see what could be done as I had noticed food being brought in by woman visitors. We then set up a food chain so that on further visits I could take in food which was allowed. We then asked the relative families to support the chain with food that I could take in being dropped off with Josie at our house. It was burgers, fruit, and small pies all heated before I left as I was now doing an almost daily run.

My embassy contacts got a message to me saying the men had been transferred to a city jail plus a Sharia hearing was imminent which did not look good. My next thought was to make contact with someone in higher authority so turned to my friend Ali who had advised me he could possibly arrange a meeting with the chief of police. This was duly done with me being instructed to meet him one evening in a large out-of-town walled house. Upon arrival I was escorted through the gates into a main large room with a large centre carpet. The police chief rose to great me in Arabic then English. I in turn greeted him the same way. He in Arabic asked if I spoke Arabic to which I replied regretfully only a little. He reverted to English for the rest of the meeting. He had with him about six men all sitting around the carpet edge to which he introduced me. They appeared to be a council of some sort. On explaining my reason for the visit and the request for assistance, he replied he was fully aware of the case. This was supported by the other men. He explained there was very little he could do to get the men and woman out of jail as the case bore very heavily on the decision of the Sharia court which was the law of the country. At that moment a large platter with half a roasted goat was brought in being placed on the centre of the carpet, followed by an assortment of salad type food. As I was the guest the eye was removed and given to me. In respect I took it stared at the wall above which I noticed woman's faces showing only the eyes staring at me. Trying to smile I bit heavily on the eye which sort of mushed into my mouth in fractured pieces. Swallowing as best I could I reached for the water trying to digest the mouthful of what felt like an onion in sauce. This appeared to satisfy the group who then continued to eat the goat by gripping handfuls of meat being sliced off with knives. I must admit the food was good but could not help but look up occasionally at the staring faces above looking out of small observation panels. I understood later they were his wives and daughters.

At the end of the meal, a discussion between the men took a serious turn. I explained to them the unfortunate situation apologizing on behalf of the prisoners including humble apologies for insulting the Sharia laws. I was then advised that they would see what could be done as this was very alien to them and the Sharia imams. Bidding goodbye in Arabic I was escorted out returning to my house in Saudi City. I had a flight to take the following day returning a day later. I got hold of my Australian friend who suggested I see the American Ambassador as some action was happening. This I did to hear that the case had been heard and deportation was on the cards for all the prisoners.

My friend Ali got hold of me to say that my meeting with the chief of police and council had been very well received. This had been followed by a few meetings with the local Sharia imams. Islamic law or Sharia law is a religious law forming part of the Islamic tradition. It is derived from the religious precepts of Islam particularly the Quran and the Hadith. Hadith for some Muslims means the words of God. It was late in the afternoon when I got a message from friends at the embassy saying that from what they understood the deportation order was about to be signed. One of the men imprisoned was a pilot friend. I have withheld names on purpose. Within an hour I got a knock at the door revealing his wife. She was ecstatic as she had just been advised that her husband was being released to be deported with the other prisoners. More information came indicating they were to be deported on that evening's flight to the U.S.A. It all happened very quickly so I donning my uniform which would allow me on board, went out to the flight line and bid goodbye to the deportees. They had been handcuffed until aboard the plane. It was very emotional goodbye by some of the woman but a very grateful handshake by the men. Over the next few months, I also got a couple of letters thanking me for the assistance I had been able to muster.

Italian Submarine and Battleships

Once the flight had departed and over the next few weeks the company set about returning the families to their homes in the USA. I would meet up with the one pilot much later when working out of Miami.

One evening while attending a small party in Jeddah we heard that one of the guests was a German sea captain who had lived there since the war. It was intriguing as I did not know that the Arab Kingdom had sanctioned German and Italian Vichy war personnel. This also brought about a rumour that South of Jeddah was a shipwreck and mysterious ghost submarine whose bow occasionally showed above the surface. Most thought it was a reef only visible at low summer tide. This intrigued Peter and I, so we set about following up on the story. What we found by going into the war history in the British archives of the Red Sea and Ethiopia was very interesting. This prompted us to consider attempting to see if the scuttled battle ships on the South shore were still there and their identity. I am going to enclose a copy of what we found as an addendum to the story of the submarine. After confirming this information, we sent a report to the Royal Navy archives supporting our findings. When Italy entered the war, she had 7 large destroyers 2 small destroyers and 8 submarines in the Red Sea, as well as a sloop, 2 auxiliary cruisers and 8 minor war vessels including 5 M.A.S. By 1st April, the British had sunk or captured 1 destroyer, the "Francesco Nullo", 4 or 5 submarines and 1 Auxiliary cruiser the "Rambi". The sloop "Eritrea" and the other auxiliary cruiser "Rambi II" succeeded in escaping and were reported to have reached Kobe on the Red Sea on March 22nd.

Between 1st April and the 10th, the remaining 8 destroyers were accounted for, largely through fine work on the part on the Swordfish aircraft of the Fleet Air Arm in order that they might cooperate in the advance on Massawa. 17 Swordfish from "HMS Eagle" led by Commander C.L. Keighly-Peach, flew from Alexandria to Port Sudan a distance of 1,200 miles in 2 days. At 09:15 on the 1st of April one of them reported a destroyer 16:09 N and at 39:49 E, this vessel appeared to be sunk 14:15 at about 16:09 N -39:55 E. This was the "Leone" which had apparently run aground or scuttled herself in shallow waters in her alarm at being sighted. There was no sign of the crew. At About 11:55 a relief Swordfish sighted a second destroyer at 16:14N – 39:49E proceeding towards Massawa at high speed, probably with survivors from the "Leone".

At 03:47 on the 3rd of April, 4 destroyers were reported by the Fleet Air Arm reconnaissance 19 miles east of Port Sudan heading north. One of them the "Nazario Suro" was sunk by bombs at 06:15. At 08:00 a Swordfish reported 2 hits on a second destroyer which was left sinking in position 38 degrees from Port Sudan at 100 miles. This was the "Daniele Manin" which sank later in the day. About 60 survivors were rescued by the HMS "Flamingo". The two "Pantera" and "Tigre" were seen heading towards Jeddah. The HMS "Kingston" was ordered to capture and tow them away, if possible, but during the afternoon Wellesley aircraft located them aground and attacked in cooperation with the Kingston. Blenheim aircraft subsequently made a further attack in which direct hits were scored with one destroyer set on fire. Two Wellesley aircraft were lost but their crew were saved. On April 4th the "Cesare Battisti" was scuttled and beached offshore near Lith south of Jeddah. This was the last of the 7 destroyers.

Ships of the Mediterranean fleet were disposed to deal with any attempt on the part of the enemy destroyers to attack shipping in the Red Sea. The destroyers HMS Greyhound and HMS Griffin plus HMS Ladybird and HMS Gnat were sent to patrol the straits of Jubla, southwest of the Sinai Peninsula. When on the 3rd of April four enemy destroyers were reported heading northwest off Port Sudan, with this information the Commander in Chief Mediterranean ordered the HMS Janus and HMS Jaguar destroyers at full speed to Port Said and be ready to proceed through the Suez Canal. The Commander in Chief East Indies however was able to report that owing to the good work of the HMS Eagle aircraft the need for these additional destroyers in the Mediterranean was probably greater than the Red Sea, so they remained at Port Said. The two small destroyers the "Vincenzo G" and the "Acerbi" were both found scuttled at Massawa. Prisoners stated that the "Acerbi" had been damaged by air attack, that her guns had been removed for use elsewhere and that she was used to provide spare parts for other destroyers. The "Ostia" a mine layer and other auxiliary craft were also scuttled. Further investigation found that no one had been able to establish what happened to two battle ships of the Vichy Italian navy that had attempted to cross over when escaping the takeover of Ethiopia by the British army. We were able over some time to establish the possible location of the ghost submarine. It appeared to be South of Jeddah about 20 kilometres near what was a small bay area called Sal. With this information we loaded our SCUBA gear into a small dingy and set off with my family for what looked like a day's outing on the coast. Locating the area we quickly donned the SCUBA gear and entered the water inside of a reef but on the open seaside. Drifting a bit we suddenly saw looming out of the depth the image of a ship deeper than us but up against the sheer reef face. This was definitely the Italian battleship "Tigre" scuttled against the reef face. Below with the stern up and bow down into the sea depth was another vessel which we understood to be the "Pantera"; it looked as if the "Pantera" had been severely damaged. This scuttled position would have allowed crew to wade ashore very easily. Remembering the reef was waist deep until about 50 meters out then a sheer drop into hundreds of fathoms into the Red Sea. Surfacing, we were confident in identifying the ships and very pleased with our find. But trouble had appeared at our camp where we had left my wife and children only 35 minutes earlier. It was an armed vehicle of the desert patrol with men looking in our direction.

Wading ashore we were met by the vehicle as we were then some distance from our camp. They immediately advised us that we were sort of under arrest. We persuaded them to allow one of us to stay at our campsite. This they did, dropping Peter at the camp and advising him to stay put until they returned. They took me, I think because I could speak a little Arabic, to a small prison-type building which we had not seen some miles away. It was obvious that from this location they could see the coastline. I was interrogated but thankfully in my broken Arabic was able to advise them that we were just a family out for the day looking at the fish life. I explained we also had a letter that we had obtained from the government indicating we were examining the fish life in an attempt to write a book. If I was returned to my car I would show it to them. This they agreed to do, returning me to the picnic camp of my family and Peter.

Peter had the sense of mind to pack our SCUBA gear out of sight as it was very possible, they would have confiscated it. Showing them the letter in Arabic and English (Enclosed) followed by some shouting and threatening we were ordered to immediately pack up and leave. They then escorted us to the road some way back in the desert indicating the direction of Jeddah. I feel the presence of a family also saved the day. We sent the information we had to the British authorities in Exeter where it was recorded. This gave the authorities the closure of where the exact position of two of the ships was plus possibly the lost submarine. It also disclosed that the Arabs had sanctioned the Vichy navy and German captains. Consequently, I never wrote or revealed this information before, except now many years later being well clear of Saudi Arabia. As for the ghost submarine, we were confident that it was there. The fact that it was only seen in the hot summer days with temperatures around the 50°c meant that possibly the air in the submarine expanded so causing a part of the hull to surface. It was not the last time that Peter and I got sort of involved in some unusual international points of interest. Argentina was one.

LEONE SUNK   SUNK   Added 1936.

3* *Ansaldo*: ***Leone, Pantera, Tigre*** (1923). 1526 tons (*standard*), 2283 tons (*full load*). Dimensions: 372 (*o.a.*), 359½ (*p.p.*) × 34 × 11·6 feet (*mean*). Guns: 8—4·7 inch (45 cal.), 2—40 mm. AA., 4 M.G. Tubes: 4—21 inch. Designed S.H.P.: 40,000 = 34 kts. (Trials, 50,000 = 35 kts.). Best recent speeds, 33 kts. or less. 2 Parsons turbines (geared). 4 Yarrow oil-burning boilers. 2 screws. Oil fuel: 200 tons *normal*, 400 tons *max.* Carry 60 mines (*normal* stowage), or 100 (*maximum*). Complement, 201.

*Leopardo and *Lince* cancelled.

Notes.—Internally these ships are most elaborately fitted. Each is equipped with a different system of fire-control—British, Italian and German respectively. 4·7 inch guns are paired very closely—only 1 foot apart. *Max.* elevation: 30°. Special apparatus for smoke screen production is fitted on starboard quarter of each.

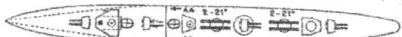

12th November, 1980

FOR SAUDI ARABIAN COAST GUARD PURPOSE

This letter serves to introduce Messrs Peter and Alan Evans employees of Saudia.

Messrs Evans are amateur underwater divers and are very interested in the sea life of the Red Sea. A letter introducing them in this capacity to Coast Guard officials would be greatly appreciated.

for SAUDI ARABIAN AIRLINES

Argentina Simulator

From a contact in British Airways there was a rumour that via a backdoor deal a surplus B747 simulator was being sold to Argentina. At the time Argentina was on the verge of war with England over the Falkland Islands issue. This information we all but confirmed as true, being supportive of the British in their endeavour not to have a war we decided to pass on this information via some diplomatic persons. They in turn revealed that this sale was very probable so instigated a motion to have it stopped. There is a very nice English bar called the London Pub in the Mumbai Hotel where crew overnighted. It sold very good ale and had a pianist for entertainment. With merging flights in Bombay Peter and I would often meet in the pub. A request to the pianist was to play "Don't cry for me Argentina". From the very first request every time he saw us meeting up, he would play "Don't cry for me Argentina." We would toast the probable success of the B747 simulator never being sold to the enemy.

Time was moving on and I was now in my 3rd year of the 5-year contract. Being on the B747 I was away a lot so financially we were doing well. I was most of the time living off my overseas per diem banking a good percent of my tax-free income. Grant was now attending the Parents Cooperative School with his brother Scott. Both now were in the swimming teams, Grant being a better sportsman doing exceptionally well. At one swimming meet he swam against the Military and won. Prince Sultan decorated him with a medal for his efforts. We had had a few nice holidays on the airline rebate tickets and were able to give my parents a trip around the world. They arrived via London being very happy to see us. Later I was flying the route to Bangkok so was able to get them upgraded to first class. They had never had an experience like that before so were thrilled. Ironically my brother was also in Thailand doing a similar backpacking trip. It was extremely good to have the family together. I had to return to Jeddah, but the folks went on to Hong

Kong, Tokyo, and Vancouver where they visited my sister Beverley plus grandchildren Mark and Troy. They then proceeded to London returning home to South Africa exhausted after a memorable 6-week holiday.

Mada'in Saleh expedition.

After World War 1 it was very clear to all that oil was as necessary as gun powder. The requirement of a guaranteed supply was imperative as although it did not support an outright victory, however, to not having a source could add to defeat. The Saudi Arabian kingdom controlled by King Abdul al Saud was fully aware of this so decided to benefit from his oil market. Saudi Arabia consisted of a small population of scattered tribes. In the middle of the eighteenth century in the Najd region of central Arabia, a Sunni Islam sect called the Wahhabism came into being. It was founded by Muhammad ibn Abd al-Wahhab who preached the fundamentalist interpretations of the Quran. To unite the people which he felt were in a moral decline, he called on them to support their true religion and its beliefs. To gain political power using this vehicle he got financial backing from the House of Muhammad ibn Saud so expanding his influence and suppressing the Shiites.

Wars came and went over the next 150 or so years but eventually Abdul Aziz who was head of the House of Saud proclaimed a Kingdom in 1932. The Saud's have since been the reigning Royal family. The new Kingdom was relatively poor but with the exploration for oil and its ultimate financial success in the neighbouring countries such as Iraq and Iran the king decided to open up his kingdom to oil exploration. At this time the kingdoms main means of income was the traffic of Muslim pilgrims coming by any way possible to pay homage to Alah at his birthplace being the holiest of places in the Islamic world Mecca. The first successful oil exploration started in 1933 when Standard Oil of California established itself and eventually found one of the biggest oil deposits in the world at Ghawar an area of about 174 miles by 19 miles wide. This put Saudi the kingdom and the royal family on a massive financial footing.

The pilgrim traffic still existed, and the Ottoman Empire in May 1900 had started to build a railway from Damascus to Mecca known as the Hejaz railway. A distance of 1,100 miles built in the blazing heat of the desert took 5 years with a workforce of 5,500 Turks, Syrians and Iraqis. Its purpose was to rail pilgrims and to open up trade. However, the 1914 – 1918 war had started, and the line was eventually destroyed. More interesting reading on this is all written in the book by Lawrence of Arabia called "The Seven Pillars of Wisdom" where he rides overland to attack Akaba a Turkish stronghold, from the inland or rear. During this ride, he comes across the Hejaz railway transporting troops and supplies. He attacked and blew up a train, mines placed on the railway shear the front axle off the engine. The Engineer managed to reverse the train enabling them to get to a maintenance station at an isolated post known as Madain Saleh. This post was built in the middle of a rock formation enclosing massive two-thousand-year-old hand-carved facades of tombs built by the first inhabitants of Arabia, the Nabataeans. They were the same nomads that eventually crossed the great Nafud desert to Petra in Jordan and carved out their settlement in the mountain rock as they did in Mada'in Saleh. These were constructed from about 100 BC to 76 AD. Originally from a simple tribe, they grew in stature to control the lucrative trading routes passing through their land by means of levying tolls on transit merchandise.

I had heard about these carvings and tombs as they had been seen by helicopter pilots. At one time a National Geographic team had attempted to find and photograph them. Historically only seen by a very few people. Not only because of their distant desert location but by their concealment amongst giant rock formations. It fascinated me so I started to compile what I could on their whereabouts and how to get there. With geographic information on every flight over the area, I mentally took note of where they might be located in reference to the railway line. Slowly I establish visually from the air the remains of the old railway. Finally, I was sure that the rock formation I could see albeit at thousands of feet, was very possibly the site Northeast of Al Ula and South of Taboo, being Mada'in Saleh. Gathering more information, I was positive an exploration would find the lost city, but it would require special permission and a couple of sturdy desert equipped vehicles. Peter Evans agreed to join me, so we started the necessary requirements to launch such a venture. When talking about our proposed adventures in the "Dead Dingo" pub at the Australian embassy two other Australians a father and son team Greg and Chris Lund asked to join us. This was good as Greg was the 1st secretary so with the Australian support 18 months later after going through numerous channels and obstacles, we finally obtained the written permission required to attempt such a desert adventure. With covering Arabic letters from the authorities, we then in theory were allowed to transit through the Holy city of Medina and out into the wild desert. Here we would attempt to follow the abandoned and almost non-existent railway line to Khaybar then out into no man's land. A good point here was that at Khaybar, a desert outpost, we could get fuel and water.

We then got a letter of introduction to the chief of the resident tribe kindly asking for assistance and safe passage. We had to accept the responsibility of being on our own with no rescue support such as a radio or a vehicle to come to our aid. Permission like this had not been given before so we were aware that should we succeed, we would be one of the first westerners to find and view the tombs. It was a risky venture, but I was sure we had covered all that was necessary including visual aerial views and information obtained from a contact with the Arab desert patrol service. We had, in anticipation of eventually getting permission, started to equip our vehicles. This we did by increasing the vehicles front end height from the axle. Then installing more external racks to carry at least 150 liters of fuel and 50 liters of water. All engine and running gear were checked, serviced and where necessary repaired. Extra tires, and spares such as wheel bearings and fan belts were obtained. Radiators were filled to 80% antifreeze with the thermostat taken out for extra cooling. Mutton cloth was tied around the carburetor intake to help filter the dust. Expansion of the roof rack adding a gas bottle for cooking.

Initially, there were going to be three vehicles with the Australian diplomatic Toyota Landcruiser driven by Greg having, his father and wife onboard. However, due to circumstances, the final number was Peter and my Chevrolet Blazer. I had my wife and our two small boys in mine, Peter and Bunty his pregnant wife of 4 months in the other Blazer with the two Australians Greg and Chris split between the two vehicles. Finally, the day came, and we set out with a good farewell from our friends. Heading towards Medina we started to climb the mountain road which by midday had an outside temperature of 45°c being about 115°f. Both vehicles were running in the red. A quick stop on a pass gave us a breath of fresh air and time to cool the engines. Proceeding on, we arrived at Medina finding ourselves approaching the main entrance gates. It was decided that we should not attempt to attract any attention so would drive to the outer limits and look for a track heading towards the mountain where we presumed the abandoned rail line remains might be found. As we were in convoy Peter was ahead of me looking for a convenient trail. I lost him in the confusion of busses and truck traffic but found a trail which I was sure he had taken as if it was heading into the mountains. Proceeding on I found that we were alone on a desert trail with no sign of Peter. Night was coming so it was decided that he must be ahead of us using the same map that we had orientated ourselves on. At this time the two women Bunty and my wife Josie were in Peter's vehicle I had my two boys, Greg and Chris. The trail led us into a mountain valley where we were forced to stop in the darkness and make camp. Fear was that Peter had proceeded into the wasteland to our right and possibly lost. Unable to travel further it was agreed we would proceed at sunrise and if we had not found Peter the woman would turn back to Medina. I was convinced Peter was on the same track as us as we had gone over the route memorizing the desired direction. With the sunrise, I was delighted to see ahead of us what looked like faint erosion in the desert soil which could resemble the rail track footing. Driving on we found Peter encamped by a hill with both women safely awaiting our arrival. Peter was sure we would be on the same trail but had turned off the Medina Road taking a trail different to ours.

Going into convoy again we moved on through the mountain cutting finding more signs of what were definitely the remains of a rail line. Old metal sleepers had been scavenged and used as fence posts with a stretch of rail line seen way off the trail. Now we were without any sign of a trail so used the geographic maps we had obtained and followed the route we felt was the right direct. At a midday stop we could see in the distance what looked like a village. Proceeding to it we arrived at Khaybar. Here we introduced ourselves to the village chief who, wearing a large dagger and a pistol at his side initially appeared very aggressive. After producing the letters of introduction, he warmed a bit and shook hands. We asked for permission to pass through and if possible, buy fuel and water. To this he agreed warning us that what was ahead was not for foreign infidels but would escort us in the right direct to Al Ula. Having filled up with fuel and water a Land cruiser appeared indicating we should follow him. Leading us out of the village he pointed to a track saying in broken English to follow it but that we would need a night stop. Thanking him we proceeded into the desert which was dusty and had a temperate around 105°f (42°c).

The kids and women were getting tired so a decision to find a place to night stop early was agreed upon. In the latter part of the afternoon, we approached a large rock outcrop. Amazing, in the middle of the outcrop was a tunnel big enough for our vehicles to pass through perfectly cut through the rock. In the middle of the tunnel was a water well hand cut into the stone with a diameter of about 10 meters. The marking on the walls of the well indicated chisel marks not associated with any mechanical machine. We would see these same marks later. The precision of the cutting was incredibly aligned all in one direction at an angle and about 2 meters in length extending down into the water. We felt it was an underground spring that had been excavated by hand with the tunnel making access to it. Fortunately, on the other side of the rocky outcrop we found an ideal camp site nestled in among the small boulders. It was hard surfaced rock and out of the perpetual wind at times bringing flying sand. Driving in the desert the vehicles have to be in convoy but not directly behind each other. The dust and sand kicked up by the preceding vehicle is choking both passengers and the engine of the trailing vehicle.

As we encamped my sons found a flock of goats which they started to chase. Immediately there was a loud chorus of what sounded like yodeling as used by Arab woman at wedding or celebrations. Within minutes we were surrounded by armed Arab Bedouin pointing their guns at us. From the direction of the goats, I immediately called my sons back at the same time seeing fleeing young children herding the goats away. Shouting at us the men indicated we were to stand together and not touch anything. Suddenly a Land Cruiser arrived with a couple of burley Bedouin men all armed. I presented myself to them asking them to let me show them a copy of the letter we had addressed to the chief. By hand signs and broken Arabic, I eventually was allowed to get the document from my vehicle. As we proceeded to discuss the matter it turned out that my kids had disturbed the children who were herding the goats back to the camp. My mind at first told me were in a bad situation with two white woman and children. If they shot the four men, the woman would have ended up on the trafficking of humans list and the kids sold to another tribe. Absolutely no one knew where we were or how to come to our aid. We did as a precautionary measure left details of our route with the Australian embassy. By trying numerous hand and Arabic means of communication I was able to put the men at ease.

As night set in I suggested to the head man that maybe he would like to have tea (chi) with us. He agreed, not saying much more but warned us against the perils of over-desert travel with no experience. He pointed in the direction of Al Ula and then instructed half of the men to leave. All night the remaining men stood guard over us only leaving at sunrise. We the men took turns at guard duty of two hours each. Moving on in the morning instead of heading for Al Ula moved east of the trail where we again found signs of the abandoned railway. To our delight at midday, we came across an old garrison building which was one of many built for fortification by the Turks and as stations to guard and supply the construction of the line. From here we drove along the old railway embankment coming across two more garrison buildings, some in remarkable condition. I estimated we could not be far from the Madain Saleh, but we were running out of time as we were only allowed 24 hours in the vicinity. About then we saw the remains of a Nabataean fort built into a mountain outcrop.

View of old Garrison fort.

Garrison fort & station

Thousands of years old Nabataean fort.

Now we knew we were on the right track. Stopping to refresh and fill our tanks suddenly out of the desert came an armed army vehicle with a mounted gun on the rear. There was no doubt they were heading toward us. On their arrival an officer got out approaching us demanding to know who we were and what we were doing there. They were a patrol of the Desert patrol units which guard the Nafud desert boundaries. Politely I again explained our being there producing the authorities officially stamped and approved letter. He examined our vehicles and asked how much fuel and water we had. Unbeknown to him the one 10 litre tank in my vehicle was full of homemade beer. He pointed to the direction of Al Ula and suggested we be out of the area by sunrise the following day.

Al Ula was previously in the early centuries called the city of Deban. Inhabited by the Lihyanites. They disappeared as quickly as they came. Within an hour's drive we found the remains of the coaches that Lawrence had destroyed when attacking and killing the Turkish soldiers. Driving on I saw ahead in the distance a giant egg-shaped rock with a large cluster of rocks forming almost a small mountain. I was certain it was Madain Saleh. Coming around the rock the sight took our breath away as the whole other side was carved into a giant 6 story tomb. Carved by the Nabataean people using the same carving technique as we had seen in the caved water well earlier. Just ahead were the main remains of the garrison village and the Turkish building which had been the supply depot, maintenance and refuel station. It was amazing and hard to believe these huge carved tombs were all done 2000 years ago by hand. Examining the derelict building we came across the maintenance shed. Here were the remains of the locomotive Lawrence of Arabia had damaged with a mine. The bogie was broken in two but as mentioned before the engineer had been able to reverse the locomotive back to Madain Saleh. There was an ancient steam engine with a broken axle and bogie. Steeped in the history of a forgotten railway and time. It was like going back in time and fascinating. A sort of time capsule which almost nobody to that date being 1983 in the western world had seen. My children most definitely were the first non-Muslim kids to see the ruins of time and history. Excitedly we explored all we could but realized that we had to depart the site by nightfall. Looking at our fuel and water it was abundantly clear we could not return by backtracking our route.

First sighting of the Nabataean tomb

Most of the tombs had been defaced with rifle fire having been used as targets by the Turkish military and curious Bedouin.

Machine casting shows date 1906 other casting shows 1834

Damaged and abandoned Turkish locomotives as in the book by Lawrence of Arabia, Seven pillars of wisdom.

Maintenance shed with broken bogie axle.

Col. T.E. Lawrence. (Lawrence of Arabia).

To the west was Al Wajh a small police and trading spot consisting of a pier and a patrol boat. This outpost would have fuel and water, but we would have to by dead reckoning find it at night 100 kilometres away across rugged open desert, wadi and quagmires.

Taking a sun shot we got our true bearing and worked out a compass direction. Setting off, we had to negotiate sliding down small sandy hills and then proceeding on into the night using only our vehicle and overhead lights. The kids were very tired and attempted to sleep in the bucking back of the Blazer where we had a mattress. The wives were becoming alarmed but confident in our ability to navigate plus being supported by our words of assurance, tried to relax on the rugged night ride. We had used our spare tires so another puncture would have put us in a very precarious position. As we pressed west very slowly a light was seen far on the horizon. It was the only light and it seemed to be blinking. This meant it had to be the Al Wajh lighthouse. It appeared to be getting brighter which was a great relief. Eventually, we arrived around midnight waking the soldiers. They showed us a toilet with a shower and where we could camp for the night. Morning came with a beautiful sunrise. All got up washed the days of desert dust and muck off then prepared a fire to have a good breakfast. The soldiers were very good to us, enabling us to fill our fuel tanks. Petrol in Saudi was only 6c a gallon. Six USA dollars filled my 100 litres. Prepared and ready for the last stretch home for a good day's drive, we thanked and bid farewell to the soldiers. The road back via Yanbu and Rabigh was good as it was hard surfaced being maintained by the military for the coastal patrols.

Arriving back in Jeddah that night we were very pleased to be at home. Soft beds and a clean kitchen, toilet and baths. Greg and Chris bid goodbye with many thanks for the adventure saying they would advise the embassy of our safe return. The Nebataeans remain a mystery of an ancient people whose ingenuity and artistry remain to be solved by Historians and Archaeologists. They lived on in Petra but were killed off by the Romans who after 100 years found their water source, put the city under siege then were able to capture the inhabitants and the rock-carved city. I have many pictures of the ruins and our adventure but too many for my memoirs.

Saudia

This was going to be one of our last adventures in the Kingdom of Saudi. I had a 5-year contract which would end that year. We had done well financially having paid off our Toronto home, bought another and by year-end could buy another developing a small rental business as a long-term investment. I was due to be upgraded to captain on the B737 which would take me onto the domestic routes which I did not particularly want as it would reduce my overseas per diem allowance. The main problem was that the social life was having a bad effect on Josie, my wife and the children. They had done well joining the swimming teams, with moderate social involvement with the children in Saudia City. One major problem developing was that in my absence Josie started taking heavily to the homebrew. This often left her sleeping for long hours locked in the bedroom. She was verging on not being able to make a day if I was away without consuming the highly alcoholic drinks we made in our homebrew recipes. The kid's well-being was at stake with me, often having to leave for an overseas trip putting alarm clocks out set for wake-up time and bus time, trusting on them to get to school on their own. If Josie was in a bad state, I would often take the children with me on short overseas trips, relieving them of the home pressure. It was affecting my work and in a discussion with Peter Evans, my close friend, we agreed that I could not realistically accept another contract with Saudia. The final incident convinced me that we had to consider leaving Saudi. This was when I returned home and found my children sitting on the pavement a mile or so from our house. Getting into the car Scott the older son explained that their mother had gone missing and had not been seen the previous day or night. They had fed each other on biscuits and cheese supported by anything in the fridge They knew the route I took home so decided to try and find or meet me. Arriving at the house I started a frantic search only to find her asleep upstairs in Brian Saunders's apartment. She had a key to his apartment to let in the batman who worked once a week as a house cleaner. She had known of Brian's home-brewed liquor stock so had devoured it causing her to pass out. At the time Brian was away on a flight and knew nothing of the invasion so I had a lot to apologize for on his return.

I was then detailed to attend the ground school for the upgrade to B737 captain. There was a lot of home pressure which at times required me to overnight at Peter Evans flat so enabling me to complete the home studies. It was at this time that fate played into the game. The chap who had originally been allocated my house had departed Saudia to take up a position with Air Lanka. He had met Brian and told him that Air Lanka was going to expand and was considering hiring contract Boeing 747 pilots possibly from Guinness Peat or Air Crew International. Both aircrew leasing companies. Peter and Brian both suggested maybe I should look into the deal and see what was up. My interest was compounded by the fact that my past relatives had come from there to South Africa. I decided I would do this imagining a better climate for the family and away from the restrictive Saudi life. From what I found lifestyle there was comfortable and reasonably economical with a good English school.

The training on the B737 had reached the end of the classroom section and now I was onto the simulator. But here I had a problem as the instructor I got was a chap called John. He had been the chap who was with me on the evacuation flight out of Iran and started a problem with the customs officer about a knife he had in his possessions. He had passed himself off to Saudia as a B737 captain from Iran Air which was not true as he had been a first officer. He knew I was aware of this so causing a bit of friction between us. With this and the home situation, I was a bit stressed. Things were not going right. The idea of maybe a position with Air Lanka looked brighter. In my next chapter, I will explain what took place. In the interim, I decided I was not going to leave Saudia without a B737 rating. I had the ground school and the simulator training all that was needed was the flight checkout to obtain the endorsement. This is covered in earlier chapters where I went to the U.S.A. and paid for the aircraft to complete my endorsement onto my American Airline Transport license.

Found this picture in an old magazine. It's one of the trains Lawrence and his rebel army with Prince Faisal, later King Faisal, destroyed on the Hejaz rail line. We found it and related it to the other train which the engineer had been able to race backwards with a broken front bogie to Madaine Salah station. The rail line in some places was intact but we did find bits of line some distance away from its original route.

Air Lanka

Being told in a specific radio message of a possible bomb threat to an Air Lanka aircraft while I was at 37,000ft over the Indian Ocean early in my contract with Air Lanka, is a bit nerve-racking. This indicates that I might be about to be blown out of the sky by terrorists. Having to continue for the next two hours with the threat can produce a very strong individual, which left me unfazed in most emergencies past and in the future. I still appeared to have that strength having to fly on heading for Dubai and very scared that maybe the bomb was a pressure bomb, which might go off as I started the descent.

 Having finally got out of Jeddah and accepted a position with Air Lanka I had broken the bonds of being a First officer and was now Captain on the B747. This had been my dream in so I was determined to fly at the time the biggest passenger airliner in the world. The feeling I had in myself was overwhelming as I and the big bird danced with the sky climbing out of Colombo airport en route to Dubai and Paris. I was in command at last of a B747 jumbo, the first jet aircraft I was to command, ironically starting at the biggest not the smallest such as the usual B737. The events leading up to this were an incredible chance that I had taken but had confidence in myself supported by the fact I had been checked out on the Singapore Airlines simulator with Air Lingus check airman Captain Gerry Young and later on the aircraft with Air Lingus training Captain Brian Noble, passing with a high standard, I felt confident in my proven professional ability. However, things did change.

To get this position I had while with Saudia as mentioned earlier, heard that Air Lanka was considering getting a B747. With my intent to leave Saudia mainly on the grounds concerning my wife plus kids, I felt we could not take much more of the living conditions plus developing family circumstances. My pending upgrade to a Captain on the domestic B737 did not appeal so I decided to visit Air Lanka. Taking my kids with me on a brief holiday, I quite by chance (fate) was very fortunate to meet the operations manager Capt. Carroll in the bar at my hotel. I put forward my intent to leave Saudia, I had B747 experience and was type-rated on my Canadian, Saudia and South African licenses. He agreed that they would need a B747 crew and promised to get in touch as soon as the B747 program was clear. Two weeks later, I got a job offer as a captain on the incoming leased aircraft. I would have to travel in 2 months to Sri Lanka and do a qualifying check flight with a certified Air Lingus B747 check airman. I confided in my good friend Peter Evans as mentioned earlier a colleague from Iran and now a training captain with Saudia. We both agreed that it was an opportunity I should not miss. Peter felt sure I would have no problem being checked out as he was a B747 training captain, so we had flown as a crew many times. My professional standards were good.

A long story short, I immediately resigned and started packing my family and possessions up into boxes. Working between flights and at night this was accomplished. Finally waging that I could pull this off, we the family departed Jeddah at the end of my five-year contract. Having to transit from N.Y to Toronto, I rented a van to carry my family and 18 boxes to La Guardia airport and then on to Toronto. The tenants had vacated our house, so we moved into an empty shell. I quickly got the family settled as best as I could. I then left them there travelling to Sri Lanka to accept the position as captain on the B747, a QANTAS 100 series. I understood they were getting it on lease from Guinness Peat aviation lessors in Ireland. Going through all the necessary paperwork which included getting a Sri Lankan license the contract crew was sent to Singapore to do the recurrent and checkout to Singapore airline standards. I must note here that one of the first officers was a certain Charl Ryan with whom I got on very well. Primarily I think because we could both drink the local potent palm brew called "Arrack". He later became the part owner/director of Ryan Air which was set up by his father who was the Mgr. Dir. of Guinness Peat Aviation in Ireland. I would later work with this company on other contracts. Their operational wing was Air Tara, having Captain Paul Plaisted as their operations manager operating one of the largest worldwide networks of leased both wet and dry aircraft known as AMIC. (aircraft, maintenance, insurance, crew) Later I would ironically do a couple of Air Tara contracts.

An interesting incident happened when we were told to go to the local aviation department with our international licenses having completed medical and simulator checks, to get a validation. The officer in charge put up verbal obstacles hindering the process. Facing him across his desk he indicated by opening his briefcase on the floor that he was not very well off, had major medical problems with his wife, was unable to afford cigarettes and certainly not whisky. I immediately left his office shot across the road and purchased a carton of cigarettes, plus a bottle of whisky. Returning with the loot in a brown paper bag, I deposited it into his reopened briefcase. Amazingly all of a sudden, the lost stamp and paperwork were miraculously found in the office next door. We all left with valid Sri Lankan ATPL licenses to allow us to operate the incoming Air Lanka B747.

Another license procurement in the Congo I will write about later. Worse than this, it was illegal.

The crews were based at the Blue Waters Hotel not far from the airport. It was called previously the Surabaya Airport but changed in 1995 to the Bandaranaike Airport. It had one runway at almost sea level surrounded by fields of tapioca plants. The approach coming out of the mountains in clouds or mist made it at times a dangerous airport. Earlier a DC8 of Icelandic airline crashed on such an approach, with 264 souls on board killing 181 and 3 crew. There was some suspicion that a generator owned by a farm on the approach had distorted the landing instruments taking the aircraft off the centre line and consequently crashing.

The humidity and heat were very high, so the rooms had air conditioning. We were able to get the hotel to give us a room above the building which had very large wooden screens that could be lifted so allowing a cooling breeze. This became our bar and social centre. Rule number one was whoever left the island brought back a bottle to add to our free bar. One afternoon while enjoying a beer or two a fellow came out onto the lagoon paddling a small boat. I was informed by the waiter he was a pilot flying the B737. On a closer look, it turned out to be Doug Eden who I had rented a room in his flat when with IRAN AIR. Calling him over, we discussed how he was able to get out of Tehran on the last plane leaving. He wondered what had happened to me knowing I brought it on the last flight from England. I explained what had happened to his left behind belongings, the eventual outcome of the dilemma the abandoned pilots were in and my escape. He understood and went back to his fishing.

The second place to obtain libation and a good cheer was the Colombo swimming club. It was, however, 20 miles away and took some time to frequent. But some of us joined and met a lot of the local fellows with distinct British colonial accents who certainly did occasionally enjoy a glass or two allowing them and us to get into a very merry state, at times visiting their homes in such a state.

Swimming club

It was at this time on a day off; that I was able to get up to "Nuwaro Eliya" passing the temple of the tooth at "Kandy" and finding my great grandfather Horas Portal's tea estate. He eventually farmed in South Africa Thereby my family link to the D'Portal. The building was still there and as I had sketches drawn by him which he had sent to his future wife in "Tonge House" the family estate in England. This enabled me to correctly identify where he had been sitting whilst drawing the sketch 100 years earlier. The estate's name was still on the stone entrance "Della Wadi" The terrain is high mountain green and very beautiful with acres of tea estates. The movie Bridge on the River Kwai was made here. The movie set bridge remains across the river.

From my Great Grandfathers estate, a picture of the Sheba's Breast Mountain.

Temple of the tooth at Kandy

The B747 went into service with Captain Carroll in charge of operations in Sri Lanka. First officer George Sinnot and I brought in the first return flight from Paris with the President of the island on board. Generally, the operation was running well. I recall a flight that required my crew to operate to Karachi, and then wait for the returning flight from Italy. We got wind from operations that there was some sort of problem with the incoming flight. It turned out that a passenger had gone berserk, attacking the Captain and First Officer's wives who were travelling in first class. Rampaging around the cabin he attempted to enter the cockpit. The male cabin attendants are not big men but had been able to corner him with his back towards to galley. They then with the flat side of the crash axe stunned him. Using the cord which holds back the curtain and some wire they bound him to the front seats by the 2nd left door. He was deranged and when I got on board, he attempted to lash out at me. The Pakistan police arrived and with the back door open, backed up a Land Rover whereupon 6 policemen hurled him into the van. The last thing I heard was his body hitting the inside of the van and the locks being secured. It appeared he had multiple entries on his passport from Asia to Italy. He was smuggling drugs in swallowed condoms, one of which had broken and sent him into a mad frame of mind. With the two wives made comfortable after their introduction to Asian ways of life and the passengers calmed, we continued with the flight to Colombo. The stewards were complimented on their efforts and to my mind their bravery.

Another incident I recall was when departing Dubai on a Paris trip; I could barely get my nose off the ground on rotation. On arrival in Paris, I demanded the weight and balance sheet I had signed be checked. Sure enough, the loaders in Dubai had incorrectly taken the load for the forward cargo hold to be in pounds whereas they were in kilos. This meant that the weight in the forward section was double its weight. Thank God for the forgiveness of the B747. There was concerning unrest with the Tamils in the north of the island and security was beefed up. Trouble was to come as Air Canada had via the aid system, sold /donated Air Lanka a couple of L1011 Tri-Stars. One of which the Tamils blew in half on the parking ramp. It was about this time that we received the mentioned bomb scare only to find out that the bomb had been loaded onto the wrong aircraft and sent to Dhaka in Bangladesh. It was unbeknown to them, offloaded as cargo which exploded in the cargo shed killing people with the collapse of the building. Another explosion took place at the plush "Oberoi Hotel" in Colombo blowing out the second floor.

Security was stepped up and this was the beginning of my problems. The operations department found out from Saudia that I was not the Captain Evans they had inquired about but was First Officer Evans. I was called into the operations department, interrogated heatedly again by Captain Carroll who upon my admission, told me that there had been a big mistake thereby cancelling my contract. Even though I had all the qualifications license-wise, been checked out by a senior Guinness Peat B747 check airman and was operating the international service having just flown the island President in from Paris. Nevertheless, they felt it better for all concerned that I be given a ticket home. So, without any further ado, I prepared to depart. Not long after this the situation became very unsettled and the B747 was withdrawn. So by in large I did not lose much but rightfully gained the long-after command seat allowing me to work in a different freelance category.

It was all very disappointing, and I had to fight off depression as I had started to prepare for the arrival of my family, so looking for accommodation and schools. The idea at last of a family life in Sri Lanka was a dream. Returning to Toronto in early winter was not a good time for freelance pilots. It looked like it was going to be a cold winter with very little workaround.

B747 Braniff.

With September almost finished and no freelance work available, I had at least been able to spend time with my family. Decisions had to be made and the outlook for B747 freelance pilots appeared the best bet. Contacting my old friend Captain Hal (Mac) McNicol of Flight Crew International, a well-established pilot leasing and contract company. He suggested that he could get me onto a B747 ground school and training program with Braniff which was about to start in Fort Worth.

This would enable me to get the B747 type rating endorsed onto my USA Airline Transport license. I had taken the opportunity after Iran Air and while waiting to join Saudia, to write my USA A.T.P. license in Dallas, thereby having a South African, British Colony (West Indies), Dutch West Indies, U.S.A. and Canadian Airline Transport Licenses. Capt. Mac much later at the age of 92, wrote a book on his life called "Flight Plan to Adventure". I sort of had emulated his life, so he sent me a copy which is well worth reading. We have remained in touch ever since.

A.T.P. Licenses.

FLIGHT OPERATIONS DEPT
Our File: 1/17

Athens Central Airport, November 4th, 1986

TO WHOM IT MAY CONCERN

This letter introduces Captain ALAN C. EVANS employed as a Captain on Olympic Airways B-747 world service.

Captain EVANS has been employed since June 1986 to November 1986 and has completed all the required base and line checks required by this company to a good standard.

Olympic Airways has no objection to recommending his services.

Captain G. PAPADOGLOU
Chief Pilot B-747

While with Saudia, I got the required training for a B737-type endorsement.

As I had resigned to go to Air Lanka, I left them without completing the flight checkout, so, to get the type rating I would have to get the flight checkout at my expense. To do this I flew SAUDIA flights to New York which had a 3-day layover, then bought a ticket down to Phoenix. Here I rented time on a B737 simulator and got checked out by Chuck Schmidt an F.A.A. check airman. I then rented from Western Airlines a B737, did a check flight and got my U.S.A rating with an F.A.A flight check airman R.A. Miranda.

Speaking again to Capt. Mac of Flight Crew International indicated that he could get me on the BRANIFF B747 training course which was becoming available very soon. It was an alternative expansion of my career. Therefore, with no immediate employment and very little cash in hand, I decided to take the chance and do the B747, F.A.A. approved endorsement rating on my U.S.A. license. This would take about 3 weeks. Arriving in Fort Worth I found a very cheap hotel near the training school. Considering I had done a B747 course with South Africans also at the Boeing training centre in Seattle with Saudia and Wardair the program was not difficult. The flight time I had gained with Saudia on the world network as a senior first officer was very much to my advantage. The hardest part of the course was that I was running out of money, and it became very evident that I was not going to have enough to complete the program. As for eating, I could not afford much being reliant on the snacks from the bar and food available at the Braniff training centre. A week before the check ride and final exam I was under huge pressure and penniless.

Depression was setting in with doubts that I could finish the course. One evening I almost broke down, fell onto the floor in tears and wanted to walk out. In the morning, I called my bank manager Mrs. McIntosh asking if I could borrow, on the strength of my bond, any cash. After I explained my situation, she gracefully agreed to forward me the funds I needed to pay for the remainder of the course, hotel and some food. I qualified by doing my check ride including all emergency drills with Captain Asray on November 1st. I was now holding American and Canadian A.T.P. licenses endorsed for B747. In those days pilots could jump seat on scheduled airlines by producing their Airline Pilots Association cards and being in uniform so getting lifts across the airline industry's networks. This I did once before with Pan Am across the Atlantic to the South Africa Airways interview and again now on my favourite EASTERN airlines which were very liberal to the airline fraternity, in so got home to Toronto.

There was no work around at all and winter was setting in, things were getting very tough. When the sleet and snow came, I made a bit of cash by waiting at the GOTRAIN commuter station near my house. Passengers disembarking would find their cars frozen or unable to start. I had a Toyota 4 x4 which I used to tow out and or start their flat-battery cars. A small flight came up to do some DC3 work but by the end of January, there was still nothing in the freelance world. We had obtained a Husky puppy named "Skeet". Much loved by the boys. He was a beautiful animal but very much a handful as he grew into maturity. We started to train him to handle a harness so to exercise him we would harness him up and let him tow us on Skies. We joined up with a Husky dog sledge club and enjoyed some great days working the teams out in the freezing snow-covered trails and forest.

Josie and Skeet our Husky sled dog on a sled dog race meet.

DeHavilland

While in the Arctic I had met the salesman Tom Appleton for DeHavilland aircraft demonstrating the Twin Otter. Locating him in Toronto I asked if he could help or knew of any freelance work. He advised that DeHavilland might be looking for some more test pilots for the DeHavilland Boeing Dash 8 and would look into it for me. The outcome was that I was duly hired as a test pilot for Boeing DeHavilland and did the conversion course onto the Dash 8. The Dash 8 was the ancestor of the old Beaver which was developed in 1947 and tested by George Neal who I believe is still alive at 92 years (date 2012). The Beaver was a great bush aircraft versatile on skis, floats and wheels, serving to open up the vast Northern territories, Yukon and Alaska. They were also used in Africa, and anywhere sturdy and hardworking machines were needed. It had a Pratt & Whitney junior engine that could lift 1320 pounds and had a speed of 140 mph. It became the large single-engine Otter with a Wright 1700 engine. Later it was developed into the twin-turbine Otter with PT6 engines again into the DASH 7 with 4 turbines and finally into the DASH 8 with 2 turbines.

The company headquarters was at Downsview Airport in the centre of Toronto. I lived at Meadowvale about 45 kilometres from the office. I would have to get on the road by 06:45 am to fight the slush, snow and heavy traffic to get to the airport office. I was given a parking spot, an I.D. and an office desk. I had a seat in the company dining hall and finished work at 4:00 pm. All looked very rosy, but the flying was something else. It consisted of taking off flying for about an hour or even less returning to reset some part of the aircraft. We wore parachutes and flying suits. Most of the time it was days of bookwork, interrupted by a small flight.

After two months of this I realized I was not cut out for office work and the office protocol. Visiting the charter section of Toronto airport almost daily, I found out that a company called SKY CHARTER operating

Dassault 10 and 20 Falcons was about to hire another pilot. They knew my credentials from Millard Air DC3 days and hired me. I immediately handed in my resignation to DeHavilland. I was never meant for an office job; I had been flying too long.

Skycharter

The company operated Falcon 10 and 20's. Fast performers who flew very much like a fighter. Their service was to collect DHL and UPS inbound mail from Willowrun; they had landed a contract to operate cross-Canada express service flying bank papers, body parts and cash. Similar to the Millard Air strike days

The service started in Toronto, Quebec then went across to Winnipeg and Regina. There an incoming service from Vancouver and Edmonton would meet up and change the crew. The crews returning via the route they had taken occasionally changing to Calgary or Ottawa. I did the conversion course adding the Falcon to my now increasing type ratings. The service was exciting and required good airmanship, flying in all weather and often getting in with urgent cargo very close to being below weather conditions.

Falcon 20

The Falcon was a real performer, one could approach the airport at the same distance as the altitude. i.e. 35,000 feet at 35 miles. Close the throttles and drop the speed brakes. Decent would be about 8,000 feet a minute, hanging in your harness and arrive over the airport at circuit height. Summer came and the flying was great. I was temporarily based at Edmonton flying a spur section to Ocean Falls. This had rather a spectacular approach and a few times I believe the first officers got a cold sweat. One of the pilots was guy called Tex was an ex-Canadian Air Force pilot who had accidently while getting into his car on a hunting trip, shot off most of the fingers on his left hand. We got on very well and as he on the Western Canada Base would meet at Winnipeg on the cross over. He had son whom he adored so we would often discuss our sons and family.

Regretfully I was to be the bearer of bad news for our friendship. A situation I hope never to be in again. While about to leave Toronto I got a call redirected from the operations department from a lady friend of Tex's in a tearful tone advised me that Tex son had been killed in an accident involving an overturned pickup in which he was travelling near his home in Calgary. She asked if I could contact Tex and break the news to him. I realized that if someone told him now the cross Canada service would be short a pilot, also there would be no way of getting him home on the airline service. I instructed the lady not to mention this to anyone until I could get in touch with Tex. He was about to leave Montréal and would be in Winnipeg in 4 hours' time. I decided to do my flight to Winnipeg swop with him so he could at least from Regina get a flight to Calgary. All concerned were advised of this; collecting a spare first officer I flew into the night to meet his flight in Winnipeg. On his arrival he walked into the pilot's lounge looking for a cup of coffee. I walked up to him and asked if he could step outside with me for a minute. This he did and we walked down the flight line a little. Stopping him I asked if he had faith in God and his mercy. He replied that he had, questioning my reason. I put my hands on his shoulders and told him his son had been killed in an accident. Tex was 6 foot 2 inches and collapsed at my feet, lifting and holding him he shook for minutes. It was midnight cold and snowy not a scene of good will, but it was all I could do. We swopped first officers with Tex flying with me to Regina. There we got him onto a flight home. I saw Tex many times after that but lost contact when I resigned from Skycharter.

It was while on this Skycharter contract, I got word that OLYMPIC Airlines, the Greek company, was looking for possible B747 freelance crews. I had staying with me an Australian friend Gary who had been with Saudia. Over the evening meal it was discussed, and I said I would pursue it as I was not happy with the present deal wanting to get back into the B747 field. My friend left that morning for Australia and unbeknown to me he had contact with OLYMPIC. It was during my attempt to speak to whoever was doing the contract that he got the deal and the job to fly the Singapore to Australia shuttle. I missed out on talking to a friend. The resignation from SKYCHATER came about when a company I heard of in Miami was looking for B707 and B737 pilots to start a new cargo and passenger company called "CHALLENGE" operating to South America. I was operating out of Edmonton at the time, so not wishing to spend another winter in the subzero weather made contact with Captain Metsker. Although I did not have a work VISA for the USA, he advised that they would be willing to sponsor me pending an interview. Getting a jump seat on Eastern to Miami I met Metsker had the interview and was offered a job.

Returning via Toronto, I submitted my resignation and proceeded to make plans to get to Miami.

Challenge.

Arriving in Miami I met some of the new hires who like me were all freelancers, pilots laid off from bankrupt airlines, or looking to relocate. The first thing was to get the signup done then look for accommodation. One guy came in a camper van, so he was set up, a chap called Bill North and I struck up a friendship and were able to find a small cabin which was part of the old Hotel on 36th street very near the Challenge offices. It was cheap, two beds and a bathroom but no privacy. 36th street had been the hub of activity with Eastern being there in force, Pan Am, Arrow and all the charter companies dotted along the street.

There were plenty of Bars, Clubs, pilot hangouts with one of the famous being "Branson's". Here you could meet 24-hours-a-day pilots of all descriptions, pilots of fortune, ex-Viet Nam ex-army and air force guys, layabouts, drunks and all kinds of rumours being the discussion of the day. It was known as Cockroach Corner with very old and some almost unflyable machines coming in from all corners of the earth. It was a breakers yard for scrapping aircraft, secondhand parts plus this mixed with pilots of all description made it an aviation circus of note. It was on this street that Adnan Khashoggi the flamboyant Saudi arms dealer had his airline called "PAN AVIATION" he flew arms to anywhere he could sell them. He had a VIP DC8 that had an omnivision dome cut in the floor allowing passengers to see while overflying the world. This modification was never registered on the aircraft's papers. The aircraft came up for sale after his company was shut down but from my knowledge, it was never sold but scrapped. He must have had Allah looking after him as it was quite likely the aircraft could have broken up in the air.

36th Street at night was not the safest of places. Gunfire was often heard, and gangs roamed the neighbourhood. One night as Bill and I were walking back to our little cabin a drive-by shooting took place with gunfire and ricocheting bullets flying above our heads. Diving behind an upturned table of one of the closed street restaurants we lay doggo until the street seemed clear, and then ran like hell for the cover of the hotel.

We completed the ground school using the back on one of Eastern's hangers. My captain checkout was done by Captain Pat Johnson using Piedmont airlines B737 simulator. We then did a Captain familiarization flight with Captain Ted Metsker. One of these was to a hair-raising airport in Venezuela called Taguchigama (Spelling may not be correct). It required the pilot to fly over the field amongst the mountains. Circle to the left around a mountain and land by using the low roof of a tavern as a right-wing marker, to facilitate touching down before the first white line on the runway. Failing this meant an immediate go-around, if not the end of the runway fell immediately off into a ravine which when inspected had quite a few aircraft wrecks in it. Some as big as C46, DC3 and whatever was left of other crashed unidentified aircraft.

Things got underway and the service was starting to mature. I had made all the applications for a work visa and green card with the companies sponsoring. I got a call from the immigration department saying my H1-work visa was ready and that I could collect a form from them to be signed by the sponsoring company Challenge. Then again, the proverbial hit the fan. Bill and I heard that the company was bankrupt, and the offices closed so if we had any hope of getting paid, we should move fast. Here I was with my papers all ready to work in the States and the sponsoring company now going under. Running down to the office in a desperate hope of getting a signature from anyone, I found the doors all locked and chained. I desperately attempted to find anyone with the appropriate stamp from the company which would enable me to stamp and sign in so getting the right to work in the USA. Everyone had vanished so there was no chance of getting the papers signed. Bill and I realized the show was over and getting paid was another thing. He packed his car and left for home. I attempted one more try with the work permit, and green card obstacle. I met again with the immigration authorities, but they explained that as I was white, owned my own home, Canadian resident, a qualified pilot there was no chance. However, if I was black, had come up the beach stark naked, illiterate, with no known nationality, they would give me a temporary work permit? Indicating I was African born did not help.

Dominicana Airlines

Down in the mouth again very little funds I started to look around to see what I could get on the illegal or legal market; anything would have to do. I had a family to feed. Little did I know fate was just about to play a very strange hand and it came out of the blue? Sitting in Branson's Bar a guy next to me struck up a conversion. He was with Arrow Air which was about to go under. He indicated he was Iranian to which I took a minor interest but indicated I had flown for Iran Air. Looking at him again he looked familiar, and then he said his name. He was Barry Hakiemin my check Captain on the B707 when I flew for Iran Air. We embraced each other and talked about what had happened to ourselves after we landed the last B707 into Tehran. The war and how I had escaped, and how he had got his family out to the USA.

I explained my precarious situation and that I was desperate to find a job. He asked me to standby for a moment, leaving to make a call. On returning he explained that a Captain from Dominican Airlines had been in contact with him as they were looking for a B707 Captain to fill a temporary vacancy. He had called them back on my behalf putting in a good word for me. The next morning, I got a call from Dominican Airlines Miami office advising there was a ticket awaiting me to leave on the midday flight for the Dominican Republic. Arriving at the airport full of anticipation and not quite sure how I was going to get around the fact I had not flown the B707 for 4 years and never as a captain. Standing at the counter the airport manager came up to me introducing himself and asking me to follow him to his office. Once there he explained that the captain due to take the flight out was ill, there was no reserve captain, he had been asked if I would take the flight to Dominican so saving the company undue expenses. The situation I was in required me to make a fast decision, chance or no chance. I agreed.

Being escorted out to the aircraft in civilian clothes I entered the cockpit to meet the crew. One did not speak good English the first Officer Gonzales thankfully did. Getting into my seat I started a regular cockpit scan frantically trying to remember my B707 system checks. All went well except when it came to start up. I asked the F/O Gonzales whether it was company procedure to start on the ramp or once out on the taxi way. He gave me a vague puzzled look, and then it hit me. Being so used to the B747 I completely forgot the B707 had no auxiliary power unit (APU). I fumbled for a second correcting myself to say whether we started all 4 on the ramp or only one and the others out on the taxi way. Without any other mishaps we got underway. I allowed the F/O to do the take-off while I tried to account for all the information I could remember and was being shown by the crew actions. The flight to the Dominican Republic was uneventful however in my earlier writing I mentioned the fact that my flight from Puerto Rico to Miami on a B707 was my first flight on a B707 jet. Little did I realize fate would have me flying for the first time as captain on B707 on the same airway as I had flown for the first time as a back packing passenger on a B707 just a few years earlier. If you find a gap, take it but be confident. Feeling comfortable I indicated I would make the landing, which was successfully completed. Walking across the ramp I got a call from a man standing on the corner of the ramp. He indicated that the chief pilot Captain Tineo wanted to see me. I thought here we go, they found out about me, and I was either meant to be sent back to Miami or jail. On entering his office, he was most cordial, he explained that he had reviewed my resume and my qualifications. He indicated that the crew on the B707 had spoken well of me, and he noted that I was B747 rated as well.

At this point I was holding my breath awaiting the inevitable sentence which could be jail. What came next nearly floored me. He explained that they had obtained a B747 which I had seen on the ramp. Continuing, he indicated that they had very few qualified crews for it and had had some problems with upgrading crews. There was a daily service going out the next day and would I please help them out by flying it for them together with their check airman Captain Brito using it as a check out on their equipment. He added that they also had a route to Milano in Italy that they wished to start up but due to lack of crew and experience it had not been started. To add would I be able to assist on this by training up some of their B747 junior first officers. I am not sure what colour I had turned by this time but nonchalantly agreed to do whatever I could to help.

A taxi took me to my hotel where I was to spend the next 6 months flying across the pond and up to New York many times, changing from the morning flight to Puerto Rico on the B707 then to the New York flight on the B747 the same day. Arriving at the hotel, I needed a double scotch fast and some time to think of what the hell I had got myself into. The time with Dominicana was great for me. My family used to visit the tropical island and I got on very well with management and the crews. There were some problems at the beginning as the first officers were not long haul experienced and were trained to treat the commander as a god. I was different, met their families and was able to find out the problems they were having on the flight deck. Mainly nerves which I totally understood caused from overpowering captains.

To keep the company afloat a little bending of the rules was the name of the game. On one occasion the New York flight was getting prepared to depart when the Flight Engineer found the pressure in number 3 was below the pass mark. I was called out to see what could be done. The flights both to and from New York were Christmas flights, full both ways with families attempting to be home with loved ones. It was imperative we get the flight operating. I decided to take the flight myself starting 3 engines on the ramp. At the holding point on the runway awaiting take off clearance we started number 3, the pressure was Ok, and I took off. At about 15,000 feet the pressure was dropping so I shut it down continuing on 3 engines. The route from Dominica to New York has many alternate airports along the way so without reporting it to Air Traffic Control I continued on only starting the number 3 engine to make a legal landing. We reported the low pressure which the engineers tested and agreed it required an engine change. The crew overnighted departing the next afternoon with a full passenger load successfully flown to the Dominican Republic.

Another incident happened on a later flight when the flight to New York was overfull. It was not uncommon to have forged tickets so ground staff had to be very vigilant in establishing which legal tickets were. On arrival in New York a child waiting in the departure lounge fell off the escalator. Regretfully she died on her way to the hospital. This set a bad mood for the delayed outgoing passengers. With an overfull aircraft and passengers without proper tickets, ground staff attempting to sort out things, a knife fight started on the spiral stairs to the upper deck. A passenger was fatally stabbed so requiring the police and immigration officers. The aircraft was towed to a hard stand and separated from the rest of the airport car park until the situation was sorted out. Finally, we departed 6 hours late with very tired, angry and disillusioned passengers plus crew.

The flights from Milano were picking up and generally running full. This meant that as we were a classic B747 one hundred series, we were very tight on fuel running against the westerly headwind across an Atlantic random track from Spain to the Dominican Republic. We used to stay South to evade the heavily congested Northern track (grid) used on the North Atlantic routes by the airlines. To make the Dominican main runway we used to have to redispatch at 52 degrees west. If we had enough fuel to make the republic, we could continue but with no reserve. The runway in Dominicana is in a rain belt and aircraft such as American and others have run off the runway. If this was to happen or the runway could not be seen in tropical rain and at night, there would be no alternative airport coming in as we had to with low fuel. Therefore at 52 degrees west a final decision had to be made to either continue or divert to Porto Rico. Occasionally we had to use the B707 on this run. It had less fuel than the B747, in fact a B747 carries the weight of B707 in fuel alone, and so a fuel stop had to be made both ways at the island of Saint Maria. This was an old fueling stop in years gone by for the big old reciprocating engine Super Constellation (super Connie's) and DC7 attempting the Atlantic jump. The halls of the almost abandoned airport echoed the sounds of now ghost aircraft and airman long gone. As an Atlantic Island it was prone to weather changes and mist. With no alternative, once the approach was started it was a very nerve-racking time with no place for error.

Santa Maria fuel stop

One good memory I have of my time in the Dominican was at Christmas. My two young sons had been to visit me transiting via Miami from Toronto. In Miami a good friend Janet Blackmore who worked for

B.A used to help them get onto one of our flights to Dominican Republic. They would then take a taxi to my hotel. The doorman knew them so would assist in them getting to my room.

They used to have a great time with the local kids plus; it was tropical, and they had a lot of freedom in my absence during the day when I was on the daily New York flights. As it was getting near Christmas there were no Christmas trees, however upon my return from a flight the boys had made me a small tree out of split palm leaves. It was a very touching present considering they were only 11 and 9 years of age, one of those wonderful memories one has with one's children.

Whilst in Dominica I got a call from an old friend who indicated he had heard that OLYMPIC Airlines out of Athens maybe looking again for a few freelance pilots to operate the B747 out of Singapore over the summer season. He gave me a name to contact, which I immediately did. The person concerned was Captain Papaloglou the chief pilot. I agreed to send posthaste all my qualifications and résumé. Within a week I was sent a ticket to Athens for an interview. I could not believe my luck as the Dominican contract was slowing down plus the B747 was due for a major check. In good faith I explained to Captain Tineo the situation and my need to continue working on the B747. He agreed with a good reference signed by Captain Frias, the operations manager I left for Athens.

Olympic Airlines.

Arriving there I had a very pleasant interview with Captain Paitakes, the operations manager. Later we did a check ride on their B747, followed a day later by a check flight with a line Captain Petru to Rhodes and back. Completing a medical and an exam on the air law I was issued with a Greek Airline Transport License so adding it to the collection of over 5 International A.T.P. Licenses most endorsed with the B747. I was briefed on the situation being that the union had requested that the crew coming into Singapore rest until the crew bringing the flight back from

Melbourne and Sydney. This meant that crew flying the sector from Singapore to Melbourne and Sydney would have a 2-day lay over in Sydney. This then required the company to have another crew in Singapore to operate the out bound flight so covering the required time for the layover of the Athens crew who had brought the flight into Singapore. All very expensive and not good crew utilization. All union and time restrictions as per their agreement. What the freelance crew was to do was to be permanently based in Singapore. Pick up the inbound flight ongoing to Melbourne and Sydney. There another freelance crew would return the flight in so not requiring the 2-day layover as per the OLYMPIC crew agreement. I was sent to Singapore and established myself in the appointed Orchard Hotel.

For the next six month the two freelance crews kept the rotation going from Singapore, Melbourne, and Sydney. There the other freelance crew would bring it back to Singapore to connect with returning Athens crews. This turned out to be one of the best contracts I did. Olympic was very good to us allowing my family to visit during the 6 months we were there. Naturally the climate and the hotel pool were just great for my wife and two sons. The freelance crews were made up of an Aussie, South African and an Englishman. It was on one of the early flights that I in a cockpit conversation found out why a certain way point in our navigation charts across central Australia was named GAFA. The answer I got from my Aussie first officer was "The Great Australian F--k All."

Knowing Australia as I did it was perfectly correct. As from here all one saw for the following 4 hours was nothing except as we flew across the Torrens area where the lights from the coast could finally be seen. Regretfully it was on this same flight that we lost a passenger. The cabin attendant came up and reported a sick passenger who was gasping for breath and very pale. Shortage of breath is not all that uncommon but I using the passenger address system, asked if there was a doctor on board. I authorized the cabin Attendant to break out the portable oxygen and administer it. The next knock on our cabin door was from the Doctor advising us the passenger had died. He believed from a heart attack and would sign the necessary papers upon our arrival in Melbourne. Without the other passenger's knowledge, we put a blanket around the now-dead passenger indicating she was sedated and sleeping so moving other passengers to vacant seats. She was identified as an Australian woman who had travelled from Ireland to London, then to Athens then to Singapore and on our flight to Melbourne, her destination. The flying time we calculated at over 16 hours. We also figured she had been travelling with the transits for over 28 hours and jet lag was a possible contributing factor.

What transpired after that was very difficult to appreciate as upon arrival the station manager advised that the husband and two young boys were waiting for her at the gate. All passengers disembarked and the hearse took the body out the back of the aircraft. The manager and I confronted the husband and invited him to the office explaining there had been a problem. There he was given the bad news. My last image of him was holding one son in his arms and the other by the hand. Tears welled in his eyes as he walked to the first-class lounge. He was not the only one attempting to hold back tears as I to had two sons. The paperwork required the company to fill out the exact time of death and location over Australia. We estimated she passed away about three hours out so over Western Australia which would put her death documents under Western Australian laws. The doctor covered the death certificate plus a report, accompanied by mine. It turned out it was deep vein thrombosis. Also called economy class disease(circulation) Today with the extended range of flights and cramped conditions it's well covered in airline knowledge. A major factor in future passenger flying.

I took the flight on to Sydney and turning it over the outgoing crew retired to the hotel bar. It had been a stressful incident. While flying this route I had been contacted by a colleague who advised that a company in the island of Vanuatu were looking for a person to help start an airline operating to Brisbane and Sydney. I followed up on this and to cut a long story short got involved in its operation. The Vanuatu company was to put up the finance and supply a B737. I was asked to find crew and hostesses. During my layovers in Sydney, I became involved and started to set up interviews for cabin staff, arrange training, get uniforms etc onto orders. Amazingly enough no advertisement for flight crew could be placed in the papers asking for a photo, or sex as apparently it was against labour rules. Things were going well when out of the blue suddenly funds failed and correspondence with the principal persons became erratic. I was very concerned as I was preparing after the OLYMPIC contract to return home, collect my family and move to Vanuatu. I had advised my wife to start packing, plus I was making temporary arrangements for the boys to be schooled in Brisbane. The project eventually collapsed as does most privately funded airlines. So, without funds and standing debts to companies in Sydney, I removed myself from the operation. I did have a problem to put it mildly, with my wife on returning to Toronto as she had all but packed up the house and our belongings.

The flights continued on as per the routine schedule then in November things started to go wrong. The Greek Airline Pilots Association was demanding more pay or something. Flights were departing late, and crews were flying to the book. There was a whisper of a pending strike in Athens with pilots and cabin attendants getting a bit aggressive. I got a call from the station manager indicating that the crew incoming from Melbourne would take the next flight back the following day to Melbourne and Sydney. There the outgoing flight would be delayed for crew rest so that the same crew could operate the return flight to Singapore. I was asked to do the incoming flights continuation to Athens as there was a strike and insufficient crews. This I did but upon my arrival in Athens I was asked to wear a civilian jacket and disembark as a passenger. The reason was that the striking crews were very aggressive and were causing major problems at the office. I was escorted out of the airport and taken to a hotel entering via the back entrance. Having just come in from an 11-hour flight with 14 hours on duty I was rather tired. I then got a call from operations asking if I would do a New York flight now delayed due the strike. I agreed as long as I got minimum rest so 12 hours later, I was on my way to New York. This to required, that I exit the hotel out the back and board as a passenger. Arriving in New York 10 hrs.35 min later I was glad to get to my hotel. Again, I was called by operations and asked to do the return flight to Athens departing in 24 hours. I agreed and so again this time in full uniform I flew the flight back to Athens now having dome 31 hours flight time in 4 days.

Arriving Athens I got a message that they required a Captain for the Johannesburg flight departing in 12 hours would I like to do it and take my crew rest in Durban instead of Johannesburg. A ticket being supplied by them. This I could not turn down so as the crew's strike got worse, I again boarded in civilian dress and operated the flight to Johannesburg allowing me to fly to Durban and spend 3 days with my old folks. I did the return flight to Athens and then again with minimum rest did another New York round trip. I had done 61 hours in 17 days which was good going and was building my B747 command time. With political situation as it was the pilot's union was winning so as a freelancer it was not the best of places to be. The company decided that as the six-month term of contract was almost up, I being now in Athens, could return home to Toronto. All the crews were paid off and returned to their respective homes so ending the contract.

B747-200

Skycharter again.

November is not a time to be looking for contractual work, especially in the freelance flying business. The usual contacts were made but as the winter deepened nothing was coming up. I walked the Toronto charter offices and sent out dozens of resumes (C.V.) local and worldwide to any and all the leads I made or heard of. The aviation business seemed to have gone dead.

Eventually as spring came about Skycharter in Toronto contacted me to see if I would join them again on the Falcon 20 flying mainly DHL and Express mail across the overnight network. With nothing else on my plate, I jumped at it and was back in the all-night flying business. Night after night, I flew the network at the same time working all the crew placement companies hoping to get back onto the heavy transport business with its generally better pay. The effect of the uncertain business and continuous irregular working hours was taking its toll on my family. Josie was having a problem with it and indulging in far too much wine and cigarettes. I would return home at 5 a.m., then get the boys up and make breakfast. Get them to school and then return to the housework. Josie would surface about 12, only then could I attempt to get some sleep. The returning kids would wake me, and I would then have to sign on at 19.00 hours to fly again all night. It was becoming harder and harder to carry on. I then found an elderly Swedish lady who agreed to move into our basement and become a sort of nanny and housekeeper. This gave me a chance to rest, and her presence was good for the boys. However Josie would take offense to it at times, and it looked as if it was not going to work.

We were in mid-winter with snow and winter activities to entertain the boys. I was battling to keep them amused and out of Josie's confused state of mind. It was at this time that Dusty Thompson, the ex-chief pilot of Quebec Air the Montreal based B707 airline I had done a contract for 10 years earlier phoned to ask if I was interested in a position on a new start up DC8 operation. I accepted the offer but realized I would have to give up the Skycharter job, which I would be very glad to do considering the effects it was having on my family. Simulator training was to start in the New Year a month away.

DC-8 training.

Ground school was held at the old Air Canada training centre, using their simulator to complete the training. By the end of January, the required training was complete and all that was needed was the airtime to be endorsed. We completed this on a D.C.8 -51 checked by inspector A. Umbach of the M.O.T, so now I had a DC8 on my Canadian license. As fate had it Dusty came in one morning and called us to an office. He explained that the funds, which the start-up operation was hoping to obtain, had failed. Therefore, we could go no further with the operation. We would be kept abreast of the situation and as soon as things developed, we would be recalled. That was the end of that dream and there I was back again on the street having terminated my job with Sky Charter who had replaced me. I took a wild decision to renew my B747 rating. To do this I went to see the Air Canada simulator instructors. A friend who was an Ex Ward-air pilot Garth Martin, now a certified instructor made the arrangements, and I did a 2-hour recurrent training session with him qualifying to the required M.O.T standards. All of which I had to pay for but gambled that I might get me back onto the heavy aircraft again. In so I was signed off now being current on DC8 and B747. I had lost a month's wages on the venture as during training there was only a small per diem covering lunch or dinner.

In desperation I started calling all the overseas crew placement companies, but nothing was materializing. It was May and at least the winter was over, but our family situation was deteriorating badly. Depression was hitting us both. I was having sleepless nights trying to keep the funds coming for the family plus I by now had bought three houses with funds earned when with SAUDIA, of which I had a loan on one. The rentals were keeping us going but only just. Josie had not worked for years and any suggestion along this path aggravated her, claiming she had the kids to tend to. Nevertheless, the wine and cigarettes were taking their toll. Then a turn of events came about. Max Ward, the owner of Ward Air heard she was in Toronto, and he was looking for a non-union person to work and to later hire stewardess in the event he was faced with a major union strike. Josie rejoined them as a junior hostess sort of incognito, a far cry from her earlier position as assistant senior hostess for the Toronto base when Wardair moved from Edmonton. Very quickly she picked up the system and became current again. She then started interviewing and hiring about 100 girls. Our good friend Peter Highfield became the chief pilot of the Toronto division.

British Midland

About this time, I got a call from Air Tara, which was the operational arm as I had mentioned before, of the worldwide leasing company, Guinness Peat. Not the brewery. They wanted B737 crews for a 6-month contract to British Midland in Tee-side England. After accepting I was sent a ticket from Miami to the U.K. which meant I then had to get to Miami at my own expense. It was a hasty call allowing very little time to make arrangements. Using my credit card, I bought a ticket to Miami chancing that this was a real deal and that there would be a ticket awaiting me. I had no funds to buy a return ticket, so it was go for broke. After quick arrangements with the Scandinavian woman who offered to be a nanny in exchange for living free in our basement, the kids and Josie, I departed for the unknown. Arriving in Miami I was relieved when I found a ticket to London and on to Tee-side. Sitting in the departure lounge a fellow walked up to me who looked vaguely familiar, he was Emile Cerisier the ground engineer who I had lent money to way back in the Seagreen days of Antigua. He had borrowed the money to put towards his pilot's license, which he had succeeded in getting. With great apologies, he explained why he had never paid me back. It was a long and sorrowful story, which I will not go into. It was pleasing to see him again and more so to find he was on the same contract as me and heading to Tee-side. We had many a tale to tell and over the next few months recounting our good times in Antigua.

Eventually, after arriving in Tee-side we were sent to Ireland to do simulator training as the aircraft was on the Irish registry so getting, our Irish licenses. It was at this point I nearly lost the job. Upon boarding the B737 to go to Ireland the check airman only found out then that I had only flown the B737 way back in May 1984, four years earlier when I obtained the rating, having been checked out by R.A. Miranda an F.A.A inspector in the USA. As this was a rush job the urgency saved my position with the operation. Subsequently, I was re-currented and started flying the British Midland routes. Another pilot who was hired was also a surprise. He was Bill Smith who I had helped get on with Dominicana as first officer on the B707. Bill had previously been an Air Traffic Controller but was made redundant when President Regan deregulated the USA airlines. We did quite a lot of charter work as well as positioning to places such as Ireland and Scotland to commence the charter flight. These usually operate to holiday places such as the Spain and the Channel Islands. It was on one of these flights that I had the opportunity to visit the Channel Island aero club; my original flying school back in 1962. I had good memories.

On a flight out of London we hit a flock of birds at 800 feet taking out our left engine, in so requiring a single engine return to the London airport with emergency equipment on standby. I was flying with a chap called Jim Koehn, an experienced pilot, so there were no problems. On an evening departure from London we had a PANAM B747, PA103 ahead of us. He was lower and heavy climbing to his initial altitude. Being lighter we passed him at the intersection which took us on a right turn towards Tee-Side. On landing at Tee-side the tower was in a bit of a frenzy asking quite a few questions as apparently the Pan Am flight had been destroyed over Lockerbie in Scotland. We would have seen it if we had been just a few minutes later. It was the Clipper "Maid of the Seas" killing all 259 aboard, as well as 11 in the town of Lockerbie.

Remains of the "Clipper Maid of the Seas"

Three years later in December 1991, Pan Am went bankrupt. Another fatal and devastating catastrophe that happened while in Tee-side was the explosion of oil rig Piper Alpha in the North Sea on the 6th of July 1988 killing hundreds of workers. The airport of Tee-Side had been a Canadian Lancaster bomber base during the war. On one side of the airport was an old, abandoned hut in which we found the remains of an officer's bar. In a very short time, we had resurrected it and it became our regular pub. Staff from the British midland started joining us and after a while staff would fly in from London to join in the Friday night parties. We had an agreement with the hotel to supply the booze. There was no charge for drinks but during the night a hat was passed around adequately filled to pay for the evening, which sometimes was held in fancy dress. As the six-month contract started to wind down there were a lot of people sorry to see us preparing to leave. For me, it was to go back to Canada and my children who I had not seen for six months. Josie had been able to fly over for a short 5-day visit courtesy of Ward Air.

Singapore (Tradewinds)

MCDONNELL DOUGLAS
TRAINING SYSTEMS AND SERVICES

Certificate of Training

This is to certify that

ALAN CHARLES EVANS

has successfully completed the

MD-80 INITIAL

Flight Crew Ground Training Program

Hours Attended: 92

from MAR 28, to APR 14, 1989

Manager, Flight Crew Ground Training
DOUGLAS AIRCRAFT COMPANY

There appeared to be no immediate contract work but out of the blue Air Tara landed a two-year agreement with Singapore Airlines to supply and operate two MD87 (DC9) aircraft to start a sort of domestic service to be called TRADEWINDS. We were all signed up to proceed to Long Beach California to start training on the MD87 in about 4 months' time. On my return to Canada, I contacted Dominicana who I had heard wanted a B707 Captain. I subsequently returned to fly for them whilst awaiting the training program in the USA to start. A call from Paul Plaisted now in charge of the Tradewinds venture, confirmed my tickets to proceed directly from Dominican Republic to Long Beach. The training program started on time with the two aircraft being prepared to go to Singapore.

During the initial days of ground school, the instructor asked what aircraft we had all been flying before. He pointed out that those on heavy aircraft such as B707 and B747 would find the transition to a glass computerized cockpit difficult. We were more hands on so not experienced with the new automated characteristics. He was right and I found the new systems very hard to accept with old basic technology clouding my scan and knowledge. Eventually we completed the course and the checkout on the aircraft. As it was a two-year contract, we were allowed to take family members and some household goods. It turned out I was the only married man who had family able to go.

On returning to Toronto, I found that Josie was not at all interested in moving to Singapore. She was well ensconced with her position at Wardair, enjoying the work she had been trained for in most of her earlier career. Our old friends Rob and Jean Mackie had divorced, and Jean had moved into our house keeping Josie and the boy's company. The situation was not good, and I could not see leaving the boys there would be good for them. She was away on flights plus the social drinking was becoming a problem to which Jean and I had attempted to get her clinical help. A tropical break from Canadian winters, social change to a foreign country plus the advantage of being able to attend a high-level private school of British background, to me appeared better for all concerned. It was then agreed that I would take the boys plus our Siberian dog "Skeet", to Singapore with Josie attempting to visit using the airline system when able. I proceeded getting the travel arrangements organized, making arrangements for the boys to follow. It turned out to be the best move I had ever made. Arriving in Singapore I was booked into the Orchard hotel for 10 days. During this time, we had to study and write the Singapore Airline Transport pilot license. I was very fortunate as I ran across a Rhodesian pilot

Our Singapore home.

I had met in Iran. He had resigned from Singapore Airlines and had a bungalow out in Changi which he would be willing to transfer the lease and furniture over to me. I was set up for the arrival of the boys as it was near the beach and airport, had three bedrooms and a small tropical garden. It was on the bus route with Changi village and market only a few miles away. We settled into a full and happy life. There were no drug or liquor problems. We joined the Changi sailing club where the boys learnt to sail. Later they joined the wind surfing club, got their SCUBA license, getting into a real nice bunch of kids all keen on healthy outdoor life.

They were admitted to the United World College mixing with 29 different nationalities some being Prince and Princess from Malaysia. We got a maid twice a week to help out with cleaning and washing. Grant started to play the guitar and I bought a piano from the local SPCA for Scott. They would travel into the city on Friday nights to join up with friends and party or go to the movies. The last train left at midnight with a bus connection to Changi. It was all safe and we hardly ever locked our doors. Thankfully the alcohol problem was in Canada not causing any harm to the boys who were free of any pressure concerning their mother. They both claim these were the best years of their schooling lives.

While living in Singapore the boys and I went across the bridge to Johor Bahru and then took a train trip through Malaysia to Kuala Lumpur. This was part of the death railway that thousands of prisoners of war died on during its construction by the Japanese during WW2. It is said there is a decapitated soldier or the body of a dead prisoner who died from disease and malnutrition or brutality every two meters of the line. It continued to Burma. Famous bridge over the river Kwai.

While in Kuala Lumpur we visited the markets and local scenery. One was to go check out the Batu Caves. A few caves have been turned into Hindu shrines. The main thing the Batu Caves are known for is Thaipusam, a festival where people pierce their skin and carry heavy offerings up the stairs and into the cave. They're usually in a trance.

Coincidently British West Indian Airlines had a strike with most of the senior pilots obtaining jobs with other airlines. Singapore hired a lot of them. Two being Junior Evans and Henry Piddack so we met up and talked about the old Caribbean days.

I would often harness up Skeet as he was a Siberian and loved to pull me on my bike usually the 5 kilometres to Changi. Occasionally he would get out of the property followed by a call from the prison nearby that our Wolf dog was on their grounds. This prison was part of the death camp prison of World War 2 where thousands of soldiers died under the brutal hand of the Japanese. It was also where drug traffickers were hanged. There was no mercy in Singapore or Malaysia, possessing drugs was a death sentence consequently a wonderful drug-free young community. The boys got on well with the local schoolmates especially the Singhalese, kids known by this as they were of mixed parents such as English fathers and Singapore mothers. The young girls found their blonde hair and blue eyes very appealing. In as much on one occasion Scott was invited to a private party aboard a young girl's father's luxury yacht. Grant was pursued by a very wealthy young Singapore girl who had her own converted van including stereo and all amenities plus a driver.

The school had organized overseas adventure trips. Scott joined one traversing India by train, bus, raft and camel ride. Grant went with a camping group to Borneo, travelling deep into the jungle on river canoes and climbing an observation mountain. I did get the chance to send the boys back to Toronto on two occasions during school holidays. Both returned glad to be back in Singapore. During their shorter school holidays, Scott being a lover of animals, got a job working for the zoo, Grant with a Chinese printing company, there was no idle time. On one lazy afternoon, Scott came rushing in saying there was a puppy trapped in a sewer pipe of an abandoned old military complex nearby. Arriving there I saw the pup stuck in the horizontal pipe about a meter down. It was moving so I returned to our house and made up a noose from a piece of wood and thin rope. Lowering the noose down I was able to snare the pup and drag it to the surface. Well with pleading eyes I agreed that Scott could keep it if he could find a home. A week later the pup now called "Happy" ran onto the road consequently being struck by a passing vehicle. It was badly mangled but was alive. The vet did not give it much hope with its one eye removed and badly injured body. Happy lived and was accepted as a household pet joining the wild cat that lived on the roof and our Siberian Skeet. About this time the school proms were getting organized. Scott in very well-dressed attire attended his with the daughter of the Australian Protective Service Chief Superintendent

Bryan Perry, whom I had met at a party I attended at the Australian High Commission.

Time was going by quickly and as we approached the end of the two years contingency programs had to be put into place regarding schooling and location. Scott had written his O levels and was therefore 6 months ahead of Grant in schooling requirements. It was decided that I would send Scott to South Africa and enroll him in one of the private Ivy League boy's boarding schools to complete his remaining two years of education. He would stay with my parents who would be able to take care of his interim needs. He agreed to go provided "Happy" went with him. I did not want him to go back to Canada as it was not a healthy situation plus the standard of school he had been attending warranted a continuation of that level to the completion of his school days. Arrangements were made, a dog kennel fabricated from two beer crates, and tranquillizers got to keep Happy calm on the long flight via Mauritius and Johannesburg to Durban with the required paperwork and tickets in order; they eventually departed for South Africa. Scott got accepted into "Michaelhouse Boys boarding school". Happy had to spend two weeks in quarantine but mixed in with the 7 large Alsatian guard dogs my parents had.

The flight crew were now advised that Guinness Peat had bought 6 of the DC8 long-range C56 powered aircraft from United Airlines. These aircraft were to be ferried over to Venice for conversion to Cargo aircraft. This meant that Air Tara was back in business and going to the United Airlines training academy in Denver to do the type of training to be endorsed on our licenses. To me, it was another license to work on the freelance market. It was now imperative that Josie come to Singapore as Grant had a few months to go before graduating. Further arrangements were made to get Grant enrolled in Kearsney Boys boarding school in South Africa. Another top private Ivy League boys' school. Josie was to put our Canadian house she was living in on the rental market which was being handled by an agent who was caring for our other two houses. She duly arrived a month or so later having tendered her leave of absence with Wardair and within a few days of me leaving for DC8 ground school in the USA.

Singapore was established by a British businessman named Stamford Raffles in 1819. Ironically the same year that Chaka founded the Zulu nation. He went on to terrorize the smaller tribes along the coast of South Africa. An Anglo-Zulu war was fought on the Tugela River the boundary of the colonial pioneers of Natal who had established themselves there many years before. I had mentioned this in my chapter about when I returned to South Africa survey flying.

Denver DC-8 with United Airlines.

Telegrams and phone calls were flying as we the crew were given the departure dates and travel arrangements to be in Denver. Then a major catastrophe happened going to the Canadian embassy in downtown Singapore. I stepped over an open gutter onto a wet pavement where I slipped and broke my ankle. I managed to get to the hospital in Changi where I phoned Grant to jump on his bike and bring me some cash, I had at the house to pay for the medical cost of the ankle x-ray and setting. This now put me in a very bad situation. If I could not attend the conversion training in Denver, I would be out of a job. I was able to convince Paul Plaisted that I was positive my ankle would be mended enough for me to continue with the rest of the crew to Denver. Sometimes when Paul's wife was in Singapore, they would come and have dinner with us, so we were on good terms which I at this point appreciated very much. I was on crutches but discarded one at the airport, finding it easier to walk assisted on one side.

The training program was set up with two weeks of ground school, then 10 hours of simulator training. Hobbling into ground school was a bit embarrassing but I managed it. My ankle at night was extremely painful and swollen. I would pack it with ice from the hotel vendor and found that the swimming pool was ice cold. I would then go from the training academy to my room via the pool where I would soak my ankle in the ice water. By the time I got to get into the simulator, I realized I would have to during the flight training apply the foot brakes. This was impossible with a cast on my ankle. The night before I started the simulator training, being barely four weeks since the break, I found a hospital and asked them to remove the cast. The break had knit but only just. The simulator training became very painful as I dared not show that I was in pain so having trouble with the flying exercise. I survived and passed the required flight test and exams. The flight checkout as a Captain was done by B. Reydee an FAA inspector. This now gave me the DC8 on my U.S.A. airline transport license plus the B737 and B747. We then proceeded to Waco Texas to ferry the DC8 to Venice where the cargo conversion would be applied. On the flight over the Atlantic to Europe we lost an engine. This was by regulation is supposed to be reported to air traffic control. We would then be required to land at the most available or nearest airport, incurring high costs and delay of delivery to the company. The aircraft was on a ferry permit with no passengers, so Paul and I decided not to report it and press on to Venice as the machines were needed there rather urgently. The DC8 had the big CF56 engines, ours was empty so on three engines we were hardly handicapped in any way.

Once we arrived in Venice, we had to make a hasty departure to catch a connecting flight to Copenhagen via Paris. Here we picked up another one of our DC8 passenger aircraft and flew to Nairobi. This was a contract with Kenya Air, so we were now based in Nairobi.

FLIGHT OPERATIONS TRAINING DEPARTMENT

PROUDLY RECOGNIZES THE ACHIEVEMENT OF

CAPTAIN A. EVANS

IN SUCCESSFULLY COMPLETING THE

DC-8 SPECIAL TRANSITION TRAINING COURSE

FEBRUARY 27, 1991

United DC 8 ferried to Venice for cargo modification.

Kenya Airways

It was great to be flying back to Africa. Our routes were to Bombay, Malawi, and Mombasa. Copenhagen with the odd charter flight into central Africa. Malaria is very high in Africa killing thousands. Cerebral Malaria which attacks the brain is a killer and has to be attended to immediately. We would very often fly down to Malawi on a special flight to bring back patients to be flown on our service to the Tropical Disease Hospital in Copenhagen. I got to know the guys at the flying club who were as usual for ex-colonials, such as myself, very friendly. More than once, I was invited to their private homes for a Braai (BBQ) and cold beer to sit and watch the African sunset sometimes with large game such as Elephant for neighbours. There was a restaurant called The Carnivore where you could buy any game meat such as crocodiles, buck, etc. Things were going well, Scott was in school, and Grant and Josie preparing to follow him to South Africa. I was building flight time on the DC8, plus the location was grand. Theft is rather high in Kenya. One of our newfound friend's wife had just had her necklace ripped from her neck at a stop street. Then one of our engineers who did a regular morning run got attacked, stripped naked, and then had to run into the hotel in a most embarrassing state urgently in need of a towel. It was not safe to be out at night. Strangely enough at the back of the Kenya Airways hanger, they had a very old B720. It had been there for years as a time-expired airline aircraft. One day we saw some mechanics working on it. Then it suddenly departed belching black smoke and disappeared. Nobody ever knew where it ended up or if it made it to its destination, which might have been South America as a drug runner or a scrap yard somewhere. On our flights to Bombay, we could see the pollution at 35,000 feet and as we approached the smell through our pressurization system could be smelt at 150 kilometres. Travelling through the city in the early hours of the morning one could see lines of people all squatting to defecate themselves in the open ground. Cattle and people all share the same territory. Sanitation in some areas is non-existent. Bombay can be a hell of a place to land with high winds and limited visibility caused a lot by airborne pollution.

Just before one of my flights to Bombay (Mumbai) I received a message from Strongfield Aviation, a pilot contracting company in London. I met Gary Jones the aviation personal manager while with British Midlands. Unable to call them from Nairobi, I got a call through to them in

Bombay. They were looking for a DC8 crew to fly and train some of the VASP pilots in Brazil. I asked Gary to stand by until I got back to Nairobi. I had to have time to think this one out, but as before fate played its hand again. On arrival back in Nairobi it a was warm afternoon when I got a call in my room asking me to please come down to the lounge as there was a company meeting being called. We all met at the lounge with cold beers in hand bought by a Guinness Peat representative who we had not met before. A brief introduction and letters were handed out. Then the shot was fired. Guinness Peat was out of business, our contracts terminated and tickets home with residual pay slips were the contents of the letter. We were a bit taken aback and the representative offered his sincere regrets as to the situation. More beers and we dispersed to our rooms to prepare to depart, closing hotel bills etc. I immediately got on the phone to book a call to Strongfield. Making contact I advised Gary of the situation and told him I would accept the VASP offer. I would need a visa for Brazil so as I was going to return to South Africa I could get it there. I would be able to fly from Johannesburg to San Paulo on VASP.

He accepted my application and advised me to contact him when In South Africa. In the next couple of days, we had all dispersed with the British, American and Irish crews flying the DC8 back to the UK. I mentioned nothing of the VASP contract to anyone. I could not afford the chance of one of the Air Tara crew hearing of it and my involvement.

VASP - Brazil

(Brazil was discovered by accident in 1500 by Pedro Cabral)

Arriving in Johannesburg I borrowed my brother's car, drove to Pretoria and got the necessary visa. Getting in contact with Strongfield I was asked if I preferred any particular flight engineer to join the crew. Some names were read out but one seemed familiar. It was Gary Wyeman who I thought I had met when flying the Falcons for Sky Charter. I agreed to have him on the crew list to be based in San Paulo. There was a requirement for two crews so a friend of mine Rob Moore an Air Canada Captain with DC8 experience took a leave of absence to make up the other crew. Ten days later I travelled to San Paulo and was met by the VASP officials and taken to the apartment which had been rented for us. There I met Gary who I recognized from my Canadian flying, with Rob Moore arriving that night. Our apartment was on the 26th floor so no matter which way one looked all that could be seen was a city and slums housing 23 million people. After meeting chief pilots, and operation managers, doing a medical and writing their air law, we got to the aircraft which was one of the Guinness Peat machines. Being very familiar with the aircraft we had no problem in doing a flight checkout. We were issued with Brazilian Airline transport license by the Department de Aviacao Civil. Signed by Fernando Cerdeira Chefe la Divisao. It was explained to us that a lot of their copilots plus some of their Captains had little or no heavy transport experience such as the DC8, which is known as a hard aircraft to fly being so long. Neither they nor Strongfield did not know that I had not been a Captain on the DC8 but flew as a first officer awaiting a command with Guinness Peat. This move to the left seat was again to my advantage for later work, albeit I had very little time on the machine. UNITED airlines restricted their female pilots from flying the 8 as they just did not have the strength to handle it with what was comically known as ARMSTRONG STEERING. The CF56 engines are very powerful so with a long aircraft tail striking was a major problem on take-off and landing. One could only pull 8 degrees up on take-off. There was a wooden skid plate under the tail, so if the paint was removed with an unknown runway touch the aircraft was grounded for inspection. We were quick to set up a training program and got to work familiarizing our routes and airports. We were scheduled to take a Miami flight so on the first flight I set up a bank account for the four of us to receive our pay cheques. This turned out to be very good as we were paid in US dollars. Returning to Brazil we could sell our dollars on the black market so living cost-free in San Paulo. The city was not a safe place, so we agreed not to be out after

08:00pm alone. Regretfully, later two of our engineers were badly injured. One was stabbed in the street with a bread knife, the other after refusing to pay for a girl's drink whom he had not invited to join him at the bar. He was badly beaten outside with a crowbar. Hospitalized and sent back to the USA. We flew all around South America up to Miami training the first officers and captains. This included Manaus in the Amazon River valley. This was one of the hottest places on earth I have ever flown to. On arrival we would wrap wet clothes around our necks, head for the hotel, jump into the swimming pool, ordering cold beers. Extracting ourselves at sunset. Manaus was a German rubber plantation city built deep up the Amazon River where the Black and White Rivers meet forming a distinct line down the centre of the river. It has a magnificent opera house but the city itself has turned into an industrial semi slum. It's a tax-free haven so the cargo we were carrying was flown in repacked and flown out with a duty-free stamp on the documents. There is a lot of infection and disease showing up in the population. This was seen in deformed people having limbs, eyes missing or stunted growth. Some had no arms or legs making a living by sitting in an old tire for support and painting with their mouths the rubber industry went broke, and the Germans moved out. Ford was involved.

DC 8 -71- f. 19 pallet cargo with CF56 engines (powerful ex-United Airlines)

Realizing that rubber had been transformed from a curiosity into a valuable commodity, explorers went into the Amazon Forest in search of the latex-bearing trees. Boomtowns sprang up. Manaus the most remarkable being accessible by river boats coming up the Amazon River. In this Brazilian city encircled by vast forest. Rubber barons built huge mansions, paraded their bejeweled mistresses, and built an ornate opera house of imported stone.

Henry Ford at this time being 1930 also built a massive city called Fordlandia intended to be the world's biggest rubber plantation. It turned out to be a catastrophe as the trees were planted too close together, the South American leaf blight hit, and he alienated his employees. He abandoned the huge project in 1945 leaving poverty and an industrial waste land. Another interesting point was that just before the war Hitler gave Ford in Germany many accolades plus there was a large German Nazi following in the USA. A possible coincidence but after the war many Nazi followers escaped to South America. Interesting that Ford shut down his rubber industry with the Germans about to lose the war. There was also J.F. Kennedys father suspected of supplying aircraft engines to the German war effort and was behind the Irish brown shirts that supported the Nazis.

There is in Brazil another place of incredible beauty which I had the opportunity to fly to. While in San Paulo a captain I was training had a brother who did helicopter sightseeing flights over the Iguazu Falls. Arriving there and meeting his brother, he gave me a free flight to see the Iguazu Falls from the air. The Iguaçu Falls, Iguazu Falls, Iguassu Falls, or Iguaçu Falls (spelling changes) are waterfalls of the Iguazu River on the border of the Argentine province of Misiones and the Brazilian state of Paraná. They are one of the largest waterfalls systems in the world. Considering I had seen Victoria Falls, Niagara Falls these were something else especially from a chopper.

Being able to get discount tickets on VASP I was able to arrange tickets for my son Scott and my brother Wallis to visit. Indicating Wallis was my older son. Flying them up to Manaus I had arranged for them to travel on the cargo river boat down the Amazon to the mouth where it joins the South Atlantic. The voyage was rough with them having to sleep on deck in hammocks. The toilet was an open hole at the rear of the ship, food was whatever they could buy when the boat stopped at the river ports, such as Obidos or Santarem. Usually bananas, river fish, chicken and rice. For them both it was a hell of an experience not to be forgotten, but reaching Belem they had survived and flew back to San Paulo then on to Rio. They also managed to get to see Iguazu Falls Halfway through the contract I flew Josie over from South Africa via Toronto. We were regretfully

not able to visit, or sight see nor tour much. This was due to my busy flying schedule. An interesting point was that I had the opportunity to meet some official dignitaries. As Brazil had been one of the wealthiest countries in South America and seemed to be going into state of decay and poverty, I took the opportunity to ask them why it was going the way it seemed to be, rather downhill. Almost everyone said it was because they had interbred with the slaves African and Indians. In so the great Portuguese culture had collapsed as had the beautiful museums, parks opera houses and infrastructure of an overcrowded population. 20 million in San Paulo alone.

At one time this city was a picturesque and flourishing Portuguese beauty. The idea of building Brasilia had also collapsed. This was to be a futuristic city shaped like an aircraft, but now an unfinished ruin. An interesting point about South America is that at the end of WW2 major Nazi leaders which may have included Hitler escaped to Argentina, Brazil, and Chile. They used the Catholic Church which harboured a lot of them to get baptized and thereby have a new biblical name. Why the Catholic church, because they did not support communism so sided with the Germans in their escape. Ireland had a strong Brown shirt movement which also was Catholic supported favouring the Nazis. It was rumoured that John Kennedy's father was removed from England apparently after attempting to sell American engines to the Germans. He was of Irish Catholic decent. They then via the Red Cross were able to get a refugee visa to South America where they established a new colony which it was learned that the movement was engaged in nuclear experiments to possibly form a 4th Reich and attack the USA. It was also known that in the USA there was a lot of commercial trade support for the Germans. So, any attack would have come from the soft belly of the south supported by Mexico attempting to get back their original land being California, Texas and New Mexico. The Nazi escape route was via Italy, Spain and Norway from which they had submarines in the Atlantic acting as tankers to supply the flying boats with fuel to reach South America.

Iguazú Falls

The contract was now coming to an end. We were thanked by the managing director for a very successfully completed contract, having trained six complete sets of Brazilian crews. It had been very difficult as the pilots did not speak much English and we had no Portuguese. I had a smattering of Spanish but it's not like Portuguese. We at times had to get translators to assist. It had been a great experience and for me an advantage as I now had the command time on the DC8, plus training captain experience to add to my resume. The addition of another A.T.P. License to my growing collection in so expanded my worldwide footprint of experience and was beneficial. Rob and Gary returned to Canada. Unbeknown to Gary or me we would meet again.

I returned to South Africa where I was needed as my ageing and ailing parents were finding things hard to handle in my absence. Regretfully Josie was on the alcohol train, and it was disrupting the family badly. The two boys and my folks could not handle it alone.

Both sons would be home for the Christmas holidays, so it was imperative that I return as early as possible. In general, I had been away too long considering the 6-month absence living in Brazil and the months before in Kenya. I was looking forward to some much-needed rest and being home with my family. Regretfully the rest was to be longer than I thought. Six months were to pass without a contract. But it was very good for our family health.

My younger son Grant was doing his last year at boarding school. The older son Scott has gone to Cyprus to study a Tourist and Hotel management course at the university. This did not appeal to him, so he returned to South Africa to manage a small hotel called Hague Hall. Wanting to get into the airline business he started working for British Airways at the Durban airport. He was also doing a correspondence diploma in Industrial Psychology but was finding things in my absence as mentioned above difficult to handle alone. The boy's support was imperative as to keep working contracts I had to have someone responsible for keeping the home fires burning.

Dubai and Time Air Sweden, OKADA, Thai, Qatar, China Airlines.

With the South American VASP Airlines contract completed, I had to return to South Africa as we, the family had now established ourselves in Hillcrest a small town about 40 kilometres from Durban on the Indian Ocean, basically my hometown. We at first rented a small cottage, later buying a 4-bed roomed house on 2 & 1/2 acres with swimming pool and bar. Months went by without any flying contracts coming in. Then suddenly my friend Garry Jones of Strongfield aviation who had got me the Brazil VASP AIR contract called me. He said say he had another pending contract in Sweden was I interested. I immediately confirmed I was so within a week or two found myself off to Stockholm. As the contract required two complete sets of DC8 cockpit crew Garry asked who I would like to join the new venture. I asked if the flight engineer could be Gary Wyman again but had no preference on the first officer. Garry suggested Greg Carroll an ex-VIP pilot from Toronto who I agreed upon as we had met years earlier on the Toronto aviation circuit. Another crew was hired from the USA so forming the all-cargo route with Swedish crews from Stockholm to Ostend and Istanbul. American crews from Istanbul to Dubai with my crew in Dubai operating across to all of India and any other charters which could be secured. The company was called Time AIR SWEDEN owned by a Swede named Johansson who turned out to be quite an entrepreneur in his aviation ventures.

Tickets were supplied to Stockholm where I met up with the other crews. It was good to see Gary again recalling some of the exploits we had in Brazil. Checking in to a hotel I offered to buy the new crews a drink at the bar. This was done and a good camaraderie was established. What I had not checked was the price of the beer. On calling for the tab I all but fainted and had to almost consider calling my bank for a loan. Compared to South Africa and Brazil it appeared that alcohol in Sweden is liquid gold. That was the last round I ever bought.

I was nominated base captain to cover the Dubai and Istanbul crews. We started well with full loads coming in from Stockholm and Belgium returning with textiles from India and flowers which were offloaded at Ostend to transship to London for the morning market. An amusing thing was that on every flight there was a small box of a dozen or so flasks of whisky, used to bribe or grease any hands that would help us along the way. This came to a stop after a while as the box would arrive from Sweden, Belgium via Istanbul inbound flight, nearly empty. We were suspicious that our fellow pilots flying the line ahead of us were helping themselves hopefully not while flying. The flying was not easy as we, from Dubai operated mostly at night flying long hours with no Inertial Navigation system or GPS, just dead reckoning. This ceased after a few months when one of our Swedish crews relieving my crew in Dubai got themselves 110 miles off course across the Indian Ocean and ventured into Pakistan airspace. We then got an INS which was kept in Dubai and installed on all aircraft flights across the Indian Ocean to India.

Loading in India had to be watched as theft was not uncommon. The trolleys bringing the textiles from the cargo section would have loaders travelling on it. It was not uncommon to see a loader dig out a shirt or two from the plastic sealed bags and throw them into the scrub alongside the ramp. Once we caught a loader walking away with what looked like rather puffy trousers. On apprehending him we found two shirts tucked into his boots. We had to lock the cockpit as theft of our engineer's handheld computer or our food in a cool box was a target. The garbage bag was often searched for our left-over sandwiches and taken. In Bombay there was a little dog that knew the tone of our engines and would scamper across amongst the loading equipment sit and beg at the bottom of the stairs for our scraps.

DC.8. Captain. CF56 engined long haul cargo.(Time) Air Sweden 1992. F/O Greg Carrol. F/E Garry Weyman

Another unusual charter we had was to pick up what we understood was Canadian drilling equipment from Italy and take it to Mombasa. However, it was not eventually for Mombasa as we were purposely diverted by the air traffic control while starting our descent into Mombasa to Mogadishu. This was a hot spot at the time, and we were asked not to reveal to anyone where we were bound for and to turn our running navigation lights out. We were requested to turn our running lights off and that the runway lights would come on once we identified ourselves. On arrival at Mogadishu, we were met by a USA army officer. He explained he would take the cargo off very smartly. This was done and I was presented with a flight plan to Aden with the departure point being Mombasa. On departure with the running light off, Nairobi Air Traffic Control on establishing who we were allowing us to join the airway to Aden for refuelling. It turned out to be a clandestine prearranged deal involving the USA.

I found out later that our cargo was cameras, movie equipment and lights to film the arrival of the American troops landing on the beach at Mogadishu.

Operating through Africa it is not uncommon to get counterfeit dollars, which we had a few in the captains' funds for landing fees, fuel etc. When I say a few, we had quite a lot. Refuelling in Aden was a task as it was at night raining and as usual fueling trucks etc are slow and time consuming however when we left and had paid for the fuel we had no counterfeit dollars.

Meantime to get home on days off my crew would fly the India round trip then fly on to Istanbul and dead head to Ostend. Then catch a train to Paris and fly home to Toronto. It would require a long day and into the night. Fatigue together with dehydration was a problem and very tiring. One of the first officers did this on his days off arrived home, sat down in his lounge and had a fatal heart attack. Occasionally the Dubai crew was required to fly on to Istanbul to do crew relief. There were also times when I flew on to Stockholm and did some passenger charter flights using the DC8 73. 9 tanker aircraft with passengers to Spain. Freelance flying is paid by the hour so it's not uncommon to be in the cockpit for very long hours.

My wife and the sons visited a few times flying from Durban, transiting Johannesburg and Nairobi to Dubai. I had a small apartment in the basement of a hotel on the Sharjah side of the Emirates. It was pleasant on the beach and had a hotel pool to cool off in. It also served as an office for crew scheduling and operations. To get any liquor we got an expat liquor book. We could go to Sharjah where there was a street of liquor stores. You could not buy any such VICE item in Dubai which all seemed rather strange. It was, I understood because of the rift between the brothers or cousins who controlled the different states of the Emirates. At one time a war almost took place between Sharjah and Dubai.

Time AIR SWEDEN DC 8

My sons were now about to leave Michaelhouse and Kearsney boarding school in South Africa so Josie my wife joined me in Dubai. Things settled down to a steady pace and all seemed at last in order. Then out of the blue, the company went bankrupt.

I had two DC 8s in on passenger charter from Sweden, 28 cabin attendants and 6 cockpit crew of theirs Time Air Sweden plus my own 3 crew and 2 flying spanners. We also had on lease a B737 which I occasionally flew for them on the Comoros and Dar-es-Salaam route, it had a crew of 2 cockpit and 2 cabin attendants. (c/a)

The hotel had not been paid nor had the landing fees for any of the aircraft. Nobody had exit visas as all were on crew general declarations. Josie, my wife came in on a visitor's visa, so she was OK. I went to all the hotels where other airlines flying back to Europe had their crews and captains. After explaining my predicament indicating that most of the crews were locked out, I eventually got all the cabin attendants back to Europe on other airlines general declarations. This with the grace of the captains and pursers, who let the girls change and sort of swop uniforms under coats to get them through the immigration without being detected as Air Sweden crew. I was then stuck with my crew and the recent inbound DC8 crew. However, the B737 was on lease and not on our operating certificate so the owners arranged for it to be flown out. I was then able to put all the remaining crew on the B737 general declaration including myself. After we pulled away from the gate the aircraft had to pass by some freight containers. We stopped and being tall I dropped out of the cargo door. Quickly getting behind some cargo containers changed my uniform shirt and put on a baseball cap with dark glasses. Not far away was a line of passengers from a Russian flight so

I tacked myself on to their line. At immigration I was questioned why my Canadian passport was not stamped with a Moscow stamp. I explained I was in transit from Quebec and somehow got through by them allowing me to buy a visitor's visa. I then ran back to the flat belonging to a friend where Josie and I had holed up, and before the authorities found out that we had all departed via clandestine means and nobody had paid the hotels, airport fees etc. We grabbed our gear and made a fast return to the airport. As Josie had a Kenya Airways ticket and I had earlier in 1992, been on contract via Air Tara to Kenya Airways, I was able to arrange per the kindness of the Air Kenya station manager a crew ticket to Nairobi and on to Johannesburg for myself. We hastily got through immigration and were safely in the transit lounge before the proverbial hit the fan and nobody could trace us. We boarded the midnight flight to Nairobi transited to Johannesburg then home to Durban and boys now with their Grandparents and at boarding school.

Air Atlanta

Those crew members all remembered me so when Air Atlanta an Icelandic company with Scandinavian connections started up out of Jeddah on B747s, I was invited to join them as one of their first B747 captains before the Icelanders and some Canadian unemployed airline flight crew, mostly ex-air force. I was duly sent a ticket to do my recurrent B747 in New York. Later a check ride with the chief pilot of Cargo Lux Capt. Hauksson who invited me to join him in California to fetch their first B747. Departing California I flew to Iceland where the owner of the company Mr. Johansson (not the same Johannson as Air

Sweden) met me. He sat in the cockpit for media news exposure as the captain. I rested for a few hours then flew the 250 new cabin attendants on to Jeddah enabling Air ATLANTA to start up the Hadj and teachers' movement airline. The first month I did 100 hours in 8 days then again, the next month 100 hours in 10 days. In the following 30 days, I had done the most allowed flight time for 90 days, 285 hours.

On return, the company gave me a ticket home after the first 3 months, so I could see the family. I was informed that on my return to Jeddah, I should travel via Manchester to pick up a B747 that was there on maintenance with some joining flight crews. This I did getting back into the routine of the Hadj flying, which was sleep, eat and fly as long as you physically could. There followed a 6-week stint based in Cairo and then the grueling teacher's movement which again required pilots to fly night and day picking up and dispatching teachers all over Saudi Arabia. All a freelance pilot's bread and butter but physically and mentally very taxing. The aircraft used were usually what was called white-tailed, old machines with engines rented by the hour from finance companies and in some cases banks. They were not always in good shape, not uncommon to get fleas maybe a rat or two (very dangerous as rats like wires) from Hadjs and baggage so requiring intermittent gassing or fogging. The pickup points of passengers varied from Africa, India, Pakistan, and Indonesia, many were illiterate and dirty all being very hard on the aircraft and cabin attendants. Some of the passengers had never used a flush toilet so they were fearful of entering or using a toilet would relieve themselves on the floor of the toilets, seat pockets or wherever possible. Airsickness would be another thing. Some attempted to bring live animals on board as food. There was a story that told of some Hadjies attempting to light a stove in the aisle to cook. It never happened to me however babies being born, passengers dying, passengers running amuck and a drug addict going berserk have, which I will relate to in another chapter.

Hadj flying is not for the feint hearted, requiring good seat of the pants pilots, real engineers, hardened cabin attendants, but where good money can be made. Later when the contract was over, I had had a disagreement with the Chief pilot a certain Captain Stone. This was after I had pulled a 3 engine, cockpit crew only night take-off out of Turkey to get a desperately needed B747 back to Jeddah and into service. I called it bending the rules and not dangerous. He was an ex-Canadian air force jockey and very much a book pilot, not having my freelance experience thought otherwise. Hadj flying is around the clock.

Although I was very respected and liked by the operations department reflecting the work I had done, I was not invited back to fly again for Air Atlanta while Stone was in office. To illustrate how backstabbing and dead man's shoes relate to a pilot's position in the industry, life security, position on the totem pole such as seniority which directly associates itself to income, relating to family happiness, marriage, (80% of pilots are divorced) not to mention job security from stress of being continually checked on one's capability or losing a medical. This same guy a year or so later was instrumental in me not getting a secure job with Air China.

Home

It was now October and winter was coming in the Northern Hemisphere. Not the place to be for an out-of-work pilot. My wife had now been diagnosed with possible cancer and my ageing parents were battling to help, together with the needs of the boys at boarding school. My dear mother was going blind, and my father was now suffering from mild dementia so restricting their movements and home safety. I had no alternative but to return home. South Africa is not the best place to be for heavy transport pilots. Any jobs that may come about are usually for light aircraft charter pilots. Pilots of my calibre and age would not find work easily available, so the USA or England was the place to be. Hoping the New Year would bring a lucrative contract I opted to return to taking up the demands of my family. Having bought a rather large house with the need to accommodate my sons who would be leaving boarding schools, I decided to build a car garage with the help of my 82year-old father, a retired building contractor. This and the need now to reorganize my life plus the necessary treatment for my wife and the homecoming of the boys got me through to the New Year.

The employment scene had not progressed much, funds were very low and there did not seem to be much work around. Hadj was coming and would start around April. I was constantly corresponding with all the agencies, but nothing was materializing. Then I got a lead on a new startup company out of Africa and a number to call. I immediately called and spoke to a fellow named Allan who put me through to a chap called Tim Steegles. He explained he was the acting chief pilot, that they were looking for B747 pilots and expected to start up soon to get onto the Hadj flying contract. I gave him my qualification indicating I could start at any time.

Okada

The contract was to be a Hadj deal operating out of out of Nigeria. The next day Steegles returned my call indicating that if I renewed my medical plus on the strength of my Canadian license, they would get me a Nigerian license and sign a contract employing me for the Hadj. I immediately renewed my Canadian medical phoned Steegles to confirm it and left two days later to do a check ride with Steegles at Stanstead where the B747 was undergoing maintenance. This completed I was introduced to the rest of the 3 crews needed to operate the service for the new company called OKADA AIR out of Lagos. I did a maintenance flight check on the aircraft with Steegles, again out of Standstead, then met another Captain Bernie Black ex B.A. who was coming onboard as check airman.

The crews were made up of 3 flight deck crews, Captain, First Officer and Flight engineer with 2 cabin attendants allotted to each crew. The other required African cabin attendants would be selected from their hometown of Lagos and trained by our contracted cabin attendants. Little did any of us know what was in store for us! Captains Bernie Black and Steegles flew the aircraft to Lagos with the rest of the crew on board as passengers. We seemed a merry bunch and the camaraderie seemed pleasant. One captain was a black Ethiopian who we named the Prince of Darkness, all in good fun. The plan was that we would fly around the clock with one crew flying a round-trip flight duty time of 16 hours, one resting. The aircraft was owned by a Nigerian known as chief Igbegian with a Hadj contract to fly the pilgrim Hadj schedule from Lagos (Nigeria) to Jeddah Saudi Arabia with some charters to Maduguri, Port Harcourt and Abuja.

Lagos can be a dangerous place. We were put up in the Continental Hotel near the airport. At 7 pm the doors were locked, and we were advised not to leave the hotel. On some occasions, we had to and that required a special taxi being obtained by the hotel which they considered safe. The driver needed Nira the local currency up front plus bribe money which he would stick into the top of the driver's side window. The military and police would pull the taxi over at gunpoint; if the Nira was there, they would allow you to continue. On one occasion two of the female cabin attendants and 4 of the crew myself included rented a VW kombi in an attempt to get to the beach being a typical hot day for a swim. On a road near the beach, we were stopped by 8-armed army men. One came to the driver's side window the other to the passenger window where one of the English girl cabin attendants was sitting. He brushed up against her arm which was half out the window, much to her objection. He took it as an offence, cocked his rifle and ordered the driver to back the kombi down a gravel bush road concealed by trees and high grass. I instinctively knew we were in trouble, especially with the two white girls. Very quickly while the driver tried to argue, out of sight of the irate soldier and below seat-level, I pushed forward all the U.S. dollar cash I had on me from my captain's float. (We could never leave anything in our hotel rooms of value). The driver grabbed it and made an offering to the upset soldier who had now got the other men agreeing to whatever he was shouting about. Slowly the driver peeled off the dollar bills till they were finished. With this, the engineer sitting in front gave him what Nira he had in his pocket. This satisfied the soldiers and they indicated we could precede, at which point the ashen-faced driver accelerated smartly with the rest of us attempting to get our nerves back and wiping sweat from our faces. It was a very close call, especially for the girls who I fear would have been the target for 8 bush soldiers. Rape in Africa is a social pastime with South Africa having a rape every 20 minutes. We did eventually get to the beach which was nothing like our wonderful beaches in South Africa. The shoreline was streaked with long lines of oil pollution, with pools of oil at the high-water line. To swim required stepping carefully around the oil and upon walking out of the water across the sand one's feet were plastered with oil residue. Thankfully enterprising young Africans arrived with coke bottles of fuel (paraffin) to wash off the oil, naturally for a fee.

Life set in with the round and round flights going on continuously day and night. The hotel had a pool, and some TV was available. The main place to be the bar where the crews consumed copious amounts of beer fueled by the heat of an intermittent air conditioner and boredom. This was the social meeting place with incoming tired, hot, and very thirsty crews heading straight for a cold beer. It also was the place for the resting crew so many a good laugh, joke and hearty singalongs sprang up. It was not uncommon to arrive back from a flight to find we had been locked out of our rooms due to lack of payment. As our arrival was often at night many nights were spent sleeping in the lounge until the matter could be sorted out with the owner in the morning.

With nowhere else to go life did become a bit tedious but the show had to go on. I started to study for my British Airline Transport licenses hoping to be able to write it and do the check ride when back in England. I had been offered a job with Virgin Atlantic provided I had the complete British A.T.P. License. I could not afford to take the time off, live in England, support my family and write the exams taking about 3 to

4 months. The crews got sort of into three groups. I had with me Allen Jones as a Flight Engineer and usually Tony Batroni as the first Officer. Allen and another flight engineer Bob Bradshaw were retired from British Airways. We became very good friends, remaining so to date, spending many an evening over beers, lots of jokes followed by some good beer drinking songs. Some songs made up around our present environment, other crews, management, and the airline owner being known as the chief. Some a bit crude but all in good fun. The service was moving fast and there was very little time to do much but sleep, eat and fly. The African continent is not the easiest of areas to fly. It's said and I agree, the most dangerous area in the world to fly is the area between the Northern boundaries of South Africa and the Southern boundaries of Egypt, Algeria and Libya. Navigation systems are poorly maintained, airways cross with inexperienced crew incorrectly advising them of their position. Some aircraft lie about their position to get priority on landing or for altitude climbing reasons. Radio reception is poor and unmaintained. The Hadj routing across Africa is specially outlined to get aircraft across on the most direct route, these sometimes-cross regular routes causing a bit of havoc to air traffic controllers and air crew.

There are cut off times for entry into Saudi airspace which if missed can be a major problem. This happened to me once, forcing me to land in Cairo. Our fuel account was for fuel at a reduced price from Jeddah, but in Cairo we had no account. Eventually the Nigerian consulate paid the fuel bill to allow us to leave, albeit 12 hours later with no food or water for the 400 Hadj passengers or crew. Our duty time was 32 hours, but that's freelance flying. Arriving in Jeddah which was a turnaround for us to return to Lagos, we were able to fill our tanks with cheaper fuel allowing the aircraft to do another round trip via Lagos back to Jeddah. Food for the Hadjie's on the flights was usually a bread roll, and a piece of chicken, and two bottles of water. For the crew we kept the upper deck cordoned off for ourselves being the two English cabin attendants and cockpit crew. This was because we were able to at least keep a clean toilet and galley for our use. Food sometimes was a tray of sandwiches, cold chicken with a flask of hot water for tea or coffee plus bottles of water. There were many times when the food did not arrive or was inedible. When this happened, we would send a runner down the street and get some grilled chicken off the street merchants, occasionally it would smell like rubber and the lord knows where it came from. Otherwise, we would go without making it a long 12 to 16 hours without sustenance. We strongly believed it was the amount of beer consumed after the flights that saved us from food poisoning.

Returning from these flights was not always easy as the drive from the airport often required us to have a security car escort the crew. In Port Harcourt we had to have the military surround the aircraft before we departed for the hotel. If we wished to use the hotel bar, we would pay the police or military to stand behind us and protect us from the prostitutes. They would invade the bar attempting to get our interest, stick their hands into our pockets and do almost anything including baring a breast or two for our attention. The hotel was damp and very unsafe. We would always have one white cabin attendant with us as the contract required 3 cockpit crew and one cabin attendant. If it was one of our girls, they would use their assigned room to wash and change but would sometimes for safety sleep in one of the cockpit crew's rooms.

My OKADA crew.

Port Harcourt was a hell of a place to not only stay but to get into. The airport is very difficult to find and has a few wrecks lying around its perimeter including one from South Africa. Regrettably, although the white girls were advised not to befriend the locals, one of our girls did. He was a policeman who regularly waited for her to return from a flight. He would at first entertain her in the hotel but one evening she went out with him. We, being the whole expat crew advised her not to do this but regrettably, she did repeatedly. Then on the morning departure, she did not answer the call for the flight. A room search found she had not used her bed. The police were advised and a search for her began. The flight departed without her by using the 3rd attendant. That evening she was found in an abandoned old building not far from the hotel. She had been repeatedly raped, with her throat cut. In my entire career as an aviator, I had never lost a cabin attendant until this unfortunate incident. The 6-month contract was completed but nobody was ever charged with her murder. Africa is lawless at a level very few realize.

One other bad incident took place in Jeddah. An African male passenger who had boarded for the return flight to Lagos suddenly went berserk in the passenger cabin. He tore off all his clothes, went running around the cabin stark naked, brandishing a Koran, screaming and shouting. The airport police guarding the aircraft rushed up the air stairs and attempted to catch him. He was able to evade them by running down the stairs and onto the ramp. From my left seat and being high I was able to see the unfolding drama. He ran for cover behind some cargo bins. By this time an army of vehicles with lights and sirens blaring surrounded him. Still ranting and holding the Koran in his hand he was attacked from all sides by Saudi police wielding batons. Some had guns drawn others standing mystified. The poor man had no chance and was beaten into unconsciousness. His blooded and battered body was removed in a police van. I never did hear what happened to the poor soul but doubt he survived the ordeal or is still rotting in a Saudi jail. Boarding Hadjs in some places the military or police would make whips from the tree branches and beat the Hadjie's into long boarding lines to expedite a quick departure.

With the aircraft now showing signs of needing major maintenance, fleas getting bad, and operating with only one side of the flight director system working correctly the contract was coming to an end. It was on our final night in Lagos as we were all enjoying a farewell party in the bar that this incident took place. There appeared to be some sort of protest or action outside the hotel. As we were drawn to see what it was all about the hotel security guards closed the curtains and locked the doors. We found out that what transpired was that there was a vigilantly killing going on in the street. For reasons we never found out the man concerned was having 6-inch nails driven through his ears, nose and eyes. Western Africa is a harsh and brutal place. They were the major slave capturers and sellers. In war they will rape a woman and then cut off her hands. Child soldiers are forced to kill their own parents and brutal torture is common. It's sort of the law of the jungle, "eat or be eaten". Don't ever question African authority. If one thinks this was bad in South Africa the political A.N.C supporters were burning people alive by placing tyres around their necks, then setting them alight. We the contract crews were very pleased to leave; it had been an exhausting ordeal but well paid.

Now with funds in my bank account I rented a small bedsitter in Horley and was able to complete the exams required for my British license plus the C.A.A check ride on the B747 simulator with British. Airways check airmen Captain Smilie and Gunn, all to B.A standards.

I now had a British, Canadian, South African, Saudi, American, Swedish, Icelandic, Sri Lankan, Greek, and Irish Airline Transport license endorsed for the B747. This would open up the freelance market especially having the big three, the British, Canadian, United States.

Scraped OKADA BAC1-11 aircraft

Thai Airways

Finishing with OKADA in October and having to write the C.A.A airline transport exams plus the similar checks had taken up all of November and most of December. With now not much money left I was attempting to get home for the festive season. I had in my possession another expired ticket which I had accumulated somewhere along the line. By smudging the date, I chatted to the counter attendant to distract her, I was able to get a flight home. New Year arrived, which had allowed me to at least have some time with the family. It brought with it a letter from Captain Graham Hawkins (Nic Name Slim) from Australian Aircrew Personnel Services saying that Thai International was looking for current B747 Captains to fill a slot while they ungraded some of their captains. The contract was for 6 months and was based in Bangkok. I immediately shot off a return message advising him I was current enclosing my British C.A.A simulator check ride report and copies of all my licenses. My résumé he had, so after some fast correspondence a day later I had a first-Class ticket on S.A.A to Hong Kong and a connecting ticket to Bangkok, Here I was met by a chap named Brown, ensconced into a hotel and set up for a simulator check ride with a Thai Check airman named Captain Chutchal a second one with a Captain Ammuny, a third and final with a Captain Vira. This was followed by a flight check out from Melbourne to Bangkok with Captain Punchai. With all going well after a 7-day ground school refresher I obtained a Thailand validation on my Airline Transport British rating. I was able to get a small flat type of room in the hotel which suited me very well. January, February, came and I went flying regular airline routes to Japan, Hong Kong, Seoul, Frankfurt, Manila and Amsterdam. Flights to Amsterdam were often stretched as the fuel required was at its limit. We used to have to step climb over the Himalayas battling to get altitude with converging B. A. and Cathay flights coming in from Hong Kong heading in the same direction. Everest is a spectacular sight but to traverse the Himalayas there are special routes to follow allowing an emergency route if an aircraft was to develop engine problems and have to descend. These routes take one out of the high mountains allowing the ability to get to a lower altitude. Flights to Amsterdam had to redispatch over Tehran and Zurich. This meant that if one was low on fuel these would be alternate airports, so when approaching them fuel was calculated to see if the destination could be made with the required three engine alternate being within 40 minutes away from the destination field. In a strange format but this system is used in the airline industry where it almost figures at departure one does not have enough fuel to make your destination. The flight crew has to build fuel by step climbing and running on long range power setting. Consequently, the need to redispatch over enrooted airports. (Step climbing is when an aircraft climbs to the altitude it can make at that weight. Then burning more fuel and getting a lighter weight climbs again to the next altitude calculated at that new weight.)

Another very intense field was Kansai off the coast of Japan near Kobe. It was feat of engineering never heard of before as an engineering marvel being able to build an airfield out in the ocean on a manmade island. Like Kai Tak (old Hong Kong) it takes a good bit of flying especially at night. I had such an approach having to come in on a wide base. The wind was very strong with rain. The airfield is just a line of lights out in a pitch-black sea. Jamaica is similar. Perception is difficult as there is no visual reference to distance or height. Upon landing the cross wind was at about 25 degrees, on touch down the wave effect of wind coming over the terminal building caused the aircraft to float cross ways to the runway. Touchdown required an almost immediate reversing of thrust with a bit of a hard landing. On the road to the hotel the remains of the great earthquake a month earlier on 17 January 1995 were still very visible with destroyed highways and buildings. The island airfield and airport are sinking. They say that eventually it may be too expensive to sustain the island.

The Thai Pilots were great guys to fly with, very efficient and polite. The general service was above average and so was the way they treated us contract pilots. Certainly not as a sort of scab pilot but rather as a pilot there to help and assist in the company progress.

Things were going fine until I got a call from Slim (Capt. Hawkins the Managing director of Australian Aircrew Personnel Services) regrettably advising me that the airline felt that the eight foreign crews they had hired were two to many.

THAI B747 -300

I and another Irish captain being the last in were then to be the first out. He advised we would be paid the contract amount, tickets home and expenses incurred would be covered. So once again I packed my bag and was taken to the airport and booked my seat not to South Africa as I have mentioned there was no work for freelance B747, and B707 fight crew there. I was waiting in the departures lounge when to my surprise along walked Tim Steegles from OKADA. He advised that they would be starting up again for the Hadj and would like to come back to operate another contract. With no work in hand, it was a case of "bird in the hand worth two in the bush." so accepted knowing full well what I was in for. I was very sorry to leave THAI International but as they say, that's the way the cookie crumbles and that's aviation. (Fate again played its hand)

Redhill.

With only a month or so to go before the Hadj start I resigned myself to the fact that I could not afford to go home. The private school fees for my sons were due, home maintenance costs had increased plus the cost of getting home was too much for my bank to carry.

I realized I had to wait it out in England for the OKADA deal to come to fruition. To do this I got a room in Redhill run by Mrs. Waters. She had a boarding house on Ladbroke Road right opposite the station. It consisted of a small room with access to a bath which had no plug but a loose shower nozzle which required one to crouch down in the bath and pour warm water from the nozzle onto oneself. It was GBP 13:50 a week with an extra pound if you wanted a breakfast of one egg, bacon and 2 toast plus tea. The name Ladbroke Road was appropriate as this lad was very broke and I had to confine myself to one pound a day to survive. The family had to come first. To amuse myself I would get a ticket to Victoria Station and ride up and back. I found a very cheap food outlet where I could get a pie and bread for less than a pound. So together with the breakfast I was able to live and must admit old Mrs. Waters was very good to me. In the interim, I also recorrected myself on the British Airways simulator so I would have six straight months of currency as a security blanket. Finally, the word came, and I reported it to the office of OKADA in London. Later with the crew we positioned back to Lagos on British Airways.

Backpack

Fortunately, this period actually gave me a chance to do a bit of father and son time. My younger son Grant when on the summer extended school holidays would buy himself a ticket to England and get work on the construction sites. This was well paid as compared to the wages for students in South Africa. I was able to meet up with him, so we bought a cheap ticket to Spain. Here we back packed staying in hostels visiting Gibraltar, Malaga, and Seville. Later in life we would have another great adventure together.

OKADA again.

On arrival in Lagos nothing much had changed, except that the B747 was worse for wear. There was a new set of crews, however to my pleasure my good friend flight engineer Bob Bradshaw was coming back. I locked onto him upon his arrival, and we spent the contract mainly flying together. Bob knew how to handle engines and between us we did very well on saving fuel plus being able to keep the now badly deteriorating aircraft together and flying.

It was the same old thing heat, dirty passengers, low on fuel, minimum maintenance, worn tyres, lack of payments for fuel and airport fees. To give an example of this when we arrived in Jeddah where we refueled on cheaper fuel, I often wondered why as we came onto our chocks and before the engines were shut down, I repeatedly saw a small pickup dart under the aircraft below the lower E and E section. (Equipment & electronics room under the first-class floor) This section had an access door to allow entry into the compartment below the first-class floor and houses the electronics room. The hatch would open and not long later close. The mystery was soon understood as we jokingly said to obtain fuel part payment was made by parrots being smuggled into Saudi inside the E and E below deck compartment. Thereafter sold by the agent to obtain fuel funds. The smuggling side was more than likely true. At this point, I wondered how long the airline would last and started to look very wearily at the operation.

Things started to come to bits; our maintenance was now almost nil. Fuel hard to get, crew wages and hotel payment not forth coming. Chief Igbegian seemed to turn against Steegles who had again been heading up the operation. Regrettably Bernie Black had died. I was sort of appointed to take over. The biggest job was trying to get money out of the chief. To do this I had to do midnight cross Lagos taxi trips, bribing soldiers to get to the chief's house. A mansion of a place with large waiting rooms and a throne seat. Guards and bodyguards were everywhere. We heard and understood he had made his money selling arms to the Government plus wheeling and dealing sort of laundering foreign currency. On arrival I would be ushered in by the guards, having to wait hours before he showed up and then gave me cash in a suitcase which I would then have to do the gauntlet back to the hotel in the early hours of the morning to pay the crew plus hotel. Carrying that amount of money was suicidal but it had to be done. As before we were locked out of our rooms many times having to sleep on the lounge floor or couch.

We had a few flights from Lagos to Tel Aviv carrying Christian pilgrims. These flights became a bit interesting to complete. As the airline had no overflying rights across Algeria or Libya we would file a flight plan across Niger to a little-known airfield in Algeria. Then upon reaching the Algerian border we would fly the border line heading for Libya. Algeria control would pick us up at the border and ask us for our destination. We would advise Tel Aviv to which they would refuse us entry without an over flight permit. Stalling our radio communication and complaining of losing contact we would race for the Libyan border. Without the correct permit number, they would threaten us with military interception. On one flight I gave them my Canadian Hudson Bay credit card number as the over flight permit number. It could not be recognized or accepted but gave us time to fly on. We would report our correct position to all other aircraft on a common frequency 122.8mhz for safety reasons so as to keep other aircraft advised of where we were.

By the time they had lost all patience we would vanish crossing the border over to Libya and ignore them. We would do the same with Libya, but it was usually a case of losing contact with them, changing transmission to the Mediterranean control out of Malta advising them we had lost contact with Libya. They in turn would scramble for a flight plan on us which could not be found. We would put full blame on Libya and request a new one to Tel Aviv. Now well in controlled airspace we could relax and head down the centre of the Mediterranean Sea working with Malta and Cyprus control direct for Israel. I loved Israel as I had some old South African friends there Helen and Tony both from Johannesburg. They were friends from our teenage years when I dated Dian a good friend of Helens'. Tony flew a few times with me back in 1965 when I was flying the Aero Commander and was heading for Durban, so giving him a lift to visit Helen. The opportunity to visit all the sacred and historic religious places is well worth a visit. The people are very friendly and polite.

A close call came on a morning when I was walking from the Hotel to buy some socks. On the way I realized I had left my wallet in the hotel. Turning back, I had walked about 100 meters when there was a hell of an explosion. A bomb had gone off in a bus shelter killing people and demolishing the shelter, cars, and shop windows. To my horror I realized that had I not turned back to get my wallet I would have been passing the bus shelter.

OKADA B747

Fate or guardian angel, who knows, but I was extremely lucky. The religious city of Jerusalem is a place to see, one is enshrouded in the spirit of the being. If one was not religious before, a pilgrimage to Jerusalem will change your thoughts. I had a few flights out of Tel Aviv and one such flight was a real gut wrencher. I had been able to get home for a few days' rest when a call from the company advising me that the B747 was in Tel Aviv for maintenance and to pick up cargo. However, they did not have a crew available to bring the aircraft back to Nigeria. Later I found out the captain and first officer had left. Could I get there to do the return flight scheduled out in 2 days' time. They had found a first officer from Air Lingus who would operate the flight as a moon lighting flight. My old flight engineer friend Allen was waiting for us. He was another great professional ex B.A. flight engineer. We remained friends and still to this day. I agreed and caught the 20:00 B.A flight to Johannesburg connecting with the B.A flight at 22:00 to London Heathrow. Here I was to meet the first officer, whose name was Butler I think and catch the B.A. flight to Tel Aviv.

This was a mad dash as I had not expected to be away and had certainly not expected to be up all night. On arrival in London Heathrow, I could not find the First Officer only to learn he had missed the flight from

Ireland. More communications were arranged and finally we met but too late for our flight to Tel Aviv.

It now transpired we had to go to Gatwick to connect with OLYMPIC'S flight to Athens. Here we were to wait for 4 hours to fly on to Tel Aviv. We finally arrived in Tel Aviv exhausted. A hotel room had been booked for us to share but we were told this flight was a special flight and had to go on time. That time was in four hours. I napped for an hour or two. Having been awake for over 24 hours I was tired. We were called and told the aircraft was ready and a vehicle would pick us up from the hotel.

Arriving at the airport the usual high security was evident with searches and document requests. It seemed strange to me that we were operating a below deck cargo only flight with the aircraft parked well away from the terminal building. The cargo and load sheet showed a full load of oranges and nothing else, not even a cabin attendant. All seemed a bit out of the ordinary. With the paperwork all complete startup was called for and taxi clearance given to the active runway. On powering up I felt the aircraft to be very heavy for a hold only cargo weight. Taxing towards the taxi way I was not happy and asked to pull over to a holding position. Calling the handling company on the radio, I requested the manager and an air stair be brought to the aircraft putting our flight plan on hold. I demanded to see the cargo, requesting the forward cargo to be opened. This they did with me climbing up a ladder to inspect the hold. The oranges were there alright in the shape of military arms packed to the roof. There were what looked like missiles all facing forward and heavy wooden trunks of ammunition.

We were very heavy, and it certainly called for a chat with the handling agent's manager. This took place in the cockpit in view of my crew. I demanded to know what was going on. He eventually informed us it was high priority for the Nigerian government to which he had been sworn to not reveal. After a discussion with my crew, we agreed to take the flight with quite a few USA cash dollars in our hands as a bonus. This after some heated radio and phone talk was agreed upon by the powers that be. We finally departed and worked our way back to Lagos on the usual pirate route but with overflying clearance given on another airline code. Arriving in Lagos we were ushered to a parking place well clear of the public's view and from the airport building itself. Here the military surrounded us, and the offloading was conducted into military vehicles. I had been on the trot since waking in my home for 52 hours. I had a cold beer with the first officer and the flight engineer crashed into bed where I slept of a whole day.

Another was when after arriving in Tel Aviv with pilgrims I was informed that there was a full load of passengers in Jeddah. This was a problem as to operate into Jeddah we could not depart Tel Aviv due to the political restrictions. We hatched a plan to file a low-level VFR (Visual Flight Rules) to depart Tel Aviv and fly to Cyprus, a short distance away. To do this we had to join an airway from Cairo to Cyprus. Upon joining this airway, we cancelled out flight plan to Cyprus and asked Malta control to allow us to join another airway incoming to Cairo. We changed our callsigns from the registration to an OKADA flight number that would be recognized by Jeddah control. After lengthy discussion with Malta, we turned back to Cyprus making contact on a new call sign. They in turn questioned our point of departure. We explained a loss of radio communication and requested a flight plan to Cairo on the inbound airway allowing us to climb into the airway route. Eventually after a lot of questions and broken radio communications we got the clearance. When in Egypt control, we advised that we wished to refile our flight plan to Jeddah explaining that Jeddah was our destination, but we had filed for Cairo to redispatch with remaining fuel.

Again, with a lot of questions and counter questions we made Jeddah so saving us the need to return to Lagos and then proceed back to Jeddah. This was all done at 3 a.m. in the morning with the hope that the controllers would not be wide awake. When working this sort of flying the tricks of the trade had to be well known. For instance, to increase speed and so use less fuel the old code was if you want speed set EPR (exhaust pressure Ratio.) if you want fuel set speed. So, to increase fuel speed had to be set. To do this I would use all the fuel from the centre tanks allowing only a small amount to be left in the wing tanks. By doing this the outboard wing or tip tanks would be kept full. I would then shut down the pacs (pressure and air-conditioning systems to pressurize the cabin) to only two and in an emergency one. This would bend the wing increasing speed, I would only open the tip tanks at the top of decent allowing myself the required amount of fuel for the landing.

Another thing I did was to put a little back pressure on the yoke when the aircraft was on cruise with the autopilot on. This would cause the autopilot to trim back a notch or two. This would give the plane of the aircraft a very slight nose down again, increasing the speed by a few knots. The situation now was getting very bad. The aircraft needed major maintenance, cash was not forthcoming, aircrew and ground personnel were agitated and the heat plus conditions were adding to the eventual breakdown I saw coming. On the strength of this, I informed the crew to always take all their personal belongings when leaving on a flight. Eventually what I expected happened on my flight to Jeddah. We were refused landing as the landing fees had not been paid. In desperation, I explained that I might have to declare an emergency as I was low on fuel. They agreed to let me land but were not allowed onto the Hadj parking area or the use of a jetway. We were sent out to a hard stand to bake in the heat. Eventually, our ground handlers arrived with an air stair and some busses to transport the passengers to the Hadj terminal. The cockpit crew and the one hostess were bused to the crew arrivals section. Here I was met by the contracted ground handling manager who explained that there was a major problem since no money was forthcoming and he had been instructed not to offer any assistance to cover landing, parking, transport, or hotels. He had been able to get permission to disembark the passengers as they were Hadjie's and had a right to be there for the Muslim Hadj. The aircraft was impounded and with some assistance, the crew could be taken to the hotel, but he could not guarantee our rooms being paid for. At the hotel, I mustered the operating foreign crew members explaining that we were in trouble as without exit visas from Jeddah we could not leave.

After a long consideration of the situation, I hatched a plan. I had noticed that coming through the crew arrival office a door led into a passage which opened out into the departure and in transit lounge. I explained that if we could get tickets out to anywhere and get into the departures or in transit lounge, we had a good chance of missing the immigration officers, then changing back into civilian clothes we might get away with boarding a flight and getting out of the country. I agreed to try it first so set off to see if I could get a ticket somewhere without producing an exit visa.

Now the aviation grapevine came into play. I had heard from a colleague that Qatar was on the verge of setting up an airline and would be needing pilots on B747 SR (short range) aircraft to start the operation. Apparently, a Captain Tabibi an Iranian was the chief pilot and the airline had been hatched by a cousin a Mr Al Baker of the Emir Sheikh Khalifa bin Hamad Al-Than. As time would have it, I was to meet this cousin who had completed an around the world flight in a light twin, written a book and gave me a copy. The Chief Executive officer was Hamad Ali Jabor Al-Thani. Another person I knew was Sheila Scott, a charming lady who had also circumnavigated the world in a light twin engines aircraft. With this in the back of my mind I considered that as Qatar was not that far away, just maybe I could get there and see what could be arranged so looking forward to them getting an airline off the ground.

Fate or luck struck again this time as I was able to find a travel agency that would sell me a ticket on GULF air to Doha, the capital city of Qatar plus could arrange a visa upon my arrival through a hotel contact. I grabbed the opportunity and raced back to the hotel calling the abandoned crew to my room. We put together a plan around the idea of getting out of the hotel in civilian clothes as they would not have let us go if we had attempted to leave in uniform. Then the management was howling in protest that the rooms and earlier rooms had not been paid for, threatening police action. I knew we had to move fast so left attempting the first getaway. I was able to slip out of the hotel with my flight bag and a small carryon bag. Got a cab and smartly headed for the airport arriving there I had donned my cap and uniform shirt with ranking and wings. Slipping into the area behind the ticket counter I put down in front of the agent my ticket on Gulf Air to Qatar. He was not sure of what to do with it but I explained I was a returning crew member and ridiculed him a little for not processing my ticket as a new captain for QATAR. This done I slipped out and did a quick sidestep into the corridor leading to the in transit and departure lounge. The guard at the end of the corridor did not notice the sudden disappearance of a crew member who was at one time on the ticket agent side and next out of sight. Quickly I got into the toilet which was very conveniently right by the door. Here I changed my shirt, putting my uniform and cap into my flight bag. Stepping out, I sat very casually in the departure lounge only to be confronted by a Gulf Air agent asking for my ticket. Handing it to her she noticed it had not been pulled. I apologized profusely and took the blame as I had missed the agent at the entrance to the departures lounge by accident. She was a bit confused and apologized for any inconvenience leaving me to enjoy the tea and coffee. I saw a phone in the corner of the room, casually walked up to it and lifted the receiver it worked, I immediately called the hotel number. Upon getting through I asked for the first officer's Jousaf room, which he answered immediately. I explained that I had got through and as the engineer was with him wished them luck. I never heard if they escaped the same way.

I swore blind I would never go back to OKADA or Nigeria. The chief called repeatedly the next year offering my job back but by then I had other work in West and Central Africa.

Qatar

My flight departed on time for Doha arriving that evening. I had an onward ticket to London I was able to pay for and collect a visa supported by my hotel booking as planned. I got to the hotel only to find it was not a 5-star but very nearly a one-star in the back end of town. I knew then why I had been able to buy or bribe if you wish a room and visa from them. The room was not clean, covered in fine dust. The toilet was broken with blood stains on the shower curtain and wall. I could not believe the bed had been changed and decided then and there I would not sleep in it. There was a small towel which looked like it had not been used. Fatigue and tension were starting to take effect so after finding a swami (rolled sandwich-type meat and vegetable mixture) street vendor I had a swami and a cup of tea, then retired to the room and fell asleep on top of the bed. In the morning, I showered under a lukewarm shower and dressed. Finding an English-speaking cab was able to find the head office of the new QATAR AIRWAYS. Here I was introduced to Captain Tabibi and presented my credentials. I now hold a B747 rating on 3 major country aviation airline transport licenses. I presented my last simulator B747 check ride and updated class one medicals. The interview went very well with a promise from him that he would be in touch as soon as things got underway. This was June 1995, and they expected the first B747 SR (SR were the short-range machines fitted with wheel brake fans) to be delivered from Japan very soon. They had hired some Iraqi pilots but would need a couple more Captains. On concluding the meeting, I understood I was in the top bracket to be hired, with Iraqis and about 4 other foreigners.

Not wishing to hang around this very desert type of town I beat a hasty retreat to the airport and got a flight on Gulf airlines to London. Here I stayed with my old friend Bob and Pam Bradshaw hoping I might get a favourable reply from QATAR. A week or so went by and nothing appeared to be materializing. I could not stay on any longer and the need for me to return home was evident. My parents were ageing with my mother losing her eyesight and father unable to cope with things in general. My younger son had had an accident and injured his back plus my wife now seemed continuously not well. On getting home to South Africa I was very tired and somewhat exhausted from the past pressure and complications, so a break was good. Time ticked by with me keeping in correspondence with Captain Tabibi.

Finally, the break came and a call from Tabibi advised me that if I could be in London the following morning and meet him at the Copethorne hotel before 08:30 I could get a lift to Qatar and start with them. I packed a fast bag, grabbed a uniform and made the SAA fight to London from Johannesburg that night. Arriving in London I got the fast train to Gatwick and then a taxi to the Copethorne Hotel. Obtaining Captain Taibbi's room number, I knocked and upon him opening the door he appeared pleased to see me considering the short time I had in getting there. Travelling back on his flight I arrived in Doha now without accommodation or very much money.

I was lucky to find a very cheap two-star hotel and was able to get a room for a couple of nights. During this time, I was relicensed with a check ride on the recently arrived B747 SR, completed medical and company paperwork. I did a line check with Captain Ruhman and settled down to fly the regular line routes to London, Cairo, Gatwick and Manila. I was then issued with a QATAR Airline transport license to add to my growing list.

B747 SR

As the company grew, we extended our routes to many parts of Africa such as Khartoum, and the Congo. A charter came up for a crew to position via Dubai and Paris to Dakar, then by a small charter aircraft to Banjul in Gambia. I was assigned the charter and left with a full crew for Banjul. The crew with me were delighted and we looked forward to a good time away from the dust and dirt of Doha now in its major transition from a camel town to a big semi western city. The charter was completed returning to Jeddah. Based temporarily now in Jeddah we flew over the next weeks Hadj charters from Dakar, Brazzaville. Banjul, to Jeddah on a back-to-back basis. Little did I know what Banjul would come to mean to me in future. The general situation of the airline grew, and services were opened to Karachi, Colombo with the main daily service to London.

It was on one of these London services that the Iraqi cockpit crew had a problem with immigration and some complicated irregular paperwork. I was operating the inbound London service that morning and was asked to see what could be done. A long story short was some sort of embargo had been served on Iraqis. I was able to get the crew released from the immigration holding room and signed a document that they would be transported out on my flight the next day. This we dually did and got the concerned crew members back to Doha. I now was happily ensconced in the company and enjoying the flying however major problem was arising. My contract stated I could work 6 weeks in and then 2 weeks home. To do this I would apply for a rebate airline ticket with Emirates, go in transit via our flight to Dubai then catch the late flight to Johannesburg and on SAA to Durban. This did not work. The flight out of Doha often left late for my connection in Dubai. Secondly as it was an airline standby ticket with the Dubai Johannesburg flight many times full. In so I would have to return the next morning back to Doha or as I did on one occasion travel all the way to Mumbai then on to Johannesburg and Durban, taking 48 hours from the point of departure. Then having to repeat the return trip often asking SAA for the captain to allow me the use of cockpit jump seat. It became almost impossible and very tiring. I had bought an old Mercedes Benz 320 from a Doha Doctor, so had wheels and on time off enjoyed travelling down to the Southern part of the coast so enjoying a good relaxing swim on long unpopulated beaches. The Sheikh Al Tani had now set up his Royal flight with a private Airbus 320. Some of the crew I had known from earlier contracts plus two of the pilots were ex Court line being part of the LIAT-COURTLINE venture in the Caribbean. I had now found a room in a house shared with 3 other guys in the oil industry. It consisted of a large main lounge which was heavily draped to keep the heat and sun out. There was an array of couches, two air conditioners and a large TV which was never turned off. The guys would come in at any time of the day or night, grab something to eat and relax in the dark lounge. Food was self-catered for with a batman to do the washing. Entertainment was very limited, but I did join the expatriate club which was in an old building part of a compound that had a swimming pool and bar. The situation was not conducive for a family, so most of the guys were on single postings.

I enjoyed the developing company and got on well with the crew. There became a need for senior flight engineers, so I put forward my friend Bob Bradshaw. To my delight he was accepted and joined the company so commuting from London often with Pam, his wife. Bob was very respected by the airline as he was an exceptional flight engineer with a wealth of engineering knowledge. One incident happened that prove pilots are not necessary always pilots but First aid attendants when needed. Bob and I had come in from a long overnight charter into Africa. We had to overnight in Jeddah for crew rest. We were standing at the reception when there was a loud bang and the sound of breaking glass. What happened was that a young man who turned out to be a Lufthansa first officer had walked through the main plate glass door. He fell to the floor almost in front of us with blood squirting out of a major gash to his thigh and lower calf. We both instinctively ran to his aid, ripping off his torn trouser leg and shoe. Bob grabbed a white linen tablecloth from the reception table tearing it into strips. I applied pressure onto the wound attempting to stop the flow of blood which was now spreading across the floor. Applying a tourniquet above and below the major gash we were able to stem the flow of blood until an ambulance and help arrived. He was taken to hospital, underwent surgery and survived. The hotel gave both Bob and I a free meal and later I got a very nice letter from Lufthansa.

However unbeknown more problems were yet to come. The principal and founding member of the airline who had conceived the company suddenly decided that except for Iranian and Iraqi pilots, they did not need foreign pilots. I believe there were 3 Americans and myself in that category. We believed they were starting to look at Airbus. It was a case of starting to pack one's bags, going through the departure requirements, getting tickets to our hometowns and collecting any pay owed. I left my car with a crew member on the promise that when sold I would be refunded. I never saw the crew member or money ever again. A few farewell drinks with Bob and newfound friends at the expatriate club finalized things. I was sorry to leave but things at home were now not on a steady keel and not being able to commute home was taking its toll.

Arriving home included a lot of home problems but in time these things were sorted out. The boys were now out of boarding school, needed cars and were in the job market. We decided that my wife's Opel was a bit long in the tooth so purchased a newer model. Grant, the younger son and I overhauled Josie's (wife) old Opel Kadet, and he became its new owner. Scott was working for British Airways at the Durban airport and studying to get his industrial Physiology degree. Grant decided to attend Durban Varsity to study for the I.M.M. (International Marketing) degree.

I put myself again on the international freelance market contacting all the agencies. One company came up with the possibility of a contract with Air Madagascar who were contemplating a service from London with a connecting service on a Saturday to Johannesburg. This suited me as I could then operate and commute home. Contracts were drawn up and signed. Anticipated start dates set, so I began to make preparations to depart for the usual crew, license and medical validation.

Early one morning I got a call from Bob Bradshaw in Doha saying that the airline had decided to re-employ the laid-off pilots. He had spoken to the company, and they had advised him that if I was not employed, I could return to Doha and continue employment with them. I was now in a dilemma as the QATAR contract was not conducive to my returning home and could they be trusted to not do the nationalization again? Whereas the Madagascan deal was closer to home and certainly more appealing? After long and deep consideration called Bob asking him to explain that I had just signed a new contract and felt I could not in good faith cancel it. It was the hardest call I ever had to make. (Bird in the hand comes to mind) This he did so it left me waiting in South Africa to start with Air Madagascar, and then another bombshell hit. Out of the blue Air Madagascar decided to move the base from London to Paris. All crews would be required to be based in London with limited turnaround time in Madagascar. In lengthy conversations on the phone with the contracting company it ended up that I could not accept the agreement by not residing in the UK or Paris. I immediately called Bob albeit some three weeks later asking if he could help in getting me back with Qatar.

Regretfully, although he tried at all levels my copybook was blackened for not accepting the first offer plus they had recruited all the B747 Captains they needed. Another reason was they were starting to look at Airbus and future crews would need airbus experience. The airline was started in 1994 in a very competitive market and succeeded in becoming one of the fastest growing airlines in the Middle East.

This put me back on the available freelance road with no immediate opportunities in sight. Not to mention two sons at college, an ill wife to support, diminishing bank funds. I was getting into a desperate situation having had the confidence of a job with QATAR and then this Madagascar upset was hard on the nerves. The chance of getting heavy transport flying contract work in South Africa as earlier explained was very rare to impossible. With the situation as it was my only chance was to get back into the overseas market. Frantic calls to every contracting agency I knew or had worked with went out. Weeks went by with no response, then late one evening I got a call from I think it was Airline Appointments an agency hiring freelance pilots, advising that China Airline needed B747 crew and was I still available. Was I, was the understatement.

China Airlines

I had to travel to London at my own expense to be selected for the interview. Money was tight so my family had to suffer a little as I found funds to get the airfare to London there I had very sincere friends such as Alan and Bunny Jones, Bob and Pam Bradshaw where I was offered a bed for a while. Bob and Alan were the best flight engineers I had the privilege of flying with. They both are on the OKADA contract and as mentioned before ex BOAC senior flight engineers working their way up off the hanger floor the hard way. Bob is now with QATAR.

I passed the interview, all the simulator tests and medicals for China Airlines in London taking over 6 weeks at my expense. The medicals are extremely harsh. Everything from balance tests, blood tests of more than 45 criteria from white blood cell counts to blood sugar levels. Vision, periphery, depth, puffer, grip tests, EKG, EEG, brain scans, stanine, ultrasounds, reflex, ears nose throat tests, and many other probes. Half the people didn't make it past the medical. I was informed I would be sent to Taiwan via a flight from Amsterdam. On the connecting flight from London the food tray consisted of a snack and three chocolate balls. After arriving in Amsterdam, I was entering the men's toilet when I, to my horror, saw in the mirror that my trousers where stained chocolate colour from my crouch to mid-thigh. One of the chocolate balls had fallen down onto my lap and melted. I now realized why I was getting unusual looks from the stewardess and passing pedestrians in the terminal. I very nearly missed the flight to Taiwan as I had to wash my trousers in the toilet sink and attempt to dry them on the dryer before setting foot out of the toilet. Even then I had damp trousers on boarding my flight but with the warmth of a blanket and my body heat they did dry.

Arriving in Taiwan I was designated a hotel. My funds were almost zero so once again relied on the ability to eat from the hotel breakfast by taking all the bread, butter jam etc. At night I would wander down the street to feed off any cheap pavement meal I could find. At their head office I satisfactory got through the hiring procedures which included another simulator check. By this time of the 10 pilots that started only 3 of us were left.

It was on this check ride that I was given a 2-engine approach into Hong Kong Kai Tak. This airport has quite a name for itself and can be very difficult to dangerous. On the final approach, which is the checkerboard approach, I was too far to the left of the final track. This happened as I had been on 3 engines then lost number 4 engine on the final turn; with trim set for 3 engines, I had my hands full. Realizing I was not in a position to make the landing I executed a two engine go around for which I had been trained. It's a critical maneuver as the landing gear must be left down, pitch no more than 5 degrees until you can get the airspeed up safely to bring up the landing gear. The gear doors would pull the speed down to below a safe landing speed. This caused a commotion in the cockpit between the check airman in the right seat a Captain Pang and a Chinese C.A.A training check airman observing from behind the flight seats a Captain Sung who was checking the check airman. It transpired that the check airman failed me but the training C.A.A. check airman had countered his decision as he had not seen a 2-engine go around from Hong Kong Kai Tak and that I had in his opinion passed a good check so indicating my competence in handling the aircraft. I still think the altercation between the two check airmen had something to do with the developing outcome. This was not long after this China Airlines lost a B747 into the water off Kai Tak.

Trouble came when they found I had not had a British C.A.A. license simulator check in the past 6 months so validating my British rating. Although I explained that I had not been able to do it through lack of funds, plus I had been under their induction and training program over the past 2 months overlapping my British license validity. Doing their initial simulator check in England instead of the British, I thought would validate a 6-month recurrence. It did not comply with their paperwork.

Later I found out that a Captain from the Air Atlanta time was now one of their training captains and had put the boot in bringing up this small misunderstanding in the paperwork. Far more possibly I believe he favoured the chief pilot's decision and not the C.A.A check airman on the two-engine missed approach, currying favour for his own job security.

An old Canadian friend of mine Garth Martin, a retired ex-B747 Captain was employed with China Airlines as a simulator instructor. I advised them he had done my last B747 simulator check the year before, using Air Canada's simulator so indicating that he could vouch for me and my qualification standards. This simulator together with the B.A. and VIRGIN's simulator I used, I paid for myself. He agreed to this and confirmed to them that he had done the simulator check

ride with me to Canadian standards, but the same Captain got in above him. A day later I was called into the office and handed a letter containing my return ticket to the UK.

I did see the C.A.A. check airman Captain Sung before I left; he was surprised and suggested I should reapply, offering his support. My funds were all but exhausted and I could not afford to wait in the UK or anywhere for another possible prolonged paper chase on the chance they would change their mind. There was a developing and pressing need for me to return to my home in South Africa.

After spending 2 months in England, doing all the necessary requirements to join China Airlines. I now found myself back on the unemployed list. I returned to London, again short of funds with none available to get home to South Africa. Such is the life of a freelance pilot.

With kindness again from Bob and Pam Bradshaw, I was able to house-sit their home as they were away visiting relations overseas. Things got desperate and there appeared to be no workaround. I was able via the aviation grapevine, to hear of a new startup company to be called Air Dabia in Gambia West Africa and would be requiring a B747 Captain. I followed up every lead and contacted a Senegali chap who appeared to be acting for the owners. After a month I was advised that I would be hired, and they would furnish me with a ticket from South Africa. In a final bid to secure my license, I did a recurrent instrument and B747 check ride with a check airman Captain J. Walker using Virgin Atlantic's simulator. It was my final pitch as far as my funds went, so with what was left I returned home to South Africa to wait things out. I had sunk my credit card to its limit. An anxious month later plus staying in contact with the representative of the new airline, I thankfully was informed that a ticket was about to be issued for me to travel to Banjul in Gambia via London. It duly arrived so once again I packed my flight bag preparing to leave family and home life at short notice. It had been 5 months without a flying contract. One was urgently needed.

Air Dabia (Banjul)

Duly arriving in Banjul I was met and taken to a hotel where I understood the crew would be based. Here I met a first Officer named Osseli who had been part of the ferry crew bringing the B747SP from the USA together with the maintenance engineers. Glen Heikkila being in charge with other guys whose names I have forgotten except Dave Gonzales with whom I together with Glen would work with again on other contracts. Later another F/O Esquirol joined us and then F/O Chris Briza a Canadian joined on more permanent bases. We operated across Africa on Charters and a lot of private flying for the owner Mr. Foutanga Dit Babani Sissoko, known as Dougie. He and I got on very well as he was attempting to start up an airline using the B747, a B727 and a couple of light twins. Dabia was the name of the town he came from which is situated in Mali near Bamako. The company had been financed and owned by Mr. Dougie Sissoko who had become a very rich man on business deals that later were to get him into jail. It involved a fraud and money laundry issue to the incredible value of $242 USA million which in the process nearly shut down the Bahrain Islamic Bank in Abu Dhabi. It was a fascinating affair, and I will enclose later a copy of the Miami

New Times publication on the matter as it is far too complicated to rewrite.

By in large Dougie was a very nice man. He bought the crew a new Toyota to use and while in Miami gave us all gold Rolex watches. Our uniforms were tailored of the highest quality bearing no expense plus we received black tailor-made suits and very expensive ties. To illustrate his financial level of trust on a flight to Toga with a football team he advised me that his daughter would be boarding the aircraft and would be handing me a suitcase to be delivered by me to him personally upon my return to Banjul. The suitcase duly arrived, and I placed it behind the captain's seat thinking nothing more of it. Arriving in Banjul I dumped it in the back of our vehicle and drove to Mr. Sissoko's house. Passing the guards I awaited his arrival in a large room fitted with a throne chair. As he walked in he immediately asked me where the suitcase was. I explained that it was in the back of the vehicle awaiting his instructions and clearance to get it into the building. Looking concerned he immediately ordered a guard to escort me to the vehicle and collect the said suitcase. Returning to the room he opened the case in so exposing its contents as pointed out by him as $3,000,000 USA in cash. I was surprised but was complimented by him as being one of the few people he could trust. (I might add that had I known there was $3, million in the case, a flight across the Atlantic to South America, landing at one of the abandoned airfields might have crossed my mind.). The crew eventually moved to a house out in the bush however before this happened, I was able to get my wife to Gambia where she was able to spend a much-needed two weeks with me. She flew with me to Dakar on one of our trips, so was able to enjoy the tropical West African experience. She had not been well for reasons we could not determine, but she was becoming a heavy drinker and it later turned to alcoholism heralded by cancer of the jaw.

The crew house in the bush was semi-furnished with a cook and housemaid. However, most of the time we frequented a pub across the fields called the "Green Parrot" It was at this pub that we heard of Princes Diane's death. To get to this pub often meant walking along a bush track in bare feet as the continuous evening rains meant shoes etc. were soaked through. The crew house had a 3-cylinder Deitch diesel engine which gave us light until 22:00, then it was turned off and we were on paraffin lanterns. Hot water was non-existent.

There was no phone so to place a call anywhere we would have to go into the local town of Banjul where on a wall exposed to the environment was a phone connected to the A.T. & T network in the USA. So, if you had an account with them a call could be made internationally. This often meant one was standing in torrential rain or with a couple of nosy kids and under continuous attack from mosquitoes. It was our only means of communication.

Edinburgh. World presidential G20 summit meeting.

One of the most interesting flights we did was to take the President of Gambia Yahya Jammeh to the Commonwealth G20 summit meeting in Edenborough. The airfield is not that long, in fact on approach it looked dam short, so getting the B747 into it was not that easy plus we were then the biggest VIP aircraft on the ramp. Being able to do this meant we were in the Government and Presidents good books. Later this saved another crew member and me from going to jail. This happened about one evening whilst driving back along the bush road to our house, when we were suddenly highjack and mugged. I was driving along the dark bush come jungle road when out of nowhere a car appeared and blocked the road. Instantly we were set upon being punched in the face, our watches, wallets and any loose jewelry was snatched. Fending off our attackers they unsuccessfully attempted to smash the car lights, and then as instantly as they appeared they vanished into the dark damp bush. Collecting ourselves and with the car still in one piece we managed to drive on to a police station that was situated near our house. Here we explained what had happened in the dim light of a musty and dark bush station. Out of nowhere some of the thieves appeared claiming we had struck their car and fought with them. Immediately the police insisted being white that they lock us up in an overcrowded cell about 2 meters wide and 10 meters long with about ten other scruffy-looking individuals. I put it to them that I was the Presidential pilot and that if they insisted on this, I would make a full report to the president. It took some time to convince the officers that I meant business and finally, after 6 hours we were released. Getting back to the house at 4 am we cleaned up and got some much-needed sleep. Later that day a police officer arrived with a radio phone indicating a senior officer wanted to speak to me. He apologized profusely and begged we did not make a report to President Yahya Jammeh. He would ensure that the culprits would be apprehended, and our goods returned. However, although we did agree not to make a report, we never saw our stolen items.

On another occasion, I had a physical fight with two African pilots who claimed they were ex-Air Afrique. Mr Dougie Sissoko's assistant came to me one day saying that there were two pilot friends of Dougie's who were to be trained on the B747. To cut a long story short this was correct as Mr. Sissoko thought that diplomatically he should have black pilots of African descent. Well, this turned out to be a bun fight of a serious nature. These two pilots claimed they were trained by Air Afrique in Dakar. They were they said Airbus pilots and would be taking over from myself and the first officer very soon. I in all good faith had attempted to train them on the B747 but after blowing two tyres, over and undershooting the runway, over boosting engines I admitted they could not possibly take control of the B747 without a lot of simulator and ground training. They were glass cockpit pilots with very little time so together with their friend it appeared wool over the eyes was taking place at the cost of my time and crew, never mind the abuse of the aircraft. Later on, an overnight in Bamako, I was called to be told that these two pilots, who were travelling with us, were at the airport preparing to take the B747 back to Banjul. Using a fast taxi I and the first officer Chris Briza arrived at the aircraft. Upon entering the cockpit these two pilots were about to start up and depart. Ordering them out of their seats they started a fistfight with Chris, my first officer and myself. Fortunately, both of us are over 6ft 4in and weigh about 102 kilos. or more each. They had no match. I was able to get a phone call through to Mr Sissoko (Dougie) using a fuel attendant's cell phone. He instructed us to wait until his brother arrived who was apparently on his way.

Upon his arrival, the two African pilots were ordered out. Later after a meeting with Dougie, we understood the matter was closed. What did transpire was the close friend of Mr. Sissiko a Senegalian was very involved in the operation for his benefit. From that day on we had a hard time with this chap, having to watch our backs constantly.

One such charter was to fly to Abidjan on the Ivory Coast and collect a football team destined for Paris. Here is what happened.

Atlantic on 2 engines

On arrival, we refueled and filed the necessary over-flight clearance together with the flight plan. We noticed there was a certain amount of civil unrest and were informed that there was a political division with opposing Government parties backing different teams. The aircraft was serviced, and passengers boarded, prefights completed, and taxi and take-off clearance were given. Upon rotation, the flight engineer advised we were losing pressure on the number one engine, followed immediately that the number one engine had failed with a possible seizure. Shutdown checks were completed and a request to return to the airfield was duly obtained. As we had fuel for Paris, I had to decide on either making an overweight landing or dumping precious fuel which we would not be able to replenish due to our fuel quote carnet being maxed out. I decided on the overweight so that at least I had fuel to get somewhere in the event I needed engineering help. The overweight was successful. On a close examination, our engineer and flying spanner came to me with alarming news. Number one engine had all but seized with serious damage. From their close examination they suspected hydraulic fluid had been put in the gearbox. We were now in a dilemma as, with no available engineering support and very little cash after having to pay landing fees etc, we were grounded. A call to our engineering support in Opa-Locka Florida USA was not very comforting so we prepared to overnight. During the night we were made very aware that the engine might possibly have been sabotaged to support the opposition Government team, in so stopping it from going to Paris. However, proof of this was non-existent but was supported by investigations done by my crew. Telephone calls and more dwindling expenses incurred during the following hours when it was decided that we should proceed back to Banjul on three engines where we had our resident engineers and better support. This we did with number one being strapped in a fixed state using cargo tie-downs. However, we were, as the engineers, aware that the number three engine was right on limits, however, it held together for takeoff and was operated at reduced thrust in an attempt to extend its life. Arriving in Banjul our engineer staff took a closer examination confirming our finding of possible sabotage with hydraulic fluid in the gear box. Attempts were now underway to find a spare engine. It appeared one was available in Paris but there was no cargo aircraft available plus stands and staff to make a change in Banjul. The main problem was the company could now not afford the accumulating cost. It was then decided that we should ferry the aircraft across to Opa Laka, Florida where engineer staff and an engine were available. I flight planned via the long way coming across the Atlantic bringing me closer to Barbados in the West Indies and up via San Juan control, rather than direct. The reason being that I was seriously concerned about the number three engine so fueled for a two-engine ferry taking the maximum I could on three. Flight clearances were obtained, and the flight plan filed for a very early departure the following morning to meet W.A.T limits with just the three-cockpit crew. It was a pitch black and semi overcast morning, cloud layer about 1,500. feet but nice and cool to get the best out of our remaining engines. Take-off clearance was given I applied the three-engine take off procedure which I had used regretfully a few times before. On lift off and gear retracting the engineer called out we were losing pressure on number three, at the same time the tower abruptly advised that we were streaming smoke. To make things worse our ground engineers came on radio frequency informing us that sparks and smoke were seen on take-off from number three engine. I reduced number three to flight idle and asked for a report from the flight engineer. He replied immediately that number three was gone but would possibly be able to hold flight idle pressure.

An immediate decision had to be made because if we returned to Banjul, we would be stuck there for eternity, possibly shutting down the operation, followed by a possible abandonment of the aircraft without crew pay and funds to cover our costs in Banjul. My thoughts had to cover the remaining crew now on their own in Gambia with the possibility that they would be forced out of their accommodation and possibly jailed. As had happened before with crews unable to meet the posting costs such as hotels, transport and unpaid aircraft handling fees. I made a quick decision supported by the flight crew and confirmed with the ground crew that we would proceed for the sake of all concerned. Leaving the number three engine in flight idle I was able to reduce some drag. I then when leaving Dakar control and in contact with Atlántico control changed my destination to Barbados. We were able to make 16,000 feet but were burning 16 tons of fuel an hour. I had crossed the Atlantic before (1963) in a 42-foot Irish fishing boat taking seven weeks, but the blackness and cold appearance of the water was a bit nerve-racking for us in the cockpit. We could not sustain ourselves on one engine so as the sun rose behind us, we became a bit more relaxed as ditching at night into the cold Atlantic was not something we wished to experience. However, the sun eased the tension and helped cheer us up and when in contact with Barbados we felt considerably better. After 6hr: 40min we sighted the island cancelling IFR we preceded VFR for a close circuit due to very low fuel landing comfortably on two engines. The idea of spending a couple of days back in Barbados was very appealing as I had flown in the West Indies for 6 years previously with LIAT and Seagreen Air Transport. My oldest son Scott was born in

Barbados. Now came the problem of getting fuel. The fuel carnet we had was all but depleted. Numerous telephone calls later to our engineering team in Florida finally got us enough fuel to proceed on using all the airfields up the islands as alternates. Refuelling completed we prepared for another take-off using two engines at max power introducing number three as able. To do this we taxied on two engines starting number three engine only when we were given take-off clearance. The take-off roll was surprisingly smooth, being very light on fuel and with an operational engine on each side. I very slowly introduced the number three engine using it to counter sway and drag. V1 was obtained with still sufficient runway left, however, just after V2 at 50 feet number three engine came to bits. Just able to climb on two and using some lift from the cliff face at the end of the runway we staggered through our engine shutdown check, after take-off checklists, at the same time turning on course. Thankfully there was no fire, but we were feeling the drag of the shutdown number three. Advising Barbados that we were on course and climbing to 12,500 feet, frequency change was approved to Martinique, Antigua and then on to San Juan. The decision to proceed was supported by the fact there were en route airports available such as St Lucia, Guadeloupe, Antigua, St Martin, and San Juan. The jump from San Juan to Florida was a bit concerning as the only airports were abandoned ex-military and then Nassau. Amusingly when in San Juan airspace aircraft on being advised that they had B747 traffic at 12,500 feet, asked why we were at that altitude. When told we were on a two-engine ferry, many comments were made such as good luck, better you than me, holy cow a B747 on two. Shit.!!!

Finally, the Florida coastline was in sight, and we were cleared directly to the Opa-Locka airfield again followed by ATC comments such as "good going". The landing was successful although we had burnt far more fuel than expected, partially due to the third engine drag. Opa-Locka Airport (OPF), for many aviation enthusiasts, was a well-known name and place where many interesting airplanes could be found. For many years this airfield was little more than a junkyard with overgrown dusty ramps where large numbers of aircraft came and spent their last dying days in hot and humid Florida weather. After the big cleanup at Miami International Airport which included the bankruptcy of PAN AM and EASTERN, the famous corrosion corner, many prop and jet aircraft arrived at OPF to spend their days awaiting a new life as cargo freighters, modified for some other service or to end up in a pile of scrap metal. The engineers started stripping the number three engine soon after shutting down. Upon leaving the cockpit we were asked to come and see what we had brought in. It was startling what we saw. The engine had almost completely disintegrated. It was later established that we had ingested something quite big. On an after briefing with my crew and the engineers, we remembered that on take-off from Barbados, a large grass cutting detail was underway on the starboard side we had to wait some time for the tractors to be removed from the runway edge to allow our take off. The First Officer Chris advised that he had taken note of the proximity of the grass cutter, and it was still in full operation as we took off. Our combined opinion was that the grass cutter had sent a stone or some kind of projectile which had been ingested by the sick engine. Pratt & Whitney are great engines, but this one did not stand a chance.

Edinburgh. World presidential G20 summit meeting.

A week later a new engine was fitted. The crew, after a good rest were mustered and we returned to Gambia to continue the contract operating many times across Africa flying Hadj to Jeddah a familiar place to me as I had been with SAUDIA. We also took the Gambian President Yahya Jammeh to Scotland being the only B747 landing at Edinburgh airport for the Presidential G20 summit meeting. It was a very short runway for a B747 which stood out against the other VIP aircraft. We the crew spent 5 good days visiting the sights of Edinburgh at the expense of the President. The protocol is very much the call of the day. Returning to Banjul I received a call from Douggie Sissoko asking us to fly to N'djamena. (Old Fort Lamy) Chad in central Africa and picked up emergency child evacuees from there as a civil war was pending. I could not believe this as when with Saudia I was a first officer on a B707 with Captain Davies and went in there with overstayed Mecca Hadjies. We were almost high jacked getting out as tanks and armed vehicles attempted to bloke the runway with civil war starting, we had to fly low for miles to evade rocket fire. This unscheduled Chad landing had been authorized by the owner. On landing, I was approached by the authorities and a Red Cross person. They begged us to take as many children as we could. Weighing up the situation I started to do some figures. We were very light and could take our maximum uplift. Children started to appear in long lines. I authorized the cabin staff to lift all the armrests and placed 5 or 6 children depending on their size in each seat. Then I started at the front placing bigger kids in twos down the floor between the seat rows. Eventually, I filled the upper deck. We got airborne with some effort and upon our arrival counted around 600 passengers disembarked, albeit children. We did Hadj flights and charters to unknown airports on dead reckoning navigation without STAR or SID charts. There are many bush-type uncontrolled airports like that across Africa. Departing often without correct weight and balance or field conditions, sort of bush flying with a B747. Some of these fields required quite a bit of nerve but the old trusty B747 performed her usual reliable self. I learnt later that this was an aircraft that had suffered a similar incident as the UNITED aircraft (shown below) that lost its main cargo door over the Pacific. The UNITED pealed up in front of the leading edge and extracted 9 passengers plus seats and cabin material in a massive decompression.

This aircraft was repaired and sold as a white tail to Air Dabia. Ironically it was the same side as engine number 3 that we had engine trouble with.

Eventually, the company was to fold. The owner Dougie Sissoko as I wrote earlier faced a jail sentence for matters regarding USA customs. He had tried to buy some USA helicopters from the military which had not been decommissioned. He bribed some customs officers and was exposed in a sting so sentenced to a jail term. With the airline now collapsing we were told to return the aircraft to Opa Locka. I advised the crew to quickly pack their belongings so able to move all the crews out of Gambia over to Opa Locka on the ferry flight This was before the Government could seize the aircraft or lock up the captain and crew for lack of landing, airport costs, fuel payment, something quite often done in Africa. A good friend of mine, Dave Gonzales, was locked up in West Africa for three months in a similar situation. A little later the engineer in charge Glen Heikkila, got permission to fly the aircraft from Opa Locka to an abandoned upstate New York Military airfield. The field was at Plattsburg and was an old B52 Bomber base. It was fully equipped with about 200 empty homes, a hospital, an operations centre and officers' quarter, movie theatres, schools, a supermarket and a mess. With no active landing or navigation equipment I was able to get into the field in a blinding snowstorm by using a cross-reference course set from another nearby active navigation station. It was touch and go, a profound seat-of-the-pants approach and landing. Here we were met by the local TB station and on the evening, news outlining the considered operation. We were put up in the old officers' quarters which were as good as a first-class hotel. Glen was attempting to build a heavy aircraft maintenance centre using the old Air Force hangers. With the contract now in pieces and nothing imminent, I was able to get a flight out of New York and home to South Africa. I was very tired and longed to get home.

This is an extract from a press release years later showing that lovely Gambia went the way of all African countries, lastly expelling its president Yahya Jammeh:

When the Prince of Wales represents the Queen at next month's Commonwealth summit for heads of government in Sri Lanka, he will no doubt be relieved to find that he no longer needs to deal with an African dictator who indulges in witchcraft and puts his foes before a firing squad.

Commonwealth conferences have a long and undistinguished history of providing dictators with a public platform they would otherwise be denied as a consequence of their murderous domestic policies. For example, Zimbabwean dictator Robert Mugabe liked nothing more than to berate the "imperialist" Western powers when he was still allowed to participate in the summits.

There have also been occasions when members of the Royal family have not covered themselves in glory, such as the time the Duke of Edinburgh, when introduced to the Nigerian secretary-general of the

Commonwealth, who was dressed in ceremonial robes for a state dinner, remarked: "You look as though you are ready for bed."

But at least Prince Charles will now be spared the discomfort of having to deal with "His Excellency Sheikh Professor Doctor President Yahya Jammeh of the Gambia" after his surprise announcement that he is ending his country's association with the Commonwealth because of its "neo-colonial" associations.

It is a moot point whether, by announcing Gambia's immediate withdrawal, Mr Jammeh jumped before he was pushed. These days, thanks to the principles set out in the 1991 Harare Declaration the Commonwealth does not tolerate repressive dictatorships. Having been initially suspended for breaching the Declaration in 2002, Zimbabwe was forced to withdraw its membership the following year.

And there was every prospect that Gambia, given its recent human rights record and Mr Jammeh's wanton disregard for the rule of law, would be only the second country to follow suit, had not its long-serving dictator spared the Commonwealth the trouble of going through the expulsion formalities.

Since seizing power as a 29-year-old lieutenant in 1994, Mr Jammeh's rule has been marked by his increasingly eccentric conduct and a ruthless determination to suppress any hint of political dissent. In a country where the average tenure of the interior minister amounts to no more than a few months, and the infamous "Mile 2 Hotel" prison on the outskirts of Banjul, the capital, is filled with political prisoners crowded into mosquito-filled cells, Mr Jammeh has established himself as one of the region's most enduring despots.

But thanks to the economic benefits, built mainly on a thriving tourism industry, that the country has experienced as a result of Mr Jammeh's political dominance, the Commonwealth has tended to turn a blind eye to his wanton disregard for some of the more important principles of the Harare Declaration, such as the rule of law and respect for individual liberties. After all, the African continent can hardly boast too many economic success stories.

It has only been in recent years, as Mr Jammeh's conduct has taken a more bizarre turn, that the outside world has begun reviewing its relations with one of Africa's more outlandish characters.

Before coming to power – a feat he achieved through the simple expedient of being the first officer to reach the presidential gates during the 1994 overthrow of his predecessor, Sir Dawda Jawara – Mr Jammeh had a reputation for blending witchcraft with statecraft. After one of his aunts died, apparently the victim of witchcraft, more than 1,000 "sorcerers" were rounded up at gunpoint by the "Green Berets", the presidential guard unit, and forced to drink hallucinogenic poisons designed to "exorcise" them.

Mr Jammeh's passion for witchcraft has also led him to claim that he has invented a herbal cure for Aids, forcing hundreds of Gambians to risk their lives by undertaking his program instead of the standard retroviral treatments used to deal with HIV.

But it is the brutal treatment meted out to Gambia's political dissidents that has caused most concern, especially after the president made the surprise decision in August last year to suspend the country's 27-year moratorium on the death penalty and executed nine prisoners by firing squad, deliberately ignoring pleas from other Commonwealth governments to show mercy.

His decision was particularly harsh given that, in Gambia, political opponents can be jailed without charge simply for questioning Mr Jammeh's declaration that he intends to rule for a "billion" years. Nor did he endear himself to world leaders at last month's UN summit when he declared that homosexuals were "very evil" and posed the greatest threat to human existence.

The dictator's irascible conduct laid the foundations for Gambia's political isolation, a process that ultimately led to the country's decision to withdraw from the Commonwealth.

Certainly, the Commonwealth, which stands to nurture the principles of democracy and the rule of law in countries where they might otherwise wither on the vine, will be strengthened by no longer having to tolerate a regime that openly treats such values with contempt. The tragedy for the Gambian people is that they must now face the vagaries of their deranged dictator on their own.

Many years later he had to flee the country, being ousted by a new government who wanted his blood. I believe he was given sanctions in Guinea Bissau West Africa.

Here is the extract on Sissiko from the BBC news writer Brigitte Scheffer.

The playboy who got away with $242m – using 'black magic'.

One day in August 1995 a man called Foutanga Babani Sissoko walked into the head office of the Dubai Islamic Bank and asked for a loan to buy a car. The manager agreed, and Sissoko invited him home for dinner. It was the prelude, writes the BBC's Brigitte Scheffer, to one of the most audacious confidence tricks of all time.

Over dinner, Sissoko made a startling claim. He told the bank manager, Mohammed Ayoub, that he had magic powers. With these powers, he could take a sum of money and double it. He invited his Emirati friend to come again and to bring some cash.

Black magic is condemned by Islam as blasphemous. Even so, there's still a widespread belief in it, and Ayoub was taken in by the colourful and mysterious businessman from a remote villa in Mali.

When he arrived at Sissoko's house the next time, carrying his money, a man burst out of a room saying a spirit - a djinn - had just attacked him.

He warned Ayoub not to anger the djinn, for fear his money would not be doubled. So Ayoub left his cash in the magic room and waited.

He said he saw lights and smoke. He heard the voices of spirits. Then there was silence.

The money had indeed doubled.

Ayoub was delighted - and the heist could begin. "He believed it was Black Magic - that Mr Sissoko could double the money," says Alan Fine, a Miami attorney the bank later asked to investigate the crime.

"So, he would send money to Mr Sissoko - the bank's money - and he expected it to come back in double the amount."

Between 1995 and 1998, Ayoub made 183 transfers into Sissoko's accounts around the world. Sissoko was also running up big credit card bills - in the millions according to Fine - which Ayoub would settle on his behalf. In 1998 I was living in Dubai, and I heard rumours that the bank was in trouble. When a newspaper reported that the bank was having cash flow problems, crowds of people gathered outside, waiting to withdraw their money.

The Dubai authorities downplayed the crisis. They called it "a little difficulty that did not lead to any financial losses either in the bank's investments or depositors' accounts". But this wasn't true.

"The people who owned the bank took a huge, huge hit. It was not covered by insurance," says Fine. "The bank was saved because the government stepped in to help. But they gave up a lot of their equity in the bank for that to happen. "And where was Foutanga Babani Sissoko? By this time, he was far away.

One of the beauties of his scheme was that he did not need to be in Dubai to keep receiving the money. In November 1995, only weeks after putting on the magic display for Mohammed Ayoub, Sissoko visited another bank in New York, and did much more than open an account.

"He walked into Citibank one day, no appointment, met a teller and he ended up marrying her," says Alan Fine. "And there's reason to believe she made his relationship with Citibank more comfortable, and he ended up opening an account there through which, from memory, I'm just going to say more than $100m was wire transferred into the United States."

In fact, according to a case brought by the Dubai Islamic Bank against Citibank, more than $151m "was debited by Citibank from DIB's correspondent account without proper authorisation". The case was later dropped. Sissoko paid his new wife more than half a million dollars for her help.

"I don't know under what legal regime he married her, but he called her a wife and she believed she was a wife," says Fine. She understood that there were many other wives. Some from Africa, some from Miami, some from New York." With the bank's money rolling in, Sissoko could fulfil his dream of opening an airline for West Africa. He bought a used Hawker-Siddeley 125 and a pair of old Boeing 727s. This was the birth of Air Dabia, named after his village in Mali.

But in July 1996, Sissoko made a serious mistake as he tried to buy two Huey helicopters dating from the Vietnam War, for reasons that remain unclear. His explanation of why he wanted them was an emergency air ambulance. But the helicopters he was looking at were pretty big, they were not the kind that you see running back and forth to hospitals and trauma centers in the United States, they were much bigger than that, says Fine. Because they could be refitted as gunships, the helicopters needed a special export license. Sissoko's men tried to speed things up by offering a $30,000 bribe to a customs officer. Instead, they got themselves arrested. Interpol issued a warrant for Sissoko's arrest too. He was caught in Geneva, where he'd gone to open another bank account.

Tom Spencer, a Miami lawyer who was asked to represent Sissoko, vividly remembers going to meet him in Geneva's Champ-Dollon prison.

"I talked with the prison warden, who asked me whether or not Sissoko was going to go to the United States," Spencer says.

"I said, "Well, you know, we'll see." And he said, "Well, please delay it as long as possible." And

I said, "Well why?" And he said, "Because he's flying in fantastic meals from Paris every night, for us." And that was my first bizarre encounter with Baba Sissoko. Sissoko was quickly extradited to the US, where he started to mobilize influential supporters.

The readiness of diplomats to vouch for Sissoko shocked the judge presiding over his bail hearing. And Tom Spencer was stunned when a former US senator, Birch Bayh, announced he was joining Sissoko's defense team.

"Well, you have to ask yourself, why would anyone get involved for a foreign national who has no apparent value to the United States?" says Fine. "I don't know the answer to the question. But it's an interesting one to pose."

The US government wanted Sissoko held in custody, but he was bailed for $20m (£14.5m) - a Florida record at the time. Then he went on a spending spree.

His defense team was rewarded with Mercedes or Jaguar cars. But that was just the start. Sissoko spent half a million dollars in one jewelry store alone, Fine recalls, and hundreds of thousands in others. In one men's clothing store, he spent more than $150,000.

"He would come in and buy two, three, four cars at the same time, come back another week and buy two, three, four cars at the same time. It was just, the money was like wind," says car dealer Ronil Dufrene.

He calculates that he sold Sissoko between 30 and 35 cars in total. Sissoko became a Miami celebrity. He already had several wives, but that didn't stop him from marrying more - and housing them in some of the 23 apartments he rented in the city.

'Playboy' is the right word to describe him. Because he is very elegant. And handsome. And he dresses with great style. He blew a lot of money in Miami," says Sissoko's cousin, Makan Mousa.

Sissoko was also giving away large sums to good causes. His trial was approaching, and he knew the value of good publicity. In one case witnessed by his cousin, he gave £300,000 ($413,000) to a high-school band that needed money to travel to New York for a Thanksgiving Day parade. Another of his defense lawyers, Prof H T Smith, remembers that on Thursdays he would drive around giving money to homeless people.

"I was thinking, is this some modern-day Robin Hood? Why would you steal money and give it away? It doesn't make any sense," he says.

"The [Miami] Herald did a story just after he left, and I think - I don't want to exaggerate but I think they said they could chronicle like $14m he gave away. He was only here for 10 months. That's over a million dollars a month." Alan Fine took a slightly more cynical view.

"So much of what he did was for image and to perpetuate a belief that he was a very powerful man and fabulously wealthy. He would give away money, but... to my knowledge it was never done in a way that he didn't get publicity for it."

Despite this PR drive, when Sissoko's case came to court he disregarded his lawyer's advice and pleaded guilty. Maybe he calculated that this would provoke fewer questions about his finances. The sentence was 43 days in prison and a $250,000 fine, paid of course, by the Dubai Islamic Bank, though without its knowledge.

After serving only half this sentence, he was given early release in return for a $1m payment to a homeless shelter. The rest he was meant to serve under house arrest in Mali. Instead, he returned home to a hero's welcome. It was around this time that the Dubai Islamic Bank's auditors noticed that something was wrong. Ayoub was getting nervous, and Sissoko had stopped answering his calls. Finally, he confessed to a colleague, who asked how much was missing. Too ashamed to say, Ayoub wrote it on a scrap of paper - 890 million dirhams, the equivalent of $242m (£175m).

He was found guilty of fraud and given three years in jail. It's rumoured he was also forced to undergo an exorcism, to cure him of his belief in black magic. Sissoko has never faced justice. In his absence, a Dubai court sentenced him to three years for fraud and practicing magic. Interpol issued an arrest warrant, and he remains a wanted man.

I found transcripts from other trials at which Sissoko failed to appear, including one in Paris. His lawyer claimed he was a scapegoat for Ayoub's actions and the bank's money had gone elsewhere, but the court didn't swallow it and convicted him of money-laundering. For 12 years, between 2002 and 2014, Sissoko was a member of parliament in Mali, which gave him immunity from prosecution. For the last four years, no longer an MP, he has been protected by the fact that Mali has no extradition treaty with any other country.

The Dubai Islamic Bank, nonetheless, is still pursuing him through the courts.

I flew to Mali's capital, Bamako, to find people who might tell me about Sissoko. I tracked down his seamstress, who remembered him fondly.

"The last time I saw him, two or three years ago, I made him a suitcase of clothes. If he didn't give out presents, he wouldn't be happy. It's his style. He loves to give things to people," she said.

I also found his driver, Lukali Ibrahim.

"The good thing about him is that when things are going well you can expect a lot of presents from him. He likes to help people with their problems," he said. "The bad things, I can tell you a few. This is someone who always gives people hope but instead of telling you the truth, he's a dreamer.

In the market, I found a goldsmith who had only praise for a client who would call and ask him to make presents for his friends.

I also heard that he could be found living near his native village, Dabia, which had given its name to Sissoko's short-lived airline, its near Mali's border with Guinea and Senegal. After a long drive I found a house that fitted the description I'd been given. Suddenly, surrounded by armed guards, there he was. Babani Sissoko, in person, now perhaps 70 years old. He agreed to an interview. The atmosphere was edgy and slightly surreal. He began by telling me about his entry into the world.

"My name is Sissoko Foutanga Dit Babani. You know, the day I was born all the villages round here burned down. The villagers went around shouting, 'Marietto has had a boy.' The fire leapt and leapt. There used to be a lot of bush around."

He then talked about his efforts to rebuild the village, which began in 1985, and about the money he made. At one point he had been worth $400m, he said. Eventually, I asked about the $242m he had received from the Dubai Islamic Bank.

"Madame, this $242m, this is a slightly crazy story. The gentlemen from the bank should explain how they lost all that money. I mean the $242m. Listen, how could that money have left the bank the way it did? That's the problem. It's not this man alone [Ayoub] who authorizes the transfers. When the bank transfers money it's not just one person who does it. Several people have to do it."

I pointed out to him that Mohammed Ayoub had claimed at his trial that Sissoko had put him under a spell.

"The gentleman you're talking about, I've seen him and met him," he said. But the heist, he denied. "The only contact I had with him was when I went to buy a car. The bank bought it for me, and I repaid the loan. It was a Japanese car. "Had he controlled people by means of black magic?

"Madame, if a person had that kind of power, why would he work? If you have that kind of power, you can stay where you are and rob all the banks of the world. In the United States, France, Germany, and everywhere. Even here in Africa. You could rob all the banks you want. "I asked him if he was still rich. His answer was blunt. "No, I'm not rich any longer. I'm poor. "Defying Interpol, Sissoko has spent a remarkable 20 years on the run, even if he has squandered all his money and can never leave Mali. He has never spent a day in jail for the black magic bank heist, only for the attempt.

A broken mirror is said to bring 7 years of bad luck

Finally, having got home I realized that it would be necessary to be grounded for a while. Things had deteriorated both with my wife's failing health and the old folk's ageing condition. My older son Scott had been working for British Airways at the Durban airport. He decided that due to the political and racial situation in South Africa he being white was going to be bypassed for any promotion work wise and wages. With this in mind he decided to migrate back to Toronto Canada. I was not in a good position to fund much of this but was able to give him all the spare cash I had to assist him on his lone venture. It was a tough decision for him but friends such as the Mutiger family offered to assist him on arrival in Toronto. He sold his car in so finding the necessary funds for his airfare.

What started out as a small toothache for Josie and a visit to the dentist ended up with visits to the oncologist, a cancer specialist. It was established that there was a small cancer growth in the lower jaw recommending radiation treatment. As we did not have medical aid it had to be self-funded. Time went by with regular visits to the oncology cancer centre with a reduction of the growth. The situation now with my folks was not looking good. Their life savings had been depleted as neither nor anyone had anticipated the rise in the cost of living. This meant that some assistance had to be included in their monthly living costs. My mother was no longer able to see very well, which required me to visit their home daily to check on them so organizing shopping, some cooking in general their wellbeing. Due to several robberies and finally with my aged father being held up at gun point we had moved them from their up-country homestead to a bungalow near my house. Fortunately, having earned an income overseas the exchange rate was to my benefit, but I could see that I was not going to be able to maintain the present situation for too much longer although being backed up by my rentals from Toronto.

The cancer seemed to subside, and this improved Josie's attitude, which had become extremely low. However, the storm had not passed and after a regular check-up it was found that the cancer had returned. It was now suggested that an operation on the jaw was very necessary, so hospital arrangements were made. Unfortunately, she would not stop smoking or imbibing rather heavily on alcohol. We attempted to help with visits to a psychiatrist who warned her that should she not resist the effects would decrease her chances of making a full recovery. The pending operation was soul destroying for her as it would scar her facial features. Considering she was a beautiful woman being in her youth a beauty queen. We and the whole family prayed this would be the end of her affliction. The operation duly took place and left her with bad scaring on the lower side of her jaw and neck. She went into a depressive state worse when she was at home and looked at the disfigurement. I now realized that it was best for me to look at getting into a business which would keep me home. Flying again appeared out of the question. It was hard to take as income was necessary and contracts became available especially on the DC8 and B747. The village we lived in was expanding fast with the centre developing bigger shops and a major road change giving a direct artery to the business area of Durban. I could see the village becoming a bedroom town as commuting for business people was on the cards. There had recently been a development of about twenty small shops named Heritage market built by the developer Hilton Cummings. Here there was an estate agency managing the sales of the shop units. The owner needed a partner to assist in its development.

After perusing and evaluating the possibilities I offered to come in as a 50% financial partner in so started my profession as an estate agent.

With my mother's ailing health, the nearest hospital was some mile away, which was of concern to me. I started to put together on a plain school notebook, doodling an idea of building a hospital for the village and the 250,000 people in the immediate 20-mile radius. Friends and family could not visualize my idea, it was too big a project. However, when I went to the local businesses and shops, there was a favourable response. It seemed impossible that I could even consider the idea. Working from the real estate office I very slowly got to grips with the development. To the ordinary person, it was impossible, but I could see a dream. Suddenly I was invited by a powerful legal company called Mooney Ford and partners to meet for lunch. I explained my idea which they approved of suggesting was a bit ambitious, but they would come on board on a risk overseeing the legal side. Things started to take place with me working feverishly attempting to self-educate myself on all the technical and legal requirements regarding getting Government permission in the way of a license to build.

Months were ticking by and at times I nearly gave up as it was one brick wall after another. The requirement to build needed a license from the minister of health not only in the province but from the government minister in parliament. Going forward I had now established all the required legal needs. It was a lengthy list being a construction company, an architect, and financial. A large construction company WBHO indicated they were interested so did an architectural business being FGG architects. Things picked up with doctors indicating they would come onboard as a lot of them lived in the area. Hillcrest was becoming fast the bedroom town I predicted. House sales were increasing at a steady rate with houses being sold at particularly good profits. A new shopping mall was being proposed with smaller sub stores starting up to service the increasing population. At this point, my son's company Health and Racket went bankrupt, so he was unemployed. He had supported the hospital idea, so we formed a company called Genuine Trading. He then became a part of the real estate business as I had bought out a silent partner forming a new estate company which included my son Grant.

To cut a long story short over a year had gone by with me self-supporting myself and the estate agency bringing in whatever my share of the sales. I reached a stage where I had to contact the minister of health, a member of the government. She was Dr. Nkosazana Zuma unbeknown to us the future corrupt president of South Africa divorced wife of five that he had. Later we dubbed her Zero Understanding Medical Association. In my telephone conversation with her she advised me that I would not get a license to build a hospital in Hillcrest as it was a white and wealthy area. I very clearly and politely advised I would, not realizing the battle ahead with its outcome. Where the new shops had been built, we, the agency now known as Heritage Properties, were managing the sales. On this same property was an empty lot on which I had decided to locate the hospital. It was ideally suited close to main roads supported by the necessary sewerage facilities, water and electrical power. The price had been negotiated with Hilton Cumming and plans were now being drawn up. Grant, now involved with the project, was collaborating with me attempting to get through all the legal jargon. The hospital was to be named The Evans Heritage hospital, being a privately owned establishment with rooms on the lower level to be a public clinic in so allowing ambulances to bring in wounded or sick and re dispatch them to government hospitals. With the project and its business plan in order we proceeded to put forward our application to the government offices in the capital of Kwa Zulu Natal Pietermaritzburg (PMB). The provincial ministers of health concerned were Dr Green Thompson and Dr. Mkhize with their offices in PMB. However, they continually travelled between Durban and PMB 96 kilometres. After repeated failed attempts to meet one of them at their offices we made a lunch appointment at the Polo Pony hotel which was halfway between the two cities. This duly took place with Dr Green Thompson arriving one hour late. This was not to be the first of the meetings at the hotel as it appeared the only way to see them was to offer lunch. This was not just for them as they had their P.A., driver, bodyguard, and usually an extra couple of staff. As soon as they had finished their meal they would get up and walk out, often leaving half-finished meals not consumed by the entourage. This was the only time I could speak to them and outlay my development with the grounds of wanting a license to build a private hospital. On two occasions I got a meeting at their head office in Pietermaritzburg, only after waiting for two hours to be told that they were not available. On the second occasion, I had my lawyers with me. The meeting was one hour late but we were able to table our plans supported by the legal requirements now being met.

A problem had arisen as Hilton Cumming had upon hearing of our progress decided to raise the price of the land we had agreed on purchasing. It was above our budget, so an urgent search was underway to find appropriate land. A particularly good site was located on Ashley Road, but it had to be converted to hospital zoning from residential. This took more paperwork and applications to the local municipality who were dragging their heels. I also had found out that there was some empty provincial land nearer the centre of the town. In my meeting with Dr. Green Thompson, I covered the problem with the land but assured him we were in the process of re-establishing to a better site. I then asked him if the vacant provincial land was available, being a better site to support the village and its inhabitancy. He slammed his fist down on the board room table, raised his voice and declared that provincial land would never be made available for a private hospital. At which point he stormed out of the meeting. We were losing the fight and some of the support we had was starting to question our success on the project. No private hospital license had been issued before so it was turning out to be a tough battle which I was determined not to give up on. I was too far committed with every penny I had plus Grant was now a year into the fight with me, so I did not want us to fail. I was now getting desperate so decided to go into the African native areas at night visiting the local bars. Here I handed out pamphlets showing the locals what my idea was and that it would create 250 regular jobs plus about five hundred during construction. It was dangerous but on one such visit I met the chief of the area. He listened intensely and said he would contact a representative in the local government body related to the outer west area of which Hillcrest was part of. At the same time the following was taking place.

Grant, having worked in London on his school holidays, had strained his back. Then riding in the back of a friend's pickup he fell off again, injuring it. He was now visiting chiropractors and therapists to try and ease the pain which seemed to be increasing. It was giving him a lot of trouble so any driving for extended periods was becoming painful so restricting his sport activities. At about this time it was established that Josie's cancer had returned so another operation was scheduled after more radiation treatment. My mother was not able to move around much, having to be assisted with a wheelchair plus with limited eyesight cooking had to be done for her and my father. I arranged a routine where I would get breakfast, settle them for the day and return at night. Grant was now almost bedridden and needing help. The second operation was undertaken, and Josie was now home but becoming more reliant on whisky and sixty cigarettes a day. Having no appetite, she was not eating a healthy meal. At times refusing to eat at all. Her condition was deteriorating at an alarming rate. No amount of pleading to stop imbibing or smoking was successful. She claimed it eased the pain. Friends coming to see her would bring in liquor although we had asked all concerned not to do so. She was in a very weak state so the inevitable happened. One evening we had some guests over for the night. I excused myself as I had an early morning appointment. Later she fell in attempting to get out of the easy chair. I was awakened by guests who helped me get her to bed. She was in excruciating pain. Morning came with a visit to the doctor to find out she had broken her hip. This meant another hospital visit with increasing costs.
I will return to this later.

Hillcrest sports club.

On returning from overseas an old friend Rob Pooley, who owned a trading store near to my folk's home, had suggested I join the local Hillcrest sports club. There was a small but nice pub where on Friday nights the locals gathered. The facility consisted of Tennis, Bowls, Rugby, Rotary, Pigeon racing and the social club. This I had done enjoying the social evening away very much from the pressure of home matters and the developing hospital. One of the members John Tyne an old friend had been proposed as chairman and asked if I would accept the vice chairman slot. I agreed, not realizing what would develop from this acceptance. Within a few weeks John had resigned handing over the chairmanship to me. In accepting this position, I realized that the club needed to be reorganized as it was in a situation of disarray from a case to many chiefs not enough Indians. The independent clubs needed to be united under one committee. This I proceeded to do plus getting a financial adviser in to assist on the matter. The club in general was in debt to about R25,000 rand with a low membership. So as not to draw out this period of my story I will shorten the outcome of what I proceeded to do. My service with the club would last 9 years during which time I would be promoted to President, bring the bank account in the first year to over R100,000. With the expansion of Hillcrest, the property neighbouring the club was sold to a supermarket chain who proceeded to develop a mall. The foundations of this building had to be dug down a great deal to establish a footing. I realized that they would have to haul the dug-out soil many kilometres away to be dumped. The club grounds had a sloping embanked area which if filled would enable the tennis club to expand in addition to allowing more parking.

In numerous and extended meetings with the builders McMurray and Roberts, I was able to make a deal with them which in the value of was worth about R1,500,000. They in turn agreed to bulldoze down our embankment remove the huge nonindigenous trees, straighten the fencing lines to our mutual advantage, fill the sunken area to facilitate the extension of level land, change and tarmac a new drive, supply an air conditioner for the club, build a new gate entrance and paint out the rugby club house. In turn we would give them 2 years' free use of the newly established and levelled plot for their construction and maintenance offices. Later the main road into Hillcrest was widened to accept a double lane. I found the man in charge of the trucks hauling the sand to be dumped. I offered him a bottle of whisky if he would dump the sand at the clubs' south side which was a swampy area. Every morning at 07:00am I was there carefully supervising the trucks to reverse into a line so I could without grading just put a roller over the dumped soil. In this way I was able to build up an unused area where later the bowling club built new greens. In all the club has six more tennis courts, a bowling green and ample parking. In general, the club was completely revamped extending the general and usable surface by 30%. This allowed the clubs to increase their membership. During this time, I was invited to an evening with some friends who were off road motor cyclists. They would meet weekly at a friend's garage. I suggested to them that they form a club. I in turn went to the trustees and asked permission to allow the motorcycle club to put a small, wooded hut on our lower ground for the purpose of fathers coming and teaching their sons the art of motorcycling. All was agreed. I then helped sponsor a small, wooded hut. We formed a club called the Chain & Sprocket agreeing that any purchase of liquor would come from our club stock. Little did I ever guess that this club would grow to a Wednesday night following over 150 people. It was the young groups' social gathering not necessary for motor bikes but just as a club. The club house was extended to a large barn with toilets and a log fire burning in the ground on winter nights. It was the spot to be for the village younger folk. The profits pushed our club finances up very quickly to the advantage of the associated sports clubs. The club ground was named after William Gillitt, a founding member of Hillcrest. I was able to get musicians to perform on Wednesday and Friday nights, urging people to dance. This prompted a large crowd every evening again pushing out profits. It became so popular that by 19:00pm the club house was full. We moved on to a Sunday afternoon BBQ and music. None of the committee believed how the expansion had blossomed. The rugby club decided to move to a better location, so I had an empty club house on the rugby field. It was separate from the main club building as was the bowls club. The local running club met at the junior school. I approached Jacque the chairman and suggested that they move into the rugby building. After a committee meeting, they agreed on expanding our liquor sales and general club membership. To assist the move, we, the main club offered to sponsor young black runners who could not afford the club fee. In addition, between the two clubs running gear was obtained for them via some outside sponsors. Regretfully we had to peruse the applications, for instance one applicant who claimed poverty turned out to be a bank manager.

Some problems arose from a neighbouring football club. They had lost the lease of the land. I was approached by them asking if we could help. With this in mind I contacted the running club asking if they might consider sharing the club house with the football club. It was agreed so the Upper Highway football club moved into the old rugby club house. Again, we increased our club membership and the liquor profits. It was a great 9 years in which I made many friends plus it was a diversion from my now non-travelling life the hospital project and attempts to build a second business. When I eventually resigned from the club in their appreciation, they presented me with the enclosed being a clock mounted into an old aircraft propeller. It was much appreciated.

The Evans Heritage Hospital.

In returning to the hospital project, I received a call from a Mr. Meshack Radebe being earlier the mayor of the outer west area and the brother of Mr. Jeff Radebe a government minister in the countries Parliament. We agreed to meet at my house where I laid out the plans I had for the building of a much-needed hospital. He supported my idea and offered to help by getting his brother Jeff Radebe assistance. He had been told of my venture by one of the chiefs from our local native area. This was just the boost we needed. Some weeks later I finally received a call from his brother from the parliament buildings in Cape Town advising him that our license had been approved. We were overjoyed but it was time to move quickly as we had only six months to start building. A major problem arose as the land we had now decided to build on had not been converted from residential to hospital marked as zone F. There appeared to be some dragging of paperwork in the local municipal officers.

Time was against us so we on risk hired a company named "Acumen" who had more experience, to take over the final stage of going on site. All was ready the construction company WBHO were eager to get on site, but the paperwork was stalled on the site rezoning, later we were led to believe that Mr Cummings had somehow got a foot in the door at the municipality officers and was opposing our rezone application. It would have forced us back onto his land being the proposed original site. After nearly three years of personal expenses plus the project I was almost bankrupt. Then the coup de grace came with six weeks to go and ready to start the foundations the government pulled the license to build. It was hell of a shock, so we turned to our legal attorneys for help. They in turn represented by Barry Garland, the senior lawyer attempted to stretch their unpaid risk assistance but regrettably to no avail. It meant going to the high court at a fee way beyond any financial figure we could meet. Grant and I had to shut down the office and I started to desperately see if I could get back into the aviation business.

The saga of the hospital did not end there. The medical body then sold the license three months later to a black empowered group of doctors. This was not legal as one cannot sell a license it has to be reapplied for in the new developer's name. The new developer must comply with all the necessary articles for an application to build. But as all the legal and detailed requirements such as roads, sewage plants, water, electricity, in fact every article required to build a hospital had been met and submitted by us to Dr Green Thompson this he had in a box which he sold to the doctors. The chairperson of the black empowered group was a lady doctor who died three months later. The project then collapsed. Eight years later the project was restarted but again after partial construction the project went bankrupt. Finally, a company headed by a Mr Ross took over and completed the hospital. It now stands as a fully functional and well-respected hospital serving the outer west community. I have to admit every time I pass by, I see my plans as copied exactly by the developer from my original hospital drawings which puts a bit of a bitter taste in my mouth.

With this hanging over my head I was at the funeral of an old friend when my father anxiously contacted me to say my mother was not well. Arriving at their home I realized she needed to see a doctor, preferably at a hospital. Lifting her into my car we departed for the nearest hospital being Crompton Hospital located at Pinetown 15 kilometres away She was admitted obtaining medical attention for what appeared to be a heart condition, but we were not to be concerned as they would keep her overnight for observation. At 04:00 am she seemed well so I decided to return my now tired and distressed father to their home. Kissing her goodnight, she appeared anxious and concerned about my father, but I assured her all was well. Returning to the folk's home I assisted my father into bed then returned to my home. Amazingly the dogs sensed something was wrong as when I lifted her into the car they attempted to get in as well, not wanting to leave her side. At 08:00 am I awoke suddenly but attempted to get more sleep.

Sometime later I was awakened again, this time with a telephone call from the hospital to say my mother had passed away at 08:00am from heart failure. Coincidental, but she was my mother. What had caused this could not be determined. However, it was brought about by a situation that had taken place a week earlier. The house next door to mine had come on the market at an incredibly decent price. I had bought it putting it into my son Grants name. In turn I would get the rental from it until the purchase price was paid. The intension was to give both my sons a house. One here for Grant the other in Canada for Scott. It was my intention to transfer my folks from their house to this as it was next door and easier for me to care for them. I in turn would get the rental from my parent's home. Regretfully we had started to move their belongings to the new house but had run out of daylight time. I had returned to now my house being the neighbour to get some sleep. In the morning, my gardener arrived to say that the house next door had been robbed. They had broken down the fence, smashed the glass front doors in and ransacked all my parents' possessions. This was the second major robbery my parents had experienced. The first a couple of years back at their country house where all our family jewelry, TV, and CB radio was stolen. One of the items stolen was my father's collection of fine whiskey. The thieves were apprehended and according to the police it took them 3 days to sober up in the cells. All this had put tremendous stress on her which possibly caused the heart failure.

I now moved my ageing father into the neighbouring house as planned but the problem was, he was not able to live alone. Fortunately, I had met a gentleman by the name of Peter Swain an ex British tank commander who at 19 was fighting in Italy in charge of five tanks. He had after the war joined the Royal Air Force who had detailed him to Salisbury Rhodesia for training. He had fallen in love with Rhodesia and got married so resigned from the air force taking up farming, Safari work and auto racing. He later was with the auto industry for some years where he traded and collected several exceptionally good cars. Such as Aston Martin, Jags, Bentley and an Alfa Romeo 3 litre Monza. When the trouble started with the Rhodesian bush war, he immigrated to South Africa starting among other things a restaurant. Regretfully his wife died so he moved in with an old friend whose husband had also died. Ironically, she was Pat Stockhill one of my first teachers at Westville School plus his father Charles Swain who had also died at 57 years of age was my physical training instructor at the same school. Having fallen on tough times with the loss of his Rhodesian properties and investments, they had survived by selling his Aston Martin, her jewelry, Persian carpets and finally their house. With his wife Maria's sudden death and being semi homeless he had taken up residence with Pat Stockhill who was going blind and had been a good friend of Peter's parents. He became her carer in payment for accommodation. He was a fine man being a true person of British army stock well-liked by all. Regrettably, Pat Stockhill died a bit earlier than my mother. The house Peter resided in was willed to Pat's nieces who evicted Peter. With my need for someone to be a companion to my father, I offered him the position which he gratefully accepted. He became a significant help to me over the following years doing odd jobs, driving, and house-sitting my own house and caring for my father. He became concerned about what would happen to him. I shook his hand and as a gentleman said I would be there for him. This relationship would last for 16 years during which time he would be solely reliant on me in his old age. I housed him, gave him a car to drive, cared for his well-being and nursed him in the final days of his life, dying at 91 years of age. The last six months of his life were extremely hard as he had developed sores on his feet that would not heal. I had to wash and dress them daily, take his blood pressure and dose him with medication. I was becoming stressed now, facing financial difficulty and had to get back into flying. To do this I renewed my medicals and sent resumes to every agency I had worked with or knew of. I got an application form from an agency looking for pilots to fly the Airbus for DHL out of Belgium. I applied immediately.

D.H.L.

Sometime later I received a call from the agency in England asking if I had any three-engine experience, plus was my UK.A.T.P. License medical current. I advised them that my license was current, and I had the Britain Norman Trilander plus I had done the ground school on the Boeing 727. They advised that there was a position available on an Airbus course for a DHL contract out of Belgium, was I interested, and how soon was I available? My reply was a definite Yes and timewise within reasonable notice. They came back to me indicating that a ticket to Belgium was being drawn up to depart Durban in a week. I then went into top gear, arranging all that was needed to meet my departure date. It was the break I had been looking desperately for and another endorsement for Airbus. Every penny I had available I had to leave it in Grant's hands to cover home costs.

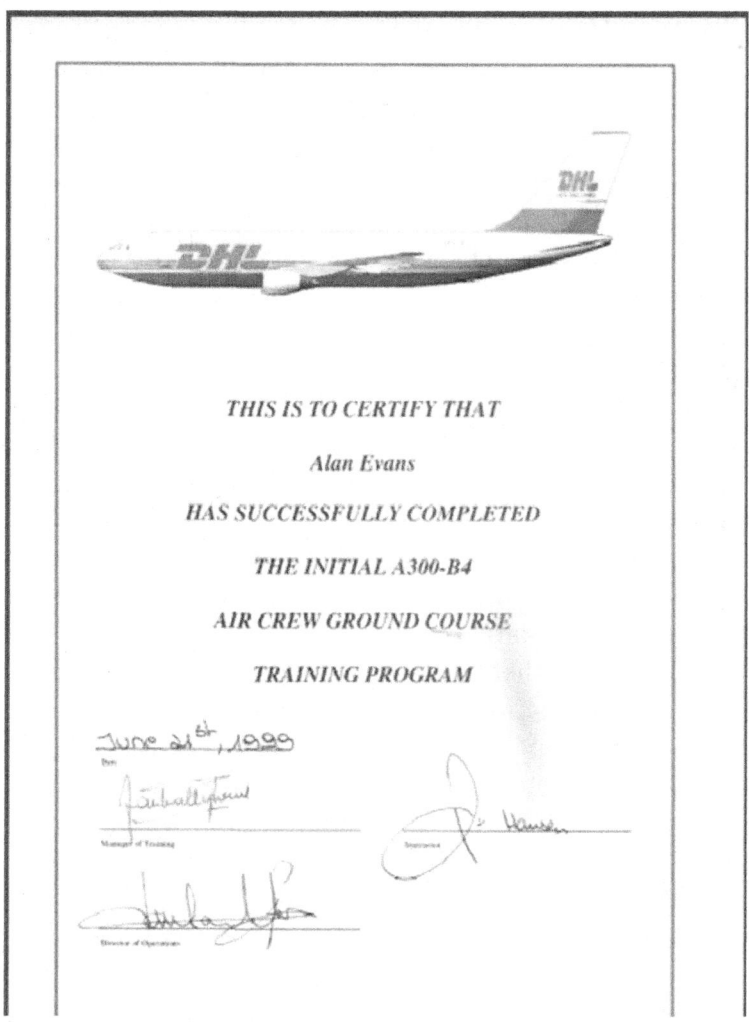

On the departure date, I travelled to Belgium where I was met by a representative who got me checked into a local hotel. He explained the procedure ahead to first meet the operations manager and then the ground school times which started the next day Following the instructions he duly met the operations manager and the regional chief pilot for DHL. The request regarding the 3engine experience was that they had B727 aircraft as well, so the more varied type endorsements they had on their flight crews the better. Ground school started on time, and the hotel was comfortable and supplied a continental breakfast which included boiled eggs. To sustain myself I used to eat as much of breakfast as I could, then put some bread rolls, butter, jam and boiled eggs into my bag. This had to be my lunch and dinner. I had an immersion heater so I could reheat the eggs and make a hot egg sandwich for dinner. I also used to go down to the local shop to buy tinned sardines and bully beef. So as not to be seen I would crouch behind a dividing wall at lunch and eat the sardines from the can. My menu was very restricted, but I was surviving on a very lean meal cost as I had no surplus money. The two-week conversion course was complete with the appropriate certificates confirming the course being given out. Then the trouble started.

I was called into the operations office to be told that the Belgium authorities would not accept my British License. Reason being they considered it a validation from my Canadian license. I explained that I had written all the exams being the performance A, written in Trinidad to get my British Colonial license and done all the required exams in England to British standards. I contact the U.K. CAA who sent a letter pointing that I currently held a full U.K license as per their requirements. The Belgium authorities indicated my three-engine experience was not on the British license but only on my Canadian license. They would not accept this so my further training on the simulator was stopped. A day later they advised me that I was to return to South Africa with a ticket to be collected at the airport office. I then asked if on their interline arrangement would they allow me to buy a 90% discounted crew return ticket to Toronto Canada. My intention was to do a check flight in Canada to renew my Canadian license. They agreed so I departed to Toronto where I caught the bus to Hamilton airport. Here was a Canadian M O.T office and a flying school that would rent me a twin-engine light aircraft to do the test flight with a ministry of transport inspector. I checked into a motel, made the necessary arrangements with the flight school and booked a test flight with the M.O.T. The night before I was to do the test my nerves packed in. I found myself in a helpless state suffering from loss of confidence, depression. unable to sleep and exhausted worrying about the situation at my home. I decided that I did not need my Canadian license to obtain future work, relying on my other international licenses, called the flight school and the M.O.T cancelling my bookings. I immediately returned to Toronto airport getting the first flight to Antwerp. With a small transit time I boarded a flight to South Africa returning home without a job.

Grant's back was causing him a lot of pain. We had seen doctors, Chiropractors, and physiotherapists all of which were not helping. It was at times so bad he could not get out of his bed, so requiring my assistance to eat or use the toilet. This meant I was caring for my ageing folks. A wife recovering from hospital after surgery and at times bedridden plus Grant to have back surgery to remove the damaged disc. It was something we were against but supported by some of the doctors. However, a surgeon was appointed, and a hospital date was set. Ironically on that day, I had a call from a gentleman in Johannesburg named Mr. Pruno. He was a Russian immigrant with a Boeing 707 that he charted out. He urgently wanted a B707 Captain and was I interested. I had kept my aviation medical certificate current so basically; all I would need was a check out on the B707 which I had not flown for 16 years. We agreed on a wage per hour plus my travel expenses. I then made frantic arrangements with our housekeeper and Peter to cover home necessities such as my father, money food, allowances, wages and petty cash then prepared to leave in two days. This meant I had to leave Grant to face the operation and hospital all on his own.

Pruno Air

The tickets duly arrived as agreed but I noticed they were from Durban to Johannesburg then on to Luanda in Angola. At the airport in Johannesburg a shortish man stool waiting at the arrivals. I presumed this was Mr. Pruno so walked towards him. He greeted me in a foreign accent and welcomed me to Johannesburg. He said he had a car waiting and suggested we go to his home where technical things could be sorted out. His invitation included a night stay at his home where I met his wife and young son. Once there and over a beer it turned out that I was to go to Angola where the aircraft was. Here I would find the crew get checked out and do a charter for the South African Government. Details of which I would get in Luanda as to date he did not have any destination. He advised me that upon returning to Johannesburg I would meet the rest of his team, another flight engineer who was the maintenance engineer as well, plus a load master. We concluded by making copies of licenses, medicals, logbooks, passports plus banking details. In the morning, I departed for Luanda where the flight engineer would meet me. Arriving in Luanda a chap introduced himself as Helder Rames a coloured African man who was to be the first officer. He explained that the B707 was owned by the Angolan Presidents' daughter and that with this connection the flight crew although not having an Angolan license had been issued with special permission to fly the aircraft on the strength of a foreign license. In my case the USA as it was the last registered B707 that I had flown. He now took me to see the aircraft and meet the other crew member a local Africa flight engineer. I stopped him at this point and asked who the captain was. His reply was that there was none, and he had been given permission to check me out on the flight scheduled to depart in the morning for Overberg in the Cape being a decommissioned South Africa military base. I could not believe what I was hearing but said no more as being a white South African I understood anything could happen in Africa.

Arriving at the aircraft I could not help but shake my head. This B707 identification SAD-FAV was one of the oldest, dilapidated aircraft I had ever seen. The tyres were thin and in a couple of places bare. It dripped oil from every old JT3D engine, was dirty with patches on numerous places of the fuselage and wings. In my mind I did a quick situation account. Here I was in Angola, no return ticket, extremely low in cash and desperately needing work to cover mounting home costs. Could I pull this off as it had been 16 years since I had flown a B707. I would have to rely on every bit of my past seat of the pants and airline training to captain this venture. Thankfully, a cargo machine with no passengers. There were still some more surprises to come as I was to find out at the apartment which had been rented for the crew. Here I was issued with a copy of my authority to fly the aircraft and some information about the pending charter. After a bit of a restless night during which I repeatedly concluded that a phone call to Pruno was an urgent necessity in the morning. This I did but he explained they had no other way of doing the special Government charter as there were no captains available with any old B707 experience. There would be no pay or return ticket or any remuneration if I refused the flight, so the problem was in my lap. Helder Ramos the first officer confided in me that he had flown the aircraft sometime back and it was not as bad as it looked. He indicated he liked me and would be pleased to do the flight together. Not sure if he got a bonus for saying that. I then got another call from Pruno asking what my intention was as the South African government was awaiting his reply on when the aircraft could be expected to arrive in Overberg. I went to the toilet, looked in the mirror and asked myself what the hell was I getting into. Now a stiff drink would have been a help. I was in a bind and needed the work so decided to go ahead and do the flight convincing myself that when we got back to Johannesburg, I would quit followed possibly by giving Pruno a black eye. Once in the cockpit I was again incredibly surprised at the shabby condition everything was in, but all was working. The flight engineer was another surprise as it turned out he was a black Angolan who was moonlighting from the air force. His experience on this aircraft was extremely limited but Helder convinced me he had flown with him before and was a good flight engineer albeit with little experience on jets. I had no choice but to continue with the flight. I was surprised at how quickly I became familiar with the cockpit layout. but there again a Boeing is a Boeing especially the older version all produced to have crews easily interchanged. Circumstances being as they were I accepted. I did the take-off very carefully, having my eyes scramble across every inch of the instrument panel. I was a bit heavy on the controls but soon felt the aviator's sensation reacting throughout my body.

At the end of the 4-hour flight, nothing much had happened whereas I had expected bits to have fallen off. In so with the help of Helder my confidence was building but now came the landing. All went well but I was a bit high on the flare out, possibly from years on the B747 having a much higher cockpit. Helder Ramos with a big smile on his face agreed on my admitted faults but indicated I had passed the necessary for a flight checkout. Overberg as earlier expressed was a decommissioned military and air force base. The runway is long having the operations buildings and living quarters approximately halfway down the runway. At the far west end is an accumulation of small buildings with a couple of hangers. We were instructed to taxi to those buildings. On parking a ladder which we carried was dropped down for the crew to disembark. We were driven to the old admin building where a briefing was held. I was instructed that the cargo was sixty tons of missiles to be flown to Biska in Algeria. This was a desert outpost consisting of a rough runway and an army base. From there we were to return to Johannesburg with damaged helicopters and used spares offloading them at the Denel arms hanger. Denel Dynamics has its roots in missile research, design and development. This was part of an agreement with the South African government but could not be transported on military aircraft for security reasons. My aircraft was privately owned and therefore registered as a private machine. This was to evade bad protocol which could become embarrassing for the South African government. I was also instructed that I could not land anywhere as the cargo might be seen. In other words, if an emergency developed and a forced landing became necessary it was to be done at sea. Our flight would be tracked by the military for safety reasons.

After a typical military meal, we were shown to our rooms being vacant officer's quarters. They were very plain, having a hard coir mattress, stiff pressed sheets, a shower but no towel. I used my T-shirt for that reason. In the morning after breakfast, we were escorted to our aircraft that had been loaded during the night. We the crew did a visual check of everything including the sixty tons of missiles now loaded securely in the rear cargo section. A flight plan had been filed directly to Biska with over-flying rights indicating we were on a private flight. The old 707 took the take-off well and the remaining flight to Biska of 10 hours 20 min went without a hitch. The navigation system put us over the airport but there was no letdown procedure, so we did a visual approach. Algerian air traffic control had expressed that we had to cancel our fight plan on their radio frequency. There was no control for Biska, the runway was long compiling of compact sand which showed drifting sand and small sand bars occasionally across the runway. With the fuel and load we had there was no alternate landing field. If a sandstorm had developed, we would have been in trouble as the runway and visibility could become obliterated with dust and sand. Being a sand strip it was more like finding and landing on a piece of sandpaper. Having flown out of Saudi
Arabia and the United Arab Emirates I had experienced this kind of seat-of-the-pants flying but not so much with a B707. While taxing in a

military vehicle approached indicating we should follow him. I had shut down engines 1 and 4 as with Cairo the outer engines create whirlpools of sand which is ingested by the engines. The outpost consisted of stacks of 45-gallon drums, a few houses and what looked like a military administration or operation building. We stopped and shut down the remaining engines at a small hanger-type building. After disembarking via our ladder, we were escorted to the admin building where an officer invited us into an office. Here with the help of an English-speaking officer, he explained that they were grateful for our arrival and that accommodation meals etc would be supplied. Fueling and offloading would take place during the night with a flight plan filed via their headquarters in Algiers direct to Johannesburg for the estimated 9-hour 30-minute flight. The aircraft would be loaded with a couple of broken-down helicopters plus crates of used and damaged spares. But they were not sure of the exact weight. However, with this uncertain information I had decided that due to the high temperature, we would plan for an early morning take-off using the low temperature for our Weight Altitude Temperature take-off calculation. Especially as I would not be sure of the actual aircraft weight.

The meal was not too bad but very Algerian. We chatted with the officers learning that they were based there for 6 months with a service aircraft every week. Where the missile went was not revealed but we presumed out to be a desert battery. We got a reasonable night's sleep although it was extremely hot. There were no air conditioners, so windows were glass-free but had sand shutters. We looked forward to getting out of there in the morning and back to civilization with hot showers and air conditioners. The departure went as planned with thankfully all four engines running. Clearing with Algerian control we proceeded as per our flight plan crossing central African countries for Johannesburg. About 4 hours into the flight the aircraft suddenly started to wallow attempting to go into Dutch roll. My immediate response was to disengage the autopilot. Things settled down for a while but repeated itself when we engaged the autopilot. Something appeared wrong with the vertical stabilizer so to stop the possibility of an uncontrolled Dutch roll we for the next five and a half hours had to hand fly the aircraft. Exceedingly difficult to do at 31,000 feet as the aircraft is inclined to pitch slowly forward and back, which in turn increases the fuel flow. Eventually, Johannesburg was in sight where we duly landed and deposited our load at the Denel hanger. Here Mr Pruno met us where I was able to give him a piece of my mind indicating where he could put the bloody aircraft hopefully in a place where he would not be able to sit down for some time. I asked for my ticket back to my hometown Durban.

Going to a restaurant for some dinner he produced at the table my remuneration in cash for services rendered. All of which I gratefully accepted and prepared to depart on the next late flight. In a departing conversation he asked if he got the local maintenance company to go over the aircraft and would I be willing to do more flying for him. He explained that he had some more government charters and needed my help as B707 pilots were hard to find. I said I would think about it but to keep in contact. Pleased to be home with cash in my pocket I searched the flying market but was not producing anything positive. A month later Pruno called asking if I would come to Johannesburg and do a test flight on the B707 as it had been cleared by the maintenance company as airworthy and operational. With nothing on the cards, I agreed as the money was good and I needed an income to cover my now heavy expenses. The test flight went well and I was satisfied with the maintenance report. In so I agreed to do another flight to Overberg and Bisk this time with an experienced South African B707 flight engineer also licensed as a ground engineer and Pruno as the first officer. He was rated on the B707 but did not have an Airline Transport License so could not fly as Captain. He was incredibly pleased with my decision. Little did I know that this was not the end of the Pruno saga.

The flight to Overberg went off as planned with no indication of any problem. The overnight followed by the loading was completed and we departed for Biska. Suddenly cruising at altitude, we started to lose pressure in the number 3 engine. With this situation developing we realized we could not continue to Biska on three engines as the fuel burn would deplete our reserve insufficient to make the destination. Secondly, we did not want to be stranded on a desert military strip in Algeria if the problem could not be fixed. The engineer reported that if we could land somewhere he was sure he could fix the problem, but we had instructions not to land anywhere but Biska. A decision had to be made quickly so Pruno decided we should land in Luanda where he was known, and we had an apartment. This we did indicating to air traffic control a minor mechanical need to be looked at, certainly not that we were losing an engine. In the parking space, we quickly put the ladder down, disembarked and removed the ladder. When the customs came Pruno talked them into not having to go aboard as we were just transiting. Fortunately, the engineer fixed the problem, so we departed again for Biska heaving a sigh of relief referring to not having the authorities on our back regarding our load. Clearing with Algerian control having the permit to land at Biska we circled trying to find the airstrip. It was late in the afternoon with visibility low and blowing desert dust. I was getting a bit concerned as after our second attempt, we could not see the strip at a low altitude. However fortunately on the second circle, a flare went up marking the desert strip. From this, I was able to align myself using a magnetic reading from the buildings which we now could identify. After landing and disembarking we had filed a flight plan back to Luanda as there was no cargo for Johannesburg.

The offloading was quick, so we decided in the failing light to depart as soon as possible. On attempting to start the number 3 engine the hydraulic pump failed. The number 3 engine is the initial start engine so without hydraulics there was a problem. Our engineer got to it but the report was not good. It was damaged beyond repair and had to be replaced. It was obvious we were there for the night so started making contingency plans. Using the military radio phone contact was made with a company in Europe that had a spare hydraulic pump. Arrangements were made to have it air freighted to Algiers marked as AOG. This meant aircraft on the ground. From there a military flight was due in two days so if the connections were made, we could look at departing into Biska in 3 days. I was able on the same phone to contact my brother in Johannesburg asking him to advise my family that I would be back later than expected. There was nothing else we could do but wait for the incoming military plane provided a desert storm did not delay them. Common so we were told but the base commander. The next two days passed not enjoying the rough military environment but well cared for. Finally, the flight arrived with the hydraulic pump. Our engineer had it fitted in about 3 hours from which we filed a flight plan via Algeria and successfully departed for Luanda. This aircraft was as explained on lease to Pruno. He had another B707 having a D check-in in Pietersburg. This is a major check so takes time. Facing his crew problem he at the apartment in Luanda asked me to consider flying on with him as he had a lot of government and private charters coming up. He increased my salary to sweeten the pot. To me, it was not my idea of a secure flying job, but work was not coming in on the B747.it was a job that got me home something I desperately needed to have. I agreed on a 6-month contract but did not know that this would be a period in my life when I would be flying some of the most daring flights into the most unsuitable airfields, flying what I called bush flying with a B707 by the seat of my pants. Over the next few months, I would have a starter failure, an engine fire on take-off, an electrical failure, a navigation failure and a burst tyre on landing. I would do dead reckoning into jungle strips that had no navigation aids. I would land on an abandoned old military field being only able to land on half the width using a parallel road as part of the runway. Flights in the Congo in some places meant arriving over the airport at 15,000 feet. Then with gear and flaps extended do a tight circle down staying within a 10-mile radius to do a final turn at three hundred feet and two miles. Take-off was at full power holding the brakes with a degree flap. Reaching minimum take-off speed, I would select take off flap rotate and climb on the stall to 15,000 feet then stabilize and proceed on route.

This was done because the war still rages in Congo. (Zaire) Their gunners would fire at any stray aircraft. Two from an associate company also flying for World Food were hit. Thankfully, both survived with a strike on one in the tail and the other in the number 2 engine. World Food Aid was one of our biggest charters. We would load up tons of wheat bags. Depart in some cases to unmarked airstrips. One was a road in which on departure one had to negotiate an uphill section which launched the aircraft into the air. Usually on arrival, a military convoy of trucks would meet you. The army would form a circle around the aircraft. On the outer circle of the army, people would appear out of the bush in ragged clothes which in some cases looked like the remains of a uniform. They would have rags sometimes wrapped around their feet and holding a tin can or plastic cup. They would attempt to get to the aircraft to grab any wheat coming from the sacks as they were offloaded onto the trucks. The army personnel would force them away using canes or in some cases rifle butts. On our departure, they would scramble to the area where the aircraft had parked. Then with small type brooms made of straw, they would attempt to sweep up the dropping of wheat from the ground before the blast from the engine swept the dropping into the bush. This was the reward they got for the civil war which most of them had fought in. At some of the strips which were abandoned Russian made with in some cases complete Mig fighters in the bush and bunkers. Derelict building with remains of tanks and armoured vehicles. It was common at some of these landing strips to have the native people rush out to the aircraft with Pepsi bottles, cans, or any container they could find. They knew where the drain plugs were on the engines so draining fuel into their containers and used the JET-A to fuel their stoves and lamps. We did not mind as the fuel they took was absolutely nothing compared to the fuel a jet engine uses. (7 tons an hour). It helped them to live as the ongoing war, poverty and abuse it causes in the Congo is terrible. Another big contract was to fly tons of Castle beer to the military outstations. On departure from Lubonga, the cargo door was unlatched. I had my hands full attempting to fly back to Luanda with the door flaying in the slipstream and threatening to tear off which could have taken part of the fuselage with it never mind what would have happened had it hit the rear vertical stabilizer.

The roads across most of the Congo, Nigeria and Angola are not passable from wars and rain, vehicles were another load which we carried across the country. On one such load, we hit a bit of severe turbulence. I asked the flight engineer to go back and check that the two vehicles we had in the cargo bay were secure. He came back with a grin on his face. Apparently as he passed his touch (flashlight) around the empty vehicle, what appeared in the back seat were a couple frightened black faces baring large eyes and a gaping mouth. These were stowaways hiding on the car's back floor. This was common but they in turn upon arrival met with a severe hiding from a police officer. In South Africa they do it in new motor vehicles being transported on car carriers to northern towns and countries. As the months went by, we started to get more work out of

Kinshasa in the Congo and finally got our own aircraft 3D ROK back from the maintenance. It was on a Swaziland registration, so we were issued validations to fly it. I was glad to see the back of the Angolan B707, it was hell bent I think on killing us.

A B707 cargo similar to Pruno Air

The Congo (Zaire) was an amazing Belgian colony with a thriving metropolis Leopoldville now named Kinshasa and Brazzaville, Lubumbashi which became Elizabethville. There were valuable mines, agriculture, coffee and in general a thriving country with a very favourable future. As in most African countries the destruction of the inner structure has been devastated by corruption, and brutal and bloody wars. In the nineteen 50s South African mercenaries led by Mike Hoare were seconded to fight in one of the worst African wars. Thousands lost their lives. One place we serviced was Bujumbura in Burundi another place of mass massacre in the streets of women and children attempting to escape the communist-supported rebel army. The main railway terminal is an abandoned graveyard of rolling stock. The huge electrical generators on the Congo River are all but non-operational. Consequently, electricity is intermittent. Back in the turn of the twentieth century Germany with two colonies, one being German South West Africa now called Namibia and German East Africa land now known as Tanzania had constructed a railway across Africa connecting the two colonies. This was to be able to ship goods across the continent eliminating the long Cape sailing route. Regretfully this line can be still seen from the air but abandoned. There was a fully operation world airline SABENA which is also a thing of the past. However, there are a few attempted upstarts of air charter and airlines. When there I heard that there was an airline starting that might need current Airline Transport Captains. In making appropriate enquiries I was able to meet with the Minister of Aviation, Mr Anicet Kitenget and the airline pilot licensing officer. I explained I might be interested showing him my numerous airline transport licenses appeared as expected I would need a Congo airline transport license, so went about asking how I could get such a license. What happened next is hard to believe but it was suggested that if I bought him a TV from Johannesburg a license might be arranged. A week or so later I returned from Johannesburg with a moderate sized TV. I planned to meet him and give him the TV. He suggested I return on my next trip and come to his office after hours. I suspected I would not see the TV money or license as promised. I met him later as suggested and was handed a fully legal (Congo) Republic Du Zaire Airline transport license authorizing me to fly B747, B707, B737, DC 3, DC 6, DC8, MD 87, Catalina, Lear DA20, HS748. registered aircraft with an instrument flight rating. Number 352/F see enclosed I never used it but the fact that a TV could get me such a license is typical of Africa and its corruption. Kinshasa was a temporary base where we resided in a hotel. One evening while leaving a small restaurant an explosion, something like a hand grenade went off at the entrance from which we had just departed. The three of us took off at a full run not knowing what was next and in search of a taxi. The reason would never be known but our driver suggested it was jealousy in respect to the owner who was dealing with the wrong political party. For me this was the second time in my life I had just missed being blown up. Remanence of the old colonial days are still present. Beautiful old cobble stone streets. Caste iron remains of bus stops, bombed out or destroyed by vagrants' lovely architectural houses in stone and imported material. The occasional flight was for the military carrying munitions and supplies to their army encampments.

Some of these were also for the Democratic Republic of the Congo (Zaire) Army up to the north which was still at war. Most of the semi-operational airfields were abandoned leaving skeletons of buildings, destroyed tanks and armament. There were hundreds of derelict and damaged MIG fighters hidden in bunkers or just pushed off into the bush. From what I understood a lot were flyable but only a very few had been removed with heavy payments to the right politician. Some had been crated getting as far as the Angolan border but there had not been enough bribe money paid as they had been there for years rotting away. Working for Pruno enabled me to get home every month or two. I would get a flight from Johannesburg arriving in Durban an hour later. At times we would arrive in Johannesburg late at night. This meant I would either try and sleep in the aircraft or get to the terminal building to enable me to get a daylight flight to Durban an hour away. My wife did not drive any distance, so I had to rely on friends or Grant to be able to collect me from the airport. Failing which I would stand in the Durban parking lot looking for a vehicle with a number plate from a town or city beyond my hometown of Hillcrest. I would approach the driver explaining that it would appear my lift had not got my message in so would they be so kind as to give me a lift? Everyone I asked did give me a lift some driving me right to my home property. The uniform helped the matter.

I flew on with Pruno for about one and a half years when unfortunately, the situation at my home, being the loosing of the hospital project, the death of my mother, my father now requiring constant nursing, plus my wife's deteriorating health which also requiring nursing, forced me to again stop flying. To add to this the operation to Grants back had failed. Twelve hours after his initial operation he was back in the theatre for a second operation. The surgeon had nicked a blood vessel causing hematoma on the spinal cord. He was semi-paralyzed from the waist down. This confined him to the hospital for three weeks supported in cone shaped structure to allow the healing of the spine without body weight. He was to suffer with intense back problems for the rest of his life. Therefore, I had to be home to deal with all these matters which I called the breaking of a mirror period bringing bad luck. The final straw of the bad luck period occurred one evening. I was at my desk having just tended to Josie by assisting her to bathe, doing her hair and getting her into bed, when I heard her call me from the bedroom.

Josies death

Arriving at her bedside she asked me to help her to the toilet. I pulled the covers back and lifted her into my arms. Suddenly she went ridged, I instinctively realized she had died in my arms. Placing her back onto the bed I attempted to find a pulse, a few minutes later Grant arrived home following my call, he came to his mother's bedside holding her hand for a few minutes. I immediately called a doctor who pronounced her dead from what he indicated as natural causes stemming from her heart, cancer and general condition. It was a misty chilly night so as the hearse came up our drive the lights pierced the mist and darkness in an ominous way. Standing together on the lawn as the hearse left the only exclamation was from Grant saying, "If only she had listened." Cigarettes. alcohol, irrational eating and the cancer had taken its toll. We arranged all the necessary funeral arrangements for a family viewing, then a service and cremation. She had asked for her ashes to be sent to Australia and scattered on the sea. Her brother Richard had his mother's ashes, so we sent Josie's to him. He scattered both his mother's and sisters' ashes onto the sea at Port Douglas. Years later Scott, my oldest son, and Richard his uncle placed a brass plaque on the rocks overlooking the ocean. She had turned 62 in April and died three weeks before our 33rd wedding anniversary in October leaving two great sons.

Scott and Grant

African International Airways.

Life now had to change, Peter was caring for my father, and Grant was working now in the ship brokering business so, at last, I could concentrate on getting back into flying. This came about suddenly when I got a call from a company in London that operated DC8 freight aircraft across Africa. It was called African International Airways looking for a DC8 rated pilot. I met up with the chief pilot in Durban so being hired to go to England to do a 6-hour simulator refresher course. The simulator and training center was at 3 Bridges West Sussex using the simulator belonging to MK Airlines, a cargo company started by Mike Kruger a Rhodesian. (Zimbabwe). Unfortunately, this air cargo company went bankrupt after two crashes one with a DC8 in Nigeria at the famous Port Harcourt and the other B747 in Canada. After completing the required refresher course and the exam I returned to Johannesburg to operate a flight to Depospasvich in Russia. This was an interesting flight as it was to carry two hundred live ostriches to the Russian airport an old semi abandoned military field. Departing Johannesburg, we refueled at Khartoum arriving at our destination on a cold misty evening. I have flown a lot of things in my life both dead and alive but never Ostriches.

They never said a word and seemed very content allowing the handlers to corral them into sectioned boxed areas. Looking back all one could see was a mass of heads with smiles bobbing around attempting to see what was going on. The airport at Despospasvich is inundated with what looks like abandoned aircraft. Some of which we got permission to board. One or two were huge inside, certainly as big as a B747 with the entrance on one via a gangplank then up some stairs done in wood. The cockpit looked like something out of a steam train with big very old-fashioned dials, large trim wheels and seating for seven men. The passenger seats were tatty but at one time must have been something like a lounge seat. We had been met by a security officer who spoke a sort of broken English but enough for us to understand. After doing some preliminary paperwork relating to the cargo and crew, he indicated we were to board a military-looking vehicle which would take us to our night's accommodation.

This accommodation was a drab looking barn type building with an uninteresting entrance door flushed with brickwork. It was a cold wet mist with bad lighting surrounding the building plus where the aircraft was parked. Entering we were introduced to two woman who looked tough but dressed in what I would describe as a maid's dress and apron in a bland dark colour. There was a wooden table in what appeared to have been at one time a small dining hall. Beyond the hall was a small kitchen with the glow of a fire. Food had been prepared so after a long 12-hour flight we, being hungry, decided to eat. The food was a type of stew with a delicious serving of thick sliced bread. Made I suspected from the smoky fired kitchen oven. Dessert was a small plate of what I think had been tinned pears. A rich black coffee followed which caused a surprise when we asked for some milk and sugar. In the bedrooms were a single military type iron bed covered by a soft mattress and heavy blankets. It was indicated that there was a bathroom for us to use and a flushing toilet. The bath was an old enamel four-legged type standing alone mid-roomed fed by a steaming hot pipe with a tap outlet into the stained bath. However, it was a hot bath followed by a good night's rest. We were woken in the morning to a breakfast of eggs. large sausage and bread followed again by black coffee. It was all an experience that made one feel as if you had passed through a time warp.

With the aircraft cleaned, the necessary paperwork completed, and a flight plan filed, we departed for Benghazi to refuel for our onward flight back to Johannesburg. Two days later we departed for a return flight to Mauritius offloading cargo meant for Singapore. This was because a load we had for Singapore was too heavy to depart Johannesburg direct to Singapore. Returning a day later we overnighted in Mauritius then flew on to Singapore. The cargo was urgently needed, medical supplies and cargo. Singapore had a virus that was spreading across the island, so the air traffic was limited to incoming aircraft carrying the necessary supplies. The island was quarantined. A night stop was planned so we departed the following day back to Mauritius to refuel then onward to Johannesburg. It was good to be visiting Singapore again. It brought back all good memories of my living there, the kids, flying for OLYMPIC and later the years for the subsidiary of Singapore Airlines "Trade winds."

Mauritius was a place I never thought I would visit as it had bad memories of the Mauritian Mr. Roger LeGes that had bankrupted my father and the tough times he had caused our family. But later you will see in the latter section of my retired life I did return to Mauritius in a wonderful time of celebration and happiness.

Transjet B747 Ferry

I had just finished dinner when I got a long-distance call that was to make my day as I had not had any flying contracts for over a year. The in-between time I had been working on the Hospital project, the death of my wife and attempting to keep myself my father and Peter Swain afloat. With all my funds lost in the hospital fiasco, plus medical costs, things were a bit tough.

It was David Gonzales, the engineer I had worked with on the Air Dabia contract. He and Glen Heikklia were in Sweden preparing two old B747s to be ferried to Muscat in Oman. Glen had been the engineer in charge with Air Dabia and had attempted to start up a B747 maintenance operation using the decommissioned Plattsburg B52 air force base that I had delivered the Air Dabia B747 too earlier. David asked if I would like to do the ferry flight, if so, could I be in Stockholm in a few days. I agreed so he advised that they arrange the necessary airline tickets. It was not a problem not being current as the aircraft would fly on a ferry permit, but I would have to renew my medical which I promptly did. I had started to see a lady named Clare who said she would keep an eye on my father and Peter for me. Grant the younger was now working for a sports operation obtaining clients to sign up for gym contract. Scott the older son was now living in Canada so between Grant and Clare I was able to leave when the tickets arrived 4 days later.

On arrival in Stockholm. I was met by Dave and filled in on the project. It was mid-winter and extremely cold. Apparently, the aircraft had been out of service for some time with the collapse of the charter company. Ironically started by the Johansson the owner of time Air Sweden back in the bankrupt Sharjah operation. We met with him recognizing me, followed by a long explanation of what had happened to Time Air Sweden. The engineers had been working feverishly to prepare the machines for departure. With the cold being around minus 20c it was a difficult and a hard job. The interior of the aircraft was in a working condition but having stood for a long time there was a lot of engineering and external work to be done. What was scheduled for a possible 2- or 3-day departure ended up with a two week wait as neither Glen nor Dave would release the machines for the ferry until they were satisfied that both aircraft would be able to complete the flight in one piece. Repeated engine runs were completed plus all control checks establishing that they were airworthy. Eventually the ferry permit was authorized, and we prepared to depart. Another problem arose as some overflying rights had been denied. This meant we had to wait until an alternate route could be flight planned. It was at this point that we were now also restricted from landing at Muscat owing to some political problem.

The new owners then arranged for us to depart and land at Fujairah in the United Arab Emirates where we would hold until the paperwork for Muscat was cleared. Our new route took us over Europe into Iran bypassing the military active Iraq. This was a bit dangerous as the B747 paints a big image on the radar. Filing a flight plan with a ferry permit could give the idea to some antiaircraft military station that we were a bomber incognito. Eventually, we departed pleased to get out of the Swedish winter and for me to get back home where I was needed. No such luck at this point as trouble started entering the Iran air space. There appeared to be a misunderstanding from the air traffic control on our handover from Turkey to Iran. We were denied entry with a threat of military intervention. With some final aid from Turkey's air traffic control, the misunderstanding was rectified allowing us to proceed.

Nearing Shiraz (Iran) we developed engine trouble so with an H.F radio contact to Glen and being cleared by Dave our fight engineer it was decided that we should divert to Bahrain where there was sufficient maintenance. This eventually took place after we went through a long explanation why we were diverting to Bahrain. Bahrain in turn had to be convinced we had a developing major engine problem which could turn into an emergency to land. The problem was bigger than we thought which meant we stayed in Bahrain for a week awaiting parts plus funds to pay landing, parking and hotel costs. I paid the hotel bill to expedite getting out of Bahrain. The flight from Bahrain to Fujairah was short. Here we were told that it was going to be about a week before the appropriate papers were cleared for the flight to continue to Muscat. The crews were now stuck as there were no scheduled flights out of Fujairah and as we were flight crew, we did not have exit visas. Secondly if we could depart, we would not get paid. The days went by with all of us becoming more concerned that the whole project had collapsed, which would make us destitute. To pass the time I started to strip the names off the aircraft using a cherry picker. There is nothing in Fujairah except an old Arab sort of fishing village. It did have a pleasant beach and a small 3-star hotel, but that was all. Finally, the clearance came, and we were allowed to depart for Muscat being two hours away. A representative from the new owners met us indicating we were to be put up at a local hotel to await air tickets for our return to our home point. There were with the flight crew now a couple of ground engineers. A day or so went by only to find that the representative had departed leaving us with no means of leaving Oman. I put through daily calls to Glen advising him of our situation. Two weeks went by before the appropriate airline tickets arrived. With them the necessary departure visas so allowing us to leave Muscat and Oman. Getting to the airport we all went through the necessary immigration and received our boarding passes. I went to the duty free and bought my lady friend in South Africa a small gift.

When I went to the boarding gate I lost my boarding pass. I presumed I may have left it duty free. However, I was unable to find it anywhere. I explained this to the boarding officer, but he refused to allow me on board. This seemed strange as I had cleared immigration and bought buy-free with my boarding pass. The Arab mind is extremely sensitive, and tunnel visioned. To board the aircraft, I had to buy a new ticket, failing which I would have to wait until the following day for a flight to Dubai. This in turn would put me in a position to miss my Johannesburg flight so having to spend another day in Dubai. We jokingly called ourselves the forgotten aircrew, however it was something I wished not to repeat. In retrospect, I was paid in full for the time away and my expenses for myself and my crew in Bahrain. This was one contract I was glad to see the back of. It was good to fly again plus the remuneration was appreciated, to say the least. To my knowledge, these aircraft were finally abandoned in India. Dave and I would work together again.

Global peace ambassadors

It was a Sunday afternoon when I got an unexpected long-distance call from my old friend David Gonzales. Dave as mentioned earlier was senior ground/flight engineer on the B747 contract with Air Dabia in Gambia and Transjet ferry. He was calling from Mumbai (Bombay) asking what I was doing and was I available for a short-term contact. The deal was that he was the engineer on a V.I.P. around the world B747 SP flight. The B747 had been chartered to an organization called "Peace Ambassadors" transporting young Indian girls and some government officials on a world flight entertaining Governments, their officials, and wealthy businessmen, to raise awareness of the poverty and need for donations to help support businessmen orphanages. The officials travelling with the troupe of girls were additionally supporting Indian investments and bilateral trade agreements. Basically, a goodwill and peace mission, with the young girls doing a traditional dance routine to entertain interested investors and donors. The aircraft was fitted out with double bed staterooms on the upper deck, a 14-seat boardroom on the front lower deck plus a lounge with wide T.V. /Movie screen and a dining area with 90 seats for staff, or any extra passengers. Indian ladies chaperoning the girls known as "Sartha Girls".

There were two captains on the initial flight, one had had a disagreement with the organizers thereby resigned, promptly leaving Mumbai so leaving the aircraft' pending flight without a full crew compliment. He asked if I was interested as he had recommended me as a freelance pilot from our Air Dabia fiasco and the Swedish B747 ferry to Muscat. I said I was but would have to renew my American medical and had not flown the B747 for 7 years. His reply was that as there was another captain who could sign me out on a check flight, but could I get a medical in two days as they were due to depart Mumbai in four days' time. Being a part government involved in flight a visa would be issued immediately so there was no problem in that matter. I asked him to give me it until the morning as medical practitioners who license flight crew don't work on Sundays. If I could get a medical urgently, yes, I would be very interested in joining up with the flight and hopefully before the fourth day. The following day I was able to get an urgent U.S.A license medical and to my amazement the following morning I was advised my VISA was at the Indian High commissioner's office in Durban. Consequently, I departed on the evening flight to Mumbai arriving the following morning, being the fourth day. An Indian representative met me and escorted me to hotel to await Dave. He arrived that evening very grateful that I had been able to join them and for him it was like old times as a team together again. Due to some minor technicalities the flight was due to depart in the morning for Syria where there would be a three day stop. I was introduced to Peter Green, the other captain, Steve Forsnan the first officer and rest of the crew being cabin attendants. The departure of the other captain had been on a personal matter and disagreement with the contractual requirements.

After a good night's sleep, we departed for the airport and plane. The aircraft looked in good shape, but I was very confident as Dave was an excellent engineer who had got the two-engine B747 Atlantic crossing back with Air Dabia prepared plus the B747 ferry flights from Stockholm to Muscat. With everything in place and the flight ready to go, the travelling contingent and the young girls started to arrive. I then met Doctor Paul who was the principal and organizer of the venture. He was escorted by numerous officials whose office or involvement I was not aware of. I had earlier in the morning developed a cough which just did not seem to go away and was a bit annoying. However, I put it down to the pollution in Mumbai. Getting back in the saddle so as to say took me about half an hour to be comfortable with the aircraft. Considering I had first flown the B747 in 1975 now being 20 years on I was very familiar with the aircraft. Dave Green had no problem in signing me out as current.

Arriving in Damascus Syria a welcoming party was awaiting us. A far cry from the last time I was in Syria being refused a seat on the evacuation flight from Tehran in 1979. My coat closet flight. The plan was a dinner with the girls doing the dance routine. They were very beautiful young girls and became very fond of me as we progressed through the itinerary of the flight. Then a day of business and political meetings followed by another dance with and for wealthy interested parties.

By this time my cough had got worse, and I was not feeling well at all, finding it a bit hard to breathe freely and a loss of energy. I thought it must be something I had picked up in Mumbai so decided to spend the day in bed dosing myself with aspirin. During the day the situation got worse, and I was seriously thinking of calling a doctor. By nightfall the chest pain had eased a bit by just getting out of bed was an effort. By morning I did feel better so advised Dave that all was on the mend.

We duly left Syria for Tripoli. My strength was returning but the cough had not eased too much and was very annoying. We flew on to Bangor Maine right in a snowstorm. From there onto Baltimore repeating the shows and meetings. Finally, on to Little Rock Arkansas where we were invited to President Clinton's house for a dinner. This was held in a hall attached to the main old-style house. After which the dignitaries arrived to see the girls dance. I did not meet President Clinton but had a tour of his home by the general manager Mr. Jay Dickey. My cough was still with me, but I was feeling stronger. We then flew on to Cincinnati where we encountered the biggest show so far. There was a huge marquee tent on a sprawling private estate. Huge limos often only with a woman or a man on board but doors were opened by footman with the dignitary being escorted into the marquee. The food was laid out in a way fit for a king. Husbands and wives flew in on their own private jets. Champagne fountains and prawns stacked in a conical manner a meter or two feet high. Waitress dressed in short evening waistcoats as in the playboy style. It was a display of wealth which was hard to believe. We were crew so we stood back against the tent wall but did get to mix and chat with a few of the guests mainly the women. This was because the men all migrated to the center of the floor with what someone described as trophy wives standing well back and not getting involved.

Once the girls had completed their song and dance routine the donations poured in with the announcement that 5 million dollars had been achieved. The function then fragmented, and people started to leave some as couples some alone in their private chauffeured limos. The girls had been hugged, kissed, and made a big fuss about being given beautiful toys and clothes. This disturbed me as I said earlier the girls were lovely and as a father myself, I could not help but feel sad or even sorry for them. They had been wined and dined to the highest level. Travelling the world, stayed in beautiful clean hotels. Given gifts they were not allowed to keep except one item as the rest went to the orphanage. This had been the norm at all the stops so lavish attention had been paid to them.

These lovely little ladies would now be sent back to the orphanage in India to a future they would have no say in. Child marriages are one of them. Not a pleasant thought when one has seen the poverty and living conditions of India never mind the poor donation-supported orphanage. It seemed cruel. However, we were informed that this was the last stop as a problem had developed between the aircraft owners and the charterers. A day later taxis arrived, and we bid farewell to the girls who left for the airport to depart for Mumbai. Most of the girls were in tears as they bid goodbye with their last song and courteous loving hugs. My eyes were damp as I had said farewell to a lot of passengers in my career, but this was very different. Where would these poor little girls end up. Had the experience been rather punishing on their future memories when back in the orphanages and inevitable slums maybe of India. Possibly servants/slaves to hierarchy or sold as unloved child brides to older or unscrupulous men. I remembered my days of flying from India and the terrible caste system. Something as bad as apartheid or worse. I turned my back and retreated to the cockpit to clear myself of any emotion.

Storage flight.

We were suddenly informed that the aircraft was to be taken out of the USA. We had to use the fuel we had on board as there was no more credit available for fuel. Secondly it had to be a dry climate as storage for the winter was being considered. It appeared there were some legal or lean charges against the owners. The nearest airport meeting these requirements for us considering the fuel we had on board was Thunder Bay Canada. The airfield at Thunder Bay is not that long but according to our airfield information we could land there with the minimum fuel we had on board. The flight was not long but when in contact with the tower at Thunder Bay they were very surprised to hear we were intending to land a B747 there. The landing was tight but successful. On taxi in a crowd started to assemble to see this jumbo on their small country airport. It hit the newspapers and local T.V.

Leaving the aircraft in the hands of Dave and the ground crew, we departed for the nearest hotel. Here we were paid off and respective tickets home issued. I chose to go via Toronto to see my son Scott and to visit some old friends from my earlier Canada days. This I did but was still not feeling very well with the continuing cough. Once in Toronto and having visited my son Scott, my good old mate Peter Highfield from Wardair days and I joined up for a beer, chat, and lunch. I had then been invited to a party at the home of some good friends Lin and Richard Mutiger who lived in the country. The party was going well but I was not, so found a quiet room and fell asleep partially from my ailment of the cough and fatigue. A very interesting fact about this aircraft was that it was a China Air machine flight number 006 with a registration N4522V that stalled and spun out of the sky from 38,000 feet to 9,000 feet of the coast of California. The crew were not paying attention when the autopilot stalled the machine. There was severe damage and injuries to passengers, but the aircraft was rebuilt then sold.

The following day I flew on to London where again I visited my very old friend, flight engineer Allen Jones and wife Bunny. They in turn drove me to visit older friends from way back in the SAUDIA days Richard and Veronica Handover living at Marlborough. I doubted I would ever see them again, so it was a good visit to the U.K. but fortunately, Lin & Rick many years later came to visit us in South Africa. We took them to the game parks, and they drove the beautiful garden route to Cape Town.

Flying back to South Africa the cough was not letting up. Once back in Hillcrest I visited my local doctor. He was not happy and suggested I see a specialist which I did and was given a CAT scan.

The specialist was the son of one of the pilots I flew with in South African Airways. On returning with the scan results he looked at me remarking that I was the luckiest son of a B—h showing me my lungs splattered with small blood clots. I had suffered a pulmonary embolism where my heart had been strong enough to deploy the clot into my lungs. Consequently, the continues coughing which might have been the saving grace by forcing manipulation of my heart, whereas I could have died at any time on the flight. To have flown in this condition was remarkable but I now had to go onto blood thinners and medication. This treatment is not conducive to holding a first-class pilot's medical certificate to maintain an Airline Transport license.

Final landing.

It was an indication that my flying time and days were coming to an end. This was supported by the slowdown and difficulty in getting contractual flying. I decided that the flight on the 13 July 2005 to Thunder Bay was my last flight. I had been flying for 43 years, had an exciting and a hell of a career with some of the greatest aviators. So, it was fate that I finished where I started in Canada. From a humble single engine aircraft to a massive 340-ton four engine 50,000-pound thrust Jumbo of the skies the B747. Yesterday is today's memory; tomorrow is today's dream. I had lived the dream. I hung my uniform up, put my cap in the top closet, took of my wings and put my flight and overnight bag in the storeroom. Remarkably as a contracting pilot I had done well. I owned a small farm in Australia, three houses in Toronto plus two houses in South Africa. A comfortable bank account in Canada, Switzerland, and South Africa. Owned everything bond free plus being able to put my sons through expensive private boy's schools. I had lost a lot at times such as the 38,000-acre farm in Australia and the devastating three-year hospital project. Gone very nearly bankrupt a couple of times and had to beg to borrow and steal once or twice to make ends meet. The wolf being at the door. Medical problems, accidents and illness had played their hand quite severely at times with the mighty reaper standing in the garden. But I took the knocker off the door with the help of the Lord. Many great men have tried and failed but many great men have never failed to try was my motto, so I stuck to it. Freelance pilots don't have airline pensions or rebate travel on retirement. So, without a pension it was time to turn to other things, possibly some sort of business venture but I was not going to stop working. Too many colleagues had died after retiring.

The idea of taking up golf and ending up in the 19th hole everyday was not on my agenda. I was widowed but was contemplating marrying again to Clare a beautiful woman that I had mentioned before, who had two young teenage daughters. This would be the start of the final chapter of my life with incredible developments all totally unexpected, fate again was working the plot and what a plot. For a contract freelance pilot, each flight is a fresh challenge and a new adventure to be places at the end of the memories

BIG BEYOND IN THE SKY.

I have shared the sky

Flown on a wing and a prayer

Felt the clash of thunder

Heard the rumbling of the slipstream

The thump of the piston

The whine of the jet

For now, the time has come

To hang up my cap

Dry my misty glasses

Till one day to take the biggest flight of all

To that big beyond in the sky

Airline Transport Pilot Licenses Land and Sea Held.

Canadian. South African. American. British. Irish. British Colonial (West Indian). Quatar. Iranian. Saudi. Sri Lankan. Singapore. Thailand. Congo. Sweden. Brazilian. Nigerian. Gambia. Swazi. Republica Dominica. Greek. Icelandic.

B747 100, 200, SP, B707, B737, DC8, DC6, DC3, B18, MD87 (DC9), PBY (Catalina), Falcon, Lear, HS748, open endorsed for 12,500lbs plus land and sea.

Postscript.

With my story of "Nomadic Wings" (By the Seat of my Pants) completed and my flying career finished I felt there was little more to say. However, with pressure from friends, it was suggested I write the second half of my adventurous life as an addendum to the story or a postscript.

Retired I was still the president of the local sports club. I also was the chairman of The Durban Early Car Club an interest I had in vintage cars, although I did not have one. This kept me quite active. One evening at the sports club a journalist friend asked if I would be interested in the position of manager for a motor vehicle promotion business needed in our province. I agreed arrangements were made for me to fly to Johannesburg to meet the company owners. I filled the position for them returning to set up an operation in our province. I was given a very large trailer equipped with promotional paraphernalia mainly to go to the large shopping malls province-wide and set up stands to promote Renault,

Honda and Jaguar. It was an early morning assignment named "insight marketing" where I hired two staff to help with the large floor mates and stands. In addition, I would hire for each show college girls in very attractive T-shirts to hand out pamphlets and talk in brief to the visiting public about cars. Their primary job was to get telephone numbers so the salesman could follow up. This was quite a financially successful business although with Jaguar and Honda, it was too much to concentrate on, thereby Renault became our main product. With this business now underway an old friend of mine named John Hatfield advised me at a cocktail party that he was about to construct storage garages and would I be interested in investing in them. I was not but as things went a year later, he had become very successful now proceeding onto mini factories. He made the same offer on these which appealed to me. I purchased 3 altogether going into an agreement with a renting and managing company Comprop to manage them for me. To purchase them I had to raise funds, so I decided to go back to Canada and sell one of my houses. Years later I bought 2 more having to sell my Australian Farm.

Mini-Factories

Me at 14000 feet, Machu Picchu, age 63

Machu Picchu and pass.

One day I and a friend John Tyne suddenly decided before we got too old now at 63 to do a backpack tour through Peru. Flying to Lima we continued down the coast by bus to NAZCA. Arriving we charted a small plane enabling us to see the huge NAZCA sand drawing of monkeys, spiders, and horizontal lines all a mystery. Then a terrifying night trip in a double-decker bus across the Andean mountains doing knife-edge turns on mountain edges, we arrived at Lake Titicaca. The highest lake in South America. This was the first time we felt the altitude. Our hotel room had oxygen bottles in them. On the lake is a large steel steam-powered ship carried piece by piece on the backs of Llamas from the coast hundreds of kilometers away. Proceeding on we headed for Cuzco. While there we witnessed the festival of the sun god, an experience I have never considered possible. The re-enactment of the sacrifice and prayers praising the sun god asking for fertility, peace and health. It's almost unnatural rehearsed by priests, followers and dancers, a thing to be seen. The priest faced the clouds at that very moment the clouds parted revealing the sun shining on him. Closing as he left the stand. As the procession started to leave a rainbow fell across the valley. The silence in the valley was ghostly, not a pin drop could be heard. John and were speechless at what we had just witnessed. If one did not believe in a god, this would maybe convince one otherwise. Finally arriving at Machu Picchu border entry, we registered. This allowed us at our risk to attempt the climb to the ruins. We accomplished the 3-day freezing climb through the mountains reaching 4,715m (15.465 feet) to the ruins of the Inca Mountain city (Machu Picchu). An incredible experience to see the remains of a very intelligent civilization and culture. Ironically destroyed by gold-hunting Spanish conquistadors in 1532. The slavery and brutality of these fortune hunters sent by Spain are beyond civilized thinking. Very slowly they destroyed the Incas. The Inca empire known by them as Tawantinsuyu extended along the Pacific coast and Andean highlands from the northern border of modern Ecuador to the Maule River in central Chile. Eventually, we flew back to San Paulo returning home. An unforgettable trip for two old buddies.

I had mentioned earlier in my story that I had met a lovely lady named Clare. She had two teenage daughters from an earlier marriage named Susan and Kathryn. They attended an up-market boarding school in Pietermaritzburg, the capital city of our province. She and I had now been dating for over a year so asked her to accompany me to Canada in so to meet my oldest son who resided there and old friends. Returning our relationship had strengthened so as a financial and practical matter I suggested she move from her apartment into my house which has 4 bedrooms, and a swimming pool all adequate for the two families. Now if one recalls my earlier story, I referred to a Jeep venture I did in my teenage years to ascend by a motor vehicle a 10,000-foot mountain pass called "Sani Pass". Since then, a small chalet and pub have been built. The pub is appropriately named "The highest pub in Africa".

I decided it would be good to go to the mountains and visit the pub. This we did where when outside viewing the magnificent mountain pass, I proposed to her, and thankfully she accepted. Clare's original family name was Reiche, she came from a large German family near a German town called Wartburg in South Africa. Returning to our hometown of Hillcrest plans were set about to amalgamate the two families. Our family and children were delighted, so a happy merger took place.

New Home and Wedding

Clare sold her Coffee shop and restaurant so with her food technologist degree she joined a chemical company as a representative. We felt now that we would like a new place of our own. Again, fate played its hand.

A good friend Penny had invited us for afternoon tea. During discussions on our fruitless search for a new home pointed out the beautiful double-story 4bedroom, 3-car garage home in front of her house. It was a forced sale as the owner had overextended himself and was facing bankruptcy. One look at it was enough, being exactly what we wanted. We offered an agreed-upon cash price which he accepted. Three months later Clare sold her apartment, and I sold my house and property, so we all moved in.

Time was going by; the girls were now preparing for University and Technical College. My younger son was in the shipping business the older one resided in Canada employed by an airline. Before the children left for their respective occupations, we had decided to get married. This was therefore planned to be a family-only wedding on our terrace at our new home. Clare came from a large family with 4 siblings, 3 sisters and a brother, all now married with children. The wedding took place with 30 people in attendance. A very joyous, happy affair with my mother-in-law, stepbrothers and sister uniting as one family.

Susan & Kathryn (New daughters)

Before the wedding, we had made a great trip across China, Thailand, Cambodia, Tibet, Singapore and Dubai. This could be considered our honeymoon in advance. We would do much more travelling later on in our lives, backpacking across Europe and Croatia, Two VIKING River boat cruises on the Danube and Rhine, plus a Mediterranean Greek, Montenegro and Italia cruise. Years later in 2024, we rented a 4-birth cabin cruiser just for ourselves so doing the "Le Midi" Cannel in South France. All the children are now married except the oldest son Scott. We now have 5 grandchildren.

Antarctic

My second to last adventure was when my younger son Grant, for my 80th birthday stood me and him on a business class flight via Argentina to Ushuaia the most Southern city in the world.

Grant & I in the Antarctic

Here we joined a luxury ship M.S. Fridtjof Nansen equipped for the ice passage. I got invited up to the bridge which was an educational experience comparing the bridge to a cockpit. This was wonderful for me as it was a father and son trip never to be forgotten.

The Sir Frances Drake passage was very rough, but the cabins were excellent, fine food with entertainment consisting of lectures on the pole and wildlife plus a coverage of the finding of the South Pole.

EXTRACT from records: *In the early 20th century, the race was on to reach the South Pole, with several explorers testing themselves in the freezing Antarctic. In 1911, Britain's Robert Falcon Scott and Norway's Roald Amundsen both launched expeditions to reach the Pole. It would end in victory for Amundsen – and tragedy for Scott.*

Amundsen got there by taking excess sledge dogs. Killing them off as the loads reduced to enable the team to extend its food supply thereby days on the ice shelf. Which unbelievably is the biggest desert in the world. At the Exploration Society celebration in London of Amundsen's success, the Chairman raised his glass to what people thought would be a toast to Amundsen, but he did not. Instead toasted the dogs. Amundsen was not amused.

I had by this trip now covered every continent of the world. (both Arctics) Not bad with one shilling and sixpence??

A close call.

Close calls with death I had had a few before but the Grim Reaper was not finished with me yet. My faithful dog "Rocky" and I did a twice-weekly run. Setting on a beautiful day I developed a pain in my chest. Taking my pulse, it seemed low, so I immediately turned for home a kilometre away. Getting there I could hardly breathe but thankfully my neighbour was washing his car. He immediately offered to drive me to the local hospital. En route, I advised him to take me to a nearer medical centre as I felt we would not make the hospital. Getting there they put me on life saving oxygen and morphine. By luck, an empty ambulance was on its way to another hospital, so it was turned around, and I was duly attended to by a doctor on board. The suggestion that the local hospital could not handle my case was put forward and my hope of survival was to get to the city heart hospital 40 kilometres away. That hospital had been advised and met the ambulance on arrival. I was rushed into the surgery unconscious; my heart was intermittent and pressure dropping. I came too with a nurse saying stay with us Mr. Evans at the same time a heart specialist Dr Gillma was monitoring two TV screens having inserted a stent. A vein had broken, and the heart was pumping blood out of the tear. To this very day, I see the doctor every year and he shows the x-ray repeating that I should not be alive. In the hospital, I resigned as president of the sports club reducing my everyday activities. Clare had met the ambulance, and my son flew in from Cape Town. It was close but Clare took me home three days later being advised to take things a bit easy.

As chairman and a lover of vintage cars, I had been looking for one of my own. Fortunately, a good friend who collected old and vintage cars knew of a 1926 Armstrong Siddeley Mendip that had been abandoned for 50 years from a farm and then to an upcountry scrap yard. It had a story to it, but too much to add here. However, I was able to buy it getting to Durban the main city, which had a small airfield and into a friend hanger. From there I built an A-frame so I am able to tow it to my home. There is a shorter story on this car enclosed, but it took me one year working every day to resurrect her to the driving and show condition she is now. A great pastime and a wonderful experience. Later the car was to be used with other Vintage car club cars in the filming of "Yellowstone" a movie partially filmed here in South Africa.

Cheers, trust you enjoyed my story.

Alan

Armstrong Siddeley Mendip Story

The Alan Evans Mendip

In 2013 I obtained the remains of an Armstrong Siddeley Mendip. This car is a Mk 2 Y Batch from the production period up to November 1926, with chassis number 24301 and car number AS24301. The radiator has a number 19641 stamped on the shell. I believe my Mendip is what was called a "doctors' car", built by the Burlington Carriage Co and owned by Armstrong Siddeley. According to the Factory Ledger Sheets available Swift & Co of Durban during 1926, received Thirty (30) Cotswold 5-seater open tourer cars. They received One (1) Mendip 2/3-Seater and amazingly this is the car I have restored.

Another company African, Eastern Trading Co. received Three Cotswold 5-seater open tourer cars in the same period. This research is limited to the information available and doesn't include private importations.

The Mendip was sold to a John Western, who was killed by his African staff. It then remained in a barn in two places for 50 years. I have now completely rebuilt the machine and am very proud of my endeavours, having won the car of the year at his Vintage Car Club in Durban, South Africa.

My Mendip is one of a variety of 14hp Mk 2 models that Armstrong Siddeley made between 1925 and 1929. Although 11,479 14hp Mk 2 cars were made during this period there are only about 70 known survivors of combined Mk1 and Mk 2 models, about half of which are roadworthy. According to Bill Smith in his book 'Armstrong Siddeley Motors', there are only two known Mendip survivors – one in excellent condition in Australia, mine, and another replica in unknown condition in the UK. (David Welsh ASOC)

Printed in Great Britain
by Amazon